SHANGHAI

SHANGHAI

CHINA'S GATEWAY TO MODERNITY

Marie-Claire Bergère

Translated by Janet Lloyd

Stanford University Press

Stanford, California

Stanford University Press
Stanford, California

Shanghai: China's Gateway to Modernity was originally published in French
under the title *Histoire de Shanghai* © Librairie Arthème Fayard, 2002.

Assistance for the translation was provided by the French Ministry of Culture.

Printed in the United States of America on acid-free,
archival-quality paper

Library of Congress Cataloging-in-Publication Data

Bergère, Marie-Claire.
[Histoire de Shanghai. English]
Shanghai : China's gateway to modernity / Marie-Claire Bergère ;
translated by Janet Lloyd.
p. cm.
"Originally published in French under the title Histoire de Shanghai,
Librairie Arthème Fayard, 2002."
Includes bibliographical references and index.
ISBN 978-0-8047-4904-6 (cloth : alk. paper) — ISBN 978-0-8047-4905-3
(pbk. : alk. paper)
1. Shanghai (China)—History. 2. China—History—19th century.
3. China—History—20th century. I. Title.
DS796.S257B4713 2009
951'.132—dc22
2009011310

Typeset by Bruce Lundquist in 10/15 Sabon

Contents

CONTENTS

Illustrations

MAPS AND PLANS

Acknowledgments

Like all works of synthesis, this book could not exist were it not for the specialist works upon which it is based. The most important of these are the works of research produced by Chinese historians, in particular those of the Shanghai Academy of Social Sciences, Fudan University, and many other Shanghai institutions. If these works are cited less often than they should be, the reason is that this book is addressed chiefly to a Western public. Let me nevertheless express my particular gratitude to Professors Zhang Zhongli and Ding Richu, who have welcomed and assisted me so generously during my periods of research in Shanghai and have themselves contributed so much to the study of this city both in their own works and through the studies of research teams that they have encouraged.

My gratitude also goes to a small group of French colleagues who have for many years shared my interest in the history of Shanghai: Alain Roux, Françoise Ged, Christian Henriot, Xiao-hong Xiao-Planes, and Wang Ju.

I cannot cite the names of all the American researchers to whom I owe so much, for they are far too numerous. Over more than twenty years Shanghai has become one of the principal subjects of research for transatlantic sinologists. Historians, sociologists, and anthropologists have trawled their way through many archives, worked on many field inquiries, and produced an abundance of highly illuminating monographs. My debt to them will be manifest from the many references to their works.

I also acknowledge a huge debt of gratitude to Lucien Bianco, whose patient and attentive rereadings of the text have greatly improved it; to Monique Abud and Wang Ju, in charge of research and documentation at the Centre d'Étude sur la Chine moderne et contemporaine de l'École des Hautes Études en Sciences Sociales, who provided valuable assistance; to Isabelle Nathan, the chief archivist, who has guided me in my exploration of the iconographical resources of the Archives of the Quai d'Orsay;

and the publisher, Agnès Fontaine, whose tenacity and competence have brought to completion a project in which I had almost ceased to believe; and finally to Wang Ju, who translated the book into Chinese and whose very careful checking of sources, transcriptions, and dates benefited the present American edition. This edition has greatly benefited from the skills of Janet Lloyd, who did the translation, from the friendly attention of Muriel Bell, and from the rigorous editing of Stacy Wagner and her colleagues at Stanford University Press. Their contributions are gratefully acknowledged.

Various individuals and institutions, including the Historical Museum of Shanghai, the Archives of the French Ministry of Foreign Affairs, the Municipal Archives of Shanghai, and Professor Qian Zonghao, have provided the illustrative material reprinted in this book. I am grateful for their collaboration.

Note on Transcription

The transcription used in this work is *pinyin*, except for a few very well-known names that are transcribed in the traditional manner.

Chronology

1879	Foundation of St. John's University
1882	Electric lighting installed in the concessions
1883	Piped water system installed in the concessions
1890	Li Hongzhang creates first Chinese cotton mill
1895	Treaty of Shimonosheki authorizes foreigners to construct factories in Shanghai and the other treaty ports
	Creation of *Shenbao* (*The Shanghai Journal*)
1896	Foundation of Shanghai's first Chinese university (*Nanyang gongxue*)
1898	Collapse of the Hundred Days' Reforms in Beijing
1898–1900	Boxer insurrection in the northern provinces
1901	New Policy of reform and modernization
1902	Creation of the Jesuit Aurora University
1903	*Subao* affair
1904	Creation of the Shanghai General Chamber of (Chinese) Commerce
1905	Abolition of the system of civil service examinations
	Sun Yat-sen founds the Revolutionary Alliance in Tokyo
	Anti-American boycott
	Creation of a Chinese municipality in Shanghai
	Foundation of (Chinese) Fudan University
	Creation of the Jiangsu Provincial Association of Education
1908	Inauguration of the Shanghai-Nanjing railway
	Inauguration of the tram service in the concessions
	Opening of the first Shanghai cinema hall
1911	Shanghai rallies to the 1911 Republican Revolution
	Establishment of a Provisional Municipal Council
1912	Sun Yat-sen founds the Chinese Republic in Nanjing
	Destruction of the old walls of Shanghai

1913	Song Jiaoren, the revolutionary leader, is assassinated at the Shanghai railway station
	Shanghai refuses to support the Second Revolution, aimed against the dictatorship of Yuan Shikai
1914	World War I
1916	Death of Yuan Shikai and the beginning of the warlords period
1917–1921	Shanghai economy booms
1917	Opening of the first department stores
1919	May Fourth Movement launched in Beijing
	May–June: Strikes by Shanghai students, merchants, and workers, within the framework of the May Fourth Movement
1921	Foundation of the Communist Party in Shanghai
	Foundation of the Creation literary society
1925	Anti-imperialist movement of May 30
	Modernist literary group formed
1926	Construction of new headquarters of the Hong Kong and Shanghai Bank on the Bund
	Construction of the new Cercle français
1927	March 21: Insurrection of the Shanghai workers and the creation of a provisional municipal government
	March 26: Nationalist troops enter Shanghai
	April 12: Chiang Kai-shek's coup against the revolutionary trade unionists and the beginning of the campaign of White Terror against the Communists
	April 18: Installation of Chiang Kai-shek's Nationalist government in Nanjing
	July: Organization of the Municipality of Greater Shanghai
1928	Construction of the Sassoon House (now the Peace Hotel)

1930	China recovers customs autonomy
	Creation of the League of Left-Wing Writers
1931	September: Japanese invade Manchuria
	Anti-Japanese boycott and birth of the Movement of National Salvation in Shanghai
	Inauguration of the ancestral temple of Du Yuesheng and the peak of the Green Gang's power
1932	January: Japanese attack against the Zhabei quarter of Shanghai
1932–1935	Serious economic crisis in Shanghai
1933	Construction of the Park Hotel
1935	Monetary reform; China abandons the silver standard
1936	May: Pan-Chinese Association for National Salvation created in Shanghai
	December: Xi'an incident and the formation of the Second United Front between the Nationalists and the Communists
1937	July: Beginning of the Sino-Japanese War
	August–November: Battle for Shanghai and the invasion of its Chinese quarters by Japanese troops
	Many Shanghai factories transferred inland
1938	Nationalist government retreats first to Hankou, then to Chongqing
1939	September: Beginning of World War II in Europe
	Rice riots in Shanghai
1940	March: Establishment of the collaborationist government of Wang Jingwei in Nanjing
	June: Defeat of France and armistice
	October: Assassination of the collaborationist mayor of Shanghai, Fu Xiao'an
	New French consul-general, Roland de Margerie, sets the French concession under the authority of the Vichy government

1941	December 7: Japanese attack on Pearl Harbor
	Outbreak of the Pacific War
	Occupation of the international settlement of Shanghai by the Japanese armed forces
1942	Internment of the British and American nationals of Shanghai
1943	January: Western powers renounce the privileges granted them by the nineteenth-century treaties
	February: Creation of the Shanghai ghetto
	July 30: French concession restored to Wang Jingwei's government
	August: Japanese return the international settlement to Wang Jingwei's government
1945	March 9: Japanese coup in Indochina; French garrison in Shanghai is disarmed and interned
	August 14: Capitulation of Japan
	September 10: Chiang Kai-shek's Nationalist troops enter Shanghai
1946	Creation of the *Guancha* review (The Observer).
	December: Student demonstrations against "American Brutalities"
1947	February: Inflation and wage freeze
	March: Democratic League banned
	May–June: Student demonstrations against "Hunger and the Civil War"
1948	February: Violent repression of the strike by female workers in the Shenxin Company's cotton mill no. 9
	April–May: Student demonstrations against "Hunger and American Aid to Japan"
	August: Reform of the gold dollar and beginning of a terror campaign against speculators
1949	May 25: Communist troops enter Shanghai

1949–1951	Reconstruction of the Shanghai economy within the framework of the united-front policy
1951	Spring: Campaign against counterrevolutionaries
	Autumn: Campaign for thought reform aimed against intellectuals
1952	Five Antis campaign against the capitalists
	Start of the construction of New Villages (designated for workers)
1953	Launch of the First Five-Year Plan, sacrificing the economic interests of Shanghai
1954	Campaign against Hu Feng
1956	January: Nationalization of the private businesses of Shanghai
	April: Mao Zedong's report on the "Ten Great Relations" and the relaunch of industrial development in Shanghai
1957	Spring: Hundred Flowers protest movement
	Anti-Rightist Campaign
1958	The Great Leap Forward
	Vast extension of the municipal territory
	Launch of the satellite towns program
1961	End of the Great Leap Forward; adoption of a policy of Readjustment
1965	Third Front policy and delocalization of Shanghai industries
	November: Start of the Cultural Revolution
1966	May–June: Mobilization of students and college pupils
	August: Red Guards carry the Cultural Revolution into the streets
	Arrival of the first radical Red Guards from Beijing
	November: Liaison between the Red Guards and workers; creation of the Workers' General Headquarters
	December: General strike

1967	January: Rebels take over power, and the municipality collapses
	February 5: Creation of the Shanghai Commune
	February 26: Creation of the Municipal Revolutionary Committee
1971	Reestablishment of the Party's Municipal Council
1973	Wang Hongwen reorganizes the trade unions and the workers' militias
1976	September 9: Death of Mao Zedong
	October: Arrest of the Gang of Four
1984	Shanghai included in the fourteen coastal towns declared open to foreign capital
1985	Jiang Zemin becomes mayor of Shanghai
1988	Zhu Rongji becomes mayor of Shanghai
1989	May–June: Demonstrations in Tian'anmen Square in Beijing
	June: Jiang Zemin becomes secretary-general of the Party
1990	Central government approves the Pudong "new zone" project
1992	Deng Xiaoping visits southern China
	Relaunch of economic reform
	Shanghai designated to pioneer new development
1993	Zhu Rongji becomes vice–prime minister
2002	January: China joins the World Trade Organization

SHANGHAI

Introduction

Shanghai and Chinese Modernity

IT WAS HARDLY LOVE AT FIRST SIGHT. The first time I set eyes on Shanghai, in October 1957, I had arrived from Beijing, where, perched on an official rostrum, I had attended the National Festival celebrations in Tian'anmen Square. Compared to Beijing, Shanghai struck me as provincial. I immediately viewed this former bastion of imperialism with a distrustful eye. I was indignant at the sight of the shantytowns, preserved in their original state to perpetuate the memory of the abject conditions to which workers had been subjected before the revolution, while I admired the gray apartment blocks built in the suburbs to rehouse some of them. I saw what people chose to show me, never realizing that an "Anti-Rightist" campaign was busy dispatching hundreds of thousands of Shanghainese to the gulags. I was the perfect "goldfish traveler," confined to its bowl.[1]

The first crack in that bowl was caused by the unease that I felt in the large hotel to which I had been assigned. From its luxurious past it had retained its huge suites of rooms, its dented silverware, and its well-trained staff. The white-suited "boy" moving about silently and speaking softly in singsong French, who was in charge of the floor where I was the sole occupant, resembled a ghost. Even more ghostlike was an elderly English couple that I passed one evening on the stairs, he clad in suit and tie, she with a permanent-waved blonde coiffure. These incongruous figures conjured up a faint vision of the vanished metropolis now masked by the austere Communist city. It was now almost ten years since Shanghai had been swept along in the Communist revolution, leaving many of its former residents and visitors with nostalgic memories. I myself had no associations with that past, but I felt a spark of curiosity and already a stirring of fascination about this city that had been engulfed by the storms of history.

During my brief stay in Shanghai, I visited the building sites, schools, and crèches of the new China. Once back in France, I immersed myself in the town's history, which, at that time, was confined to that of its foreign concessions: the international settlement, with its trading companies, banks, naval yards, and factories that had turned Shanghai into a world metropolis; and the French concession, the international settlement's younger sister, whose shady streets, fashion houses, literary bohemia, and militant revolutionaries had caused the town to be known as "the Paris of the East." Later, as my research probed deeper, I began to appreciate the degree to which Shanghai had all along been above all a Chinese town. The old concessions teemed with Chinese inhabitants, and no business project could go ahead without their cooperation or assent. The originality of the town and the attraction that it exerted lay not in the implantation of a colonial modernity, many other examples of which were provided by Asia and Africa, but rather in the welcome that its local society had given to that implantation, adopting and adapting it, and turning it into a modernity that was Chinese.

In the 1960s, the concept of modernization prompted only distrust. It chimed all too well with westernization and, it was said, served simply as a sorry excuse for imperialism. The few specialists who took an interest in the history of Shanghai laid the emphasis on the phenomenon of foreign domination: the town was no more than a foreign enclave, a thorn in China's side.[2] Nowadays Shanghai modernity is no longer contested, but specialists try to present it as the consequence of an autochthonous evolution that preceded the arrival of the Westerners by several centuries.[3] Chinese nationalism and culturalist history are well satisfied with this new interpretation. However, the role that foreigners played in the rise of Shanghai is no easier to obscure than that the Chinese played. The interaction, cooperation, and rivalry between the two groups turned Shanghai into the capital of "another" China, one that was cosmopolitan and entrepreneurial.[4] Within an empire dominated by a long rural and bureaucratic tradition, Shanghai thus became the model of a modernity founded upon Western contributions but adapted to the national Chinese culture.

Contrary to the long-standing belief of Westerners, in the mid-nineteenth century Shanghai had not been a wretched fishing village just waiting for foreign intervention to wave a magic wand and transform it into a major economic and financial center. With a population of around 200,000 inhabitants, it was a relatively important administrative center, an active regional market town, and a seaport thronged by junks that sailed up and down the coastline and even all the way to Japan. In the thriving region of the lower Yangzi, it was, however, eclipsed by many richer, more dynamic, and more highly cultured towns.

Shanghai's destiny was sealed in 1842, when the treaty of Nanjing designated it one of the five Chinese ports to be opened up to Western trade. Until that date, the Chinese Empire had refused to enter into any economic or political relations with the West, and it was only in consequence of the First Opium War (1839–1842) that it had been forced to relent. The British had waged this Opium War. What was immediately at stake was the importation of opium, which the imperial authorities wished to prohibit but foreign merchants continued to pursue, since the drug represented for them the major commodity that they could exchange for tea and silk. More generally, though, the Europeans' objective was to force the Empire of the Middle Kingdom to agree to the establishment of regular relations with themselves. Among the ports that were "opened up" in this way, Shanghai rapidly affirmed its preeminence, not so much because of its really quite mediocre situation as a river port on the Huangpu (a tributary of the Yangzi that flowed into the estuary of the latter), but thanks to its position at the mouth of this great river that served a huge surrounding basin right at the center of China. Within a few decades, Shanghai became the preferred place of residence for the foreign entrepreneurs who, with the aid of Chinese merchants, set up their businesses there. Thanks to the privileges granted by the treaties and the autonomy that the concessions thus acquired, the foreign residents, together with the Chinese who now settled alongside them, found themselves protected from the troubles that beset the decline of the last imperial dynasty and the fraught birth of the Republican regime after the 1911 Revolution.

As the country's chief center for international commerce and an islet of relative safety in a deeply troubled China, Shanghai provided many opportunities for intercultural contacts between merchants whose chief concerns were their material interests. The Jesuits' arrival in the Beijing Court at the beginning of the seventeenth century had prompted a highly intellectual dialogue between the mandarins and the missionaries; three centuries later, the establishment of European and American entrepreneurs in Shanghai gave rise to interchanges that focused essentially upon commercial practices, financial techniques, and production processes. Shanghai had never been a great center of intellectual influences. The meeting of Chinese civilization and Western modernity took a pragmatic form. The local society's reception of foreign novelties and the foreigners' adaptation to their new place of work and living conditions progressed more smoothly than might have been expected given that, on both sides, the interested parties were not particularly highly educated individuals but merchants and adventurers eager to justify their ventures by whatever profit possible. The adaptability and flexibility of these men injected an extraordinary dynamism into Shanghai society. Positioned on the margins of the Chinese Empire and at the antipodes of the Western world, this was a society of pioneers. The lawlessness that reigned within it was tempered to varying degrees by the way in which the various groups organized their respective communities—merchants or vagrants, Chinese or foreign—and also by interventions on the part of the Beijing government and the governments of the imperialist powers involved.

However, those interventions were by no means symmetrically balanced, as the position of the Chinese authorities was far weaker than that of the Western powers. The disproportion of the forces involved definitely favored the foreign merchants, supported, as they were, by their consuls and their gunboats, rather than the Chinese merchants, who were not so much supported but exploited by the declining imperial power and were then, following the 1911 Revolution, abandoned to their own devices by the Republican regime that was struggling to establish itself. However, actually there, on the spot, the privileges extorted by diplomatic and military pressure were not invariably translated into economic advantages. The relations between the foreign and Chinese communities were by no means always weighted in favor of the former, as claimed by nationalist Chinese historiography and suggested by our own guilty consciences as former imperialists.

Shanghai and its surrounding region, the rich Yangzi delta, constituted a long-standing commercial civilization, crisscrossed by a very dense network of communicating river routes, market trading, and channels of finance controlled by extremely well-organized guilds. In order to develop relations with the Chinese interior, where they were for a long time not permitted to establish themselves, the foreigners were obliged to cooperate with these guilds and frequently had to accept their conditions. In the face of the trump cards that their European or American competitors held (tax exemptions, technological superiority, and so on), the Chinese made the most of their own familiarity with the local environment and the extreme cohesion of their professional organizations. Although the foreigners dominated relations between Shanghai and the Western markets, the Chinese still controlled the commercial circuits linking the treaty port with the inland provinces. The economy of Shanghai functioned because of the cooperation between the two groups, a negotiated cooperation from which stemmed advantages that were divided less unequally than has frequently been claimed.

On the other hand, the cultural exchanges implied by such cooperation were rather more uneven. The foreigners were regarded as models from whom the Chinese borrowed production techniques as well as economic, social, and political institutions. Such borrowing was, however, not the same as imitation pure and simple. Western practices came to be grafted onto traditional systems, modifying the way that these functioned and themselves being changed by this transplantation. The acculturation that accompanied such borrowings was rendered the more humiliating by the arrogance of the foreigners and the privileges they enjoyed. But in Shanghai, the customary xenophobia took the form of a modern nationalism that aimed to take up the Western challenge on its own terms: it aspired to economic modernization, material prosperity, and social progress. Shanghai, the most "foreign" of all Chinese towns, was also the one where nationalist awareness and the revolutionary mobilization of the masses first developed.

The myth of Shanghai evokes prostitution, drugs, and mafia activities. Yet the role that the town played in the definition of Chinese modernity was far more important. So in the first part of this book, "The Treaty Port," we shall see how the town itself became a pole of modernity. This evolution begins with the arrival and establishment of the foreigners (Chapter 1) and the creation in the concessions of a Sino-foreign society that was quasi autonomous, thanks to the disturbances that were at that time disrupting the

Chinese Empire (Chapter 2). The compradors, who constituted the crucial link in the cooperation between the Chinese and the foreign merchant communities, played a major role in the development of Shanghai capitalism during the second half of the nineteenth century and the first half of the twentieth (Chapter 3). The men who made this development possible came from various provinces of China, from the principal nations of Europe, the United States, Japan, and other Asian countries already colonized by the West. The relative importance of these communities varied from one period to another, but the barriers that separated them—languages, customs, and interests—all contributed to the fragmentation of the local society (Chapter 4). The foreign presence polarized those divisions, superimposing on them the fundamental distinction between the Chinese and the non-Chinese, but to a certain extent transcending them by providing the model of concessions that most Chinese aspired to imitate, the better to compete with it (Chapter 5). Meanwhile, Shanghai presented itself as an example to the rest of China when, following the 1911 Revolution, it endeavored, despite many difficulties, to commit itself to the Republican way forward (Chapter 6).

The second part of this book, "The Metropolis," is devoted to the period between the two world wars, in the course of which the success of Shanghai reached its peak and the city extended its modernizing influence not only to other coastal regions but also, increasingly, to inland China. This was the golden age of Chinese capitalism (Chapter 7), at a time when mass movements, led by political parties (the Guomindang and the Chinese Communist Party) were fast developing. Both the manner of their organization and, in some cases, their managers or organizers, came from the West (Chapter 8). From 1927 onward, the effect of the growth of central power that resulted from Chiang Kai-shek's creation of the Nanjing government was to integrate Shanghai more closely into the political life of the nation. Shanghai now became the modern showcase of a regime that, however, was itself by no means modern (Chapter 9). These years of relative prosperity and order saw a flowering of popular culture, namely, *Haipai*, which significantly boosted both foreign influence and mercantile interests (Chapter 10).

In 1937, the Sino-Japanese War ushered in "the end of a world," as described in the third part of this book. Shanghai, occupied by the Japanese armed forces, lost its international status, and its concessions reverted to the collaborating government of Wang Jingwei, a Chinese version of France's Vichy government. For the city of Shanghai, bruised, humiliated, and starving, this was a dark period (Chapter 11) to which the Japanese defeat and the 1945 liberation brought no more than brief relief. While Mao Zedong's peasant armies pursued their conquest of China, Shanghai, left to suffer inflation and the corruption and arbitrary whims of Guomindang officials, looked on passively as the Communist revolution triumphed (Chapter 12).

The history of "Shanghai under Communism," which is the subject of the last section of this book, is that of a city disliked by the Maoist regime, which never forgave it for its cosmopolitan past and rejected the modernity founded upon trade and individual initiative that it had exemplified for an entire century (Chapter 13). However, the policy of reform and openness that the Chinese regime has adopted from 1980 onward has allowed Shanghai to embark upon a renaissance (Chapter 14). With the government's plans for it to become once again a great economic and financial metropolis, maybe Shanghai will recover its destiny.

PART ONE

The Treaty Port
(1842–1911)

CHAPTER I

Foreigners in the Town
(1843–1853)

T HE OPENING UP OF SHANGHAI TO FOREIGNERS, decreed by the treaty of Nanjing, which in 1842 brought the First Opium War to an end, proceeded over more than two decades. Dictated by the prevailing circumstances and the influence of a number of strong personalities, the forms taken by the Western presence in the course of those years crystallized, producing institutions of a very particular kind, which then rapidly spread to other Chinese treaty ports. Shanghai thus became the laboratory in which the "treaty system" evolved. It was to rule relations between China and the West for a century.

THE ARRIVAL OF THE BARBARIANS

On the evening of November 8, 1843, a small British steamer dropped anchor at the Huangpu riverside, beneath the walls of Shanghai. On board was George Balfour (1809–1894), an Indian Army captain of artillery. He had come to take up his post as consul and to open up Shanghai to foreign trade, in conformity with the stipulations of the Nanjing treaty, which had been signed fifteen months earlier. The officer was young and had no previous experience of China. However, the small staff that accompanied him included, along with a doctor and a secretary, a missionary-interpreter, Walter H. Medhurst.

Nobody was there to greet the British party, so they decided to spend the night on board. At dinner, they drank a toast to "the future greatness and glory of the port." The following morning, the highest local official, *daotai* (circuit intendant) Gong Mujiu, was alerted to their arrival. He sent a few old sedan chairs to meet them. In these, the new consul and his companions made their entry into the town amid crowds of onlookers. In the administrator's *yamen* they were given a polite but cool welcome.*

---

* In Chinese, *yamen* means an official's office.

When the captain asked if he could rent a house to live in and set up his offices, he met with a blank refusal: no lodgings in the town were vacant. The mandarin remained impervious to the pressure exercised by Balfour, a seasoned soldier who declared himself ready to pitch his tent in the courtyard of a temple. But when the interview was over and firecrackers were exploding in the crowd clustering around the foreigners, a richly clad man approached the consul, offering to rent him his own dwelling, a vast house comprising fifty-two rooms. The stranger's name was Koo, and he was one of the town's wealthiest merchants. He was of Cantonese origin but had interests in Hong Kong and was keen to profit from the opening of the port to expand his trading.

The deal was agreed upon, and Captain Balfour and his team were soon installed. Their residence, although luxurious, was not comfortable, mainly because from dawn to dusk crowds of curious visitors invaded, who came to watch the foreigners working, dining, or even bathing. Merchant Koo showed them around. At dinner, the servants crossed the room in single file, marching in time to their chanted songs, "as if, instead of platters of food and plates, they were carrying bales of silk or cotton."[1] But Balfour belonged to a race of empire builders. Overcoming the reticence of the mandarin and moderating the indiscreet ardor of the merchant, he adapted to the peculiarities of his new environment. On November 17, he announced the official opening of the port to foreign trade and set about negotiating the concession of plots of land where British residents could settle. Most were merchants, and by late December there were twenty-five of them.

Four years later, in November 1847, Charles de Montigny (1805–1868) had the task of opening a French consulate in Shanghai. He was from southern Brittany, the son of an émigré who had in the past fought in support of the Greeks. His temperament and policies were to make a lasting impact on the French presence in Shanghai.[2] Upon arrival, the new consul settled some distance from the Chinese town and the British concession, in a house belonging to the Catholic missionaries. "It is small," he said, "but I shall be at home in France here."[3] The national flag, which Montigny hastened to hoist, floated above a "shed," a "barracks," a "frog's nest,"* the floors of which were regularly flooded in the summer rains and the approaches to which were littered with corpses.[4] No curious visitors came here, but plenty of thieves on the prowl, against whom he had to mount a nightly armed guard. Nor did the French consul have a team of assistants at his disposal, only a wife and children, whom he requisitioned to assist him as secretaries. He was also provided an interpreter of Polish origin, Count Michel-Alexandre Kleczkowski, who was a good linguist but had a difficult disposition. In contrast to the prosperity of the British community and the luxury of its consulate, Montigny could count on little apart from himself, his belligerent temperament, and the vivacity of his political imagination.

Since there were as yet neither French traders nor French residents in Shanghai, Montigny, showing remarkable zeal for a "Bonapartist Republican,"[5] set about becoming the official defender of the Catholic missions and their flocks in the town's suburbs and the neighboring provinces of Jiangsu and Zhejiang.** Montigny was of the opinion that protecting the missions could well further the diffusion of French influence. "Allow me to repeat, Minister, all the missionaries here are instruments of the future preponderance and success of France. . . . It is not religious sentiment that prompts me to speak and act in their favor . . . but the interests of my country."[6]

In those times of famine and banditry, his efforts were nothing if not hazardous. As soon as some incident blew up, the consul would set out in a sedan chair or a boat, accompanied only by Kleczkowski. He would organize the defense of the good fathers, harangue the pillagers, admonish the local magistrates, and generally achieve his ends, "half by reasoning and half by

---

* These were the terms used by those who had occasion to visit this earliest French consulate.

** The Jesuits first arrived in China in the late sixteenth century. They were very active in Beijing, where they mingled with the Imperial Court's elite groups. Their settlement in the lower Yangzi basin, at the beginning of the seventeenth century, owed much to the friendship between Matteo Ricci (1562–1610) and a great scholar of Shanghai, Xu Guangqi (Paul Hsu). The latter's conversion triggered that of his extended family and his tenant farmers. When China ejected the missionaries in the following century, the Jiangsu Catholics continued to practice their religion secretly. When the Jesuits returned, in the mid-nineteenth century, they depended very much on these Catholic communities and set up their mission in Zikkawei, to the southwest of Shanghai in the village of the Xu family (Xujiahui in Mandarin).

intimidation."[7] He commanded the respect of crowds thousands strong that were "being pushed about and pushing back" by "brushing aside a hand here, a foot there, with his rifle butt."[8] The very sight of his rifle was usually enough to scare off the brigands. But when pirates attacked the consul at sea while he was returning from one of his expeditions to Ningbo, he opened fire, killing eight of his assailants.[9] In the spring of 1851, he learned that a French whaler had been wrecked off the coast of Korea. He immediately embarked on a Portuguese *lorcha* in search of the crew, which he eventually managed to save after weathering the stormy waves and the hostility of the Korean authorities.[10]

Montigny was equally bold in his diplomatic undertakings. June 1848 saw the arrival of the first Frenchman wishing to settle in Shanghai. He was a young man named Dominique Rémi, a native of Besançon and a clockmaker by profession. The consul immediately seized upon this opportunity: he solicited a territorial concession from the Chinese authorities in order to facilitate the establishment of several dozen large-scale merchants. Montigny found little favor among his hierarchical superiors, who criticized his independent nature and his frequently risky initiatives. But he persisted in pleading his cause: "The distances that separate us, the irregularity of communications, . . . the inevitable delays in the solution of the slightest problem are facts that will always prevent fully united action on the part of Shanghai and the legation, on any urgent matter (and unfortunately nearly all matters here *are* urgent)."[11] Eventually he had his way.

Many of those, whether Chinese or foreign, who held official posts of responsibility in Shanghai in the second half of the nineteenth century or the beginning of the twentieth, might well have resorted to a similar argument. In Shanghai, a frontier town on the edge of the empire and at the antipodes of Europe, adventurers (in the most noble as well as the most abject sense of the term) could allow free rein to their talents. It was they who were to forge the town's destiny. And it was a destiny that would become part of the history of the new geopolitical order that was being set in place.

The foreigners who arrived in China from 1843 onward were not the first to do so. In 1832, the British in Canton, anxious to extend their trade northward, had sent out a reconnaissance party headed by Hugh H.

Lindsay, who took with him both merchants and missionaries aboard the *Lord Amherst* in which he sailed. He was followed by more missionaries and subsequently by the British fleet and army. In the course of the Opium War, Shanghai was occupied on June 19, 1842, without a shot fired, by 4,000 soldiers who then engaged in a four-day-long pillaging rampage before proceeding northward. However, after 1843, it was no longer a matter of commercial explorations or bellicose incursions. Now, the foreigners who came intended to stay. Their presence signaled that times had changed. It was at once a consequence and a symbol of the opening up of China.

FROM THE TRIBUTE SYSTEM
TO THE TREATY SYSTEM

Until the mid-nineteenth century, relations between China and Europe had been limited. It was not that China remained "closed," as merchants, diplomats, and missionaries tended to complain. On the contrary, China engaged in active relations with a number of Asian countries, but those relations operated according to a tribute system in which Westerners were unable to find a position that suited them.[12]

For centuries, the ideas that dictated China's relations with the outside world had rested upon Confucian doctrine. The universe was conceived to be a homogeneous whole within which phenomena were ordered according to a precise and imperative hierarchy. The Son of Heaven was a figure of cosmic dimensions, who performed rites indispensable for the maintenance of universal harmony. He was also a sovereign emperor, placed at the top of a civilized society, who acted as the family head for a number of countries. Chinese tradition made no distinction between internal and external politics. The same rules that fixed human relations within a family also fixed relations within a state or the international community.

Given that the emperor was considered to rule the entire world, his dominion extended to both civilized society and barbarian regions. However, a barbarian society was defined not so much by belonging to an ethnic or religious culture as by an absence of cultural achievements. Barbarians were people who knew nothing of civilization (civilization being identified exclusively with Chinese civilization). If barbarians adopted the rites, ceremonies, and music of China, they could be integrated into the Chinese world. In the meantime, the relations between those poor, deprived peoples of the outer margins and China remained governed by the tribute system.

The states that paid tribute signaled their recognition of the superiority of (Chinese) civilization by periodically sending representatives bearing gifts to Beijing. In return, the emperor manifested his goodwill toward the tribute bearers, along with his desire to ensure that peace reigned among all peoples, thanks to the giving of gifts. Essentially, the tribute system was a ritualistic and symbolic means of communication, designed to encourage the progressive assimilation of barbarians. In practice, it sometimes opened up the possibility of conquest and domination, but at the same time it provided the framework for many peaceful exchanges of both a cultural and a commercial nature. It always implied an attentive surveillance of the barbarians, whose direct contacts with the Chinese population were strictly limited to avoid any risk of contamination of the civilized Chinese mores and to preserve the peace and supremacy of the heavenly empire.

However, the Western barbarians, obeying the logic behind their own capitalist growth, were crowding in ever greater numbers into the coastal regions of southern China. They promoted a quite different concept of the world and international relations, a concept founded on recognition of the equality between nations, the primacy of law in the regulation of their relations, and a belief that closer contacts would naturally be likely to prevent conflicts in the future. Barbarians such as these were not ready to adapt to Chinese ways, so the empire held them at a distance.

Since the end of the eighteenth century, trade between Britain and China had nevertheless been developing, but it did so without any contact between their respective governments and according to an institutional system that isolated the British merchants. Canton was the only port open to them. There, transactions took place under the aegis of the monopolizing East India Company on the British side and the Co-hong guild on the Chinese side.* The Co-hong merchants, who had been granted their

---

* The Cantonese Co-hong was a corporation of merchants with special rights. These alone could communicate with foreign traders, who were allowed no direct contacts with the general population or with Chinese officials. The Co-hong merchants were responsible for concluding commercial transactions with the foreigners and, in the name of the imperial administration, also for charging them customs dues. They made the most of this monopoly to make money by both illegal and legal means.

privileges by the imperial bureaucracy, were answerable to the latter for every foreign ship that docked in the port. The foreigners were isolated and confined to the periphery of the Chinese territory, and control was exercised through a system of collective responsibility, the very features that characterized the tribute system.

In the earliest decades of the nineteenth century, the traditional Sino-centric order had succeeded, although with some difficulty, in engulfing the outposts of European capitalism, whose growing vigor nevertheless gradually undermined "the Canton system," which was bypassed by the agents of "country trade" and smugglers and weakened by the corruption and predations of Chinese officials.* In 1834, the suppression of Britain's East India Company precipitated a crisis, for the adoption of a "laissez-faire" policy on the part of the British called for the suppression of monopolies on the Chinese side. The enormous technical progress achieved in the fields of transport, armaments, and industrial production provided the Westerners with the means to impose upon China the opening up that they had been clamoring for and that China was refusing them. The principal objective of the First Opium War, which broke out in 1839, was precisely to force China to recognize and accept the new capitalist order of the world.

Great Britain engaged in hostilities on its own. Later, in 1856, in the Second Opium War, it was to be joined by France. But the principal European powers, as well as the United States, were all party to the conventions and Sino-foreign treaties that followed in quick succession in the 1840s and 1850s. These were ostensibly bilateral, but in the end they in fact created a multilateral system because there were so many of them and because of the way in which they applied the clause of most-favored nation, extending to all nations the concessions granted to any one of them.

The treaty system was to govern Sino-Western relations for almost a century. By 1842, the broad lines of it were established in Nanjing. Five ports, one of which was Shanghai, were now opened up to British merchants, who

---

* The "country trade" that developed in the territories controlled by the East India Company was carried on by private entrepreneurs, and it linked the company's commercial network and the local trading circuits. Along the Chinese coastline, the company's agents devoted themselves essentially to the sale of Indian opium, which imperial administration prohibitions had banned from legal circuits. The profits from this trade were nevertheless plowed back into legal trading circuits and financed purchases of tea and silk.

could reside there "without suffering bad treatment or restrictions on their activities." Freedom of trade was to be respected. The merchants would no longer be obliged to treat solely with the organizations and agents that the imperial authorities designated. They would no longer be subjected to arbitrary fees but would instead pay taxes; and information concerning the moderate and uniform sum of these would be widely circulated. Finally, British residents would enjoy extraterritoriality and would be subject solely to the jurisdiction of their consul. Curiously enough, the Nanjing treaty made no mention of opium smuggling, even though this had been at the very beginning of the 1839–1842 war. However, the trafficking continued, apparently regulated by informal agreements with the Chinese authorities. Offshore from the treaty ports, foreign ships were always present: anchored a short distance from the coast, they constituted so many "floating stations," which ensured deliveries of the drug to local traders.

The treaties signed with the other powers repeated the same stipulations. The Franco-Chinese treaty of 1844 also included clauses concerning the missionaries, whose presence was now accepted by the imperial government. It revoked the banishment edicts and even undertook to return some of the churches confiscated in the preceding century.

A DOUBLE MISUNDERSTANDING

The agreement sanctioned by the Nanjing treaty was based upon a double misunderstanding. Westerners regarded it as a prelude to the establishment of far more solid commercial and diplomatic relations, similar to those that European nations maintained with one another or with other countries overseas. The Chinese saw it simply as a matter of calming the appetites and turbulence of the new barbarians by making a few specific concessions and cutting one's losses.

At the point when China began to open up to Westerners, the two sides knew very little about each other. The missionaries, who had been expelled from China by an eighteenth-century edict, no longer played the role of cultural intermediaries. The diplomats that the London Court sent as ambassadors to Beijing at the turn of the nineteenth century had run into a blank wall of nonrecognition. Such information as the British possessed was thus drawn from their experiences in Canton, from a number of commercial and religious explorations, and from their recent military expeditions. The Chinese were ignorant of not only the political constitutions and economic activities of the principal Western powers but also the location of the latter and, quite often, even their names.

Now forced to have dealings with one another, the British and Chinese officials thus proceeded to select from their respective funds of experience and political ideas those that they determined would be the most helpful to them in the management of the unknown, hoping in this fashion to reduce unprecedented situations to familiar schemata. The most valuable reference for the British was to be the dominance they had already established in India.[13] Most of their diplomats and military men came to China fresh from a furlough in India, where they had refined the style, ideas, and values of a self-confident elite whose authority rested upon its prestige and its reputation as the possessor of a reserve of superior military power and its determination to deploy that power whenever the need arose.

In Shanghai, the consul, John Rutherford Alcock, epitomized this policy. Unlike Balfour, whom he succeeded in 1846, Alcock was not an Indian Army officer but a former military doctor who had become a career diplomat. Alcock based his position upon a dubious interpretation of the treaties but drew his strength from the presence of the British warships anchored in the Huangpu River. The Qingpu affair—the first in a long series of incidents involving missionaries—illustrates the gunboat diplomacy that foreigners in China were to implement over many decades. In 1848, three British missionaries set off to preach in Qingpu, 40 or so kilometers to the southwest of Shanghai. There they were attacked and seriously molested by some out-of-work sailors. The local magistrates' intervention saved them in the nick of time. Consul Alcock demanded reparation. The Shanghai authorities refused it, claiming that the missionaries should never have gone to Qingpu, a town situated outside the zone authorized for foreign residents, who were not allowed to venture beyond a distance that it was possible to cover in both directions in a single day's journey. The consul, however, maintained that Qingpu did fall inside this zone, and he immediately ordered the brig *Childers* to blockade inside the port 4,000 junks that were ready to set to sea to deliver the imperial quota of grain tribute. For two weeks, the port of Shanghai was paralyzed by the threat that ten cannons represented. A handful of British sailors were facing thousands of Chinese seamen. The consul's initiative was risky, but it was justified when the governor-general of Nanjing stepped in to arbitrate.* He ruled against the local Chinese authorities and insisted that Alcock's claims be satisfied.

The military force to which the consul had resorted was to a large extent symbolic. What made the crew of the *Childers* so redoubtable was the fact that behind it lurked the entire might of the British Empire. This was what also explained definite reservations on the part of the Foreign Office: Alcock was accused of having overstepped his prerogatives and received the approval of his hierarchical superiors only once success was assured. This episode provides an early example of the kind of conflict that quite frequently in the future would set expatriates, who favored gunboat diplomacy, in opposition to the administrations of their respective native countries, which were often considerably more reticent.

Obliged to give way before force, the Chinese authorities tried to regain the upper hand in the field of negotiation and manipulation. The long history of their relations with the countries of central Asia had taught them that when barbarians possessed the upper hand militarily, it was necessary to calm them down with specific concessions, winning them over by treating them well and neutralizing them by setting them against each other or by coopting them and integrating them into the administrative structures of the empire. This strategy, known in the Chinese political vocabulary as the strategy of "loose reins" (*jimi*), was the one adopted by the Chinese negotiators of the opening-up treaties. From the point of view of international law, some clauses in these treaties appeared to threaten Chinese sovereignty: in particular, exterritoriality, which deprived the state of its jurisdiction over part of the resident population; likewise, the clause referring to the most-favored nation, which, when systematically applied, made it quite impossible for China to structure its diplomacy to suit its own interests.

---

* The title of governor-general was given to provincial officials of the highest rank. China had eight governors-general, each of whom supervised the administration of two or three provinces. The governor-general in residence in Nanjing exercised authority over the provinces of Jiangsu, Jiangxi, and Anhui.

Privileges such as these, which nowadays appear outrageous, were not always judged to be so by the Chinese bureaucracy. At the time when the treaties were concluded, the exterritoriality conceded to foreigners may perhaps appear to constitute an extension of a practice that was classic in China, where the concept of personal law outweighed that of territorial jurisdiction and where barbarian residents or frontier dwellers had almost always retained the right to manage their internal affairs in accordance with their own customs. By keeping the reins "loose," the empire avoided becoming embroiled in private conflicts that had nothing to do with its own direct interests. The authority conferred upon the British and French consuls, who were made responsible for laying down the law and applying it among their compatriots, resembled that of the tribal chieftains who, as the Chinese authorities saw it, were responsible for the behavior of their own communities. The establishment of the five treaty ports could, furthermore, be regarded as a means of limiting, rather than developing, commercial transactions. Similarly, the clause concerning the most-favored nation could be seen both as a manifestation of the supreme imperial impartiality and benevolence with regard to all barbarian nations and, at the same time, as a strategy designed to divide the nations, the better to control them. What the foreigners regarded as "a charter of privileges," the Chinese apparently perceived as "a series of limitation measures."[14]

Until the occupation of Beijing by Franco-British troops in 1860, the imperial government was therefore relatively unconcerned about the settlement of Westerners on the country's southern coast. The only problem that it could detect was the minor one of maintaining order along its maritime frontiers. Rather than resolve this by force, it was perfectly possible to defuse it by allowing the foreigners to take their place among the leading local elite groups. In accordance with this "laissez-faire" policy, the management of the Western presence in the treaty ports was left to the local officials, who negotiated agreements and compromises with the foreign consuls. Meanwhile, however, the political visions of the two sides were totally divergent. To the Chinese, it seemed a matter of organizing ghettoes or keeping foreign troublemakers in quarantine. For the Europeans, the aim was to lay the foundations of an eventually triumphant imperialism. On the basis of this misunderstanding the treaty ports began to develop.

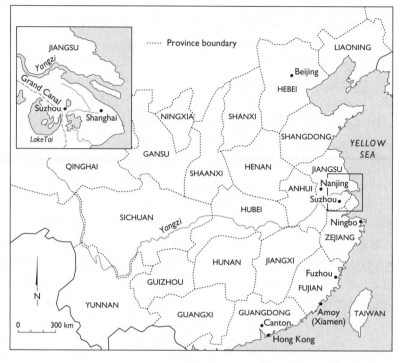

China

WHY SHANGHAI?

At first sight, Shanghai seemed the most modest and least attractive of the five new treaty ports. So why Shanghai rather than Canton, Fuzhou, Amoy (Xiamen), or Ningbo? Why did this particular town, described by its first Western residents as a filthy place, become the laboratory in which the treaty system was invented? It was not a provincial capital, as Canton was, but simply a circuit capital. The port was not positioned within a bay protected by offshore islands, as Amoy and Ningbo were. It was situated on the left bank of the Huangpu, about 18 kilometers from the river's confluence with the Yangzi. The surrounding countryside, which rose hardly higher than sea level, was furrowed by rivers and canals whose waters rose and fell with the tides and frequently overflowed, causing floods. Despite their agricultural richness, these delta fields presented an austere landscape that filled Captain Jurien de la Gravière with melancholy feelings and strange political reflections: "You cannot imagine anything flatter or more monotonous than the vast alluvial expanses between which the sinuous course of this river [the Huangpu] wanders. The Camargue and the banks of the lower reaches of the Charente are picturesque in comparison to these half-drowned fields that present the eye with nothing but a featureless expanse. The level is as low as that of democracy: rich harvests but no trees, fertile land but not the slightest hill, holding magnificent promise to the eye of a cultivator but absolutely nothing for the soul of a poet."[15]

Nor was the town itself much to look at. All the same, it was not just "a fishing village," as one long-standing myth would have it.[16] Shanghai boasted between 200,000 and 300,000 inhabitants. Bustling commercial quarters bordered immediately upon the river, and beyond them stood a walled town surrounded by three-centuries-old ramparts on the point of collapse; within, a maze of narrow streets, the most important of which, 3 or 4 meters wide, were paved with bricks and lined by stalls. The network of streets interlaced with that of the canals, beds of mud and rubbish periodically flushed out by floods. The pointed roofs of a few temples rose above a horizon of low houses covered by thatch, reeds, or tiles. There was no sign of any town planning reflecting a political will or any ritual or ideological preoccupations, such as are suggested by the regular grid pattern of the cities of northern China.

Until the beginning of the nineteenth century, Shanghai attracted the attention of no foreigners: no Catholic missionaries in the days of Matteo Ricci and no East India Company agents later on. It was not until 1832 and Lindsay's expedition on the *Lord Amherst* that news of the town began to circulate among merchants and missionaries. Now praise was voiced for the busy port in which Lindsay, in a single week, counted more than four hundred junks from northern China laden with beans and flour.[17] Fifteen years later, Captain Balfour, the first British consul, was praising the strategic position of the town, on the estuary of the vast Yangzi River basin, which provided access to markets in the inland provinces.

William Jardine played the determining role in the choice of Shanghai as a treaty port. This opium merchant, who became a member of Parliament in London in 1841, produced the best analysis of the possibilities that the port offered for the development of international trade. As the head of a company engaged in "country trade" and the sale of opium, William Jardine had had occasion to trade with private merchants and entrepreneurs whom the imperial bureaucracy ignored, frequently dismissing them as pirates and smugglers. He thus had a chance to assess the dynamism of a society that made the most of the imperial officials' inability to control the full range of economic mechanisms: it was upon precisely the booming business of these zones of autonomy that the destiny of Shanghai was to be constructed.

The town's commercial development was closely intertwined with that of the surrounding Jiangnan region.* Shanghai had been a market town since the fifteenth century. Its rise was propelled by that of the provinces that specialized in the production of cotton in the lower Yangzi basin, where the richness of the agricultural produce and the early development of craftsmanship were favorable to both local and regional trade. At an early date Shanghai began to export raw cotton, woven fabrics, and other textiles, including silk, to other provinces and to import rice, tea, and soya cake (used as fertilizer). In 1684, when the emperor lifted the two-century-old ban on maritime trade, Shanghai added to its functions as a market town those of a major coastal port. While Canton monopolized trade with the West, Shanghai traded with Japan and the Nanyang (the countries of Southeast Asia). But some products made in Shanghai, such as silks and nankins (thick cotton fabrics, dyed blue), made their way to European and American markets via Canton.

Trade continued to expand throughout the eighteenth century, right up to the beginning of the nineteenth century. At this point difficulties surrounding the navigation of the Great Canal caused the delivery of grain tribute to be rerouted by sea.** Shanghai now became the starting point of

---

* Jiangnan was the name for the southern part of Jiangsu.
** The Great Canal, the construction of which had begun in the seventh century and took several hundred years, linked the lower Yangzi region with Beijing. For a long time it was the great axis for trade between central/southern and northern China. It was the route along which, every year, hundreds of thousands of tons of cereals were delivered to the capital, as grain tribute. In the mid-nineteenth century, when floods and alluvium were disrupting navigation and rebellions in the interior threatened transport security, the Great Canal was abandoned in favor of transport by sea.

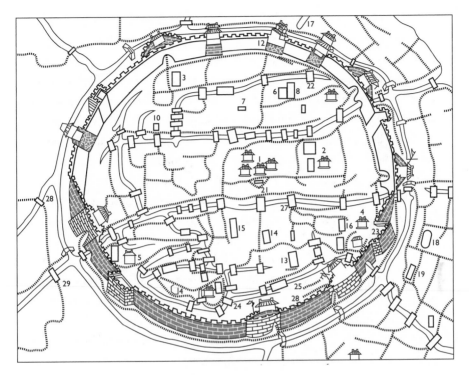

The old walled town

a new network of transportation, and its shipbuilders launched into the construction of large seagoing junks. Its success led to a greater demand for money, to which private banking and credit endeavored to respond. By the end of the eighteenth century, the town boasted 125 *qianzhuang* (money houses). In accordance with a system of credit that had been in operation for many decades among the merchants of Ningbo, the bills and notes produced by these traditional banks constituted nothing less than veritable bank money. Even before the opening up of China, many of these banks used opium as security in the (illegal) trade in which the qianzhuang were heavily involved.

Up to a point, the public authorities adjusted to the town's economic expansion. From being a mere district capital (*xian*), Shanghai, as early as 1730, became the capital of a circuit (*dao*) with a resident daotai. He was placed directly under the authority of the provincial governor and controlled the administration of twenty or so districts. He was, furthermore, in charge of the management of the river and maritime customs posts that levied taxes on external trading.* The transfer of this office to Shanghai (in 1637), followed by that of the office for grain tribute, reflected and stimulated the increasingly important role that the port played in both external and internal trading. The fact is that the imperial bureaucracy seemed, above all, intent on garnering the fiscal benefits of the town's economic expansion. Its major contribution to this was probably the policy of maintaining peace and public order that it had pursued throughout the eighteenth century.

The mainspring of growth was private enterprise. Its agents were recruited from a mass of artisans, porters, shopkeepers, itinerant agents detailed to explore the local markets, manufacturers, wholesalers, exporters, shipbuilders, and bankers. Many had come from provinces near and far, eager to profit from the possibilities of enrichment that Shanghai's rise offered. These exiles gathered in native-place associations (*huiguan*), the network of which structured the local merchant community. Their growing number (twenty-one by 1830) was an indication of the economic importance of Shanghai. Initially, these native-place associations recruited members from various social categories on the basis of their provincial or regional origins; in the eighteenth century they had been dominated by merchants and tended to merge with the professional guilds (*gongsuo*) and to reflect the specific activities of the entrepreneurs of this or that region. The native-place association of merchants from southern Manchuria and Shandong, for example, was made up of merchants dealing in beans and soya cow cake. The Ningbo native-place association dominated banking activities. That of the merchants of Fujian specialized in the sugar trade and the sale of wood for building. The native-place association of the Cantonese merchants of Shantou (Swatow) specialized in opium trafficking.

These native-place associations and professional guilds guaranteed the regularity of transactions in the sectors of their competence and played an essential role in promoting the cohesion of the local economy and in the development of an interregional economy. They also took on social

---

* In the eighteenth century, four Maritime Customs Offices, upon which many agencies depended, levied taxation on external Chinese trade.

responsibilities, organizing charitable and philanthropic activities, some of which were restricted to their own members whereas others extended to the community of urban residents as a whole. Their power and wealth left their mark on the landscape, for these institutions acquired vast tracts of land, mostly situated beyond the walled town. On these, they erected temples, pavilions, funerary halls, cemeteries, and dormitories, the better to cater for the needs of their members.

Thanks to its material resources and institutional structures, the merchant society of Shanghai enjoyed relative autonomy; but it did not rate as a power when faced with the imperial bureaucracy. Its political weakness stood in sharp contrast to its economic dynamism, and its wealth did not compensate for its low status. The Shanghai merchants remained subordinate to imperial officials and to the gentry class that produced the latter. They played no part in the refined culture that provided Jiangnan its identity and political clout within the empire. A deep gap separated them from the literate elite living in the countryside, the big country towns, and Suzhou, the provincial capital. That gap was not impassable, for some wealthy merchants did manage to become assimilated by passing civil service examinations, purchasing official titles, or being awarded them in recognition of their large contributions to the public treasury. But the mechanisms for such assimilation continued to be governed by Confucian values and remained under the control of the imperial authorities who stood as guarantors of their orthodoxy.

This made for complicated relations between the political power, embodied by imperial officials, and the economic and social power held by the major guilds and regionalist associations. In general, their aim was cooperation, but the merchant organizations, which usually behaved as auxiliaries to the public authorities, occasionally managed to convert themselves into redoubtable "lobbies," and this made it necessary for the representatives of imperial authority to extend them understanding and flexibility. Westerners landing in Shanghai found it hard to understand how this society and this bureaucracy interacted. They were inclined to ally themselves with the former (hence the—extremely symbolic—agreement reached between the merchant Koo and Consul Balfour in November 1843), but they never ceased meanwhile to seek the support of the latter.

QUARTERS RESERVED FOR THE FOREIGNERS

The opening-up treaties granted the right of residence to foreigners but did not make it clear where they should establish themselves. The concessions were the result of local agreements that, in the first instance, specified the procedures for transferring those foreigners' land rights. In the course of time, those ad hoc arrangements served as the basis upon which to develop veritable colonial enclaves.

In Shanghai, the idea of installing the foreigners in a separate quarter, outside the walled town, came from Daotai Gong. Once the port was opened up, the circuit intendant was obliged to add to his administrative and fiscal responsibilities "barbarian management" (*yi wu*), that is, relations with the foreigners.* Daotai Gong was a traditionally trained Confucian scholar and a competent administrator. He was supposed to see that the treaty terms were respected as were the claims of the merchants of Guangdong and Fujian, who were keen to do business with the British. But his main preoccupation was to avoid Sino-foreign altercations about which the imperial authorities did not wish to be bothered. The best policy seemed to him to be segregation, for, unlike the merchants, the people of Shanghai were hostile to the presence of these "long-nosed" devils who had sacked the town in 1842 and who made use of dangerous firearms with singular unconcern.**

Daotai Gong therefore drew up the *Land Regulations* of 1845, which granted the British the right to install themselves in a zone measuring 832 *mu* (56 hectares); the area was increased to 2,820 *mu* (199 hectares) in 1848. The zone was situated to the north of the walled town and its suburbs, along the bank of the Huangpu, where gunboats and merchant vessels could anchor. To the north and the south, the Suzhou River and the Yangjingbang delimited the area. To the west, the frontier, initially marked by a boundary post, was extended in 1848 to the banks of another watercourse: Zhoujingbang (Defence Creek).

---

* The *dao*, or circuit, was an intermediary administrative unit under the authority of the provincial government. The authority of the circuit intendant (*daotai*) extended to the lower employees of the prefecture (*fu*) and the district (*xian*). It also covered the fields of justice, finance, education, and military affairs. Gong Mujiu was the daotai of Shanghai from 1843 to 1846.[18]
** In a "hunting incident" on November 20, 1843, a sailor hunting in the Shanghai neighborhood had accidentally killed two young boys.

The daotai of Shanghai meting out justice

The *Land Regulations* laid down detailed rules governing the acquisition of land and buildings, essentially fields and marshes dotted with
farms, huts, and tombs. Provided they paid compensation to the Chinese
proprietors, the foreigners could obtain perpetual rights, but China reserved an overriding property right, to be recognized by the payment of
an annual tax known as "rent." Individuals were supposed to carry out
such transactions. Very soon, however, the British merchants, discouraged
by linguistic difficulties and complex administrative procedures, opted instead to have their consul negotiate with the Chinese administration, which
itself acted in the name of the landowning peasants.* The merchants also

---

* Despite the intermediary role played by the consul and the daotai in the conclusion of
permanent leases, transfers of land took place between individuals, for example, between
a Chinese landowner and a British merchant. The legal and institutional structure of the
settlement that they reached thus differed from that of the concessions, where the land was
ceded by the Chinese government to a foreign power that then passed it on to the merchants. In French, in this instance was less precise than the English language, no
distinction was made between these different forms of settlement, all of which were termed
"concessions."

used their consul as an intermediary in the annual payment of both their rent to the imperial government and the customs dues on their merchandise. The consul thus, in effect, acted with regard to his compatriots as an agent of the Chinese government.

In his management of foreign affairs, Daotai Gong thus adopted the classic Chinese strategies for controlling barbarians: segregation, collective responsibility, and partial integration into the Chinese administrative structures. At the local level, the establishment of British merchants outside the walled town resembled the treatment meted out to merchants from other provinces within the empire. They too were foreigners, although not barbarians. The British, like the merchants of Fujian or Zhejiang, Anhui or Guangdong, were confined to a sector where they could build their homes and their warehouses, conduct their business and practice their religion, speak their own language, organize their own entertainment (horse racing), and obey their own laws. The British Guild (*Yingguo huiguan*), to borrow the expression then used by the Shanghainese to designate the British business community, "easily found its place within the already existing frameworks of Chinese commercial organization."[19]

The *Land Regulations* explicitly stipulated that no Chinese could claim ownership of land or buildings in the settlement, but they did not specify the procedures to be observed by Western buyers who were not British. As Consul Balfour saw it, there could be no doubt that, because the "settlement" was placed under the exclusive authority of Great Britain, all foreigners who wished to settle there had to apply to him as an intermediary and would remain under his jurisdiction. The French and the Americans did not agree. The clashes that arose over this point soon resulted in the creation of new concessions.

The property over which Consul Montigny raised the French flag upon his arrival in the spring of 1848 belonged to Catholic missionaries.* It was situated on Chinese territory, in an as yet barely built-up zone squeezed between the walls of the old town to the south and the British concession to the north. Montigny set his sights upon this quar-

---

* It had been ceded to the Catholic missionaries in 1847 as compensation for the confiscations of the previous century.

ter, close to what was then the town's business center (the Chinese town and its suburbs). As soon as a single French merchant, Dominique Rémi, indicated his intention to buy a plot of land, the consul presented the daotai with an official request for a concession. Negotiations dragged on, however. The administration played the card of dividing the foreigners and offered Montigny land within the British enclave, provided Consul Alcock agreed. Montigny rejected such a solution with indignation: "It is altogether unseemly that you, the Taontae (daotai) should offer me, the representative of the great French nation, a plot of land that already belongs to the British nation."[20] Eventually the matter was resolved. On April 6, 1849, a proclamation established the boundaries of the French concession: it was bordered on the south by the canal that wound around the town walls, on the north by the Yangjingbang, on the east by the banks of the Huangpu, and on the west it extended roughly as far as the British concession did. However, it was smaller than the latter (measuring only 986 mu, 66 hectares) and, instead of the wide river frontage that the British had succeeded in acquiring, its access to the Huangpu was relatively restricted.

The French consul, like his British colleague, was granted the exclusive right to farm out land to his own nationals, or possibly even to other Westerners, in accordance with the conditions already laid down by the *Land Regulations* of 1845, and he alone exercised jurisdiction over the concession's foreign residents. The conditions that the opening-up treaties granted the Western powers for the exercise of consular jurisdiction were, in fact, one of the principal arguments that Montigny put forward in favor of the creation of a French concession. The maintenance of order among the cosmopolitan population of adventurers—sailors, deserters, receivers of stolen goods—attracted by the opening of the port, certainly entailed increasingly frequent interventions on the part of the various consuls, and the danger was that clashes over jurisdiction would multiply. For Montigny, as for Balfour several years earlier, "everyone needs to be in his own home and responsible for his own actions vis-à-vis the Chinese authorities."[21]

However, the American consul, John N. Alsop Griswold, protested against the creation of the French concession and the existence of exclusive privileges and rights: "Imagine if there were fifty consuls in Shanghai and each one . . . obtained a portion of territory as extensive as that obtained by the consul of Great Britain, . . . how could enough land be found to answer the demand for it?"[22] Defending lofty principles while at the same time applying the "me-too" policy and profiting from the advantages obtained by other powers, the Americans abstained from negotiating for the concession of a particular zone for themselves. They settled in large numbers to the north of the Suzhou River, in the Hongkou quarter that, de facto, became the American concession. This "Cinderella concession" did not gain official recognition of its existence and boundaries until 1863, only a few months before it merged with the British concession.[23]

A TOWN WITH TWO FACES

The eighteenth-century expansion of the town caused it to spill over its walls and populated its eastern suburbs. In the nineteenth century, opening up the port to foreigners and creating the concessions extended the town northward. The structure of the new quarters and the regular layout of their streets running from west to east and south to north presented a stark contrast to the maze of tiny alleys in the walled town. However, this quadrangular network that spread westward did not reflect any deliberate overall planning. It was simply a legacy of the rural way of dividing up the land, which the system of land concessions, agreed between individuals, respected: it followed the pattern of waterways and paths that led to the fields and hamlets.[24]

These new quarters developed at a very uneven rhythm. The American merchants were dissatisfied with Hongkou, which at that time was served by no bridges over the Suzhou River, and they abandoned that distant, muddy quarter to impoverished missionaries, preferring to settle in the British concession. Meanwhile, the French concession, four years after its creation, was still an empty shell. Montigny's aspirations were apparently exaggerated: since Dominique Rémi, no merchant had asked to settle there. The Chinese peasants were still there in their mud huts, scattered amid the wastelands, cemeteries, and scrub. To the west, there were a few Protestant missions, already established before the creation of the concession, but the French quarter itself consisted of no more than the property of the Jesuit mission of Jiangnan, which covered about 7 hectares, in the middle of which lay the house that Montigny had rented and converted into a consulate. Rémi's land was close by. All around, local merchants and artisans lived in squalor; and along the banks of the Yangjingbang, all the immigrant thieves—people from Guangdong and Fujian—lured by the gaming houses, opium dens, and general debauchery, made the French quarter "a dangerous and unsavory place."[25] The only architectural contributions the French made to Shanghai between 1840 and 1850 were the baroque cathedral of Saint Francis-Xavier and the church of Saint Ignatius, built in the form of "a Greek temple, topped with a Chinese lantern."[26] Both, however, were situated outside the French concession, the former in Dongjiadu (Tongkadou), the latter in Xujiahui (Zikkawei), on land the Chinese authorities restored or sold to the missionaries.

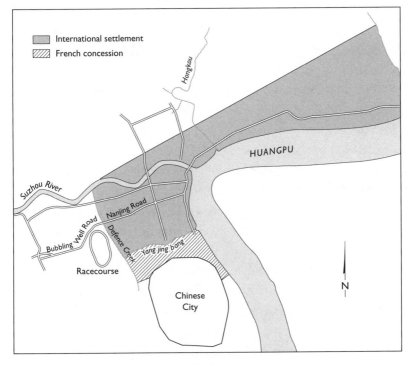

Shanghai in 1881

Upon scrambling over the humpbacked bridge spanning the Yangjing-bang, one reached the British concession and the residences of the proprietors and representatives of the major trading companies, some of which had been operating in East Asia for decades. These were the merchant princes whom the Chinese called *taipan*. Their wealth and opulent way of life conferred a dazzling glamour upon the early "romantic period" of the European and American establishments of Shanghai.[27] Those "were the days when commercial life was marked by romance and a veritable oriental splendor."[28] The Europeans and the Americans were the first to acquire plots of land in the British concession, and they proceeded to install themselves along the edge of the Huangpu. Plot no. 1 was allotted to the Jardine and Matheson Company; its rival, the Dent Company, acquired plots 8 and 9, a little further south. Within a few years, the line of foreign *hong* extended right along the curve of the river.*

These early constructions, built in the Anglo-Indian style familiar everywhere from Calcutta to Macao, which in Shanghai became known as the "comprador" style, possessed a certain simple grandeur. In the absence of architects, the merchants themselves drew up plans for them and spared neither money nor space. The main one-story residence would be set in the middle of a vast square or rectangular precinct. It would be surrounded by a veranda with wide arches opening to a garden in which English roses mingled with magnolias and tulip trees. At the rear would be the outhouses, a kitchen, servants' quarters, stables, and warehouses. The main facade, set back from the bank, looked onto the river. The 1845 *Land Regulations* reserved a right of way between the course of the Huangpu and the riverside mansions. In those days this was a towpath about 10 meters wide and so muddy that people had to wear waders to venture onto it. Later, the riverfront was to become the Bund promenade, the very symbol of the grandeur and elegance of the town of Shanghai. In the meantime, jetties set on stilts linked every hong to the river.

From 1852 on, the British Consulate occupied a remarkable site of about 15 hectares at the extreme northern end of the Bund, from which

---

* *Hong* was the term applied to all the buildings needed for commercial activities: offices, warehouses, and residences.[29]

it appeared to watch over the interests of both the merchants and the empire. The other public edifices consisted of an Anglican church and a racecourse. The design of the concession did not as yet suggest any aspirations to colonial grandeur. It simply reflected the preoccupations of the merchants and aimed to answer their needs. The Committee on Roads and Jetties, created in 1846, set out to consolidate the banks of the Huangpu, thereby laying the foundations of the future Bund, and to improve the roads by straightening out a number of the curves inherited from the sinuous course of rivers and streams (which they had replaced) and by widening the principal thoroughfares to 3 meters. Its objective was to facilitate the transport of merchandise from and to the port. But above all, the committee aimed to avoid having to increase the then very low quayside dues and land taxes that fed its coffers.

Within about ten years from the opening up of the port, the face of Shanghai had thus changed considerably. Its territory had been expanded by the addition, to its north, of new quarters, in theory reserved for Westerners.* Although increasing rapidly, these were still quite few in number: about one hundred in 1846 but almost three times as many by 1854. This small community had at its disposal a territory of 650 hectares, which it by no means completely occupied, whereas as many as 200,000 people were crammed within the walls of the old town. The vast European residences, set in their flower-filled gardens, and the regular network of the streets in the concessions contrasted strongly with the cramped buildings of the town and the higgledy-piggledy confusion of its alleyways.

There were now two towns in Shanghai, linked by commercial interests but living apart. Should this early European settlement be seen as an illustration of the history of the colonial towns that Western powers created in Asia?[30] Across the board, from Delhi to Saigon, there were many such double towns to be found, in which the native and the European quarters were juxtaposed. In Shanghai, the segregation of the communities was decided by the Chinese authorities just as much as or perhaps

---

* In fact, though, many of the original Chinese inhabitants still lived in the British and, even more, in the French concessions.

even more than by the foreign consuls and merchants. The Chinese were anxious to avoid cultural contaminations and diplomatic difficulties; the Europeans wished to safeguard their commodities and their standards of hygiene. However, that segregation failed to prevent the serious disturbances that were soon to upset the Chinese town, modify its relations with the concessions, and, more generally, change the relations between the Chinese Empire and the foreign powers.

CHAPTER 2

Local Diplomacy and National Politics
(1853–1864)

THE TAIPING UPRISING, which erupted in 1851 in southern China and spread rapidly toward the Yangzi valley, began a period of major rebellions from which the Manchu dynasty was to emerge weakened and by which the ideological and political landscape of China was to be transformed. A number of elements were in play in this revolt: a traditional insurrection, the inroads that Christianity was making, Western technology, and a number of forms of utopian socialism, and it marked China's first steps in its pursuit of modernity. In the course of this long decade of civil wars (1851–1864), Shanghai experienced an unremitting series of violent disorders, rebellions, massacres, looting, and repression. In 1853, the walled town fell into the hands of the secret society of the Small Swords (*Xiaodaohui*). In 1860 and then again in 1862, it was attacked by the main body of the Taiping forces.

For over ten years Shanghai thus lived amid violence and confusion. The authority of the imperial bureaucracy hardly made itself felt. The local administration and society were thus left dependent upon their own forces to organize resistance and negotiate compromises. But the presence of foreigners seriously complicated the classic Chinese pattern of rebellion and repression. At first simply spectators of the clashes and not unsympathetic to the rebels, the foreigners progressively intervened in order to defend their own interests. They ended up making common cause with the imperial administration and forces, to whose triumph in 1862–1863 they were able to contribute. With the agreement of the daotai and the local Chinese administration, they then proceeded to take a series of measures designed to ensure the application of the opening-up treaties and the security and smooth management of the concessions.

THE CHINESE WALLED TOWN GIVEN OVER TO
THE SMALL SWORDS (OR RED TURBANS)

The insurrection that from September 1853 to February 1855 placed the Chinese town in the hands of the Small Swords took place in a context of general disorder and reflected the destabilization of Shanghai society in the wake of the opening up. The rebels were attached to the Triads of southern China, among which the ideology of the Taiping was evolving and spreading. The elements of the Taiping ideology that the Triads embraced were Christian egalitarianism, the Confucian utopia of universal harmony, and, above all, the plan to overthrow the Manchu dynasty.

The Small Swords occupied Shanghai in the wake of the great crusade that carried the Taiping as far as Nanjing, where they established their capital in March 1853. But their uprising was also a response to particular circumstances. Once it became a frontier town that served to bring China and the West into contact, Shanghai attracted many Chinese from the southern provinces. The local administration, already weakened by the pressures that the Western consuls and merchants exerted on it, now had to face up to the growing appetites of these provincial groups. The most wealthy and the most powerful were the Cantonese.[1] Even before the First Opium War, when Canton was the only port open to Western trade, they had acquired an experience of international contacts that gave them an important advantage over their Ningbo and Jiangsu rivals. They were organized into powerful regional guilds (*huiguan*) that gathered together merchants specializing in the trading of opium, tea, and silk; compradors who had followed British companies initially established in Canton when these moved to Shanghai; and officials whose knowledge of "barbarian management" qualified them for the administration of the treaty ports. But alongside these elite groups, Shanghai attracted many other Cantonese, who were then closely followed by people from Fujian: out-of-work sailors and workers reduced to vagrancy, adventurers, people with no particular loyalties grouped into gangs and belonging to secret societies (*banghui, huidang*). Many notables and vagabonds were linked by their common origins, and such links created a solidarity that was further strengthened by the risks and profits shared in opium smuggling, a domain that these immigrants monopolized.

The notables who headed the Cantonese guilds were men with two faces, or, to use the Chinese image, they were like rats in that the positioning of their eyes allowed them to see two sides at once. Sometimes they were prepared to assist the local administration by mediating in the many conflicts that disrupted this ill-policed society. However, in certain circumstances and in order to protect their own interests, they would not hesitate to switch camps and turn for support to the secret societies. This was precisely what happened in 1853. The Shanghai daotai was then Wu Jianzhang, a Cantonese social climber who had purchased his post and made the most of his official functions to favor the affairs of his compatriots. To strengthen the administration's and the local militia's loyalty to himself, he packed them with men from his own province and even from his native village, but this Cantonization of Shanghai did not produce the hoped-for results. On September 7, strong-arm men from Guangdong and Fujian seized the Chinese town without having to strike a single blow. Daotai Wu then owed his safety solely to the intervention of American merchants, who helped to organize his escape by concealing him in a large basket let down from the ramparts.

The rebels' success depended essentially upon the support and structures that the regional guilds provided. In this ill-governed town, prey to opium trafficking and all the corruption that accompanied it, the guilds played an important but ambivalent role. The mechanisms they set in place to strengthen the public authorities—for example, the militia—could be turned against those same authorities suddenly and without warning, whenever geographical and intracommunity solidarities overrode loyalty to the imperial dynasty and administration. Neither their personalities nor their careers disposed the principal guild leaders to defend the public interest or even to consider doing so. Upstart notables, as they were, in possession of fortunes amassed from one day to the next, they were parvenus with shady pasts, racketeers as much as protectors of their respective merchant communities. The absence of ideology among the Shanghai rebels stood in sharp contrast to the vigorous theological, social, and political aspirations of the Taiping. For that reason, once the Small Swords had seized the walled town, the Taiping rejected the allegiance that the rebels offered them.

At the end of September 1853, the imperial government sent troops to expel the rebels. This mediocre militia, recruited locally, which pitched camp beneath the town walls, made many incursions into the foreign concessions. To the foreigners, the imperial soldiers were just as daunting as the rebels. The consuls and commanders of the ships anchored in the Huangpu had opted for neutrality but had no way of getting it respected. Both Chinese camps were using Western mercenaries. Moreover, the merchants kept the besieged rebels supplied with arms, thereby helping to prolong their resistance: "The meeting of East and West, so often romanced upon, resulted in this case in the demoralization of both; the results were more sordid than romantic. In the ensuing months of 1853–1855 officials became merchants, imperialists supported the rebels, consuls neglected their trust, neutrals profited from the arms traffic."[2]

On two occasions, the foreigners made military interventions. The first time, on April 4, 1854, British and American marines assisted by a few volunteers recruited locally—380 men in all—attacked the imperial troops encamped close to the racecourse to force them to desist from their incursions in the concessions. Profiting from a sortie made by the besieged rebels, the Westerners forced 10,000 imperial soldiers to withdraw to the south of the walled town, well away from the concessions. This skirmish, glorified by the longtime residents, entered into history under the name of the Battle of Muddy Flat. The French, who at that time had no warships in the Huangpu, were not able to take part in the action but morally associated themselves with it. Consul Benoît Edan wrote as follows to his colleague Alcock: "Allow me, sir, by supporting the act of justice and imperious prudence that you have accomplished, to congratulate you."[3]

A few days later, the arrival of the *Colbert*, soon joined by the frigate *Jeanne d'Arc*, enabled Edan to reinforce security measures in the French concession. This territory, situated very close to the walled town, was regularly visited by the rebels, crossed by the European and American adventurers in their pay, and invaded by bands of imperial soldiers. It had become the scene of disorders of every kind—brigandage, assassinations, and arson. However, it now found a defender in the person of Rear-Admiral Laguerre. Indignant at the many incidents of complicity between the rebels and the British and Americans, the admiral took the side of the imperial troops. He prohibited all communications with the besieged town, and eventually, on January 6, 1855, he led 250 sailors mustered from among the landing troops in an attack on it. Laguerre and his men managed to take the walls but not the town. Although this attack was not successful, it spelled the end of the insurrection. On February 17, 1855, the rebels, subjected to an increasingly rigorous blockade, finally fled. The town then fell to the imperial soldiers, who proceeded to sack it and massacre the inhabitants.

Despite their proclaimed neutrality, the foreigners had played an important role in the rebellion. The complicity between the British and Americans and the Red Turbans had allowed the latter to prolong their resistance for seventeen months, and they were eventually overcome only because of the alliance between the French and the Imperial Army. In the course of this dramatic episode, many cracks appeared in what was known as Western imperialism. On all sides merchants, consuls, naval officers, Catholics, Protestants, the British, the Americans, and the French raised discordant voices. Long after the events, mutual accusations continued to fly. One side denounced "the hostile intrigues of the Jesuits . . . , the consul of France, the commander of the French navy . . . both of them bigots . . . who had sold themselves to the priests."[4] The other side was meanwhile deploring all "the illusions . . . , the immoral and mercantile calculations"[5] and "that fatal policy of . . . nonintervention."[6] Admiral Laguerre was disgraced. But the interventionist policy that he had recommended and practiced was readopted a few years later, this time with unanimous approval, when the major contingents of the Taiping troops threatened Shanghai.

THE TAIPING ATTACKS (1860–1862)

When the Small Swords were ejected from Shanghai, the Taiping rebels were also sustaining serious reverses. In 1855, their progress northward was halted at Tianjin, and dissension within their ranks led to a series of military setbacks. In 1860, the rebellion nevertheless acquired renewed vigor under a new leader, Hong Rengan, who decided to deflect the insurgents' march eastward. His objective was the lower Yangzi, whose riches he coveted and where he planned to make an alliance with the Westerners. His long familiarity with missionaries in Hong Kong had introduced him to Western culture and technology, and he was hoping to acquire ships and arms on which to found his power.

After capturing Suzhou in June 1860, the Taiping saw the route to Shanghai opening up before them. This time the Westerners were no longer faced with a local revolt but with a movement of national dimensions with institutions of its own, which was the rival of the imperial government with which they themselves had been at loggerheads since the outbreak of the Second Opium War in 1856. Contrary to the old adage that the enemy of one's enemy becomes one's friend and despite the sympathy that the Taipings' Christian-tinged ideology attracted and other more mercantile complicities, British and French diplomacy remained officially neutral, although their neutrality was qualified by the need to defend their concessions and their economic interests. In the months that followed, British diplomats negotiated with the Taiping as with a de facto power in a bid to safeguard the trade of the lower Yangzi. Then, from 1862 onward, the reorganization of the imperial forces and their improved situation under the leadership of two impressive mandarins, Zeng Guofan and Li Hongzhang, along with the partisans of peace triumphing in Beijing, opened up the way for true cooperation between the foreigners and the imperial forces against the Taiping.*

In the summer of 1860, when the Taiping appeared beneath the walls of Shanghai and set up their headquarters in Zikkawei, from which they ousted the good fathers, the foreigners were ready to ensure on their own the defense of the concessions and the Chinese town. The presence in the vicinity of both French and British expeditionary forces on their way to fight the imperial troops in Beijing provided them with the means to do so. "What would appear impossible in Europe, namely, separating the cause of a sovereign from that of his subjects and the cause of one province from that of another in this manner, raises no difficulties at all here," a Shanghai priest commented at the time.[7]

The Chinese merchants also mobilized and raised a militia. Introducing adaptations to their traditions of self-defense, they even decided, with the

---

* Changing relations in the balance of power in the Imperial Court made possible the ratification of the treaties of Tianjin (1858) and Beijing (1860) and also the accession to power of Prince Gong, who advocated respect for the treaties and peace with the Westerners.

approval of the local mandarins, to engage foreign mercenaries, entrusting their recruitment to a certain Frederick T. Ward. This American adventurer, with dreams of building himself an empire in Asia, lacked neither boldness nor skill. He was the son-in-law of an important comprador banker from Zhejiang named Yang Fang, and he worked hard to implement a local defense policy supported and financed by the Chinese elite groups of the lower Yangzi. At the head of several hundred Filipinos, men from Manila and Macao, and Chinese, led by deserters from British and American ships, Ward campaigned in the vicinity of Shanghai, thereby distancing the threat hanging over the town. His little band of men, given the name The Ever Victorious Army, was then officially integrated into the ranks of the imperial forces.

However, the danger, more acute now, reemerged in 1862 when the Taiping launched a new offensive. In Shanghai, the defense of the town was organized. The French and British troops pooled their efforts with those of Ward and his mercenaries, and reinforcements were brought in from India and France. The objective was not only to protect the town— both the concessions and the Chinese walled town—but also to pacify the surrounding countryside within a radius of 30 miles (45 kilometers), destroying the bases from which the Taiping launched their attacks and restoring free passage for commercial goods. The campaign was taxing for the French and the British.[8] They suffered from the hot, wet climate, fell victim to dysentery and cholera, and struggled hard to move their artillery around the rice paddies. They were dependent on the Jesuits and their converts for information, and in order to scale the ramparts of walled towns, they were frequently reduced to the use of rope ladders. The commander of the French forces, Rear-Admiral Auguste-Leopold Protet, was killed in action on May 17 while leading an attack on a country town. Shanghai honored him with a solemn funeral ceremony attended by the foreign consuls and the daotai, who read out an imperial proclamation ordering "the dispatch of one hundred sheepskins and three lengths of fine velvet to the admiral's widow."[9]

But the imperial garrisons entrusted with guarding the liberated areas were not up to their task. Pressure from the Taiping increased during the summer. In September Ward, too, was killed. The American adventurer was replaced at the head of The Ever Victorious Army by a British Army officer, Captain Charles G. Gordon, whose government authorized him to serve under Chinese command. Gordon, a good organizer and a good soldier, set about reconquering the "30-mile zone." Unlike Ward, he fought truly within the framework of the Chinese Empire, to which Li Hongzhang, now the governor of Jiangsu, was imparting new energy and efficiency. In December 1863, the Taiping were expelled from the lower Yangzi. Six months later, in Nanjing, they were definitively crushed.

The firm hold over the imperial forces reestablished by strong regional mandarins, Li Hongzhang among them, played an essential role in these successes. But one of those mandarins' trump cards was military cooperation with the Westerners that had been established in Shanghai. Thanks to the British and American mercenaries whose services they had hired, and to the rifles and light artillery that these had provided for the imperial armies, the generals of the imperial forces succeeded in vanquishing the rebels. The modernization of military technology just beginning was soon to point the way to far more ambitious policies in the field of economic modernization.

The misfortunes of those days had encouraged many Chinese to take refuge in the foreign concessions: by 1854, they already numbered 20,000.[10] Poor and rich alike, all were in search of shelter. The concessions were soon to change from quarters reserved for Westerners into Sino-foreign towns. This massive wave of immigration soon turned the life of residents and the organization of the concessions upside down.

THE CHINESE INSTALL THEMSELVES
IN THE CONCESSIONS

Initially, both the foreign and Chinese authorities endeavored to repulse the new arrivals, invoking the regulations and sometimes employing force: in January 1855, a squatter quarter was razed to the ground, and its occupants were ejected. But faced with the determination of the Chinese, who were spurred on by their desire for security, and that of the foreigners, who were motivated by their thirst for profits, the authorities soon gave up the struggle.

Speculation was taking over. A hectare of land that had fetched 1 tael in the 1840s was worth over 30 some twenty years later (or even 60, if it bordered the Bund).[11] In these circumstances nobody paid any attention to the warnings proffered by the British consul, Sir Rutherford Alcock, who was pointing out the risks of Sino-foreign cohabitation for the future of the concessions. "What difference can that make to me or to other proprietors and speculators like me?" was the response the consul received from one of the principal residents, who went on, "My problem is how to amass a fortune as quickly as possible by renting plots of land to the Chinese and by constructing dwellings for them, which will bring me 30% to 40% profits. . . . Within two or three years at the most, I hope to leave. What do I care if Shanghai is subsequently engulfed in fire or floods?"[12]

It was good-bye to the gardens of roses and magnolias and to the aristocratic Shanghai of great mansions. The concessions now mushroomed with *lilong* intended for Chinese tenants. These housing developments, hurriedly constructed using cheap materials, were composed of "terraced houses of one or two stories, arranged in parallel rows, and served by a network of alleyways of varying widths. The houses presented a continuous built-up facade giving onto the street, with alleys here and there leading inward through gates or porches."[13] In 1860, the British and American concessions contained 8,740 lilong and 269 European-style houses.

Despite the influx of Chinese residents, the concessions remained outside imperial jurisdiction. Given that, the local bureaucracy had ceased to function at all levels; the British, French, and American consuls had to shoulder the task of inventing institutions to make up for the shortcomings of the imperial administration and to cater to the needs of the new Sino-foreign community. To this end, they obtained the collaboration of Daotai Wu Jianzhang, who had himself been ejected from the Chinese walled town by the Small Swords and had then taken refuge in the concessions. Shanghai was thus on the way to turning into a republic of merchants, placed under the jurisdiction of foreign consuls.

The administrative regime of the concessions, whose birth resulted from the prevailing circumstances, took shape in the course of the adoption of a series of urgent measures. The first, as early as 1854, was the creation of the Shanghai Municipal Council. This was made responsible for ensuring the security of the concessions under threat from the rebels and for improving an administration whose efficiency had been undermined by the influx of new arrivals. Chinese refugees were not alone in crowding into the territory of the concessions. The rebellion, along with all the opportunities of enrichment that it offered, ranging from smuggling to pillage, attracted many new immigrants. Hard on the heels of the diplomats, merchants, and missionaries came mercenaries, fugitives, absconding sailors, and criminals who had broken the law. The risks of epidemics and fires linked with overpopulation were now compounded by delinquency and criminality.

In July 1854, the British, French, and American consuls elaborated new municipal regulations known as the *Land Regulations*. These regulations, which were valid for all three concessions and applicable to all foreigners resident there, without distinction of nationality, gave the foreign community, represented by "land renters," the right to self-government. The Shanghai Municipal Council, elected by the assembly of land renters from which all Chinese were excluded, thus received the right to levy a tax on all residents, the Chinese included, in order to finance urban development and the upkeep of a police force. This municipal mini-constitution, which was the fruit of local initiative and the concerted action of the various consuls, Daotai Wu Jianzhang, and the concession residents, was set up without any consultation with either the diplomatic corps or the Beijing government.

The creation of the Shanghai Municipal Council and the prerogatives that it assumed were ad hoc arrangements not actually covered by the treaties but just tacked on. It would be twenty years before the British government got around to recognizing their validity. The French government simply refused to ratify them, even though they had been countersigned by its own consul. The administration of the French concession, which was placed directly under the authority of the consul and the Quai d'Orsay, thus always remained distinctive; and it was in the international settlement, created in 1863 from the fusion of the British and American concessions, that the original institutions defined by the 1854 *Land Regulations* were to evolve. The imperial government de facto lost the right to tax the concession's Chinese residents and retained no more than a limited right of jurisdiction over them: the Mixed Court, set up in 1864 to adjudicate cases involving Chinese residents, was—it is true—chaired by an imperial official, but this magistrate's assistant was a member of a consular staff.

Making the most of weakening imperial power, the residents and their consuls thus seized the initiative and transformed the Shanghai concessions from mere residential zones into veritable enclaves that eluded Chinese sovereignty. Despite the considerable autonomy that it allowed the foreign residents, the 1854 municipal constitution was integrated into the general provisions of the treaties, with the administration of the international settlement remaining subordinate to consular jurisdiction. The latter factor indicates a certain discrepancy between the policies elaborated locally by the foreign residents and consuls, intent upon protecting local interests, on the one hand, and the diplomatic action pursued by the great powers, on the other. The fact that Shanghai was "different" was indicated even more clearly by the negotiations that eventually led to the creation of a (foreign) General Inspectorate of Maritime Customs.

In 1854, the Small Swords had sacked and destroyed the Chinese Customs office, and Wu Jianzhang, whose functions as daotai included those of customs superintendent, had been ejected from the Chinese walled town. After that, taxation of imported merchandise became very irregular. Many Western merchants determined that, in view of the weakness of the imperial authorities, there was no longer any need to observe the treaties or to pay dues. Many of the consuls shared their views, including the French consul: "Until such time as I see established and recognized in Shanghai a regular authority able to guarantee the observation of the treaty articles . . . relating to the protection of commerce and the properties and persons of my nationals, I consider myself free to allow my nationals' vessels to enter and leave without paying any dues."[14]

Some went even further, judging that the rebellion presented a good opportunity to turn Shanghai into a free port. Indeed, the *North China Herald*, the organ of British interests in Shanghai, proposed this. It suggested that the Chinese merchants should be left to find a way "to organize the levying of taxes with their own corrupt government."[15] Daotai Wu Jianzhang, who needed customs revenues in order to finance his administrative (and personal) expenses, opposed such suggestions. Moreover, the British consul, instructed by his government to safeguard the maintenance of the judicial framework established by the treaties, was equally opposed. For what would become of such a free port, which the Chinese authorities would certainly cut off from the inland provinces by erecting a multitude of tax barriers?

A compromise was found in July 1854: the foreigners would take over the collection of maritime customs taxes on behalf of the Chinese administration. The consuls appointed three officials to manage the new Maritime Customs Service and to fix the amount of the dues, which were to be directly payable into Chinese banks. Daotai Wu and the provincial authorities ratified this arrangement without referring the matter to Beijing. However, the Chinese administration now found itself with a source of local revenue, which was all the more valuable given that the rebellion had wiped out most others. Meanwhile, the British saved the treaties system from disintegration. The General Inspectorate of Maritime Customs, whose responsibilities were later extended to the other treaty ports, eventually became the very keystone of the system. It acquired a reputation for integrity and professionalism and established a new model for public service in China, maintaining equality of treatment for all the empire's commercial partners.

Although the merchants were keen to exploit the weakness of the Beijing government, with a view to making immediate profits, the British diplomats, aided by their American colleagues, thus succeeded in consolidating a legal framework that guaranteed free and regular commercial transactions. This system was to favor Shanghai's prosperity for decades to come. But there was a price to pay for the salvation of the imperial administration's fiscal prerogatives: namely, the control that the foreigners thereafter retained over the maritime customs revenues—a control that later became a redoubtable means of applying political pressure.

THE SHANGHAI MODEL AND THE TREATY SYSTEM

Foreign diplomats and imperial officials, united in defense of the economic interests of Shanghai, thus began to cooperate. On the Western side, the cooperation was part of a plan to universalize free trade. On the Chinese side, Daotai Wu Jianzhang was condemned as a traitor first in 1854 by the Beijing government and thereafter by historians of the period. Nowadays, however, he appears more as an opportunist who made the most of the large measure of autonomy enjoyed by local officials specializing in the management of "barbarian" affairs, in the face of the lack of interest that the Imperial Court manifested for what it judged to be mere frontier problems with little political impact.

While Beijing ignored the foreigners and Canton continued to reject them, Shanghai accommodated them. For that reason, Shanghainese did not consider themselves involved in the Second Opium War, which broke out in 1856 in Canton and later took Franco-British troops all the way to Beijing. "Shanghai has been on good terms with the foreigners," the daotai reported, going on to say, "It would be unwise [for Shanghai] to get involved in a war between the Cantonese and the barbarians. Any open conflict at Shanghai would certainly damage Shanghai's economic stability, and the government's income from the customs taxes would be drastically reduced. . . . Cantonese affairs must be sorted out in Canton."[16] The episode might be summed up as "Shanghai, or the triumph of local interests."

It was not long before the model of Sino-Western relations elaborated as early as the 1850s began to be imitated on a national scale. The commercial clauses of the treaty of Tianjin, which in 1858 brought the Second Opium War to a provisional end, were inspired by the arrangements earlier approved in Shanghai: the system whereby foreign inspectors collected maritime customs dues was extended to all the treaty ports. Then, in 1860, the Beijing treaty, which confirmed the clauses of the Tianjin treaty, brought two decades of opening-up wars to an end. By this date the treaty system had evolved considerably: the arrangements envisaged by the first diplomatic agreements had been amplified by other measures inspired by Shanghai practices, such as the foreigners' administrative control over their concessions, which thus de facto eluded Chinese sovereignty; and also the transfer of the service of Maritime Customs, which was a major provider of public funds, into the hands of foreign officials. But the influence of Shanghai practice on "barbarian management" faded after the end of the Taiping revolt. From 1862 on, the Beijing government formulated foreign policy and applied it within the framework of institutions specially created for the purpose. Shanghai's pioneering role was now confirmed in the economic and social domain.

CHAPTER 3

The Birth of Shanghai Capitalism
(1860–1911)

I N   T H E   C O U R S E   O F   T H E   H A L F   C E N T U R Y that separated the crushing of the Taiping from the triumph of the 1911 Republican Revolution, Shanghai became a modern city, the capital of new economic activities founded on external trade and the importation of foreign technology and capital. This evolution was directed by no political plan but was brought about simply by the interplay of material interests. Neither the Chinese nor the foreign authorities played a major part in it, nor were they its principal beneficiaries: the scene was played out between increasingly numerous, diverse, and autonomous actors on the social stage. The development of the modern sector of Shanghai is often described as the manifestation of a triumphant imperialism and an example of Western exploitation of the Chinese labor force and Chinese resources. But in truth that development was fueled by the town's relations with the Chinese hinterland just as much as by its contacts with markets overseas, and by the vitality of Chinese firms and economic institutions just as much as by innovations linked with the Western presence. In Shanghai, tradition—the tradition of merchants, money lenders, and manufacturers—was not an enemy of modernization. The two went hand in hand and interacted, unaffected by any ideological constructions.

FOREIGN TRADE, THE MAINSPRING OF GROWTH

For a long time trade, finance, and property speculation dominated the economy of Shanghai. As early as 1861, the opening up of the lower and middle reaches of the Yangzi to foreign ships and merchants extended the existing trading circuits, increasing both what was on offer and demand for it.* During this same period, the opening of the ports of the north and northeast enhanced the position of Shanghai, to the detriment

---

* This opening up was ratified by the treaties of Tianjin and Beijing in 1858 and 1860, respectively.

of Canton and Hong Kong. In thirty years the value of Shanghai foreign trade doubled, increasing from 74 million to 155 million HkTl between 1861 and 1894.* Between 1895 and 1911, it doubled again, to 378 million HkTl.[1] On the other hand, Shanghai's relative share of the overall value of foreign Chinese trade was slowly declining (from over 60% between 1860 and 1870 to about 55% at the turn of the century and 45% ten years later).[2]

Initially, Shanghai exported mainly tea and silk. But Chinese teas, often poorly processed, competed badly with Indian and Japanese teas. Silk was also under heavy competition from Japan. Even before the end of the century, products of agricultural origin were taking over: soya, leather, pig bristles, eggs, and their derivatives.[3] Above all, the importation of opium continued to play an essential role into the 1880s, even though for a long time the Chinese government continued to prohibit it. The fact was that contraband opium remained the only exchange commodity that enabled British and American merchants to offset their purchases of tea and silk. Clandestine deliveries therefore continued throughout the 1850s, to the knowledge and in the sight of all and sundry, including the local Chinese officials, anxious for their share of the profits from smuggling.

Shanghai was at this time the Chinese Empire's major port for importation of the drug, and its commercial rise, along with the fortunes of its large-scale merchants—Chinese and foreigners alike—was based on this trafficking. At Wusong at the mouth of the Huangpu, the British and the Americans would anchor "receiving ships" to which cargo ships would transfer their crates of opium before sailing upriver to deliver the rest of their cargo in Shanghai. The Chinese smugglers who ensured the resale of the opium would come straight to Wusong to load up from the receiving ships. Transactions took place under the protection of foreign navy cannons, as pirates would frequently try to intercept the precious merchandise. In 1854, illegal imports accounted for as much as 72% of the total value of imports.[4] The quantity of opium imported through Shanghai increased still further when the treaties of Tianjin and Beijing legalized the opium trade

---

* The Customs tael, or Haiguan tael (HkTl), was a unit used in the accounts of the Maritime Customs. It represented 38.40 grams of pure silver and in 1911 was worth 3.4 francs.

(and taxed it to profit the central government) in 1858–1860. These imports now accounted for 60% to 70% of all the opium introduced into China, depending on whether it was a good or bad year.[5] But from the 1880s on, those imports suffered competition from Chinese opium—its production was authorized at the same time that its sale was legalized, and its price was much lower. Furthermore, Chinese public opinion—and increasingly that of Great Britain—deplored the trafficking and consumption of opium ever more vigorously. From 1908 on, Great Britain, with a view to supporting the Beijing government's efforts to eradicate the use of opium, was year by year cutting the sale of Indian opium on the Chinese market by 10%, in the expectation of its total suppression by 1917. However, opium still did not disappear from Shanghai: quite the contrary. But it now no longer served as the principal exchange currency in Western trade with China.

Over the last decades of the nineteenth century, Shanghai imports diversified. They did so partly as a consequence of the progress of Western penetration and the growing complexity of the local economy but also as a result of the appearance of new needs and new markets both in the town itself and in the hinterland. The category "miscellaneous goods," which in 1893 covered 30% of the value of imports, included many consumer items—cigarettes, matches, bazaar articles, and so on—as well as kerosene, coal, industrial equipment, and, above all, cotton products.[6] For years the Chinese had been content with the cotton yarn and cloth that their own thriving craft industry produced, but the situation changed with the rise of industrial cotton mills in British India, whose goods—of high quality but at the same time cheap—presented serious competition for those of the traditional Chinese weavers. Indian yarns, joined by Japanese yarns at the turn of the century, won over the Chinese weavers' immense clientele. In Shanghai, where the merchants of the huge Yangzi basin came for their supplies, imports of cotton yarn increased by leaps and bounds. By the early twentieth century, they represented 40% of the value of all imports.[7]

ONE OF THE WORLD'S FOREMOST PORTS

The development of commercial activities in Shanghai was favored by modern means of transport and communication, which shortened distances and brought continents closer together. The era of sailing ships was nearing its end in the second half of the nineteenth century, although agile clippers continued to compete with steamships for a long time. Clippers had been built in the United States since 1841 and, later, also in Great Britain. They were easily recognizable from their elegant silhouettes, the exotic woods used in their construction, their metal hulls, and their white sails. They were solid enough to confront typhoons, and their speed could outdistance pirate vessels; however, it took them 148 days to travel from London to Shanghai. Their limited tonnage could cope with the transport of opium, which was their original purpose, and also with that of tea. In the early 1870s they were still to be seen at anchor in the Huangpu, even though twenty years had already elapsed since the first appearance of steamships in the port of Shanghai.

The triumph of steamships was ensured by the opening of the Suez Canal, which was inaccessible to clippers. Not only were the steamers speedier but they could transport far larger cargoes than the sailing ships, and this made it possible for them to lower their freight and insurance charges. As the clippers disappeared, so too did the great seagoing junks (*shachuan*), some of which had been sailing as far as Japan, Manila, and Singapore. Shanghai now became the center of a vast web of maritime relations, dominated by the foreign navigation companies that plied their way between Korea, Japan, the southern seas, Hong Kong, Europe, and America.

The early modernization of coastal shipping and some rivercraft was also linked to foreign business, which continued to develop, in violation of the sovereign rights of China, according to the terms of the international treaties that opened up the river routes of the empire to foreign steamers between 1858 and 1898.[8] The first companies to operate in Chinese territorial waters were set up by the major British and American trading houses of Shanghai, which from 1873 onward operated in competition with the China Merchants' Steam Navigation Company, a semipublic enterprise created under the aegis of Governor-General Li Hongzhang. Once the Yangzi was opened up and as coastal navigation developed, the Shanghai market was extended to a vast inland region.

The port did not offer particularly favorable natural conditions for commercial activities. Being an estuary port, it tended to silt up. Furthermore, at Wusong, where the Huangpu joined the Yangzi, a sandbar denied access to the largest vessels. Between 1906 and 1910, the Chinese administration, assisted by foreign engineers, undertook and financed improvements that would turn Shanghai into one of the world's foremost ports.[9] Railways played a somewhat belated and limited role. The first attempt, financed by British merchants, aimed to create a local line to Wusong, which served as an outer harbor to Shanghai and where many cargoes were transferred. In 1875, just as the project neared completion, it had to be abandoned because the Chinese authorities, who had from the start refused to grant permission for its construction, bought back the line and demolished it. Not until 1908 did the Shanghai-Nanjing railway line come into service. This connected with the railways of northern China and created a link between the country's economic metropolis and its political capital.

The construction in April 1870 of telegraphic links between Shanghai, Hong Kong, and London transformed Shanghai's commercial import-export operations, making it possible to speed up orders, reduce stocks, and diminish the risks run by buyers. Initially, the Chinese administration also opposed this foreign initiative. But the imperial government soon became convinced of the utility—which it regarded as essentially of a strategic nature—of such connections and itself proceeded to install lines between Shanghai and Tianjin (in 1881) and between Shanghai and Canton (in 1882), thereby consolidating the string of coastal treaty ports' newfound unity and identity.

BANKS AND SPECULATION

The development of foreign trading brought in its wake that of credit. As the growing demand for money provoked by the intensification of commercial activities could not be satisfied solely by importing foreign silver or producing Chinese copper, local private banks proceeded to produce an abundance of fiduciary money, which conferred an indispensable flexibility upon a system until then founded solely on silver and copper. The financing of transactions between Shanghai and Western markets, along with the operations of money changing and buying insurance, were undertaken solely by foreigners. Initially, such activities took place within the framework of the great trading companies, which set up special departments to organize them. The first British bank opened in Shanghai in 1848. Thereafter the British held a dominant position thanks to the presence of the Chartered Bank of India, Australia, and China, which began to operate in 1858, and, above all, the Hong Kong and Shanghai Banking Corporation (generally known as the Hong Kong and Shanghai Bank), a local branch of which opened in Shanghai in 1865. Over the following decades, half a dozen other establishments, most of them European, opened for business in Shanghai, but the British preeminence was never challenged.

These foreign banks did not operate as merchant banks, at least not for the Chinese clientele, as the Chinese were discouraged by the complexity of their procedures and the need to provide mortgage guarantees. Nevertheless, they were profoundly influential to the extent that, with a monopoly over external deals, they fixed international exchange rates and the rate of exchange between the Chinese tael, based on silver, and the gold-standard currencies of China's Western partners. Furthermore, because of their extra-territorial privilege, they attracted into their coffers deposits from wealthy Chinese who wished to protect their fortunes from the exactions of the imperial administration. That same privilege allowed them to issue banknotes without ever receiving authorization to do so from the Chinese authorities. Their banknotes circulated widely in Shanghai and were even accepted in other treaty ports. These banks financed direct investments by the Westerners, particularly from the turn of the century onward, when the latter invested heavily in mines and railways. They also injected large sums of money into the commercial circuits controlled by Chinese merchants through the intermediary of local traditional banks (*qianzhuang*), which constituted the principal sources of finance for private Chinese enterprises.

Qianzhuang already existed in Shanghai in the early nineteenth century, and they prospered once the port was opened up to foreign trade. They financed the collection of products destined for exportation and the distribution of imported products, opium in particular. The rise of the qianzhuang was closely associated with the success of opium sales. Initially the qianzhuang were located inside the walled town, but at about the same time as the first foreign banks, they established themselves in the international settlement. They were extremely sensitive to the ups and downs of the commercial and monetary situation, appearing and disappearing as successive crises came and went, but their numbers tended on the whole to increase, rising from fifty or so in the 1880s to over one hundred by the beginning of the twentieth century. Then, during the speculative crisis of 1911, their number fell to fifty once more.[10] Their clientele was drawn from the Chinese merchants, to whom they were prepared to issue loans known as "trust loans," without insisting on any guarantee other than that of the borrower's good reputation. The qianzhuang either operated independently or served as intermediaries to the foreign banks, whose credits they redistributed. The foreign establishments allowed the better-established traditional banks short-term credits without guarantees (chop loans), although they were not prepared to grant them to individual merchants, considering these to be too difficult to identify and assess.

The flexibility of these traditional institutions, which managed to adapt to an economic and financial scene still in the process of evolving and which themselves contributed to that evolution, goes some way toward explaining why modern Chinese banks developed so late and why they played such a limited role until the beginning of the twentieth century. The first modern Chinese bank was created in Shanghai in 1897 on the initiative of the mandarin-entrepreneur Sheng Xuanhuai. This was the Chinese Bank of External Commerce (*Zhongguo tongshang yinhang*), better known by its English name, the Imperial Bank of China. Sheng Xuanhuai's plan was to use this bank "as foreigners use their banks: to provide capital for economic development" and, in particular, to finance railways.[11] Very soon, however, Sheng realized that Chinese merchants were not prepared to risk their money in long-term projects of uncertain outcome. The Imperial Bank of China vegetated, and foreign establishments and the qianzhuang continued to dominate the local financial market.

The development of credit in Shanghai was also based on the real estate market, in which both the banks and the qianzhuang operated actively. This market had originated in 1853–1854 when the Small Swords occupied the Chinese walled town and during the Taiping attacks of 1860–1862. The influx of refugees, which wiped out the segregation between the Chinese and the foreigners envisaged in the initial agreements, led to a strong demand for lodgings inside the concessions. Foreign proprietors acquired plots there where they constructed rental apartments. Alongside the patrician residences of the major merchants or, in many cases, supplanting them, rows of two-story houses now appeared, separated by alleyways and forming residential precincts known as *lilong*.

Until the 1880s, property transactions in the concessions remained in the hands of foreigners, who alone were legally permitted to acquire plots of land there. Everyone wanted to profit from the rising prices: residents, merchants, religious communities, adventurers, and other professional operators. The French consul no longer needed to advertise, as offers to buy

An alleyway in a lilong in the 1930s (courtesy of Qian Zonghao)

were now multiplying fast. "Long-disdained plots of land in the French concession have suddenly acquired value. . . . Not a square inch of the area remains available. Once triggered, speculation really took off. Plots of land bought for 1,000 taels per *mow* (mu), after changing hands several times, were sold for 2,500 taels. . . . We French have made our fortunes out of our land."[12] As the cost of land rose, so did rents. Naturally, the Chinese were attracted by speculations of such a profitable nature. One of the first to launch himself into speculation was Xu Run, comprador for the British Dent Company. In 1883, he acquired 2,900 mu in the international settlement; now his real estate properties made up two-thirds of his fortune, which was estimated at 3.3 million taels.[13]

At the beginning of the twentieth century, the real estate market was still just as prosperous: in the heart of the international settlement, the price for 1 mu of land rose from 13,500 taels to 34,700 between 1903 and 1907,[14] while the annual dividends paid out by real estate companies oscillated between 7% and 14%. Demographic pressure, economic success, and general speculation all contributed to the soaring prices of land and leases. Real estate played an essential role in the formation of the fortunes of individuals as well as that of the assets of banks and commercial firms. The real estate market was certainly one of the sources of Shanghai prosperity, but the speculative nature of transactions made that prosperity vulnerable.

THE BEGINNINGS OF INDUSTRIALIZATION
(1860–1895)

The treaty of Shimonoseki, signed in 1895, brought the Sino-Japanese War to an end and authorized foreigners to set up industries in the treaty ports. It marked a crucial turning point in the economic modernization of the town, which within two decades was to become a major center of industry. This success owed much to the familiarity with technological innovation and capitalist management that many had acquired between 1860 and 1895 in the course of their individual pursuits.

The preliminary phase of industrialization resulted from the combined efforts of foreigners, mandarins, and Chinese merchants. At this time, the establishment of foreign factories was not authorized by the treaties but was often enough tolerated by the local authorities. Shanghai was furthermore one of the principal centers of the Foreign Affairs Movement (*Yangwu yundong*) and of the policy of industrialization that had been introduced in the early 1860s by a number of high-ranking mandarins after their victory over the Taiping. From their experiences on the ground and their military cooperation with the foreigners, Zeng Guofan (1811–1872), Zuo Zongfang (1812–1885), and Li Hongzhang (1823–1901) had derived a conviction that economic modernization was indispensable for the survival of the empire. Moreover, beginning in the 1870s, a number of Chinese merchants, most of them compradors, created their own businesses.

In 1894, Shanghai boasted 108 modern industrial businesses representing a combined capital of 30 million dollars.* Most of them were foreign businesses, but it was within the framework of the Foreign Affairs Movement that most of the capital was invested. The private Chinese sector appeared weak,[15] but the statistics did not take into account the extremely large sums merchants invested in foreign firms and those created by mandarins.

The first modern industrial businesses were naval repair yards set up by foreigners. The importance that the latter attached to external trade and maritime transport explains why these were the first investments to be made. The Boyd and the Farnham yards dominated the shipbuilding sector into the twentieth century: in the early 1890s, each of these firms employed over 1,000 workers. The complexity of the techniques used in this industry had the effect of limiting Chinese competition. Although large, the Jiangnan Arsenal could not rival the foreigners in the domain of civil shipbuilding. It was set up under the aegis of Li Hongzhang in 1865 and included a department for naval repairs and construction, but in the course of thirty years it produced only eight vessels, all destined to become warships and all of moderate tonnage.[16]

In 1894, the (mechanical) weaving of silk, with sixteen factories and an overall capital of 8 million dollars, represented Shanghai's principal

---

* Although the tael was an accounting unit, the silver dollar was used in commercial transactions. This was a silver coin whose nominal worth and weight varied and whose value, expressed in taels, fluctuated around 0.70, depending on the market. Unless otherwise specified, the dollars mentioned in the text refer to this Chinese silver dollar.

modern industry.[17] This was also the branch of industry in which foreigners invested most heavily: 5.5 million dollars divided among eight mills. However, as silk production was one of the strong points of the traditional production of the lower Yangzi, the foreigners clashed with many local interests. Peasant silkworm farmers, merchants, local officials, and notables all conspired to hamper cocoon collection and drying in the silk-producing districts. Fresh cocoons (inside which the silkworm is still alive) were the only kind then used by the Chinese peasants and craftsmen, but such cocoons had to be treated within ten days of harvest, after which time the chrysalis split its sheath. The time needed to transport cocoons to Shanghai thus made it necessary for mechanical mills to use dry cocoons, inside which the silkworm had died. The Chinese producers were not familiar with the technique for drying, so the foreigners were obliged to carry out this operation themselves. The persistent difficulties in acquiring supplies of cocoons led the foreign investors to withdraw almost completely from the silk mills.[18] By the beginning of the twentieth century they had abandoned this sector to the Chinese entrepreneurs.

Cotton mills made their appearance in 1880 in response to Chinese demand. Their establishment, somewhat later than that of the silk mills, was prompted by the realization by merchants and mandarins alike of the importance of the local and regional market for cotton cloth and cotton yarn, an importance signaled by the sharp rise in Shanghai imports of cotton products: 1,900 piculs in 1870, and 100,000 piculs in 1886.* The most remarkable creation in this period was the Shanghai Cotton Cloth Mill (*Shanghai jiqi zhibuju*) by Li Hongzhang and the promoters of the Foreign Affairs Movement. The Beijing government granted it a production monopoly for ten years and exempted it from payment of the internal *lijin* tax. It took an entire decade to set up this mill, and it did not start production until 1890. The Shanghai Cotton Cloth Mill enjoyed a monopoly that the administration fiercely defended and that prevented the creation of any competitors until 1895, at which point the treaty of Shimonoseki cleared the way for foreigners to enter this branch of industry.

---

* The picul was a unit of weight equivalent to about 60 kilograms.

Viceroy Li Hongzhang, the promoter of modern industry in Shanghai

Apart from a few major investments in naval yards and silk or cotton mills, the industrialization of Shanghai was limited to the creation of small workshops, modern to the extent that they used mechanical means in some of their operations. Closely linked with external trade, most businesses were founded by foreigners and regarded as activities annexed to the major export-import firms. Most engaged in conditioning processes applied to imports, for example, kerosene. The treatment of agricultural raw materials destined for exportation also generated a few industrial activities, such as ginning cotton and tanning leather. Light industries intended to satisfy the needs of the foreign and Chinese population found it difficult to take root, for they encountered competition from both imported products and local craftsmanship. However, foreign printing works both prospered and multiplied; the earliest, connected with missionary activities, appeared in the 1840s. Thanks to the modest prices of their products, match factories also managed to find a market. The manufacture of cigarettes, which later became one of Shanghai's principal industries, was established quite late, in particular when the American Trading Company was set up in 1892.

Also worth mentioning are the public utility services. The Shanghai Waterworks, a private company, introduced a supply of running water in 1882–1883 in the international settlement. Public gas lighting, which appeared in both concessions as early as 1865,[19] was progressively replaced by electric lighting beginning in 1883. In this respect, Shanghai had a twenty- to thirty-year start on the other treaty ports of China. As manifestations of material progress made possible by the development of science and technology, these municipal achievements made a considerable, stimulating impact.

A NEW INDUSTRIAL LEAP FORWARD (1895–1911)

Although it produced limited results, this initial wave of industrialization laid the foundations for further development that took off at the turn of the twentieth century. Shanghai's new industries benefited from relatively abundant capital, the existence of a pool of labor already trained to perform the complex procedures used by highly skilled craftsmen, and the vigorous entrepreneurial spirit of the local merchants. It was likewise stimulated by favorable international circumstances and the many orders brought in by the Russo-Japanese War of 1904–1905. But the treaty of Shimonoseki, by opening the door to Western and Japanese capital, sealed the downfall of the Foreign Affairs Movement that had encouraged the creation of businesses in both the official and the semiofficial sectors. It spelled the end of a period of protection and monopolies.

Private capitalism now established itself as the moving force behind industrial development. Foreign investment diversified: British preeminence waned as Japanese investment, in particular, intensified. From 1895 onward, foreign investment increased by about 10%, reaching 63 million dollars by 1913.[20] The major businesses that had been founded illegally before 1894—the shipyards of Boyd and Farnham, the Shanghai Waterworks, and the international settlement's Central Electricity Company—strengthened their capital and increased production. Their example stimulated the private Chinese sector. At first it profited from the reconversion of official and semiofficial businesses, now privatized by the mandarins responsible for their management; later, from 1901 onward, it benefited from reforms introduced by the imperial government within the framework of the New Policy (*Xinzheng*).* The sixty-six Chinese firms created between 1895 and 1911 together held capital worth 20 million dollars.[21]

The industries born at the turn of the century were no longer as closely linked to external trade. They now aimed to satisfy the needs of local and interregional markets. These were light industries that provided consumer goods intended for not just a small fringe, composed of the foreign population, but also a more or less well-to-do Chinese clientele. In some domains demand already existed—for example, for industrially produced yarn, which was widely used by weavers in the interior. Following the treaty of Shimonoseki, the Westerners had increased their investments: in 1895 there were already four foreign cotton mills in Shanghai; by 1910 their number had increased to thirteen, with a total of 320,000 spindles.[22] There were only half as many Chinese mills and spindles.[23] High-ranking officials such as Sheng Xuanhuai and Nie Qigui (a former Shanghai daotai who had become the governor of Zhejiang), educated entrepreneurs such as Zhang Jian, or wealthy compradors such as Zhu Zhiyao and Zhu Dachun had set up these mills. Meanwhile, however, the Chinese were rapidly taking over silk industries abandoned by foreign entrepreneurs. At the beginning of the twentieth century twenty-four of Shanghai's twenty-seven silk mills were Chinese.[24]

---

* This New Policy was the name for the raft of institutional, legal, and social reforms that the empire introduced between 1901 and 1911 during the last decade of its existence.

Food-processing industries—oil works and grain mills—were also set up in response to local demand. But the Russo-Japanese War, when both sides turned to these for supplies, also considerably increased their sales and profits. After 1895, the production of consumer goods—essentially textiles and food—was added to the activities that had developed in response to the needs of external trade.

Supplies of machinery were more limited. Only one sector, spare parts, really took off, which subcontracted with the foreign naval yards or with the Japanese arsenal. By the eve of World War I, there were ninety-one workshops, most of which were tiny and specialized in repairs to shipping or the maintenance of industrial machinery. The Qiuxin workshops were an exception. The comprador Zhu Zhiyao founded them in 1904 and immediately launched a major industrial adventure, within a few years moving from maintenance to the production of engines and even railway carriages.[25] In the long term, however, the existence of dozens of small workshops probably proved more crucial for the spread of technology and the further development of Shanghai industry.

In the last days of the empire, Shanghai's modern economic sector was thus weak and was playing no more than a marginal role in the Chinese economy. But the town had already placed itself at the head of the modernization movement: it handled over half of the country's external trade and was home to the Chinese or East Asian headquarters of the principal banks and foreign businesses, which in the other treaty ports were represented by mere agencies. About one-third of the modern factories created by Chinese capital between 1895 and 1911 in the treaty ports were based in Shanghai, where they represented investment estimated at between 14 and 20 million dollars.[26]

The development of this small modern sector posed a series of problems relating to economic institutions, the role of the public authorities, relations with the internal market, and those between the foreign entrepreneurs and the Chinese. Attention has often focused mainly on the contradictions and differences involved (modernity against tradition, foreigners competing with the Chinese), and it has been thought that imperialism, with all its positive side effects and all its negative consequences, was the principal force at work. Yet what is most striking is the juxtaposition of all the different institutions and organizations that presided over the accumulation of capital and the earliest implantations of technology. In this crowded scene, the profile of Western capitalism on its triumphant onward march is certainly visible. But whether it was really the orchestrating agent of all the forces at work is by no means certain. There appears to have been no chief agent at work, not even market forces. For among all these forces adjusting to the situation and in competition with one another, the quest for profit was frequently obliged to come to terms with diplomatic privileges, bureaucratic constraints, and the defense of already established interests. What was developing was a Sino-foreign form of capitalism.

HONG AND GUILDS

The earliest foreign merchants operating in Shanghai for the most part belonged to large trading companies known as *hong*. By 1852, forty or so of these were already in place, more than half of which were British.[27] Within this group, recruitment followed criteria based on native origins: the Jardines chose their partners—Mathesons and Keswicks—from among their Scottish compatriots, as did Butterfield and Swire, also of Scottish origin. Middle Eastern Jews, such as the Sassoons, and the Parsees of Bombay between them controlled eight firms. Other pioneering companies were American, the Russell Company being the largest. Germans arrived on the scene in the 1850s. The foreign businesses of Shanghai were becoming increasingly cosmopolitan. But even if the British lost their quasi monopoly, they still retained their predominant position.

The first Shanghai hongs developed as offshoots of companies already established in Hong Kong and rich in experience from their long years of commercial activities in the China seas. Their well-oiled organizations were strictly hierarchical and founded on family solidarity. The company partners and managers, who in many cases overlapped, belonged to families allied through marriages. Generation after generation, only the first names of individuals would change. Some dynasties went back to the beginning of the nineteenth century: the Jardines, for example, whose founder, William Jardine, began his career as a ship's doctor working for the East India Company. The directors of these great houses resided in

London or in Boston. Usually, the partner responsible for the management of business in China would live in Hong Kong, and the head of the company's agency in Shanghai would be subordinate to him. But these agency heads in fact enjoyed a large measure of autonomy and possessed the authority of big business bosses, as their Chinese title of taipan indicated. Until 1870 that authority was enhanced by the slowness of communications with Europe and America, which made them responsible for keeping an eye on the evolution of the local market as well as in their respective metropolis. In the general import-export business, their functions were those of agents working for a commission, while the company directors in England or the United States made the decisions, as well as taking the risks. The hongs, in which commissions ranged from 0.5% to 5%, depending on the circumstances, would often increase their profits by entering into other operations on their own account.

The taipans were assisted by young collaborators known as "griffins," named after the wild ponies imported into China from Mongolia that, like them, had to adapt to a new environment.* Griffins were generally initiated into Chinese trading in the company's headquarters. In Shanghai they would work as accountants or managers, in the hope of one day becoming taipans themselves. Right at the bottom of the hierarchy was the "gooser" (the word was of Portuguese derivation) or "white boy" (actually, usually a Eurasian from Macao), who did copying work and performed other menial tasks. Far from home, the griffins would live a communal life within their respective hongs; the effect was to strengthen cohesion within the business. Faced with a difficult environment, the various hongs would enter into a certain degree of cooperation, but naturally this did not rule out rivalries fueled by national or religious differences or simply by competitiveness.

In the early 1870s, the general introduction of steamers and telegraphic communications turned the structures of the foreign firms in Shanghai upside down. The major hongs lost their monopoly, and the taipans were eclipsed by merchants who operated on a far smaller scale, on their own

---

* The literal meaning of *griffin* was a Mongolian pony that had to undergo training before being accepted on the Shanghai racecourse.

and with capital that they topped up with local loans from foreign banks. These "brokers" did business at their own risk, specializing in one or another branch of activity. The taipans bitterly noted that the newcomers benefited from at least one considerable advantage: they had "little to lose and much to gain."[28] The golden age of the taipans, financially self-sufficient and shouldering moral as well as economic responsibilities, was succeeded by the age of individualistic entrepreneurs, whose spirit of initiative was not always ruled by considerations of honesty. The old hongs tried to put up resistance by diversifying their activities. They liberated their former departments specializing in navigation, banking, or insurance, creating separate businesses out of what had until then been no more than accessory services. Furthermore, after 1870 these Western companies transferred their Asian directors' offices from Hong Kong to Shanghai, thereby conferring greater prestige upon the taipans. This northward shift of regional headquarters reflected the triumph of Shanghai commerce over that of Canton: foreign interests were now centered at the heart of China rather than on its margins.

Naturally enough, Chinese businessmen were far more numerous, but their origins were equally diverse. Shanghai natives represented no more than a small minority. Even before the First Opium War, the presence in Shanghai of twenty-six regional guilds composed of merchants from other provinces testified to the town's role in local and interregional trade. As external trade developed and the chances of making a fortune out of it increased, further waves of immigrants arrived: Cantonese in the 1840s, merchants from Zhejiang fleeing the Taiping rebellion in the following decade, and then at the turn of the 1860s, people from Jiangsu, also fleeing before rebels.

The new arrivals joined regionalist associations, swelling their memberships. The effect of opening up Shanghai to the foreigners brought about or stimulated many new activities—in particular opium trafficking—that were far less regulated than the traditional ones. Among the recent immigrant merchants were many smugglers, adventurers who depended on support from their compatriots to defend their interests, if necessary by using force. We have already noted the role the Cantonese played in the Small Swords uprising. After the suppression of the

Taiping, the regionalist guilds stabilized. The legalization of the opium trade in 1860 turned traffickers into merchants. Former adventurers became notables and proceeded to turn the native-place associations into their own power bases in their dealings not only with Chinese and foreign competitors but also with the imperial administration and the consuls of the great powers. Because these associations reflected the activities of the merchants who controlled them, they often became confused with the professional guilds (*gongsuo*): the trading of sugar and opium for the merchants of Chaozhou (Swatow) in eastern Guangdong, tea for the merchants of Canton and central Guangdong, silk for the merchants of Zhejiang, and banking for the people of Ningbo. In 1852, the Cantonese guild was the largest, with 80,000 members; in the 1860s, the membership of the Ningbo guild was even greater. Right into the mid-twentieth century, both these guilds played a fundamental role in Shanghai economic development.

Within the native-place associations, merchants represented no more than a minority. However, under cover of a consensus, if necessary a "discreetly imposed" one, from that minority came the twenty to thirty directors, who assumed decision-making powers.* The guilds performed many economic functions in their respective branches of activity: they fixed prices and wages, supervised the payment of debts, negotiated in cases of bankruptcy, and in certain circumstances acted as commercial courts of justice. To combat smuggling and tax evasion, in the 1860s local officials decided to entrust the merchants themselves with collecting the lijin, the major trading tax imposed on the transport of merchandise to the hinterland. It was not long before this system turned into a veritable tax-farming procedure that strengthened the authority of the associations and their monopolistic control over the economic activities of their own respective domains.[29]

Shored up by their bureaucratic privileges and strengthened by their internal cohesion, the guilds controlled the trading circuits operating between Shanghai and the interior. However, the foreigners controlled the

---

* Historians have interpreted the nature of this consensus in divergent ways: Mark Elvin regards it as an embryonic but basic form of democracy, whereas for Bryna Goodman it is a conventional disguise for directorial oligarchic power.

trading networks operating between Shanghai and overseas markets. Import and export trading thus functioned within separate circuits. Although military victories and diplomatic treaties had made it possible for foreigners to gain a foothold in Shanghai, their attempts to penetrate the Chinese interior ran up against the hostility of the imperial bureaucracy, and even more important, they were blocked by the cohesion of traditional Chinese economic institutions. Between 1860 and 1890, the major hongs tried hard to get around the monopolistic power of the guilds, thereby provoking many clashes. One of the most violent occurred in 1877 between the British Jardine and Matheson Company and the Shanghai silk guild, which wished to prevent foreigners from buying cocoons directly from the producers in Zhejiang.

Distribution circuits were equally jealously guarded and defended. Between 1870 and 1880, the Chaozhou guild repeatedly challenged the British opium importers who were attempting to deliver their opium directly to Zhenjiang on the Yangzi. In 1887, the Chaozhou merchants finally did

Foreign hongs lining the Bund circa 1880 (courtesy of Qian Zonghao)

lose their trading monopoly.[30] But the networks of geographical, family, and professional solidarity continued to block foreign penetration into the interior. Not until the end of the nineteenth century, under pressure first from the Japanese, then from the Germans, did the resistance of the guilds slacken. Even in the twentieth century, foreign firms continued to encounter numerous difficulties as soon as they ventured outside Shanghai or the other treaty ports.

The explanation for the deep gap separating the letter of the treaties and daily practice lies with the autonomy and organization of Chinese society. International law, dictated by the strongest party, did not always cut much ice in a society organized according to a system of personal relations. The Chinese merchants' ability to retain control of the internal trading circuits was probably one of the main reasons for the economic rise of Shanghai. In 1875, the inspector general of Maritime Customs, Robert Hart, a qualified observer of trade with China if ever there was one, took a gloomy view of the port's future. He noted that even after the opening up of the Yangzi basin in 1860, imports and exports had continued to pass through the town because of the already existing interests and capital invested there. But he predicted that eventually Hankou, on the mid-Yangzi, would become the terminus for trade with Europe and went on to announce "the commercial death of Shanghai within ten or twenty years."[31] As often happens, history failed to confirm the expert's predictions. Shanghai, situated at the intersection of the internal trading circuits dominated by the Chinese and the overseas networks under foreign control, became the major center for the collection and redistribution of import-export products.

In the conflicts over the control of trading circuits between Shanghai and the interior, the most detested enemies of the guilds were probably not the foreigners but other Chinese merchants, "outsiders" who, profiting from their links with the foreigners, tried to get around monopolies and ignore regulations. One may even wonder whether the foreign merchants were not simply used by those within Chinese society who were opposed to the established trading system and who set out to make the most of the advantages of the opening up without having to submit to the authority and exactions of the guilds and their allies, the local officials.

THE COMPRADORS

The relations between the Chinese merchants and the foreigners produced both conflicts and instances of close cooperation. That cooperation depended upon an institution whose role remained fundamental until World War I: namely, the institution of the compradors. Originally, compradors were simply domestic servants or overseers responsible for supplying the foreign ships and warehouses of Canton. But when the Nanjing treaty eventually liberalized trade, they became veritable assistants and partners of the foreign merchants. Their presence was necessary to overcome language difficulties and the complexities of the monetary system and also to penetrate local business communities.

Thanks to their experience of external trade and their expertise with tea, the Cantonese were destined to become the first compradors of Shanghai. They arrived there in the company of foreign traders between the 1840s and the 1860s. In those days there were as many compradors in Shanghai as there were foreign hongs. This was a period of trusting relations. "Business conducted honorably, as gentlemen. A man's word was his bond and could be thoroughly relied on," Augustine Heard reminisced, not without nostalgia.*[32]

The comprador was generally responsible for his hong's financial transactions. He guaranteed the honesty of the Chinese staff placed under his authority, as he also guaranteed the solvency of local partners, traders, and qianzhuang banks; and likewise he managed the treasury, verified the value of coins and crated bullion, and calculated the exchange rate between the local unit of value, the tael, and the coin in everyday use, the silver dollar. The discredit that the Nationalists later cast upon the compradors, vilifying them as the "running dogs" of imperialism, should not obscure the importance of the latters' functions or the respected status that they held in both the Chinese and foreign business communities. In this period, compradors also stood as guarantors, which was the reason

---

* Augustine Heard was originally a partner in, then a rival of, the Boston-based Russell Company and was one of the pioneers of American trade with China. Before the opening up, he worked in Canton, buying tea and silk and selling opium, which he imported from Turkey. In the 1850s, he opened an office in Shanghai. His company disappeared in 1874, along with a number of other American companies established early in China.

Foreign merchants and their compradors sharing a Western-style meal

they were recruited from among well-to-do and esteemed merchants. They continued to engage in commercial activities on their own account. Their status was extremely ambiguous: they were at once salaried employees of the foreign hongs, intermediaries who earned a commission, and sometimes independent brokers operating for themselves.

The first-generation Cantonese compradors left their mark upon their period. Those who worked for Jardine, such as Yakee (in the late 1850s), Acum (in the 1860s), and Tong King-sing (from 1863 to 1873), were as well known and as respected as the British taipans for whom they worked. But as the years passed, the institution of the compradors evolved. As trading trends diversified, regional recruitment changed, and their responsibilities multiplied and became more specific. The Cantonese came into competition with compradors from Zhejiang and Jiangsu provinces, who specialized in silk and banking. Compradors came to manage more and more important elements in business and were now employed also by industrial firms. But at the same time, the intensification of transactions, the increasing numbers of economic actors, and the periodic outbreaks of financial crises undermined the erstwhile trusting relations between compradors and the foreigners. Hongs began demanding that their comprador bring with him capital and collateral guarantees.[33] After 1870, when Shanghai was attracting large numbers of independent entrepreneurs, many of whom lacked funds of their own, compradors often found themselves the victims of the dishonesty of their foreign partners, and lawsuits before the Mixed Court of the international settlement multiplied.

By the turn of the century, the Chinese and the foreign merchants were on a more familiar footing. Knowledge of English began to spread, and the study of Chinese was encouraged in both Western and Japanese firms. As a result, compradors now seemed less indispensable. The Mitsui Company was the first company to dispense with one, in 1899. Little by little, Western firms followed suit. Chinese collaborators and associates still played their part, but the role of intermediary that they assumed no longer implied that they were personal guarantors of transactions with local partners, and the services that they organized no longer represented a personal stake in the business.

Compradors generally exercised their functions for no more than the few years needed to establish precious contacts and to salt away serious profits. But did the division of profits engendered by external trade really favor them at the expense of the foreign merchants, as many contemporaries believed? It is true that a comprador was expensive and the money spent on him helped limit the profits of the foreign capitalists to about the same level as earnings in Great Britain and the United States.* It is therefore not particularly surprising that in the years between 1874 and 1914, when movements of international capital were intensifying, the countries that we should now describe as "developing" were not themselves the main recipients of Western investments. In Shanghai, modernization and, especially, industrialization were only partially financed by foreign direct investments. The principal investors were recruited from among taipans, who reinvested their profits locally, and Chinese businessmen, especially compradors. Unlike traditional merchants, the latter did

---

* The interest rate earned by foreign firms in China between 1872 and 1932 oscillated between 5% and 20%.[34]

not hesitate to throw themselves into long-term projects and to increase their fortunes through such productive investments.

According to contemporary historiography, modern businesses financed and managed by the Chinese blocked the advance of imperialism. But Chinese entrepreneurs were investing just as heavily in foreign companies. When the American Russell Company launched the Shanghai Steam Navigation Company in 1862 with capital of 1 million taels, compradors employed by the company itself underwrote over one-third of the shares. Jardine likewise obtained Chinese capital to found the China Coast Steam Navigation Company. Subsequently, mixed enterprises were set up in many other domains: insurance, modern banking, public utility services, naval repair yards, and manufacturing.[35] Even if the fact that they were registered in the international settlement gave them the status of foreign businesses, they were in truth Sino-foreign firms. These businesses, which eluded all Chinese governmental and foreign controls, were prime mediators of technology for both production and management. They constituted the crucible of the economic modernization for which the Chinese compradors, alongside the foreigners, were the principal agents.

A SINO-FOREIGN CAPITALISM

The foreign entrepreneurs were obliged to operate in an economic and cultural context that they found difficult to understand and that was often hostile to them. The privileges that the treaties had granted them did not suffice to remove all obstacles in their path. Locally, it was essential for them to obtain the cooperation of Chinese merchants. To attract the most skillful and the most worthy of them, the foreigners had no hesitation in extending them the tax exemptions that they themselves enjoyed, as well as the legislative and institutional devices they had set up to regulate their own economic activities. By so doing, they extricated a number of Chinese entrepreneurs—those who, with more or less good reason, claimed to be their assistants and associates—from the authority of the monopolistic guilds and a corrupt bureaucracy. The Chinese entrepreneurs thus became quasi-autonomous economic agents who, like the foreigners themselves, were subject only to explicit and minimal rules that aimed to encourage the progress of business, not to control it. The fact that they were able to benefit from such a juridico-administrative framework played just as important a role in the modernization of the town as did the injection of capital and the transmission of technology.

The exemption from lijin dues (an internal tax) from which the foreigners benefited according to the terms of the treaties was thus extended first to the compradors and subsequently to the Chinese shareholders of Western companies and all those who worked in liaison with them. The foreigners generously dispensed many transit passes, particularly to those engaged in the sale of silk and cotton.[36] In 1876, the inspector general of customs, Robert Hart, deplored these abuses.[37] The consuls followed suit. But the foreign merchants persisted in their ways. Quite apart from the financial advantage involved, they perceived this as a means to counter the obstacles that blocked the freedom of trade. Their strategy made it easier to supply Shanghai with raw materials destined for exportation or for local factories. It also had the effect of opening up new transaction possibilities to Chinese producers and traders, placing them beyond the reach of the guilds and allowing them to elude the monopolistic control for which the lijin provided the basis and symbol. As has been noted previously, the guilds tried to resist. However, by the 1890s they were losing the battle, and as the transit passes system continued to spread, their monopoly eroded.

What the Shanghai guilds feared and opposed even more than the foreigners were the Chinese traders who were operating outside the traditional institutional framework and whose profits were steadily growing, eluding all the levies through which the imperial administration tapped commercial revenues. The guilds mobilized local officials against these uncontrollable economic operators. But in order to rescue their compradors and associates from the pressures of the Chinese bureaucracy, the foreigners showed no compunction in playing the card of the Extraterritoriality Clause. In 1882, the American Frazer Company thus refused to hand over its comprador, Wang Keming, for whom the Shanghai daotai had issued a warrant of arrest.[38]

The foreign merchants furthermore offered their Chinese associates all the advantages of modern commercial legislation designed to encourage and protect long-term investments. In 1878, thirty-three British hongs demanded that the English Joint Company Act of 1862 be applied to the international settlement. Their purpose was, above all, to protect their interests against the dire financial consequences that might stem from their association with Chinese merchants. In Chinese business circles the predominant form of partnership, that of general partnership (*hegu* or *hehuo*), implied unlimited liability on the part of each of the company's partners. In 1881, the British government decided to authorize that the joint-stock companies of the international settlement be registered with the British Consular Court of Shanghai and that the terms of the 1862 law be extended to cover all Chinese shareholders, making the liability of each proportionate to the size of his investments. The new legal measure attracted many Chinese investors who, like the foreigners, felt reassured by the guarantees that it offered. It favored the reorientation, toward productive ends, of the merchant fortunes traditionally used to purchase official titles, to finance philanthropic works, or even to purchase bureaucratic favors.

By extending some of the privileges granted by the treaties to their Chinese trading partners and arranging for the latter to benefit from a legislative and institutional framework that reconciled the freedom to trade with the authority of the law, the foreigners presented those partners with the opportunity to escape constraints, monopolies, and exactions without being obliged, as in the past, to exclude themselves from the public order by resorting to contraband and smuggling. Chinese merchants were quick to seize these opportunities. In Shanghai, in circles of business interlopers, heirs to coastal China's vigorous entrepreneurial tradition, the graft of capitalism effected by the Western intruders found a particularly favorable terrain. The second half of the nineteenth century witnessed the emergence of Shanghai capitalism out of this Sino-foreign symbiosis.

These days, historiography tends to support the idea of economic aggression perpetrated by foreign governments, in particular that of Britain, as the first blow in a campaign for imperial domination. In other words, the suggestion is that the Western intrusion paralyzed China's development. But that thesis is totally at odds with the symbiotic phenomena described previously. Such interpretations, widely disseminated since the nineteenth century, result more from the history of current ideologies, political movements, and diplomatic maneuvers than from the history of economic development.

THE FOREIGN CONSULS, AT TIMES
RETICENT ACTORS ON THE ECONOMIC STAGE

In Shanghai, business contacts between Chinese and foreigners almost always resulted from private initiatives on the part of individuals or groups prompted by a common desire for profit, who all used pragmatic devices to achieve their ends: reciprocal investments, borrowed identities, false foreign company names. Every situation called for a flexible and negotiable solution.

China and Shanghai were not the preserves of any great power in particular. The treaty system and the clause relating to the most-favored nation that constituted its backbone created a many-sided framework within which the representatives and nationals of the European powers and the United States, joined at the end of the century by those of Japan, all evolved. These were world powers with complex interests, and relations between them were often affected by crises. Yet in Shanghai, in the face of an unfamiliar Chinese world that was at once feared and despised, their respective representatives usually maintained a degree of solidarity. The foreign consuls would either intervene with the Chinese authorities on their own or as a united group, led by their most venerable doyen, in pursuit of some kind of collective action. The most thorny files would be sent on to their national ministers and diplomatic corps in Beijing, there to be negotiated directly with the Imperial Court.

In the nineteenth century, three consuls dominated the Shanghai scene, those of Great Britain, the United States, and France. The problem of harmonizing economic interests with diplomatic objectives hardly affected the latter two. There were very few French businesses in Shanghai, and the French consul devoted most of his energies to improving the territorial and administrative situation of his concession and the defense of missionaries rather than merchants. The American consul represented a young country with no diplomatic traditions and still absorbed in settling its own internal conflicts. The protection of immediate economic interests, initially entrusted to a merchant, Edward Cunningham of the Russell Company, was as far as American diplomacy went. The creation in 1854 of a regular consular service did no more than replace merchants by "poorly paid" officials with "fleeting interests."[39] Moreover, after a promising start made between 1840 and 1860, Sino-American trade slowed down, as capital was then attracted by the boom in internal American markets, and one after another, the great American hongs closed down: Heard in 1874, Olyphant in 1878, Russell in 1891. Secretary of State John Hay's formulation of an American open-door policy in 1899 certainly indicated the emergence of a U.S. Chinese policy, but this was founded on the defense of cultural values rather than economic and strategic interests, which were then considered to be of little importance. In Shanghai, American representatives therefore mostly limited themselves to following in the steps of British diplomacy and seeing that American nationals benefited from the advantages that this secured.

Essentially, the defense of the foreign merchants in Shanghai depended on the British government. However, that defense was but one part of a policy of imperial expansion that led Foreign Office staff to take into account political and geopolitical factors that were frequently alien to the preoccupations of the expatriate merchants. The interests of the British Empire did not necessarily coincide with those of the Shanghai hongs, and the perspective from London differed from those that emerged locally. Consuls, sandwiched between the Foreign Office hierarchy, whose objectives they supported, and the residents of Shanghai, whose living conditions and preoccupations they shared, sometimes had a difficult role. Depending on their own temperaments and the prevailing circumstances, consuls would arbitrate in favor now of private interests, now of political imperatives.

In the mid-nineteenth century at the time of the disturbances, when some British merchants, like other Western ones, sought to take advantage of the Chinese administrative paralysis and avoid payment of customs dues, Consul Alcock had opposed them.* On September 9, 1853, he had solemnly declared that the Small Swords' capture of Shanghai did not suffice to invalidate the treaties signed by China and the Western powers and that consequently the obligations that those treaties imposed upon merchants still stood. The plenipotentiary minister, Sir John Bowring,

---

* We should remember that immediately after the opening up, Chinese officials collected Maritime Customs dues.

supported his consul: to suspend payment of customs dues because of the Chinese administration's inability to collect them would be to "consent to the abrogation of all treaties and to the utter destruction of our trade with China." He could not "consent to 'opiumize' so valuable a commerce."[40] Sir John therefore supported Alcock's plan to establish a foreign inspectorate to manage the Maritime Customs on behalf of the imperial administration.

During the decades that followed, conflicts repeatedly broke out between the expatriate merchants, anxious to exploit the weakness of the imperial government, and the Foreign Office diplomats, determined to preserve long-term commercial development and therefore also the legal framework of the treaties that guaranteed that development. The British residents of Shanghai frequently complained that their government did not intervene energetically enough to preserve freedom of trade and to prevent the exactions and abuses of the Chinese administration.[41] They formed residents' associations and other bodies designed to bring pressure to bear on the British consul, his hierarchical superiors, and the British government. But the latter offered them little support, in accordance with the philosophy and practice of a system to which both the governed and governors must adhere: "British enterprise in China must be independent and individual and self-reliant. The moment it ceases to be this and leans too much on State assistance, . . . it ceases to be enterprise; in fact, . . . it ceases to be British."[42]

AN OFFICIAL MODERNIZATION MOVEMENT
WITH NO FUTURE

In the seventeenth and eighteenth centuries, when the Chinese Empire was prospering and the Manchu dynasty reached its peak, both philosophical policy and administrative practice tended to minimize direct state involvement in the processes of production and trade. At this time, the devolution of an increasing number of leadership tasks to a para-public sector filled with local notables led to a veritable privatization of the economy.

The arrival of Westerners in the 1840s did not immediately overturn that philosophy and those practices. But from 1860 on, as has been noted, a number of important mandarins, warlords, and officials responsible for putting down the Taiping uprising became aware of the need to modernize the economic system. They thought that the public authorities should take the initiative in such modernization. Their motto, "Self-strengthening" (*Ziqiang*), was inspired by the Legalist tradition, which was both interventionist and pragmatic and recommended enriching the country and developing the armed forces (*fuguo, qiangbing*). Very soon, their objectives moved from the manufacture of weapons to industrial development and from the adoption of new technology to that of new institutional and cultural models. Self-strengthening thus nurtured the Foreign Affairs Movement, which remained active until 1895, at which point China's defeat at the hands of the Japanese sealed its collapse.

It was in Shanghai, where in 1860–1862 Chinese military leaders made common cause with the foreigners against the Taiping, that those leaders discovered Western firepower and the efficacy of new military technology. To Li Hongzhang's mind, "shells that explode before touching the ground are indeed a device of the gods," while Zeng Guofan remarked in his private diary that "the Chinese must learn the casting of cannons and the construction of steamships."[43] But the prestige and influence that their victory over the rebels conferred upon these military leaders did not suffice to rally the Court behind their reforms nor to turn the modernization plan into imperial policy. Nevertheless, the reformers did obtain enough support from Beijing to implement their program in the provinces over which they had some jurisdiction as governors or governors-general. The Foreign Affairs Movement thus moved ahead under the aegis of regional authorities and achieved a fragmentary modernization, frequently lacking in coherence as projects were launched, then abandoned, as the administrative postings of their promoters dictated.

Shanghai, however, was not affected by these ups and downs. From 1860 to 1884, the posts of governor-general in the provinces of Jiangsu, Jiangxi, and Anhui were successively held by the top leaders of the Foreign Affairs Movement, Zeng Guofan, Li Hongzhang, and Zuo Zongfang. Li Hongzhang, the principal architect of the movement, made Shanghai his base. Initially, he concentrated within his own hands all the administrative powers that would facilitate the implementation of his plans: he began as the governor of Jiangsu, then also became the temporary governor-general and trade commissioner for the ports of the south (*nanyang tongshang dachen*).* In 1870 he was appointed governor-general of the metropolitan province of Zhili, a post to which he added that of trade commissioner for the ports of the north. But even with all these responsibilities, he continued to oversee the modernization of Shanghai.

Authority on this scale, extending from one province to another and establishing a horizontal link between two administrative entities, ran counter to imperial policy, which traditionally preferred to keep each province as an isolated unit in dealings with the central imperial authorities. It was an exception that may be explained partly by Li Hongzhang's own personality, for he dominated the Chinese political scene at the time and, even more, by the fact that there was no precedent (*wuli kexun*) for dealing with "barbarian affairs," and this had the effect of minimizing constraints. Li Hongzhang kept a firm hold on the program for the economic modernization of Shanghai and retained the right to appoint the managers of all pilot schemes. He supervised the development of both the northern and southern ports, thereby attracting attention to the uniqueness and unity of the Shanghai-Tianjin corridor.

Li Hongzhang was lucky enough to be able to rely on an excellent administrator, Sheng Xuanhuai, who became his principal collaborator on economic matters, as he was involved as a promoter, shareholder, or manager in nearly all the official business ventures set up in Shanghai between 1871 and 1895. At a local level, Li Hongzhang could count on the collaboration of both provincial governors and local daotai, most of whom were appointed upon his recommendation. For example, in 1865 Daotai Ding Richang contributed actively to the foundation of the Jiangnan Arsenal, of which he became the director. In Shanghai, Li Hongzhang benefited from support not only from the somewhat unreliable local bureaucracy but also from other quarters. Thanks to his powerful networks

---

* The post of trade commissioner for the treaty ports was created in the aftermath of the First Opium War. With the opening of new ports in 1860, the responsibilities of this post were split in two. There were now two commissioners: one for the ports of the south (including those of the Yangzi), the other for the ports of the north. These commissioners, whose responsibilities extended to all types of relations (economic, diplomatic, and so on) with foreigners within the framework of the treaty ports, held authority over the local daotai.

of personal relations and his links with former disciples or colleagues or even with his compatriots from Anhui, his native province, he was also able to form alliances with merchant and scholar elites who proceeded to provide the ventures set up by the Foreign Affairs Movement with most of their funding and their managers.

The public sector that played an important role in the early modernization of Shanghai was therefore unusual in a number of respects. Its creation did not result from any state policy, for local and regional authorities in cooperation with some local elites ensured its funding and management. The importance of this modernized public sector in Shanghai stemmed from two main factors: the will of the great mandarin, Li Hongzhang, and the presence of local elite groups that were more numerous, more wealthy, and more open-minded than anywhere else in China.

By the end of the three decades that the Foreign Affairs Movement lasted, Shanghai could, admittedly, boast no more than four official or semiofficial businesses. But those four together commanded capital of 14 million dollars and employed 14,600 workers: 40% of the total capital and 30% of the workforce of Shanghai's modern industrial sector.[44] The first of those business concerns, created in 1865, was the Jiangnan Arsenal. It was also the only one that possessed the distinguishing features of a public enterprise with regard to both its funding and management. The Maritime Customs of Shanghai provided its funding, and the Shanghai daotai was, ex officio, its director. The arsenal manufactured arms and munitions and built a few small gunboats. But costs were too high, the quality of production left much to be desired, and the top-heavy managerial staff was constantly changing, since each newly appointed governor or governor-general used the arsenal as a reserve of sinecures to be distributed among his own particular clients.

Li Hongzhang founded the China Merchants' Steam Navigation Company in 1872 to compete with the British and American companies that dominated the maritime transport market. This was the first Chinese steamship company and also the prototype of mixed companies "supervised by officials and managed by merchants" (*guandu shangban*). Its system of organization subsequently served as a model for that of the Shanghai Cotton Cloth Mill and, later, that of the Imperial Bank of China.

Despite the enthusiasm of their founders and the talent of some of their managers, these mixed ventures suffered from the same drawbacks as the imperial administration: insufficient funds, corruption, and nepotism. They survived thanks only to their powerful patron, Li Hongzhang, and to the monopolies that he arranged to have conceded to them. After Japan defeated China in 1895, Li Hongzhang fell into disgrace, and the installation of foreign industries put an end to state monopolies. Once this happened, the official and semiofficial establishments could no longer survive: some closed down; the rest were privatized. But their eventual failure should not cause us to underestimate the role they played in the process of introducing modern technology and training a skilled workforce. For example, most of the small-scale entrepreneurs who created Shanghai's booming mechanical industries in the first half of the twentieth century had learned their trades while working in the Jiangnan Arsenal. Furthermore, those mixed enterprises, which facilitated contact between mandarins and compradors, inaugurated a form of modern bureaucratic capitalism that was to reappear whenever the public authorities felt strong enough to try to orient economic modernization to their advantage. However, such was not the case in the first decade of the twentieth century, for at that time the imperial regime was able to impose its authority upon neither its own bureaucracy nor the new social forces that had made their appearance since the opening up of China. In this period, the modernization of the Shanghai economy was to stem from private initiatives, some of them made by officials acting in a private capacity.

The rapid modernization of the Shanghai economy in the second half of the nineteenth century was reflected in the evolution of local society. This modernization maintained the extreme geographical and social mobility of the urban population at a time when the anarchy and violence of the pioneering period were beginning to slacken.

CHAPTER 4

The Kaleidoscope of Shanghai Society

A T THE BEGINNING OF THE TWENTIETH CENTURY, almost three-quarters of Shanghai's inhabitants were not natives of the town. They had come there from the Chinese provinces, Europe, the United States and, toward the end of the century, Japan. The population was fragmented into communities that had virtually no communication with each other. Shanghai was a Tower of Babel where provincial dialects created as many barriers between the Chinese as national languages did between the Europeans. The image of a patchwork or a mosaic has often been used in this connection.[1] But that of a kaleidoscope would be more appropriate, for the different communities changed as the economic and political circumstances did.

In this society of largely temporary residents, the mechanisms of control did not function well either on the Chinese side, where individuals tended to elude the discipline imposed by traditional solidarities, or on the Western side, where they depended on many different administrative authorities and consular jurisdictions. In the absence of a strong and unified local government, authority resided principally with organizations that represented specific regional or professional interests: chambers of commerce, clubs, residents' associations, guilds, secret societies, and gangs, all of which led largely autonomous lives.

Yet, despite everything, a Shanghai identity began to emerge in the last years of the nineteenth century. On the side of the foreigners, the pioneers of a society established on the margins of the Western world gave way to longer-term expatriates who welcomed a much-improved urban environment. On the Chinese side, there were detectable signs of a nascent patriotism that, although confused by particularist loyalties, to a certain extent transcended them.

THE FIRST SHANGHAILANDERS

Within this fragmented society the major cleavage that separated Chinese and Westerners remained. Westerners were now more numerous: about 15,000 in 1910, compared to 250 in 1855, but they represented barely 1% of the 1.3 million inhabitants who now made up Shanghai. Nevertheless, their presence acted as a catalyst upon a number of social and institutional upheavals that were to make Shanghai the first modern Chinese city. Their influence on local life can be explained not only by their numbers, relatively large in comparison to those of other treaty ports, but also by the high caliber of some of them. Once the Taiping uprising died down, traffickers, passing adventurers, and filibusters were replaced by more respectable notables. The small bourgeois republic that became established in the international settlement was in many ways reminiscent of the Hanseatic towns of the sixteenth and seventeenth centuries, jealous of their autonomy, keen on material comfort, and more or less entrenched in their own particular social customs.

Before World War I, Shanghai's foreign society was a privileged one. Even as they loudly proclaimed their allegiance to this or that national or confessional group, the foreigners were beginning to feel a certain attachment to this port in which their establishment was becoming increasingly stable. The terms "Shanghailanders" (mainly referring to the local British and Americans) and "old Shanghai hands" reflected their burgeoning identification with their place of residence.

However, the foreign community only appeared homogeneous in comparison to the Chinese society at the heart of which it had settled. In reality it was sundered by deep national, professional, and religious rifts. Although the relative importance of the British had declined, in 1910 they still represented the largest group (4,500 strong) and also the most influential, thanks to the de facto control that its members held over the municipal institutions of the international settlement and to the prestige they enjoyed as members of the greatest imperial power of the day. Around the British establishment gravitated an Indian community of about 1,250 individuals, most of whom were Sikhs employed as policemen by the municipality of the international settlement, and many merchants from the region of Bombay who had arrived in Shanghai at the same time as the first British firms. Between 1840 and 1870 a number of Parsees succeeded in acquiring large fortunes; but in the following decades their economic role declined at the same time as the opium trade. Most of Shanghai's Indians were municipal employees or small-scale shopkeepers, and their influence on local life was slight. The only exception was a group of Sephardic Jews, also from Bombay but originally natives of Baghdad, such as the Sassoons.[2]

Among the other national groups, the Japanese, who began to flock in around 1900, numbered about 3,400 at the time of the collapse of the empire. They lived in isolation in the Hongkou district, to the north of the international settlement, and rarely mingled with the other foreign residents. Next most numerous were the French, installed in their own concession. The American group was almost as large. Germans were slightly less numerous; Russians, even fewer. The 1,500 Portuguese formed a group apart: they had come from Macao, and many were half-castes, the concessions' so-called poor whites. Each of these groups stressed its own cultural and religious individuality, for national feeling was strong among these expatriates. However, the British, who were at the top of the tree and put their mark upon social relations both within the international community and with the neighboring Chinese society, set the tone. The British influence was manifest in the rhythm of daily activities, the organization of the living environment, the development of leisure occupations and sport, and the use of English as the lingua franca of the foreign communities.

The professional hierarchy reflected the national one. The most highly respected notables were the merchants and the bankers, many of whom were either English or Scottish: 40% of the 643 foreign businesses in Shanghai in 1911 were British. These British businessmen had arrived as youths in Shanghai and worked as griffins before becoming bosses and taipans. The most important of them represented companies based in London or New York; the rest busied themselves making their own capital bear fruit.[3] From the 1880s onward, the improved living conditions in the concessions made it possible for them to bring their families out to join them. They were able to remain for longer periods in Shanghai, and increasing numbers stayed there throughout their careers. The development of transoceanic shipping lines and the establishment of intercontinental telegraphic communications reduced their isolation. "Shanghaians" would from time to time return to their native lands on holiday and could now keep in closer touch with what was happening in the rest of the world.

Diplomatic staff represented a different circle of influence. Each of the fifteen or so great powers covered by the treaty system maintained a consulate-general or a consulate in Shanghai. In the last years of the empire, three consulates-general were remarkable for their competence and influence: those of Britain, France, and Russia. The preeminence of the British consulate-general was marked by its location in the urban landscape. Its premises, which extended over 43 mu (3.5 hectares), stood at the entrance to the Bund, close to the confluence of the Suzhou River and the Huangpu. Lawns surrounded the residence of the consul-general and the administration offices, buildings in the classical style erected between 1870 and 1880. The British consuls, who competed for their appointment, were skilled diplomats, many of whom specialized in Chinese affairs. French consuls were for the most part appointed to Shanghai and elsewhere in China for shorter periods in their careers, which were more diversified than those of their British colleagues. But they benefited from the assistance of good sinologists working alongside them, many of whom later became professors in the School of Oriental Languages in Paris. Similarly, the Russian consulate employed a number of experts who had attended courses in the Oriental Faculty of Saint Petersburg. In 1910, one of the secretaries, V. V. Hagelstrom, coauthored a work that, in its English translation, *Present Day Political Organization of China*, served as a reference for generations of officials, journalists, and historians.[4]

Members of professional classes were still underrepresented. Many of the earliest doctors had begun as ship's doctors, the French François Sabatier and Paul-Édouard Galle, for instance. Many worked only for a short time in Shanghai. Others did settle there, combining a private practice, hospital work, and administrative functions. Doctor Edward Henderson, who practiced in Shanghai from 1868 until the end of the century, working for the municipal council of the international settlement, became an expert in problems of public hygiene. Doctor Louis Pichon worked in a similar capacity in the French concession, while Doctor Robert A. Jamieson ran a medical practice and at the same time published *Medical Reports* for the imperial administration of the Maritime Customs. Those reports soon came to be regarded as international reference documents.[5]

The small circle of professional men thus sometimes intersected with that of local foreign officials and, more often, with that of the missionaries, especially after 1877, when a conference of Protestant missions in China decided to lay greater emphasis on works promoting education and health than on evangelization. Over the years leading up to World War I, Christian missionaries, buoyed by guarantees granted them by the opening-up treaties, particularly the 1860 Beijing treaty, rapidly extended their influence.

All the Catholic orders and every Protestant denomination were represented in Shanghai, which was the principal center for missionaries in China. The Reverends W. H. Medhurst and William Lockhart, of the London Missionary Society, were established there even before the arrival of Captain Balfour.[6] Half a century later, Shanghai was home to over one hundred Protestant missionaries, most of them British or American. They ran many educational institutions, hospitals, dispensaries, printing works, and publishing houses that produced not only Bibles but also translations of Western scientific works. Their ranks included many men of remarkable talent and character, such as the American educator W. A. P. Martin; the writer Young Allen; John Fryer, who headed the translation department of the Jiangnan Arsenal from 1869 to 1889; and Alex Wylie (1815–1887) of the British and Foreign Bible Society, who set up Shanghai's first large, semimodern printing works during the 1850s.[7] Jesuit influence dominated the Catholic missions. From 1842 on, these renewed their links with the tradition bequeathed by Matteo Ricci. Their great center at Zikkawei, in the southwestern suburbs, contained, alongside Saint Ignatius College, an orphanage, a printing works, and a meteorological observatory to which Aurora University was added in 1903. The French supplied the main contingent of missionary priests. In 1860, the Beijing convention had made France the protector of the Catholic missions. The Shanghai consuls fulfilled their obligations in this domain with zeal until the separation between church and state in 1905 caused them to distinguish more sharply between diplomatic action and missionary activities.

Numerous violent rivalries divided the missionaries, both between Catholics and Protestants and among their various orders and denominations, but on the whole they lived happily enough alongside business and diplomatic circles. Indeed, they contributed to the running of the concessions, whose economic success helped them to pursue their own undertakings. In the last decade of the nineteenth century, the names of several pastors appear in the list of members of the municipal council of the international settlement. The major trading companies financed many of the missions' charitable works: in 1844, the London Missionary Society founded the Chinese Hospital, thanks to the generosity of companies such as Dent, Jardine and Matheson, and Russell. The Catholic missions were among the largest landowners in the French concession, and their members maintained many institutional and personal connections with the consulate, the municipality, and commercial businesses. The Jesuits' Saint Ignatius College, for example, provided training for many Chinese translators and collaborators who worked for the administration and the French banks and trading companies. The career of Nicolas Tsu (Zhu Zhiyao), recruited as a comprador to the Bank of Indochina in 1897 before becoming one of Shanghai's foremost Chinese industrialists, benefited greatly from the Jesuits' protection of his family,* in particular his uncles Ma Xiangbo and Ma Jianzhong, who were two of the earliest and most illustrious Zikkawei students.

The everyday functioning of the foreign community also depended on the presence of other Westerners, ones who did not belong to the high society of the concessions. Many Portuguese were entrusted with accounting and copying work in foreign companies in which they had no hope of promotion. Several dozen demobilized or deserter soldiers from the expeditionary forces became artisans or small-scale shopkeepers.** Others worked in the police forces of the concessions. Many were drunkards and poorly disciplined, and their behavior tended to provoke scandal. In 1863, the

---

* The Zhu family, whose conversion dated from the seventeenth century, had remained faithful to the Catholic religion, despite its being banned by the imperial authorities in the following century. The family's support was crucial to the Jesuits on their return to Shanghai, when it was opened up.
** At the time of the Taiping rebellion, British and French expeditionary forces were sent to Shanghai, where they remained until the mid-1860s.

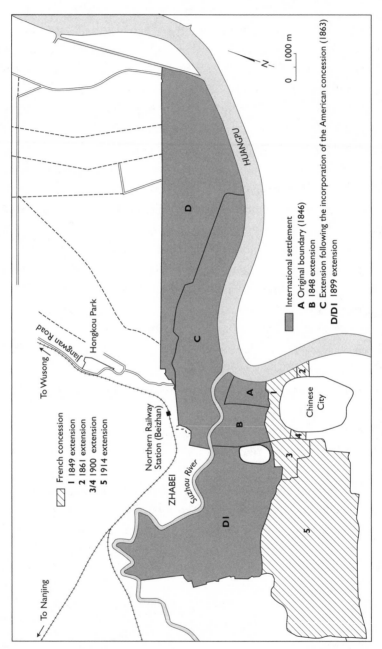

The foreign concessions and successive extensions

International settlement
A Original boundary (1846)
B 1848 extension
C Extension following the incorporation of the American concession (1863)
D/D1 1899 extension

French concession
1 1849 extension
2 1861 extension
3/4 1900 extension
5 1914 extension

HUANGPU

Chinese City

ZHABEI

Suzhou River

Northern Railway Station (Beizhan)

Hongkou Park

Jiangwan Road

To Wusong

To Nanjing

N

0   1000 m

municipal council of the French concession accordingly decided to recruit men of a more respectable caliber directly in France, and the following year saw the consequent arrival of a thirty-strong contingent of Corsicans in Shanghai. The remedy proved worse than the problem.[8] Subsequently, the municipal council of the French concession turned for help to Annamites, while that of the international settlement appealed to Sikhs. However, the police forces of the concessions did continue to employ a number of Europeans: 143 in the French concession in 1900, and 245 in the international settlement by 1883.[9] And the sisters of charity lavished their unassuming devotion on hospitals, orphanages, and educational institutions, such as a dozen or so Saint Vincent de Paul sisters in the Shanghai General Hospital, founded in 1864, which provided care for Western residents of all nations and religions. Finally, the foreign community could also count on the services of a dozen or so prostitutes of Western origin.[10] The crews of warships and merchant shipping, who made up the most numerous and most turbulent section of Western society, stayed in Shanghai only long enough for a few drinking bouts and brawls.

Before World War I, "poor whites" were rare in Shanghai and were neither interested in nor capable of challenging the order imposed by the oligarchy of merchants and local elites. The latter formed a tight community of their own, maintaining with the surrounding Chinese world just enough contacts to enable them to pursue their own economic, political, and missionary objectives.

DAILY LIFE IN THE CONCESSIONS

Since the mid-nineteenth century, living conditions in the foreign concessions had greatly improved, thanks to the residents' efforts to increase the security, health, and comforts of their living quarters. Major epidemics of typhus, cholera, and typhoid fever were combated by the development of sanitary and medical infrastructures, in particular the installation of a drainage system in 1862 and, twenty years later, a system for the distribution of running water. By the end of the century, the quality of the infrastructures of Shanghai equaled or almost equaled those of large European and American towns, and the death rate of the whole foreign population, resident and nonresident, fell to around 2%.[11]

Some building work undertaken for sanitary purposes improved the appearance of the concessions. The Bund was no longer a stinking towpath bordering the river but a well-constructed wharf, extended to the rear by an esplanade, covered by a lawn in the 1880s, which opened to the facades and colonnades that now adorned banks, trading houses, and official buildings. The alleyways of the past, in which there had barely been room for two coolies laden with crates of tea to pass, had been widened, in some cases as much as 10 meters, with the carriageway paved in stone and somewhat raised to avoid flooding at high tide. The former Maloo (the road leading to the racecourse) became the Nanjing Road, an avenue bordered by both Chinese and foreign shops. With the influx of residents and increasing numbers of businesses, the territory of the concessions expanded northward and westward. Wealthy foreigners built their villas in the airiest quarters of Bubbling Well Road, beyond the racecourse, or along the quiet, shady avenues created in the early years of the twentieth century inside the French concession, such as Xijianglu Avenue, which, renamed Avenue Joffre during World War I, later became Shanghai's elegant Champs-Élysées.[12]

During the 1890s, electric streetlights began to replace the gas lamps along major thoroughfares. Horses and horse-drawn carriages came into

The Nanjing Road in 1905

The Nanjing Road in the interwar period

increasingly fierce competition with new modes of transport. Rickshaws (from the Japanese *jin-riki-sha*, vehicles pulled along by a man) were introduced in 1873 and became very popular. They were subsequently made more comfortable by the addition of pneumatic tires and in this form survived the arrival of electric trams in 1908. At this time, cars were still a curiosity (the first two were imported in 1902), and the telephone, a very recent innovation, was still reserved for professional use.

In this foreign Shanghai, painstakingly modeled on the image of the capitals of Europe, residents tried to re-create the amusements and way of life of their own class in their native societies. Long gone were the days of the 1860s, when young griffins who arrived, unmarried, in Shanghai would live communally in premises provided for them by their employers, and when women were conspicuous for their absence at grand dinners and even at balls. Now, many residents enjoyed a family life: the number of Western women in Shanghai rose from 296 in 1880 to 3,207 in 1905.[13] In the villas of Bubbling Well Road and the French concession, the presence of many Chinese servants made daily life easier. Women, relieved of domestic duties, now took an active part in social life. Their husbands,

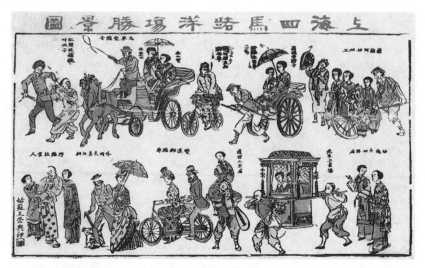

Street scenes at Fuzhoulu, a place of entertainment and culture

who would usually devote only the mornings to their business affairs, also enjoyed plenty of leisure.

In a predominantly masculine and British society, leisure time centered around the clubs and sporting activities. The "Shanghai Club," which was the most exclusive, had set up its premises on the Bund as early as 1864. In 1901, it treated itself to a new building with a neoclassical facade. On the exterior, a pediment crowned two stories of colonnades; inside, the bar, the billiards room, the dining room, and the library were all adorned with marble and ornate woodwork. The Shanghai Club was famous for the length of its bar—which stretched for over 30 meters—and the quality of its members, recruited from among the prominent British and American taipans. The French and the Germans preferred to gather in their own clubs, the former at the Cercle sportif français located near the French Park of Koukaza (moved to Rue du cardinal Mercier in the 1920s), the latter at the Concordia Club, which opened new premises on the Bund in 1907—complete with neogothic turrets and gables.[14] The Scots joined the Saint Andrew's Society, the Irish the Saint Patrick's Society. Other clubs catered to men of a particular profession (for example, the Customs Club, reserved for the staff of the Maritime Customs service) or to groups with shared political or philosophical inclinations: one such was the Masonic

Club, open to members from the various Shanghai lodges. These clubs played an essential role in the lives of the foreign residents. There they would meet, drink, dine, exchange their news, and read the newspapers, in particular the ultraconservative *North China Daily News*, the voice of British interests in Shanghai and China generally. The clubs also organized parties. As early as the 1870s, the Caledonian Ball, organized by the Saint Andrew's Society, was one of the key events of the social season: hundreds of male kilt wearers and just a few dozen women attended.[15]

The foreign residents also devoted much of their time to sport, particularly the British, who regarded sport as an antidote to the clammy, unhealthy climate and depended upon it as a means of "reviving their livers."[16] In the early days of the concessions, they had to content themselves with wheelbarrow races along the Bund or shooting parties on the track of pheasants or wild duck, or sometimes simply gatherings in the neighboring countryside, to which they traveled on horseback or in junks. Later, sporting activities became more organized. Among the griffins, the favorites were cricket, tennis, and rowing. They were also keen on training Mongolian ponies with a view to running them in the races that took place between

The Shanghai Club circa 1910

May and November, attracting elegant crowds to the racecourse constructed in 1861. Replacing a series of tracks closer to the Bund, this covered an area of some 30 hectares, at the junction of Nanjing Road and Bubbling Well Road.[17] The Racing Club building and its clock tower added in 1890 stood out as landmarks in the Shanghai landscape.

The Western residents of Shanghai were very keen on the theater. They amused themselves by putting on amateur dramatics, as there were no professional actors' companies. The Amateur Dramatic Club, created in 1867 by some English residents, put on plays in the Lyceum Theatre, then a simple wooden building on the Bund. The French entered into competition by creating their own dramatic society: in 1872, the major silk merchant and ex-president of the municipal council of the French concession, Napoléon-Auguste Buissonnet, took to the boards, accompanied by Henri Cordier and other local elites, in a performance of *Le bourreau des crânes*. Meanwhile, the Philharmonic Society recruited musicians, mainly from among the German residents.[18] On the other hand, literary, philological, and historical research interested a few missionaries, diplomats, and administrators of the Maritime Customs. These organized themselves around the North China branch of the Royal Asiatic Society that had been set up in Shanghai in 1858. This published a review and possessed a fine library: Alexander Wylie, one of the best missionary sinologists of his day, created a collection containing 1,000 works in Chinese and 1,300 volumes in Western languages. They were catalogued in 1872 by Henri Cordier, then an employee of the American Russell Company but taking his first steps as a bibliographer and historian.[19] Fifteen or so years later, another future historian of China, Horsea B. Morse, then working for the Maritime Customs service, became secretary of the society and tried to breathe new life into intellectual enterprises that most Shanghai residents considered to be respectable but dry as dust.[20]

Even leaving aside the Japanese, who as yet involved themselves very little in the activities of the Westerners of Shanghai, could it be said that the various national groups thrown together in the concessions made up a real community? For a long time, the standoffishness of the French, preoccupied with the survival of their own concession, and the national and religious particularities of other groups blocked the emergence of a wider sense of community membership and the development of a spirit of local citizenship. The Shanghai of the foreigners was from the start defined by its opposition to its Chinese environment, and this conferred upon it a negative kind of identity.

On November 17 and 18, 1893, the international settlement celebrated the fiftieth anniversary of the opening of the port, with a great show of illuminations and fireworks. On the Bund, a streamer proclaimed, "In what region of the world is Shanghai not known?" However, the collective memory often functioned in a somewhat patchy way. To commemorate the Western fighters who fell in the struggle against the Taiping, in 1870 the French erected a statue to Admiral Protet in front of the municipal offices of their concession; on the Bund, close to the British consulate, stood a monument to the dead soldiers of Ward's Ever Victorious Army. Each national group celebrated the history of Shanghai by commemorating the part that its most distinguished nationals had played. In conformity with history, foreign Shanghai was essentially British in the general collective memory. And the policy of the municipality of the French concession, which

Jubilee celebrations in Shanghai (1893) for the
anniversary of the international settlement

from 1900 onward named all its streets and avenues after its own consuls, missionaries, and obscure councillors, was unable to change that.

In such circumstances, it was hard for the foreign residents of Shanghai to entertain the notion of a shared destiny. The various expatriate communities continued to gear their lives to the rhythms of their respective mother countries. The French celebrated July 14; the Americans, July 4. The British got together to celebrate Queen Victoria's diamond jubilee in 1897 and King Edward VII's coronation in 1901; the Germans celebrated the visit of Prince Henry of Prussia in 1898.[21] But until World War I, such demonstrations were above all occasions for rejoicing, and the atmosphere was usually one of cosmopolitan conviviality.

Closeness and complicity among the foreign residents of Shanghai were forged elsewhere, in a shared sense of belonging to a pioneer community and coping with difficulties beyond the ken of their compatriots in the mother country and also in the satisfaction of leading a life of luxury; in the shared pleasure of freely flowing alcohol, banquets, and grand receptions; or, more simply, in the charm of evenings spent together as families taking the air along the Bund and amid the groves and flower beds of the Public Gardens, listening to the concerts played on the bandstands, waving to friends aboard junks, the better to savor the falling dusk and the river breeze. The "old Shanghai hands" or "Shanghailanders," as they were beginning to call themselves, were not ideologues, but their attachment to Shanghai and identification with it grew ever stronger as they rose to the challenges of the difficult environment and created the conditions for a privileged existence.

CHINESE SOCIETY

In the mid-1860s, when Taiping turbulence died down, many of the refugees who had sought shelter in Shanghai returned to their native provinces. But many of them decided to settle definitively in the town, which by 1865 contained 700,000 Chinese. In the following years, regular and sustained immigration swelled that population, carrying it to 1.3 million by 1910.

The merchants and adventurers from Guangdong and Fujian who had flocked to Shanghai at the time of the opening up were succeeded by people from Zhejiang and Jiangsu, many of whom were likewise merchants. But other social groups carried in by the migratory influx also appeared: land-owners and scholars driven out of Jiangsu (Jiangnan) by the Taiping rebels, bankers from Ningbo, attracted by Shanghai's booming trade, craftsmen and peasant laborers in search of work. Most of the newcomers settled in the foreign concessions or on their peripheries. In 1910, the old Chinese quarters held 672,000 inhabitants; the concessions, 616,000 (500,000 in the international settlement, 116,000 in the French concession).[22]

People with the same provincial origin liked to cluster together in particular quarters and streets. In the international settlement the natives of Jiangsu made up the most numerous group (about 180,000). The next largest was that of the natives of Zhejiang (168,000). The Cantonese numbered only 40,000;[23] they no longer played a predominant role, for their merchants, compradors, and artisans had been supplanted by competitors from Zhejiang or Jiangnan.[24] These immigrants, who maintained strong family, clan, and religious links with their native regions, were considered, and indeed considered themselves, temporary residents. Each group was distinguished from the local population and other immigrant groups by its own dialect, its cuisine, its cults and rituals, and, in many cases, by its professional activities. The very multiplicity of local cultures constituted a formidable obstacle to the formation of a Shanghai identity.

The diversity of dialects played a key role in the segregation of the various communities. Except among elite literate groups with some knowledge of the language of the imperial bureaucracy, very little, if any, communication took place between residents from different backgrounds. They spoke mainly—in many cases, only—with fellow countrymen hailing from the same province or even the same district, so fragmented was the geographical distribution of dialects in eastern and southeastern China. Diet was an equally important criterion of identity. The richness of Chinese gastronomy is well known. In Shanghai, restaurants were classified not in terms of the quality and prices of their menus but according to the regional character of their cuisine. And, unlike contemporary Parisian gourmets, keen to discover different tastes from different regions, Shanghai diners kept to their accustomed habits and flavors. Even the hierarchy of everyday dishes and those of luxurious banquets kept well within the framework of regional specialties. In a restaurant, the ground-floor rooms, opening

The small trades of Shanghai, from cigarette-card illustrations
(courtesy of Qian Zonghao)

to the street, would receive the working-class clientele, whereas the upper stories, where more refined menus were served, were reserved for better-off diners. Provincial and regional characteristics also marked religious practices, for each community brought to Shanghai the cults of its own village deities and celebrated the great festivals of the Chinese calendar in its own particular way. Depending on whether one came from Suzhou, Guangdong, or Anhui, one would eat a particular type of cake, take part in particular processions, and go to hear particular operas.[25]

The various native-place associations were organized in accordance with a strict hierarchy that reflected the importance of the individuals involved, their economic functions, and the renown and influence of their leaders. In many cases this hierarchy overlapped with that of the professions, for the various communities tended to specialize in particular branches of activity. Among the most respected groups were the bankers of Zhejiang and the silk merchants of Guangdong and Fujian. At the bottom of the social ladder were the people from Subei (the northern part of Jiangsu), among whom cesspool attendants and rickshaw pullers were recruited; these were completely ostracized.[26]

Regional and professional solidarities were constructed around native-place associations (*huiguan*) financed and run by a few dozen leaders. These associations, which protected the interests of their community (*tongxianghui*), assumed a role that was originally of a religious nature. They built temples dedicated to tutelary deities, organized festivals and rituals, helped to send the coffins of those who died in Shanghai back to their ancestors' native land, and provided for the upkeep of cemeteries in which the poorest could enjoy eternal rest in a plot of land symbolically attached to their provincial birthplace. Such philanthropic works, initially closely associated with religious functions, assumed increasing importance and autonomy as the nineteenth century came to an end. The huiguan now opened schools and dispensaries, helped their members to find work or obtain capital, and came to their assistance when they fell into need. Although the huiguan represented entire communities, welcoming all who shared the same geographical origin, they were nevertheless elitist institutions managed by a handful of notables. This combination of hierarchical elements on the one hand, and a sense of collective responsibilities and social closeness on the other, gave these institutions a traditional appearance, but, as we shall see later, the huiguan also played an important role in the town's economic modernization and development of political awareness among its inhabitants.

Leading merchants undertook the management of the huiguan, which involved large property transactions and a wide range of financial operations.[27] Regional specialization in economic activities made for a certain assimilation between the huiguan and the professional guilds (*gongsuo*). Native-place associations shared with the guilds many responsibilities in the management of the local economy: they monitored the regularity of operations in the sectors of activity in which they were competent, arbitrated in conflicts between their members, and served as mediators with other communities or with the imperial administration. Their power was reflected in the urban framework. Every community was keen to acquire a social headquarters of a kind to promote the smooth running of its services and to symbolize the prestige of the group that it represented. Within the town precinct, temples and altars, meeting rooms, offices, small theaters, schools, and cemeteries sprang up amid gardens and courtyards. The planning of these buildings was reminiscent of that of the offices (*yamen*) of the imperial administration. But the headquarters of the native-place associations were more luxurious than those official buildings, for the Shanghai merchants were quite prepared to bring in exotic woods and precious materials from afar to embellish and increase their own prestige as well as that of their communities.

Did these communities identify their own particular destinies with that of the Shanghai metropolis? Or did they regard the town simply as a place of residence in which to conduct business or seek work, while their hearts remained back in their native birthplaces where, as the saying went, "the wine was better and the moon fuller"?[28] The truth is that the strength of regional loyalties did paralyze the development of a collective consciousness, and Shanghai remained for the most part a "patchwork" of more or less willing and temporary exiles.[29] Even at the end of the nineteenth century, middle classes (*xiao shimin*)—with their cohorts of employees, minor officials, schoolmasters, and qualified out-of-work students, all with a definite urban identity—had hardly begun to appear. Their rise would not begin until the 1920s, when a relatively modern economy and educational system would develop.

The working world had not yet been turned upside down by industrialization and the appearance of a workers' proletariat. In 1895, the shipyards, factories, and workshops of Shanghai employed no more than 37,000 people. By the eve of the 1911 Revolution, the number of workers in the modern and semimodern industrial sectors had increased, but not beyond a total of 150,000.[30] The vast majority of the urban commoners was composed of laborers, coolies, dockers, rickshaw pullers, beggars, vagrants, and thieves and other criminals. The existence of these poverty-stricken people was precarious. They lived on junks anchored along the banks of the Suzhou River or crowded along the edges of the concessions and the walled town, in the shantytowns of Yangshupu and Pudong, where the huts constructed out of mud, straw, and bamboo were repeatedly ravaged by fires or destroyed in police raids. This was where immigrant workers squatted, essentially living from day to day, many of them employed in temporary seasonal jobs. When workers were laid off or an economic crisis or other family accidents arose, the men would return to their respective villages. They could not have survived without regional solidarity. Immigrants from one particular region all lived together (the shantytowns of Pudong and Hongkou were known as "the villages of the people of Subei," *Subei cun*). They tended to work in the same sectors: peasants chased out of Anhui, Shandong, or Subei by famine or flooding took up the hard labor of coolies and night-soil carriers; those from the countrysides of Jiangnan, where an old tradition of craftsmanship used to flourish, found more gratifying and better-paid work as carpenters or weavers.

These people's closeness to their rural origins favored the development of popular cultures rich with all the diverse village traditions by which they were fueled. In the great town of Shanghai, immigrants remained faithful to the deities of their native communities. They built them temples, marking out the precincts by processions and summoning from their native homelands Daoist priests to conduct rituals and organize carnivals designed to appease the souls of wandering ghosts. Wandering ghosts! Theirs was precisely the fate that these workers far from home feared for themselves, should they ever die in a foreign land, for that is just what Shanghai seemed to them.

The elite groups, too, were recent arrivals and of diverse origins. But more affected by the upheavals that the opening up introduced, they found a measure of agreement regarding the idea that change was necessary, for they all intended to make the most of the economic conditions and to assume unprecedented social and political responsibilities. The influence of the outside (non-Chinese) world and the apparently imperious necessity to modernize introduced a factor of unity among the new elites of the treaty ports, albeit one certainly more fragile than the Confucian orthodoxy that had preserved the cohesion of the gentry for centuries.

Shanghai had never been a cultural center such as those to which the province of Jiangsu owed its rich scholarly tradition. Prior to the opening up, its merchants could not compete with those of great centers such as Canton and Hankou. Not until the second half of the nineteenth century did scholars, landowners, and wealthy merchants come together in the town. According to the Confucian orthodoxy, scholars stood at the top of the social hierarchy and merchants at the bottom, but the two groups gradually grew closer together and formed a class of "scholar-officials/ merchants" (*shenshang*). Such an integration of elite groups was not a new phenomenon. Merchants had always employed a variety of strategies (buying official titles, making large donations to the public coffers, giving their sons a classical education) for acquiring acceptance in the established mandarin order. But in Shanghai, this integration came about not so much on the basis of the Confucian values landowners and scholars praised but on the values that merchants recognized, namely, pragmatism and modernism.

At the end of the 1850s, the Taiping rebellion had swept into Shanghai many landowners, distinguished scholars, retired officials, and powerful lineage heads—all of them members of the class that Western historians of China have labeled "the gentry." Their arrival tempered the predominance of the merchants, for they brought with them the prestige of their academic titles and connections, their experience as local managers, their Confucian zeal, and their respect for traditional morality. Their influence on the political and social life of Shanghai soon made itself felt. They founded academies, fought against the decadence of urban mores, and created and directed philanthropic institutions (*shantang*). These landowner/scholars also recognized the challenge presented by the presence and technical superiority of the foreigners, and they provided the Foreign Affairs Movement with some of its best theorists. One was Feng Guifen (1809–1874), a native of the Suzhou region, a graduate of the metropolitan examinations, and a member of the prestigious Hanlin Academy, who arrived in Shanghai in 1859 and whom Li Hongzhang made one of his chief advisers on the implementation of his policies for regional modernization.[31]

The members of the gentry who streamed into Shanghai brought with them a more refined lifestyle than that of the local merchants. They were cultured men of leisure who enjoyed meeting their friends around a table, in concert halls (*shuchang*), or at the theater to share their appreciation of the talents of the singers and the quality of the operas.* They would often spend evenings in restaurants with courtesans they had invited to entertain them with songs and games. The most elegant teahouses, particularly those in Fuzhou Road in the international settlement, were much-frequented haunts of the courtesans. In a society in which wives and concubines were traditionally confined to the home, courtesans brought a note of elegance and conviviality to such masculine gatherings. With their white, powdered faces, reddened lips, and carefully traced eyebrows, they embodied an impersonal kind of beauty that was further enhanced by the splendor of their costumes. They were the aristocrats of the world of prostitution, on whose margins they operated. Scholars delighted in extolling the flower-ladies in their poems and in special reviews with suggestive titles such as *The Journal of Leisure Pastimes*, *The Forest of Smiles*, or *The World of Flowers*.[32]

All this was a far cry from the world of the opium traffickers who had invaded Shanghai in the wake of the first foreigners. But that world, too, had calmed down. The profits from opium had been reinvested in banks or workshops, and the traffickers had become respectable traders. These nouveaux riches shared the scholar/landowners' respect for Confucian morality. Like them, they were committed to filial piety, family and clan

---

* In concert halls and traditional theaters, performances took place in front of tables where the public would sit to enjoy food and drink.

A westernized Shanghai home. The chandelier, clock, fireplace, and table setting are all foreign. (courtesy of Qian Zonghao)

solidarity, and mutual assistance for compatriots. However, Confucian culture, of which they had limited understanding, did not create among them the common tastes and views—the kind of Pan-Chinese cosmopolitanism—that existed within the mandarin class. The merchants remained in a provincial mold, their provincialism confirmed by the role that they played at the head of the huiguan, their preference for local rather than Beijing opera (that of the Imperial Court), and the custom that many of them followed of maintaining their principal family home in their native province while entrusting the running of another household in Shanghai to a secondary wife.

The wealthier merchants, in particular the compradors, who were more exposed to contacts with the foreigners, adopted a partially Westernized lifestyle. Their horizons widened beyond China itself to encompass the outside world. Although they continued to respect Confucian precepts, they rejected some long-standing customs, such as not schooling girls and binding feet, and embraced the leisure distractions of the foreigners: sports and horse racing. Their culture was hybrid, as were their wardrobes, where long silk robes would hang beside European-style suits and Chinese skull caps would be stacked alongside Western headgear; and as, too, was the pidgin that they used to communicate with their Western partners, a language that combined Chinese sentence structure with an Anglo-Indian or Portuguese vocabulary.

Shanghai merchants wishing to become integrated into the elite groups were still buying themselves official titles and posts. However, the decline of the mandarin system and the suppression of the official examinations in 1905 deprived the gentry of their criteria of social distinction.* The prestige of wealth now tended to eclipse that of education, and the pursuit of profit became more important than the practice of virtue. Initiation into "barbarian affairs," for a long time perceived as a factor of social exclusion, was now seen as a privilege and became a condition of personal success and the good management of public matters. The classic trajectory that propelled an individual and his family out of trade and into the mandarinate was no longer such an absolute requirement. Major entrepreneurs gave up the idea of transforming their sons into scholars; instead, they had them educated in missionary schools or abroad to turn them into modern businessmen. A diversion by way of the mandarinate came to seem increasingly unnecessary in order to convert economic success into social success. On the other hand, across the board, from mandarins who combined their official tasks with entrepreneurial activities to those who abandoned a public career altogether in order to devote themselves to business, there were now many members of the gentry joining the ranks of the merchants. The most famous case was that of Zhang Jian (1853–1926), a graduate of the

---

* The system of mandarin examinations, organized by the public authorities, had since the thirteenth century associated intellectual activity, conceived as the study of the Confucian classics, with service to the state; officials were recruited from those who passed the examinations with the highest scores. The examinations were fundamental to the existence and unity of the class of scholar-officials. The system could not rise to the challenge of modernization and was suppressed in 1905, within the framework of the reforms launched by the imperial authorities under the name of the "New Policy."

metropolitan examinations who became the founder and owner of one of the major Shanghai textile mills without, however, abandoning the world of scholars.

Despite the diversity of their origins and careers, the Chinese elites of Shanghai manifested a concerted determination to modernize. This conscious decision and mobilization did not wipe out their regionalist loyalties, but it did affect their policymaking within institutions such as the huiguan by transcending the latter and thereby contributing to the creation of both a Shanghai identity and Chinese nationalism. The fact is that although they often referred in their discourse to the superior interests of the nation, their options were conditioned by the concrete situation that prevailed in Shanghai and by the presence of its foreigners. No doubt that proximity did not make the initiation into modernity any less painful, but it did confer upon it a remarkable efficacy and at the same time a specifically Shanghai character.

CHAPTER 5

The Concessions as a Model

B Y THE END OF THE NINETEENTH CENTURY, Shanghai rivaled the great cities of the West—that is, of course, foreign Shanghai did, the Shanghai that in 1893 with great pomp celebrated the fiftieth anniversary of the opening up of the port and that had at its disposal all the public facilities that the technological progress of the period could provide. Quite unlike some colonial cities, stranded at the very ends of the earth where, amid the humidity of exotic climes, the marks of civilization seemed doomed to degeneration, foreign Shanghai exhibited a vigorous modernizing energy. Its residents wished to raise the town "to the scientific and useful level of the West" and have it benefit from the progress evident in the improvements made since the 1830s and 1840s in the great cities of Europe.[1] Shanghai, London, and Paris were all waging the same battle against dirt, epidemics, and prostitution.

That dynamism, which aimed above all to ensure the well-being of the foreign residents, also influenced the aspirations of the Chinese population both beyond and inside the concessions. The existence of enclaves that eluded imperial authority offered Chinese residents the possibility of being Chinese in a new, different fashion. It broke the monopoly over power and thought upon which Confucian orthodoxy was based, abolished the notion of "barbarians," and established the theoretical possibility of a dialogue between different civilizations. The cultural arrogance that had long bedeviled Sino-foreign contacts gave way to interest, comparisons, and second thoughts. But new and productive though these developments were, they were often painful, for that cultural arrogance now frequently seemed to switch camps and become a feature of the foreigners. Hence the vigorous nationalism very soon manifested by the elite groups of Shanghai, in their headlong race toward modernization. Out of these twofold aspirations, at once modernizing and nationalistic, came the initially reformist, then revolutionary movement that would eventually topple the imperial regime in 1911.

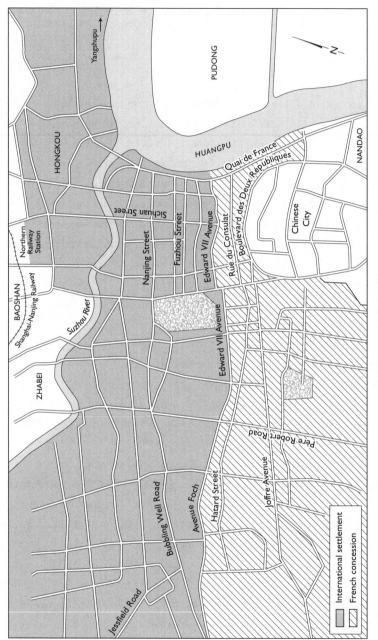

The streets of Shanghai

THE INTERNATIONAL SETTLEMENT

The concessions that, at the time of the opening of the port, had been relegated to an area set apart from the walled town expanded at a steady rate until 1914, when the foreigners, in this case the French, for the last time obtained permission to extend their territory. The area of the concessions had grown from 0.56 square kilometers in the mid-nineteenth century to almost 33 square kilometers, two-thirds of which were taken up by the international settlement, the remainder by the French concession. The concessions now sheltered 640,000 people, 98% of whom were Chinese. The territory and population of the Chinese town, in contrast, had remained relatively stable.

The spatial growth of the town throughout that half century had been a response to the needs created by the commercial and industrial boom of the treaty port. It had been effected by successive additions, secured in the course of diplomatic negotiations whose targets in many cases transcended local interests. In the course of that growth, Shanghai's center of gravity slipped from the old fortified town to the foreign concessions, in particular the Bund. New industrial and commercial Chinese suburbs developed to the north of the concessions, out toward Zhabei, and to the south of the walled town in the direction of Nanshi. The relatively compact block formed by the concessions thus constituted the heart of the urban zone. All around it stretched the scattered quarters that came under Chinese administration.

The two concessions enjoyed a status of extraterritoriality that removed them from the authority of imperial power. They were also unified by the nature of their management, which was modeled on that of Western institutions, and made the most of scientific and technical progress to promote the collective well-being. However, the foreigners' town remained split in two, since the French government's opposition had scuppered the plan to create a single, united concession. The international and the French concessions manifested now rivalry, now solidarity, with the one drawing upon British liberalism, the other upon the French Jacobin tradition: on the one hand an oligarchy of merchants keen to defend their community interests, on the other a bureaucratic autocracy proclaiming to serve the republican ideal.

By 1854, the foreign residents had set up the Shanghai Municipal Council (SMC) and laid down the foundations of what was to become the government of the international settlement. The Association of Ratepayers (the Ratepayers' Meeting) held the power, the Municipal Council being originally composed of seven members elected yearly by the association; in 1865, the number of councillors was increased to nine. It held all the prerogatives of a municipal government but had no power to intervene in judicial matters: foreigners were answerable to the jurisdiction of their respective consulates, the Chinese to imperial courts. To be qualified to take part in ratepayers' meetings and vote in the election of council members, one had to be a landowner or householder paying high annual taxes or rent. Based on poll tax, the voting system excluded 80% to 90% of the foreign population living in the concession, not to mention its Chinese residents, who were deprived of all representation.* Chinese residents remained theoretically subject to the authority of the imperial administration, but over the years the latter lost taxing and legal power over Chinese nationals established in the concession. The Mixed Court, created in 1864 to pass judgment on lawsuits between Chinese residents or between Chinese residents and foreigners, was, it is true, presided over by a magistrate representing the daotai, but his foreign assistants constantly encroached upon his prerogatives. By the beginning of the twentieth century, the Chinese magistrate had lost the power to arrest Chinese residents or even to extradite them to bring them before imperial justice. In 1911, the consular corps assumed the right to appoint and pay the president of the Mixed Court, which thus passed under foreign control.

The settlement's government thus came to be delegated to an elected executive organ responsible to its constituents, whose attributes were fixed by a written municipal constitution, namely, the *Land Regulations*, which had been drawn up by men "imbued with the modern municipal spirit of England" and attached to the principles of self-government.[2] The Shanghai Municipal Council had no power to modify these regulations: the Shanghai consular corps or, as a last resort, the diplomatic corps

---

* Only taxpayers could take part in the association, and only foreigners who owned property worth 500 taels or more or who paid rent of an equivalent value were eligible for the council; by the end of the empire, the number of taxpayers had risen to about 2,000.

based in Beijing, had to sanction any amendment.* In practice, the SMC enjoyed considerable liberty, since the international settlement was home to foreigners of a variety of nationalities and was subject to no power in particular. Its powers were therefore not limited by the controls to which a central government usually subjects its local administrations.

The policy of the Shanghai Municipal Council was inspired by the spirit of the founding fathers, the handful of taipans and missionaries who engineered the opening up of the port and ensured its early success. The British influence left its mark on the recruitment of councillors and administrative staff, the style of management and its objectives, and the particular importance attached to relations with Her Gracious Majesty's consul. All the same, the SMC was not an instrument of the British government. It served the majority group of leading British entrepreneurs who, intent above all on defending their own interests, by no means always shared the views of the Foreign Office. In the last resort, however, the powers of the oligarchs of the international municipality rested upon the armed might of the world's greatest imperial power. The public resources of the settlement stemmed from the local taxes, the weight of which fell mostly upon the foreign residents until the 1890s.** In the early days, municipal budgets were modest—between 60,000 and 70,000 taels—and they were devoted above all to the maintenance of security.

Initially, the small group of entrepreneurs who dominated the international municipality sought to create, at the lowest possible cost, conditions favorable to the expansion of its economic activities, the preservation of its health, and the improvement of its comfort. The installation of the first urban infrastructures thus by and large resulted from private initiatives. Until 1880, apart from the Bund and a few other major thoroughfares, the construction of urban roads depended upon the local inhabitants. Gas lighting in 1862, an electricity network in 1882, the installation of running water in the following year, and the construction of tram lines

---

* New *Land Regulations*, introduced in 1869 and 1898, clarified and completed the initial ones.
** According to the treaty, only foreigners could register the deeds of their properties with the consular services, so only they were liable to real estate taxation. On the other hand, a rental tax also applied to Chinese residents.

from 1902 on were all innovations achieved by private companies. Their headquarters were in London, but they recruited their shareholders from among local bankers and entrepreneurs, with the objective of making a profit from their investments by responding to the needs of a solvent clientele that was, in the early years at least, exclusively foreign.

The Shanghai Municipal Council adopted the same policy concerning infrastructures such as hospitals and educational establishments. The first institution designed to cater to foreign residents was the Shanghai General Hospital, founded by the Jesuits in the French concession in 1862 and later transferred to the international settlement. But the SMC refused to assume responsibility for it, contenting itself with making a few donations from time to time. As for schools, there was not felt to be much need for them. Few families even considered having their children educated locally. The British in particular preferred to send their sons back to England to board at private establishments ("public schools").

From the 1890s onward, however, with the influx of Chinese merchants into the settlement, the idea of public services began to gain ground. Now in possession of a bigger budget,* the Shanghai Municipal Council felt more obliged to devote part of the municipal resources to the needs of a foreign population that was now more cosmopolitan and less wealthy, as well as a Chinese population that was contributing over half of the municipal taxes. Until this point the Chinese residents had hardly benefited at all from the progress achieved in the settlement. The guilds and charitable associations had been assuming the responsibility for providing medical, social, and educational assistance. Meanwhile, the prices of gas, water, and electricity had been too high for most Chinese, who were consequently unaffected by these new public amenities. It was only thanks to private initiatives—essentially those of religious organizations funded by donations from wealthy Chinese and foreign merchants—that a small proportion of the Chinese residents had limited access to modern medicine and

---

* Income from taxation increased, reaching 633,000 taels in 1900 and 1.8 million in 1911. The increase was due partly to demographic growth and the fact that residents paying rental tax were more numerous and partly to the extension of real estate taxation to Chinese landowners. Commercial patents and wharf dues, which rose along with economic activity, also contributed to the increase.

Western education. Under the impact of the forceful proselytizing of both Protestant and Catholic missions, religious schools multiplied. Jesuits, the American Episcopal Church, Baptists, Presbyterians, and Methodists all competed in their ardor to open elementary and secondary schools, most of them for boys. But there were also a few universities: St. John's, founded in 1879 by American Episcopalians, and Aurora University, opened in 1903 by the Jesuits.

By the turn of the century, the Shanghai Municipal Council recognized that it was no longer possible to continue to ignore the well-being of Chinese residents. In April 1900, F. Anderson, its president, declared at the ratepayers' meeting that it was not only "right and equitable" but also "politic and expedient to do for the Chinese what we do for ourselves."[3] This new policy produced the construction of a Public School for Chinese and, in the same year, a municipal hospital reserved solely for the Chinese to care for contagious diseases.

The international settlement's success rested upon the presence of a large community of merchants who were either British or influenced by the Anglo-Saxon civilization, such as Americans and Jews from the Middle East. These rich entrepreneurs wished above all to defend their economic interests, but they also entertained philanthropic and religious initiatives. Furthermore, they all shared the same respect for the smooth functioning of the limited form of democracy that they themselves had established. The defense of economic interests, philanthropy, and community action were all practices familiar to the Chinese elite groups, who often collaborated in projects that foreign merchants set on track. However, what were altogether new to them were democratic procedures—in particular the majority vote, the scientific interests that governed the actions of the Shanghai Municipal Council, and the opportunity of being introduced to modern endeavors through cooperation with foreigners with whom they sat on the boards of various firms and foundations. The Chinese elite groups accepted Western values not so much because they rallied to the principles embodied in them but rather by reason of the examples of patent material progress that the international settlement daily offered.

THE FRENCH DIFFERENCE

The French concession was not a mirror image of the international settlement. It was not only smaller but also less populated: in 1910, it housed 116,000 inhabitants, about 1,500 of whom were foreigners, although for the most part not French. Above all, its economic activities were far less developed, for it sheltered no more than a few major companies. Nevertheless, the pace of modernization in the French concession more or less matched that in the international settlement. The modernization achievements, in some cases as a result of a combination of French and international efforts, were very similar; the same kinds of urban infrastructures were introduced: roads, drains, electricity, and a bit later, telephone and tram lines. For that reason, the French concession has often been regarded simply as the younger sister of the international settlement, an appendage with no character of its own that played no particular role except perhaps that of complicating the tasks of its elder sister both in the area of municipal management and in relations with Chinese authorities.

City Hall in the French concession, constructed between 1863 and 1865
(Archives of the Ministry of Foreign Affairs)

Residence of the secretary of the French municipality

Judging by the criteria of British pragmatism, liberalism, and morality, the management of the French concession may indeed seem somewhat unsatisfactory. It was very much dependent on the consul and, through him, the French government; and the budget that the French Ministry of Foreign Affairs provided for it was inadequate. Given that its revenues from taxation were more modest than those of the international settlement, since it was less densely populated and less active, it was obliged to increase its resources by taxing opium dens, gaming houses, and brothels, which it was consequently in its interest to encourage or at least to tolerate. Nor could it count on the many philanthropic initiatives that came to the support of the international settlement. However, in the domains of education and medical care, it could at least rely on the cooperation of the Catholic missions.

The values of the French concession were not those of Anglo-American civilization. In keeping with the Jacobin tradition, it was organized in such a way as to entrust to the state the responsibility for securing the triumph of universal values. The concession's most remarkable figures were to be found among its administrators, doctors, and missionaries. If there were no great entrepreneurs in this enclave of expatriates, that was probably because of the still-rural and bureaucratic nature of French society at the end of the nineteenth century and the beginning of the twentieth. Their absence was also connected with the origins of the concession, which had resulted from determined efforts on the part of a few French officials more or less supported by their government.

In the very earliest days, the consul was the sole administrator of the concession, but it was not long before he was obliged to appeal to land-owners, whose financial aid was essential if the municipal projects were to be completed. The creation of the Municipal Council in 1862 to which a number of powers were delegated formally sealed that collaboration. But the council soon objected to the consul appointing its members and also claimed authority over the police force. The rivalry between the consul-ate and the council led to an open clash and the promulgation in 1866 of *Regulations Covering Municipal Organization*. These, which were ap-proved by the Minister of Foreign Affairs and periodically revised, served as a charter for the French concession. According to these regulations, eligible voters were to elect the Municipal Council. The council was to be responsible solely to the consul, and its functions were to be deliberative. In the event of any clashes, the consul could dissolve it.

Unlike the municipal system of the international settlement, which rec-ognized the quasi autonomy of a merchant community, the management of the French concession depended on the consul. Whereas the status of the international settlement resembled that of a free port, the French conces-sion was more like a colonial enclave managed under the authority of the French government. In other words, the personality of the consul-general was of utmost importance: if the consul were too weak, he would allow those under his administration to encroach upon his prerogatives; if he were too authoritarian, he would antagonize the notables of the French community, who were always quick to accuse the Paris government and its representative of turning a blind eye to local realities. The relations be-tween the Municipal Council and consular authorities were consequently regularly punctuated by crises fueled by personal animosities, often violent in small expatriate communities.

Yoke-bearing porters on the French wharf circa 1880 (Archives of the Ministry of Foreign Affairs)

Despite its weaknesses, this system promoted the values that had characterized French political culture since the 1789 Revolution. Paris exported to the French concession not only its centralizing administrative procedures but also its principles geared to the public interest, to general access to the new well-being made possible by scientific progress, and to equality before the law for all categories of individuals. These universalist principles could not prevent racism from affecting everyday relations just as much as in the international settlement, but they did find expression in a certain concern for the general interest: for instance, in the French concession, the construction of public roads and wharves was planned as early as 1862. While the international settlement was busy creating public parks that continued to exclude the Chinese until 1928, the French municipality was beginning to line the concession's streets with the plane trees that would lend such a leafy charm to its residential quarters. These efforts at planning and urban embellishment may be regarded as an exotic extension to Georges-Eugène Haussmann's remodeling of Paris. The installation of running water presents another example of the conceptual difference between Anglo-American "public utilities" and public services in the French manner. Instead of a private company drawing up private contracts with potential users that were solvent, as the Shanghai Water-works had in the international settlement, in the French concession the municipality purchased water from the British company and then distributed it through public fountains, free of charge, to the entire population, Chinese residents included.

This idea of an authoritarian bureaucracy representing the general interest was often hard to apply in an extremely heterogeneous society dominated by community interests. On two occasions, in 1874 and 1898, the municipality clashed with the powerful Ningbo guild, which refused to transfer its cemetery, then situated in a densely populated zone, to the south of the concession on the edge of the old walled town. The guild protested that it did not wish to disturb the repose of its dead by exhuming and moving their remains. The Municipal Council did not "believe it should depart from the European custom that, in the name of health, . . . dictated that cemeteries should be moved away from populated areas."[4] The violent riots that erupted during these clashes forced the municipality to backpedal and then to negotiate.

From 1914 onward, two notables who were invited to join the council as consultative members represented the Chinese community on the French concession's Municipal Council. This initiative was taken a full twelve years before Chinese were allowed to sit on the council of the international settlement. Given the extremely limited powers that the Municipal Council of the French concession possessed, the importance of the presence of Chinese councillors in its midst was more symbolic than real. The same could well be said of numerous aspects of the actions of the French consulate and the French concession's Municipal Council.

Nowadays, when liberalism, culturalism, and respect for community values are supposed to be triumphant, the management of the French concession may seem to reflect narrow, chauvinist notions. However, the universalist values that that management claimed to be serving, in its authoritarian fashion, certainly contained an element of rationality and generosity. Leading Chinese intellectuals, such as the grammarian, jurist, and modernizer Ma Jianzhong (1844–1904) and his brother, the educator Ma

Xiangbo (1840–1939), both appreciated this. Perhaps that was because those values partly coincided with those of a mandarin tradition that lived on among many intellectuals, allowing them to escape the limitations of the community system to which the Chinese merchants preferred to confine themselves.

THE GRADUAL MOBILIZATION OF
THE CHINESE LOCAL ELITES

Once the port was opened up, the commercial ventures, workshops, hospitals, schools, and municipal services that the foreigners created all served to introduce modernity to the Chinese who acquired responsibilities in them, whether as compradors, shareholders, members of the board of directors, or at a more modest level, simply as assistants performing practical tasks.

However, most of Shanghai's Chinese had no direct contact with the foreigners. The influence of the foreign institutions, as places of apprenticeship, was limited to a few particular sectors of society. This purely pragmatic modernization remained marginal, the more so given that, ideologically and politically, its impact was weak upon an urban culture in which Confucian values had been revitalized by the presence of many scholars and notables from the surrounding provinces, Jiangsu and Zhejiang, who flocked into the town at the time of the Taiping uprising.

But in the course of the first decades following the opening up, Shanghai certainly did see the birth of an incipient Sino-foreign culture. The missions worked hard to diffuse "Western science" (*xixue*). To this end, they set up modern printing works such as the London Missionary Press and produced many translations of scholarly works and technical handbooks. Within the framework of the Foreign Affairs Movement, the Chinese administration supported those efforts. Governor-General Li Hongzhang opened a modern language school (1863), a school of military engineering (1874), and a school of telegraphy (1882). He also attached a translation office to the Jiangnan Arsenal; in the course of its forty years of existence, it published 160 works, mostly relating to the applied sciences.

Among the missionaries, as in the arsenal, translation work was based on close cooperation between Western sinologists and Chinese scholars.

The former would produce an oral translation that the latter then rendered into classical Chinese, the only medium recognized by the educated public. A number of famous collaborations thus developed, among them that between the British missionary Alexander Wylie (1815–1887) and the mathematician Li Shanlan (1810–1882). With close links through many intellectual, professional, and social contacts, these translators embraced their role as cultural transmitters with great enthusiasm. With funding from both Western and Chinese notables, they founded a number of educational institutes, in particular Shanghai Polytechnic Institution (*Gezhi shuyuan*), created in 1874, and published popular anthologies and reviews such as *The Globe Magazine* (*Wanguo gongbao*). However, these Sino-Western circles made scant impact on local society, as they included too few people: there were at that time no more than a few dozen missionaries and fewer than one hundred Chinese working together. The latter included many talented intellectuals, but their failure in the upper-level mandarin exams; their eccentric lifestyle; their taste for wine, women, and in some cases, opium; not to mention, in many cases, their conversion (whether sincere or opportunist) to Christianity robbed them of any prestige in the eyes of other scholars.

In general, the scholar class remained impervious to "Western science" and consequently also to the imitation of Western models. In Hong Kong, another frontier region but one where elite groups and institutions carried little weight, "Her Majesty's Chinese" adopted Western values without reticence. In Shanghai, in contrast, the presence of a large scholar class inhibited a straightforward adoption of the new ways of behaving. Some changes were made, but the need for change generally was not yet widely accepted. To be sure, a few individual modern practices appeared here and there, but modernization could not develop further until the dominant class, the scholars and the bureaucrats, accepted its objectives.

Not until the turn of the century, under the pressure from circumstances that were disastrous for the empire, did scholars and the imperial bureaucracy rally to the policy of modernization and Westernization. In 1895, China's defeat at the hands of the Japanese put paid to the Foreign Affairs Movement, with its instrumental concept of a modernity limited to the military and economic domains. That failure stimulated the rise of a patriotic and reformist trend, led by a number of Cantonese intellectuals of great talent, such as Kang Youwei (1858–1927) and Liang Qichao (1873–1929), who clamored for institutional changes inspired by Western and Japanese examples. Their program was beginning to make an impact in 1898, at the time of the One Hundred Days, during which a strong reformist gust of wind swept through the Chinese systems of education, administration, and production. However, the reforms turned into a fiasco. The subsequent restoration of a conservative government coincided with the anti-foreigner Boxer uprising, which in its turn provoked military intervention by the great powers. They spared the dynasty but imposed the humiliating protocol of 1901 upon China.* Following these catastrophes, Chinese leaders and scholar-elite groups at last agreed on the need to modernize institutions. The imperial authorities now took over the ideas of the reformists of 1898 and launched themselves into the New Policy, posing as the architects of modernization and the defenders of the nation.

Shanghai was not at the center of these developments, but when the official policies reverberated there, they found a particularly favorable reception. The notables mobilized, spreading the idea that Western political culture possessed an intrinsic value.

Urban elite groups discovered a new form of participation in the debates organized by study groups (*xuehui*) in which discussions on technological questions (agricultural modernization, teaching improvements, and so on) presented them with an opportunity to tackle the problems of social and political reform. *The Shanghai Journal* (*Shenbao*) helped them to learn about modern problems. This commercial newspaper, founded in 1895 by a British businessman but produced by the best Chinese journalists, broke with the religious and scientific priorities of the missionary press and instead devoted itself to investigations of local problems and national and international news. Interaction between this society, already prepared for change by several decades of open trade, and the modernizing policy that the authorities and most officials and gentry had now adopted

---

* The protocol stipulated, among other conditions, the execution or banishment of the principal leaders of the Boxer uprising, the stationing of a foreign military force to guard the Legation Quarter in Beijing, and the payment of an indemnity of 450 million taels, payable in gold over thirty-nine years and guaranteed by Maritime Customs receipts.

was to turn Shanghai into the center of a movement of modernizing and nationalistic reform. The same members of the gentry and rich merchants founded many study groups that did research on institutions and economic and educational systems. These men found that they all shared an ambition to modernize the economy and bring society up to date in order to save their country. In their search for models, they turned to the West and also, increasingly, to the Japan of the Meiji era.

Borne along by this wave of reformism, the charitable associations of the gentry and the native-place associations and professional guilds of the merchants broadened the scope of their activities. Philanthropy, the maintenance of order, and the upkeep of hydraulic machinery all involved discussions about the management of the town and the port. Traditional community institutions placed themselves at the service of the town as a whole and set out to provide the Chinese districts with all the equipment on which the concessions prided themselves, and to ensure for the residents of those districts the same services that benefited their neighbors in the fields of education and health. Casting aside corporatist and geographical limitations, the guilds now devoted themselves to building new urban thoroughfares and organizing the municipal police force. The "Efficient Care" charitable association funded a brigade of fifty firemen; the "Impartial Altruism" organization took charge of street cleanliness and the installation of public lighting. Philanthropy, always popular among the richer notables, began to operate within the framework of this modernizing activism: local elites drew on their own resources to create modern schools and vaccination centers.

The modernist elite groups' takeover of various sectors of the municipal management usually occurred with the agreement and cooperation of local officials. The latter were accustomed to delegating part of their powers to the local elites, within the framework of offices (*ju*) responsible for implementing specific projects, such as hydraulic works, maintenance of public facilities, and so on; during the last decades of the nineteenth century, the flexibility of partnerships of this type made it possible for private initiatives to take over the activities of a weakening bureaucracy. In 1895, for example, the Office for Commercial Affairs was set up to coordinate the economic initiatives of community institutions and the administration, as was the Office for the Construction of Roads in the city, which became responsible for extending the Bund into the neighborhood to the south of the French concession.

Although these offices were originally conceived as extensions of the administrative apparatus, it was not long before they threw off the officials' supervision and were, respectively, transformed into the General Chamber of Commerce (in 1904) and a municipal government for the Chinese City (in 1905). These two institutions extended the notion of local autonomy, until then conceived simply as a collection of community management centers, and rooted it in the service of the entire territorial collectivity. However, even if their objectives were modern, both institutions remained affected by the fragmentation of local society: bankers and merchants of the Ningbo (*Zhejiang*) guild dominated the General Chamber of Commerce; entrepreneurs from Jiangsu and Shanghai itself, the Chinese Municipality.

The synergy of private community and official initiatives thus gave rise to a series of changes that, within fifteen years or so, began to transform life in the Chinese districts of the city and also the thinking of their inhabitants.

CHANGING ATTITUDES AND THE MODERNIZATION OF THE TOWN

The modernization of the Chinese districts of Shanghai was the work of the municipal government created in 1905 and managed by scholar/merchants (*shenshang*) such as Li Pingshu, a former district magistrate and the proprietor of a number of insurance companies, and Wang Yiting, the comprador of a Japanese shipping company. These men had had occasion to become initiated into Western civilization, were recognized by officials, and had held posts of responsibility in community organizations. They had testified to their interest in Western-inspired modernization: Li Pingshu, for example, had invested in the construction of modern hospitals. Under the authority, more symbolic than practical, of the daotai, they were now to introduce a new style of municipal management.

The new municipality, originally known as the General Office of Public Works, borrowed its structure from the model of the Shanghai Municipal Council. Eligible taxpayers elected the sixty members of its council. Decisions were made on the basis of majority votes instead of by the traditional consensus. The execution of tasks was entrusted to employees whom the municipality recruited and paid, unlike the employees of the imperial administration, who were paid directly by their hierarchical superiors out of the latter's personal funds: the distinction thus introduced between private and public funds made for more transparent accounting and deterred corruption. Furthermore, the municipality had the right to levy various local taxes to increase its budget. It maintained a police force of eight hundred men and a court of justice in which the judges, who were independent, were expected to examine cases involving infraction of the municipal regulations. The separation of powers, financial regularity, and the clear definition of structures all contributed to the success of this early experiment in administrative modernization.

The territorial jurisdiction of the General Office of Public Works was confined to the Chinese quarters situated to the south of the foreign settlements, that is, to the old walled precinct and its suburbs. But very soon similar institutions sprang up in Zhabei, in the northern industrial quarters, and in Pudong to the east of the river.

The municipality took charge of the dredging of canals, construction of roads and bridges, removal of refuse, public lighting, regulation of building permits, and so on. It also planned more ambitious projects, such as installation of a tram system and demolition of the ramparts that surrounded the old Chinese town, which paralyzed its economic development. But these were not to be realized until after the upheavals of the 1911 Revolution.

The remarkable planning zeal of these local elites owed much to their patriotism. For them, it was a matter not only of modernizing the town but also of blocking interference from the foreigners and denying them the slightest pretext to intervene outside their own concessions, which they were all too prone to do. Unlike the Provincial Assembly created in 1909 on the initiative of the Imperial Court, the Shanghai municipal offices took no part in national political life. Nevertheless, their actions certainly appeared to express a modern variety of nationalism that set out, in concrete fashion, to meet the imperialistic challenge as it was posed, that is, in terms of material progress.

All the same, in the case of educated elite groups such as the Shanghai shenshang, such pragmatic ways of proceeding called for changes in peoples' attitudes. These elite groups ardently espoused and frequently preempted projects for the renovation of teaching methods, which occupied a central place in the designs of the reformists of 1898 and the engineers of the New Policy. In 1901, imperial decrees called for the creation of "new schools" that would include in their programs foreign languages and Western sciences; and in 1905, the Imperial Court abolished the system of mandarin exams. Meanwhile, the Shanghai gentry and merchants were already mobilizing. Within ten years, they created 220 institutions. The Jiangsu General Education Society, founded in 1905, with Zhang Jian as its president, coordinated the community initiatives, some private, some official.

The directors of this society and the town's business circles shared the conviction that development of scientific and professional training was an essential condition of economic modernization. An extremely dense network of subsidiaries supported their efforts: in every district, intellectuals of more modest rank—schoolteachers, students, and minor scholars—strove to implement the reformist programs. It fell to the society to coordinate all these efforts and to arbitrate in the conflicts that invariably tend to arise whenever the status quo changes. The field of education reflected the solidarity that existed between Shanghai and its neighboring districts— a solidarity that pervaded the economic development of the treaty port and that negated any interpretation suggesting that the metropolis was an enclave of exoticism, a malignant tumor in China's flank.

The implementation of the reforms linked with the New Policy constituted a response both to the demands of Shanghai society and to official expectations. Establishments of general education were flanked by technical institutes, teachers' training colleges, courses for adults, and schools for girls, all of which strove to satisfy new needs. Publishing companies such as the Commercial Press (1897) were founded, specializing in the publication of school textbooks suited to the new teaching programs. The overhaul of the schooling system was furthermore well served by the emergence of a modern intelligentsia of teachers, journalists, and writers, increasing numbers of whom went to Japan for their training.

All these efforts produced unequal results. The standards of many teaching establishments were mediocre. This was nevertheless the period that saw the foundation of a number of universities that would later come to rival those of Beijing: Jiaotong University or University of Communications (created in 1897 under the name Nanyang College) and Fudan University, created in 1905 when some Chinese students and professors seceded from Jesuit Aurora University. Shanghai now assumed a new role as the metropolis of cosmopolitan culture, and its renown began to eclipse that of Suzhou and Changzhou, the great scholarly centers of Jiangnan.

Local elite groups did not mobilize against the imperial authorities. On the contrary, they tried to assist the central government and to make its efforts at modernization and the struggle against imperialism more effective. Zhang Jian declared, "It is up to the government to decide on the general line, while the people must devote themselves to constructing the bases of local autonomy by promoting economic and educational development. Instead of wasting time talking, everyone should endeavor to move forward bit by bit."[5]

Despite their political misgivings, the Shanghai merchants and, more generally, the elite groups of the treaty ports did not turn their backs on all forms of commitment. The shenshang supported the New Policy; they hoped it would strengthen the state, believing this to be indispensable for the modernization of the country, for they attributed the economic and military successes of the Western powers and Japan to the representative institutions that they possessed. They therefore actively encouraged the efforts of the Imperial Court, and when, in 1906, it at last announced the establishment of provincial and national assemblies, they immediately created an association to prepare for a constitutional regime. It was an elitist organization with between two hundred and three hundred members, among whom were the presidents of the Chinese municipality, Li Pingshu; the General Society of Education, Zhang Jian; the General Chamber of Commerce; and the Fujian native-place association.[6] Compared with the other societies of a similar type that were then springing up all over the country, this Shanghai association was remarkable for its dynamism and its desire to link institutional reform to economic development.

However, in the elections of 1909, the representatives of the rural gentry were swept to the center of the public stage, not the merchants of Shanghai.* All the same, the Jiangsu Assembly, led by the scholar/entrepreneur Zhang Jian, did play an extremely active part in the campaign of petitions clamoring for the convocation of a parliament that the Beijing government was constantly announcing yet constantly deferring. Faced with the procrastinations of the Imperial Court, the elite groups of Shanghai became more pressing and laid down their own conditions. But it was not from their elitist circles that the wind of revolution was now blowing.

---

* Many of the major merchants of Shanghai, who were natives of distant provinces, were excluded from voting by a ruling that imposed strict conditions of residence. Others were unwilling to reveal the size of their fortunes to satisfy the wealth conditions, which were fixed by the same ruling.

CHAPTER 6

The 1911 Revolution

T HE REVOLUTION THAT TOPPLED the imperial regime in 1911
was one of the high points in the history of Shanghai. For one thing,
the town contributed greatly to the success of the movement: it both advanced funds and mobilized men, thereby enabling the insurrection to
spread into the Yangzi delta; and above all, it provided the leaders and
programs that bestowed a modern look upon an antidynastic uprising
in many other respects similar to those that had preceded it. At the same
time, in the town itself the revolution liberated minds and energies just
as it demolished the feudal walls surrounding the old Chinese precinct.
Only the Shanghai experience to some extent justified the epithet "bourgeois" that Chinese historiography applied to the 1911 Revolution. Free
from all central authority, Shanghai now advanced on the path of modernization and democracy. It was an exalting but ephemeral venture,
for the rest of China did not follow its lead. The republic proclaimed
on January 1, 1912, soon gave way to the military dictatorship of Yuan
Shikai. Shanghai was then obliged to fall into line. The 1911 Revolution testified to the lead that the town had seized in terms of arousing
national consciousness and promoting popular participation in political life. It also revealed the chasm that separated coastal China from the
Chinese interior and the still crucial weight that the latter exerted upon
the country's destiny.

"ALL PRESS AHEAD! . . . KILL! KILL!"

The quotation was the exhortation of a young pamphleteer, urging his
fellow citizens to wipe out the foreign imperialists and their Manchu accomplices.[1] In the first decade of the twentieth century, the politicization
of Shanghai society was stimulated by the radicalism of intellectuals such
as he, whose writings inflamed public opinion. They were few in number
and occupied center stage for only a few years, until 1904. All the same,

they played an important role, for they launched the idea of a revolution to which, ten years later, the whole town would eventually rally.

These young people certainly did not mince their words. The insults that they flung at the enemy were interspersed with flights of an incantatory kind of lyricism: "Revolution, revolution! Achieve it, then you may live . . . fail in it, then you may die."[2] Their ages ranged between twenty and thirty, and most were not natives of Shanghai. Their political awareness had developed in Japan amid the circles of Chinese émigrés. In this period, the two-way movement of both ideas and men was weaving close relations between Shanghai and Tokyo. Young students from the provinces, in quest of modern training, passed through Shanghai on their way to Japan, whence they would return every time China's political and diplomatic setbacks rekindled their desire for commitment and concrete action. The freedom of speech that they enjoyed abroad was complemented in Shanghai by the right to political asylum that the concessions de facto offered.*

The presence in Shanghai of well-known scholars who had fled Beijing, disappointed by the failure of the One Hundred Days of 1898, also stimulated development of the Shanghai-Tokyo revolutionary axis. Cai Yuanpei and Zhang Binglin were the masters who directed the thinking of the first generation of revolutionary intellectuals.** These prestigious older men offered the young radicals patronage and social protection.

The radicals' activities—meetings, petitions, the formation of militia—were developed around the Patriotic School, founded in 1902 by Cai Yuanpei. This establishment, with a program that concentrated almost exclusively on political education and physical training designed to mold citizen-soldiers, attracted many rebel students. *The Jiangsu Journal (Subao)*, the press organ associated with the Patriotic School, opened its columns to them. In 1903, Zou Rong published his "Revolutionary Army" in it. With

---

* The authorities of the concessions partially extended the privilege of extraterritoriality that foreigners enjoyed to Chinese residents, in contravention of the treaty clauses that recognized the imperial government's sovereignty and jurisdiction over those residents.

** Cai Yuanpei (1867–1940) had achieved the very highest grades in the mandarin examinations. As a man imbued with classical Confucian culture and at the same time open to Western influences, he won over the students of Nanyang College, where he taught from 1901 to 1902. Zhang Binglin (1869–1936), who was an expert on both the Confucian classics and Buddhist philosophy, was one of the principal thinkers of the period.

a preface by Zhang Binglin, who provided anti-Manchu nationalism with its theoretical bases, this article, overflowing with youthful and romantic ardor, diffused a new kind of hostility toward the Manchu dynasty. Until then, the latter had been criticized for its weakness in the face of imperialist aggression. Now, the opposition to the Manchus was founded on racial, cultural, and historical arguments. These barbarians who had conquered China in the seventeenth century and since then had never ceased to oppress and "violate her" had to be ejected. China must be returned to the Chinese. Zou Rong's cry came straight from the heart.

It was not long before the imperial magistrates accused and sought Zou and Zhang, nicknamed "the Mazzinis of China" by their contemporaries. But the Mixed Court of the international settlement, rejecting the idea that the death penalty could be applied for holding offensive opinions, decided not to hand over the two pamphleteers and simply passed prison sentences on them. This decision, which was contrary to the letter of the treaties but in conformity with a certain idea of justice and the relation of forces, provoked a violent clash between the authorities of the international settlement and the Chinese administration. The polemics surrounding "the *Subao* affair" increased the popularity of "The Revolutionary Army" still further, and the martyrdom of Zou Rong, who committed suicide in his prison cell two years later, turned this twenty-year-old into the symbol of the early Chinese revolutionary movement.

Following the *Subao* affair, repression fell upon the radical groups. After 1905, most of the radicals, with the exception of Zhang Binglin, disappeared from the public life of Shanghai and from the Chinese political scene. But their ideas continued to inspire popular nationalism, which, moving on from meetings to demonstrations, acquired an ever-growing vigor. "There was no day without meetings and no meeting without indignation."[3]

Whereas in the West the creation of a public sphere was conditioned, from the seventeenth century on, by autonomous social institutions acting in partnership with the political authorities, in Shanghai the politicization of society took the form of a succession of major movements of popular mobilization. There were as yet no parties, trade unions, or permanent representative structures, but when particular incidents and problems arose, there were rallies, proclamations, petitions, boycotts, and occasionally strikes and attacks on public buildings. For weeks and months on end, the entire urban population would mobilize: the common people (*xiao shimin*), office workers, students, and artisans, as well as wealthy merchants and elite scholars. Although there was no modern proletariat as such yet, many workers were to be found in the ranks of the professional guilds and native-place associations, which played an active part in organizing these movements.

The rapidity with which these movements succeeded one another, all using the same nationalistic and anti-imperialistic slogans, made up for the potential ephemerality of this kind of political commitment and at the same time kept the town in a recurrent state of agitation. Local conflicts triggered some of these great waves of mobilization, but most took place in either a national context (for example, the anti-American boycott of 1905) or an interprovincial one (for example, the struggle against foreigners by the movement for the Return of Railway Rights). But wherever they started, all the movements took on a particular intensity in Shanghai, where they were supported by the extremely dense network of community organizations. Here, they also benefited from above-average coherent political discourse and from the abundance of urban sites suitable for mass gatherings: the native-place associations would make their huge precincts available, the chambers of commerce would throw open their assembly halls, and the Zhang Gardens could accommodate an audience more than 1,000 strong.*

The anti-American boycott in 1905 that affected all the large treaty ports was a movement of protest against the renewal of treaties limiting Chinese immigration to the United States. In Shanghai, the regionalist associations and the chambers of commerce took the initiative. The students and educational societies supported the boycott, which was led by a merchant of Fujian origin, Zeng Shaoqing (1848–1908). However, it lasted only from July to August and barely affected the importation of American merchandise. Guilds traditionally used boycotts to force into line merchants who infringed the corporate regulations or to put pressure on

---

* The Zhang Gardens, the property of a wealthy merchant and newspaper proprietor, were situated in the western sector of the international settlement. In the early twentieth century, Shanghai's most important political meetings were held there amid the trees and pavilions.

abusive officials, but on this occasion boycott was turned into a political weapon serving the anti-imperialist struggle. Hardly was the boycott over than unrest again broke out when, in December, the Mixed Court of the international settlement, overstepping its powers, proposed to imprison a sentenced woman of Cantonese origin in the settlement instead of handing her over to the Chinese police and prisons where, it claimed, conditions were barbaric. The unrest, led by the Cantonese guild, always prompt to fly to the aid of a compatriot, spread to commercial circles and students, as well as to a number of associations. Telegrams, petitions, and meetings were followed by shops closing, rioting in the markets, and finally an attack on a police station and the municipality headquarters. The repression by the settlement's police force resulted in fifteen deaths.

The nationalistic upsurge of 1905 hastened the creation of a number of volunteer corps. Midway between the militia habitually organized by merchants for self-protection in troubled times and the groups undergoing physical and military training that patriotic students set up to resist any fragmentation of the national territory, these groups were organized on

Sentence being passed by the Mixed Court (courtesy of Qian Zonghao)

the model of the volunteer groups of the foreign concessions. They were paid with money raised in Chinese business circles and were recruited from among the owners and employees of commercial firms. Aware of the danger posed by these quasi-autonomous groups, the Shanghai Municipal Council hastened to neutralize those located in the international settlement by integrating them into its own volunteer corps. But in the Chinese districts, the volunteer organizations remained under the authority of the municipality's elites. When the revolution broke out, these men provided the bulk of the insurrectional armed forces.

The movement for the Return of Railway Rights (1905–1907), which spread to numerous provinces, provides an example of the anti-imperialist consensus that existed between urban elite groups and the rest of the population and also of the links between nationalism, on the one hand, and autonomist and constitutional claims, on the other. It was a matter of preventing the British and Americans from building and exploiting the provincial railways of Jiangsu and Zhejiang. The local gentry demanded that the Beijing Court annul the concessions ceded to the foreigners in 1898. It had created railway companies of its own with investments from the major Shanghai capitalists, the leaders of the chambers of commerce, the Chinese municipality, and the principal guilds. A desire to avoid competition was here combined with a determination to preserve national integrity. In November 1907, following another capitulation on the part of the Beijing government, the mobilization of elite groups escalated into popular fury. Students, shopkeepers, and office workers—who had become small shareholders in a bid to support the provincial railway companies—were making antidynastic pronouncements that were echoed in meetings, telegrams, and petitions. The disturbance had originally arisen in the provinces, but it was in Shanghai that this torrent of words was unleashed, paving the way for action.

In Shanghai from 1905 until the 1911 Revolution, every year saw the birth of movements of mobilization provoked by a variety of incidents but always ones that touched upon sovereignty and the national interest. Although intellectuals were not absent from the political scene, it was not ideology that presided over the mobilization of public opinion but the force of a modern nationalism generated by contact with the foreigners.

A BOURGEOIS REVOLUTION WITHOUT A FUTURE

The Shanghai elite groups' progressive alienation from the imperial regime was a response to the latter's increasingly patent incompetence and impotence. The shenshang were frustrated by the repeated procrastinations of the Beijing government, which refused to implement the promised constitutional reforms in 1909–1910. They were indignant at the weakness of the court when faced with the foreign powers and felt betrayed by the nationalization of the railways decreed in May 1911 and funded by loans from the foreigners. In Shanghai itself, the merchants were violently scathing about Daotai Cai Naihuang's behavior in the "rubber crisis." This episode, which in 1910 rocked the town's financial system, brought many traditional Chinese banks and their clients to the brink of ruination.[4] After covering his own losses and the debts of traditional qianzhuang banks to the foreign banks, thanks to contracting loans from those very banks, the daotai fled to Singapore, leaving the General Chamber of Commerce to bail out the Chinese merchants, whose losses came to as much as 4 million taels.

The growing dissatisfaction of the shenshang and the activists who followed in their wake coincided with the arrival in Shanghai of a new group of revolutionary leaders trained, like their elders, in the circles of émigrés. The Shanghai-Tokyo axis still functioned, but in Japan the political landscape had changed. Under Sun Yat-sen's leadership, in 1905 the small revolutionary groups had united to form the Revolutionary Alliance (*Tongmenghui*), which had elaborated statutes for itself and a program known as the Three Principles of the People (*Sanminzhuyi*). The new revolutionary leaders who now arrived in Shanghai were members of this party. Compared to the humanist intellectuals who had preceded them, they had the air of professional politicians, for what preoccupied them was organization and the raising of both funds and troops. One of their principal objectives was to rally the shenshang, whose power in Shanghai was increasing, and to this end they employed various strategies, all equally effective.[5]

In Shanghai, Song Jiaoren, considered to represent Sun Yat-sen's party, set up the office of the Revolutionary Alliance for Central China.* Its

---

* Song Jiaoren (1882–1913), who came from Hunan Province, took part in revolutionary activities in the Yangzi basin before departing for Japan, where he studied law.

relations with Sun Yat-sen were quite loose. With Song Jiaoren's encouragement, it adopted an ideological and political line based on moderation and opening up. It called for the overthrow of the Manchus and the foundation of a republican regime in accordance with the first two of the Three Principles of the People. But on the third principle, the introduction of equal rights to the land, it remained silent so as not to alienate the many landowners among the shenshang of Shanghai and the gentry of the lower Yangzi.

Song Jiaoren's battle of ideas stood in sharp contrast to the underground maneuvers of the other Shanghai revolutionary leader, Chen Qimei, who depended on a number of networks and knew how to manipulate them all.* When he returned to Shanghai in 1909 as a representative of the Revolutionary Alliance, Chen Qimei benefited from the support of his compatriots from Zhejiang, who included several wealthy bankers and entrepreneurs. At the same time, he entered into relations with one of the principal secret societies of the town, the Green Gang (*Qing bang*), of which he himself seems to have become a member, the better to establish his authority over the local gangsters.**

On the eve of the revolution, the shenshang and the revolutionaries were already establishing closer relations. Merchants financed *The People's Stand* (*Minlibao*), a newspaper published by Song Jiaoren, which appeared in the international settlement. Some merchants even joined the Revolutionary Alliance. These early supporters included a number of men of influence: directors of the General Chamber of Commerce, councillors from the Chinese Municipal Council, compradors, bankers, and guild leaders, most of whom came from the merchant and compradorial wing of the local elite, but no serious sociological or political cleavage separated them from the reformist elites, who were closer to the gentry. In June 1911, the creation of the Association of Chinese Citizens (*Zhongguo guomin zonghui*) set

---

* Chen Qimei (1878–1916), the son of a small-scale merchant from Zhejiang, had learned English and worked in a Shanghai shop before departing to study military arts and policing techniques in Japan.
** The Green Gang made its appearance in Shanghai at the end of the nineteenth century. In the decades that followed, it rose to power thanks to the control that it managed to acquire over a variety of criminal activities—gambling, prostitution, opium trafficking—and the relations that linked its godfathers with the police of the concessions.

the seal on the cooperation between the local elites and the revolutionaries. Its avowed objective was "to promote a militant spirit and the formation of militias." But in reality it served as a cover for the members of the Revolutionary Alliance who were flocking in from Tokyo. By facilitating contacts between the revolutionaries and the Chinese Municipal Council, this association also helped to reorganize the Chinese merchant militia, the membership of which now rose to 2,000 men, integrated into a volunteer corps under the command of Li Pingshu. In Shanghai, unlike in the rest of China, cooperation between local elites and revolutionaries did not follow the uprising but preceded and prepared for it.

The 1911 Revolution began on October 10 in the heart of the country, with the insurrection of the Wuchang (Hubei) garrison, which set off a vast movement of provincial secessions and local power seizures. Three weeks separated the Shanghai insurrection from that of Wuchang, three weeks that Chen Qimei put to use, completing his forces by recruiting several thousand secret-society members, gangsters, and hooligans and grouping them together to form a "Dare-to-die" brigade, and by negotiating with Li Pingshu to secure the neutralization of the Chinese municipal police and the imperial troops that were stationed close to the town. The only obstacle was the imperial garrison holed up in the Jiangnan Arsenal in the southern suburbs of the walled town. On November 3, Chen Qimei launched an attack on the arsenal, and its defenders soon capitulated. The governor of the province had rallied to the movement, and the daotai had fled. Never had a revolution been less bloody.

The 1911 Revolution in Shanghai strengthened the power of the local elites to whom it owed its success. It liberated the municipality and the chambers of commerce from all administrative supervision and installed their leaders in key posts in the local revolutionary government. In the Provisional Military Government that he organized in early November, Chen Qimei entrusted many responsibilities to the merchants of Shanghai: he put Li Pingshu in charge of civil administration; the banker Shen Manyun in charge of general finances; the merchant Wang Yiting in charge of agriculture, industry, and the Treasury; and he appointed the comprador Yu Xiaqing vice-minister of foreign affairs. The presence of merchants in the new government reassured the foreign consuls who, since the disappearance of imperial officials, had been cooperating with the General Chamber of Commerce in the running of day-to-day affairs. The merchants' involvement also facilitated raising the funds that the new authorities urgently needed. Li Pingshu and Shen Manyun set an example by contributing 300,000 taels each.[6] The shenshang made the most of the circumstances to speed up modernization of the town and urban society: it was at this point that the walls of the old town were demolished and tram lines were installed to serve the Chinese districts.

The new authorities raised no obstacles to check this society's initiatives carried forward by the wind of optimism and liberty that the revolution had engendered. Shanghai now experienced a brief but remarkable period of intellectual and political fervor. By 1912 the town had produced more than thirty political groups and parties with both local and national importance, reflecting the new social forces that had arisen.[7] The Chinese Socialist Party (*Zhongguo shehuidang*) was formed in November 1911 by the members of a small study circle recently created by Jiang Kanghu (1885–1945), a young scholar who had visited Japan and Europe, where he had come under anarchist influences. Anarchism remained a noticeable influence on this party, which launched a series of attacks against the family system, repudiated any idea of hierarchy, and set more store in virtuous practices such as vegetarianism and chastity than in political mobilization. The creation of the Labor Party (*Gongdang*) marked the appearance of a working-class consciousness. This was an interprofessional organization that recruited its members from among the skilled workers of the various guilds. It was in favor of industrial progress, education, political participation, and military training for workers; it furthermore supported the strikes (of foundry workers and carpenters) that broke out in 1912 and called for the formation of trade unions.[8]

The revolution also stimulated feminism. Behind the already familiar figure of the "female student" (*nü xuesheng*) there now emerged that of the "female revolutionary" (*nü gemingjia*). Since the creation in 1903 of a Women's Department attached to the Patriotic School and the 1907 visit to Shanghai of the heroine Qiu Jin, who was executed soon after in the wake of an anti-Manchu plot, feminism and revolutionary fervor

Women demonstrating during the 1911 Revolution

had gone hand in hand.* In the summer of 1911, the Association of Chinese Women-Citizens (*Zhongguo nüzi guominhui*) was formed, to match the Association of Chinese Citizens. The masculine revolutionary militia were now flanked by feminine "dare-to-die" brigades. The activists—daughters, sisters, and wives of enlightened elites and radical intellectuals—called for an end to their domestic enslavement. Following the revolution, numerous feminine parties thus sprang up: the Women's League for Political Participation, the Feminine League, the Republican Alliance of Chinese Women, and so on. The success of the magazine *The Time of Women* (*Funü shibao*), founded in 1912, testified to the impact that the feminist cause made on public opinion.

By involving themselves in the organization of the revolutionary up-

---

* Qiu Jin, born in 1875 into a family of minor scholar-officials in Zhejiang Province, at the age of twenty-eight broke away from those circles and the constraints of traditional family life and committed herself to the nationalist struggle. After a year of studies and militancy in Japan, she returned to China, where she became a pioneering feminist and a professional revolutionary. In 1907, she was beheaded for her participation in a failed plot that had caused the death of a high-ranking provincial official.[9]

rising, the shenshang had hoped to spare their town disturbances and armed clashes that would hamper the progress of business. When they took power within the framework of the Provisional Military Government, their intention was to speed up the work of urban modernization begun in the last years of the ancien régime. Their interests were, above all, local. Their social origins, the values they defended, and the success that they achieved gave credence to the idea of a bourgeois revolution similar to those in eighteenth- and nineteenth-century Europe. However, in the long run, their impact failed to influence either the destiny of the town or that of the country.

THE DISENCHANTMENT THAT FOLLOWED

It was not long before the shenshang became paralyzed as a result of the degenerating local situation and the turn taken by the revolution nationwide. Within a few weeks, the fragile alliance between the professional revolutionaries and the shenshang began to unravel. The principal cause of the clash between the head of the Provisional Military Government, Chen Qimei, and the local elites managing the town in the name of that government was money, or rather the lack of it. The merchants' gifts had not sufficed to fill the coffers of Chen, who had engaged in a costly policy of intervention in provincial and national affairs. To obtain funds, Chen Qimei therefore resorted to blackmail and kidnapping, even seizing the director of Shanghai's Bank of China, Song Hanzhang. The military government entrusted this dirty work to henchmen recruited among the members of the Green Gang. This period saw the beginning of the special relationship between the Guomindang, the party that had emerged from the Revolutionary Alliance, and the Shanghai underworld. It was a relationship that was to bedevil the history of the Chinese Republic until 1949.

Rivalries that developed between different revolutionary factions also fostered insecurity and violence. In January 1912, two visitors arrived in a private ward in the Sainte-Marie Hospital, where Tao Chengzhang, one of the historical leaders of the revolution, was convalescing.* A

---

* The sisters of Saint Vincent de Paul managed the Sainte-Marie Hospital, created by the French municipality in the French concession in 1908.

conversation began, voices rose, and then a shot rang out. Tao Chengzhang's death suited Chen Qimei's interests too well for the idea of an
assassination not to gain ground: after all, the man who had fired the
gun was a young officer totally committed to Chen; his name was Chiang
Kai-shek. Over 4,000 people joined the funeral procession of Tao Chengzhang through the streets of Shanghai. Two years later, the revolutionary
period was over.

The incidents that brought bloodshed to Shanghai did not relate solely
to the ups and downs of local politics. The town had been solidly supportive
of the dramatic progress of the revolution further afield, in the rest of the
country. Initially, the elites, co-organizers of the Shanghai insurrection, had
been concerned with local interests, but they very soon became involved
in the struggles taking place at the top. The strategic position of Shanghai,
the prosperity of its economy and finances, and its close foreign contacts
all made the town a factor of importance in national politics.

A consequence of the revolutionary experience of Shanghai was the
establishment of the Chinese Republic in Nanjing on January 1, 1912.
The Shanghai shenshang, with their loans, evaluated at 7 million dollars,
made possible the establishment of the Provisional National Government
with Sun Yat-sen as its president. However, the new government dashed
the hopes of the Shanghai elites and business circles, for it proved incapable of consolidating its position and finding further sources of financial support.

The weakness of the Provisional National Government played into
the hands of Yuan Shikai (1859–1916). This former high-ranking imperial official turned against the Manchu dynasty and by February 1912 had
supplanted Sun Yat-sen at the head of the republic. The republican torch
was then taken up by Song Jiaoren, who, allying himself with moderate
political elements, turned the Revolutionary Alliance into the Guomindang
and won the national elections organized in the winter of 1912–1913.
His assassination on March 20, 1913, right in the middle of the Shanghai
railway station as he was about to leave for Beijing to take up his duties
as prime minister, caused the revolutionaries to break with Yuan Shikai
and led to the "Second Revolution," which Yuan Shikai crushed four
months later.

The disappointments of their revolutionary experiences, the attraction of a regime strong on order, and the hopes encouraged by the new dictator's promises of economic expansion persuaded the elite groups of Shanghai to repudiate their support for Sun Yat-sen and his camp. When the "Second Revolution" broke out, Shanghai refused to support the southern insurgents, recommended a negotiated solution, and became absorbed in the preservation of its immediate interests. The leaders of the General Chamber of Commerce announced: "As Shanghai is a trading port and not a battlefield . . . , whatever party opens hostilities will be considered an enemy of the people."[10]

The abstention of Shanghai's elite groups and the passivity of the population caused the failure of the attack that Chen Qimei tried to launch against the Jiangnan Arsenal, which was loyal to Yuan Shikai. At this, the Shanghai elites did not so much rally to the authority of the new dictator as resign themselves to it. Yuan Shikai wasted no time in suppressing not only the institutions created by the revolution but also the organs of local autonomy produced by the reforms on the eve of the empire's collapse. In Shanghai the merchant militias were disbanded, and the municipal authorities were forced to make way for an administrative office.

The manner in which the revolution had unfolded in Shanghai between 1911 and 1913 drew attention to the originality of this town where modernization had progressed more rapidly than in the rest of the country. But that had not caused Shanghai to be cut off from its Chinese roots. The reformists and revolutionaries had won their victory by mobilizing traditional institutions—the scholar circles, regional associations, and merchant guilds—and these had employed new procedures (elections, popular mobilization) in the service of new objectives. The policies of local autonomy, then at its peak, which had made it possible to encourage the modernist and revolutionary projects, did not imply any split from the nation as a whole. On the contrary, Shanghai had presented itself as an example: when it assisted the republican government of Sun Yat-sen, it hoped to carry the rest of the country in its wake. When the failures of the local revolutionary movement and the fall of Sun made it face up to the reality of a backward China in which an authoritarian central power seemed the only alternative to disintegration and chaos, the Shanghainese gave up the struggle of persisting along a path to which only they were committed. Unlike the more southern and extrovert Guangdong, Shanghai maintained solidarity with the national destiny.* It was that solidarity, as much as an element of social conservatism among the elite, that prompted it to rally, albeit somewhat unwillingly, to the regime of order imposed by Yuan Shikai.

---

* Making the most of Guangdong's quasi independence since the end of 1911, the local revolutionary leader, Hu Hanmin, worked to consolidate the revolution and socialism in his province, hoping that circumstances would allow the experiment to be extended to China as a whole.

PART TWO

The Metropolis
(1912–1937)

CHAPTER 7

The Golden Age of Shanghai Capitalism
(1912–1937)

THE BOOM OF SHANGHAI CAPITALISM started immediately after the 1911 Revolution that produced the Chinese Republic; it was
to continue until the early battles of the Sino-Japanese War in 1937. The
combination of international circumstances and private initiative played
an important role in the economic miracle of the 1920s. However, that
miracle was a fragile one. A new generation of entrepreneurs now came to
constitute a business bourgeoisie, but the absence of institutional frameworks in which to root the economic growth soon reduced them to impotence. After 1927, Chiang Kai-shek's restoration of central power was
brought about with the cooperation of businessmen but operated against
the latter, for it cleared the way for a state capitalism, which for the most
part then degenerated into bureaucratic capitalism.*

THE ECONOMIC MIRACLE OF THE 1920S

The rapid growth of the modern sector of the Shanghai economy during
World War I and the immediate postwar period resulted in part from international circumstances. Upon the outbreak of war, the great powers
that were its protagonists immediately turned their backs on China and
Shanghai. Many foreign companies, whose staffs were affected by mobilization, either closed down or reduced their activities. Thanks to the decline of imports, the Chinese market now benefited from protection that
it had until then been denied by the terms of the treaties.

At the same time, the belligerents asked China and India to supply them
with nonferrous minerals, vegetable oils, flour, eggs, and so on, and this
caused a rise in the rate of silver on the international market since China

---

* The republic founded in the aftermath of the revolution soon sank into chaos. From 1917
on, warlords, local potentates who ruled by force over one or several provinces, engaged in
constant civil wars. In 1927, General Chiang Kai-shek, who had placed himself at the head
of the Nationalist Party (*Guomindang*), reconquered the country by military force and reunified it under a new central government installed in Nanjing.

and India were also countries that used silver money. The tael now became a strong currency: in 1919 it was worth 1.4 U.S. dollars (as compared to 0.7 U.S. dollars in 1914). However, certain obstacles, also resulting from the world conflict, such as the difficulty in obtaining supplies of machinery from the Western markets and the shortage and expense of maritime transport, limited the advantages that the Shanghai industries might derive from the international situation.[1]

After 1919, European demand remained strong, as the needs of reconstruction replaced those of warfare. The return to normal shipping and the reconversion of armament industries made it possible once again to obtain supplies of machinery. At the same time, the reconversion crisis led the great powers to defer their reconquest of the Chinese market, which thus remained relatively protected.

Within a few years, the external trade of Shanghai went through the roof, its value increasing from 407 million HkTl in 1917 to 958 million in 1926.[2] Between 1920 and 1930 Shanghai, now served by the river transport network, coastal traffic, and transoceanic connections, was handling 40% to 50% of all China's external trade. Products from the provinces destined for export all passed through the town: silk from Zhejiang, tea from Fujian, vegetable oil and pig bristles from Sichuan. Imports destined for the interior were handled by 340 warehouses grouped together according to their geographical origins: for instance, the seventy-four wholesalers from Sichuan who supplied their province with foreign cotton yarn were all situated on Fuzhou Road.[3] The expansion of external trade caused changes in its structure: imports of spare machine parts now competed with those of consumer goods, and the purchase of textile machinery doubled between 1918 and 1919 in response to the needs of fast-expanding industries.

The industrialization of the 1920s was based on the production of consumer goods and private initiative. Its development was rapid: between 1912 and 1920, the growth rate of national industries reached 13.8% per year. Shanghai was the main center of this new wave of industrialization, in which cotton goods led the way: the number of spindles owned by Chinese capital in the metropolis increased from 147,000 to 500,000 between 1913 and 1921.[4] The capital of many new firms exceeded 1 mil-

A young girl working in a textile workshop

lion dollars, and entrepreneurs such as Mu Ouchu (1876–1942) and
the Rong bothers of the Shenxin Company each controlled more than
100,000 spindles.

Another major sector of national industry, flour milling, started up
and developed during the war. Before 1914, only about a dozen modern
mills existed in China, mostly in the hands of foreigners, and the major
part of the wheat flour consumed in large towns was imported. By 1920,
Shanghai possessed twenty or so mills, most of them backed by large
amounts of capital (over 1 million dollars), and they were responsible
for 30% of the national production. This increase was largely due to the
successful industrial empire of the Rong brothers, who owned the Maoxin and Fuxin flour mills as well as the Shenxin textile mills. Oil works
were developed next, although on a smaller scale. Finally, Shanghai also
became the major center for the production of cigarettes when the company owned by the Nanyang brothers transferred its headquarters there
from Canton in 1919. In other sectors of light industry, expansion resulted
chiefly from the installation of many small factories producing hats, soap,
paper, glass, and so on.

*Rong Zongjing, founder of the Shenxin textile mills and
the Maoxin flour mills (courtesy of Qian Zonghao)*

In the domain of machinery, progress was much slower, amounting mainly to the creation of mechanical workshops (over two hundred between 1912 and 1924) and the manufacture of knitting machines and small-scale equipment used in the processing of agricultural produce and in a number of semi-craftsmanlike activities. These workshops employed on average no more than twenty or so workers, and only the best equipped of them possessed electric motors. The Qiuxin Company was an exception in the size of its capital, its modern equipment, and its ambitious objectives.

During this period of prosperity, the rise in prices and profits stimulated growth of trade and production. It was also supported by the development of credit. Because of the diminished activity of the foreign banks, elite groups and compradors, who for reasons of security had previously deposited their funds in foreign establishments, now switched to Chinese banks.

During World War I modern Chinese banks began to grow. Although most preserved their close links with the central or regional authorities, a dozen or so of them, almost all established in Shanghai, were managed on a purely commercial basis. However, the archaic structure of the market did not make it easy for them to penetrate the financing of national ventures. The Shanghai Stock Exchange in the international settlement transacted only foreign shares. The creation of the Chinese Stock Exchange in 1920 served only to spark a great wave of speculation, "The Stock-Exchange Storm" (*xinjiao fengchao*), which culminated in a general debacle one year later.

To finance commercial ventures, the modern banks, like the traditional banks, or *qianzhuang*, resorted to direct loans. But they had to insist on guarantees (in the form of real estate mortgages or pledges in the form of merchandise), so they compared unfavorably with the qianzhuang, which operated according to their customary rules, on the basis of personal relations, and dispensed with formal guarantees. The modern banks preferred to turn toward the extremely speculative purchase of state bonds. The qianzhuang thus remained the principal business banks. During the war, their number increased by 130%, and their total capital, by 500%. By 1920, Shanghai could boast seventy-one qianzhuang, with an overall capital of 7.7 million dollars. Alongside the compradors, the principal investors and depositors were the dye and opium merchants, enriched by their wartime speculations. The qianzhuang financed the expansion of large firms and workshops, advancing them short-term loans of quite limited sums: the purpose of these loans was to top up the funds of firms that as a general rule used their capital to finance their fixed investments, spent their profits on dividends, and kept their working capital to a minimum.

The entrepreneurs profited most from the prosperity. Between 1914 and 1919, the average profit made by cotton mills increased by 70%, as did that of the qianzhuang, and dividends rose to between 30% and 40%. Euphoria reigned. But for how long?

The prosperity of the early 1920s created the hopeful mirage of a decisive economic transformation. However, this was blocked by many obstacles—first, by an aggressive return of imperialism. The collapse of the Washington Conference in 1921–1922 demolished any hopes of Western disengagement from China.* In the name of realism, foreign banks and firms now demanded the retention of the politico-military apparatus on which they had relied since the nineteenth century in order to exploit the Chinese market.

The miracle was also fragile because of the underdevelopment of the Chinese economy and the structural imbalance brought about by Shanghai's very growth. The war, which had distanced the foreign powers from the market, had not caused foreign competition to disappear entirely. The United States and Japan had made the most of the decline in British influence to pursue policies of expansion that sowed the seeds of many difficulties and even conflicts. The Americans had increased their shares in Chinese businesses and their role in external trade. Japan had made even more rapid progress. Japanese banks opened many branches in Shanghai. In 1921, Japan's share in Shanghai's external trade rose to 23% (equaling Britain's share). Moreover, Japanese companies had multiplied their direct industrial investments: the number of Japanese spindles installed in Shanghai rose from 112,000 in 1913 to 939,000 in 1925. They were now five times as numerous as the British spindles and greatly exceeded the 677,000 spindles backed by Chinese capital.[5]

The hope that the miracle would become deep rooted was also dashed by the absence of any unified national market, an absence perpetuated by local disturbances, the antiquated means of transport, and the archaism of financial structures. The fragmentation of the market and all its uncertainties encouraged entrepreneurs to make their fortunes rapidly, mainly through speculation. In external trade operations, entrepreneurs speculated on the variations in the value of silver, and hence of the tael, in the course of the few months that elapsed between the signing of contracts and delivery of European or American merchandise in Shanghai.** Chinese traders could have protected themselves had they immediately cov-

---

* In conjunction with the U.S. initiative, the objective of the Washington Conference was to check the development of Japanese influence in China and the Pacific generally and to build up new relations between China and the major powers.
** China, which until 1935 still used a currency based on silver, traded with European, American, and Japanese partners, whose currencies were linked to gold. Hence the importance of variations in the values of silver and gold in determining the terms of trade and the rate of the tael on the exchange market. It is worth noting that in contracts signed by Chinese importers and foreign companies, the sums involved were stipulated in the currency of the supplier, in other words, usually in currencies linked to the gold standard.

ered their positions by buying foreign currencies. But having been favored since 1915 by the steady rise of silver, they continued to bank on adding to their commercial profits the gains to be made by speculating on variations in the exchange rates. Similarly, the desire to maximize immediate profits influenced the management of firms that sacrificed their working capital, long-term investments, and reserves to the avidity of shareholders, thereby leaving themselves defenseless in the face of any contingencies that might arise.

Finally, difficulties also arose from the very speed of the industrial growth that was founded on the production of consumer goods, which necessitated ever more abundant supplies of agricultural raw materials: cotton, tobacco, and oil-bearing products. The inability of Chinese agriculture to progress at the same rate as the modern industrial sector created many blockages and imposed structural limitations upon the miracle engendered by the international situation.

All these handicaps conferred a somewhat chaotic character upon Shanghai's industrial growth. Many crises interrupted its prosperity, such as the Stock Exchange debacle of 1921. This crisis was the consequence of a fall in Shanghai imports that left much capital uninvested and led to a huge wave of speculation: within just a few months, 140 stock exchanges appeared in Shanghai, but these private companies, with overall capital of several million dollars, sold no bonds or items of merchandise and simply contented themselves with speculating on their own shares. The wave of speculation soon died down, but it left in its wake quite a few bankruptcies and a lasting distrust of stock-exchange transactions. Businesses were also vulnerable in other ways. In 1923, the Shanghai textile mills went through a crisis provoked by the scarcity of raw cotton following a poor harvest and massive purchases by the Japanese. Within two years, the price of raw cotton rose by over 70%, and most of the textile mills were operating at a loss. One-third closed down, whereas others kept afloat by obtaining mortgage loans from rival Japanese companies.

THE NEW SHANGHAI ENTREPRENEURS

The 1920s miracle corresponded to a spontaneous growth supported by a combination of private efforts and private interests. The native capitalism flourishing in the midst of an underdeveloped economy was based on the presence of elite groups whose growing professionalism, rapid enrichment, and membership in a number of employers' associations set them apart from the traditional urban notables. The members of these elite groups appear to have been the principal promoters and beneficiaries of the economic development. Shanghai, the capital of the economic miracle, was also the capital of a new bourgeoisie of businessmen.

This group of new entrepreneurs made its mark primarily by its material power. The industrial and commercial fortunes of that time could be counted in millions of dollars: 10 million for the Jian brothers, the proprietors of the Nanyang Tobacco Company; 40 million for the Guo family, who owned the Wing On Department Store and the Wing On cotton mills. Rural land property no longer figured much in the patrimonies of these families, who preferred to reinvest their profits in the development of their own firms or in the speculative purchase of land and houses situated in the

Guo Biao, cofounder with his brothers of the Wing On Department Store, surrounded by his family at his home in Shanghai

concessions. The entrepreneurs of this golden age were thus quite different from the class of urban notables (*shenshang*) who had dominated Shanghai society at the end of the empire.

The earlier elites had engaged in economic activities quite different from those of the rural gentry, but they had remained linked to the structures of the ancien régime through their rural properties and the close contacts they maintained with local or central authorities. The 1920s business bourgeoisie distanced itself from the authorities. Without breaking away from the group of notables from which it had mostly sprung, with which it continued to share many common interests and upon whose help it frequently relied, this new bourgeoisie was happy to embrace methods imported from the West: technological innovations, rationalized management, and an entrepreneurial culture. When it involved itself in politics, it was not so much in order to acquire social prestige or administrative status but to affirm the power that it already possessed in the economic domain. The new bosses no longer regarded their entrepreneurial activities simply as a source of income or as a stepping-stone toward other activities of a more prestigious nature; rather, they regarded them as a vocation with an aim that transcended all considerations of private interest and was ennobled by its service to society and the nation. Many of these families provided their children with an expensive education abroad, the better to prepare them to manage the family business.

These men, all of whom shared an appetite for modernity, had emerged from a variety of backgrounds and launched themselves forward along various paths. The textile manufacturer Mu Ouchu had worked hard for many years to master foreign techniques. He was born in Shanghai to a father who was a cotton wholesaler, and he had entered an apprenticeship at the age of fifteen. Later, he returned to his studies, learned English, and successfully passed the entrance examination to the Maritime Customs service. While serving in this administration, he familiarized himself with Western management methods. In 1909, aged thirty-two, he left for the United States to learn about the production of cotton and mechanical spinning. Upon his return to Shanghai in 1915, he founded several textile firms. Nie Yuntai (1880–1953) came from a family of high-ranking mandarins. Private tutors gave him a classical education, but at an early age he learned English and studied mechanics and electricity on his own. While running a small textile mill that his father, the governor of Zhejiang, had entrusted to him, he took his first steps as an entrepreneur. His business successes during the war enabled him to increase his capital considerably and to set up a series of other textile mills in the early 1920s. Although he remained proud of his background, Nie Yuntai chose the business world and seems to have been very well suited to it. At about the same time, the two Rong brothers were building a veritable industrial empire made up of twelve flour mills and seven textile mills. They came to the business world in the wake of their father, a minor official who had become the proprietor of several qianzhuang; but they had no specialized experience apart from that afforded by an early apprenticeship working within a circle of merchants pursuing a wide range of activities.

Directors of the Sincere Department Store on their company's twenty-fifth anniversary (courtesy of Qian Zonghao)

Cai Chang, founder of the Dah Sun Department Store,
with his partners, 1936 (courtesy of Qian Zonghao)

The Shanghai entrepreneurs of the golden age had a taste for technological innovation and a knack of exploiting it, whereas Cantonese businessmen were more drawn to trading or managing money. Among the
Shanghai bosses, the one who best embodied that technological ambition
was Zhu Zhiyao (1863–1955).* He was the proprietor of the Qiuxin

---

* Zhu Zhiyao was known in Shanghai French circles as Nicolas Tsu. His family had converted to Catholicism in the seventeenth century.

mechanical construction workshops. The very name of his business, which meant "searching for innovation," indicated his agenda. During World War I, his firm was remarkably successful, manufacturing railway carriages, metal bridges, factory chimneys, and engines. Zhu Zhiyao held a number of trump cards. He came from a prominent and longtime Catholic family and benefited from the experience that his father had acquired as a fitter of large seagoing junks, and also from the protection of his two uncles, both famous scholars with many contacts among both mandarins and Jesuits. Thanks to his uncles, he was offered the opportunity to travel to France on a journey of scientific and technical discovery, and upon his return he obtained the post of comprador for the Bank of Indochina in Shanghai. But Zhu was committed to his bold vision of Chinese industrialization and dreamed of supplying the machinery indispensable for its success. In the end, financial difficulties got the better of this industrial adventurer, and in 1918 he went dramatically bankrupt. Through their experiences in the business world, these employers were introduced to modernity. But it was not enough simply to take over the techniques of production and management picked up from the West; these then had to be adapted to the local social and cultural environment. The modernity of the Chinese bourgeoisie was owed not to its break with tradition but to its ability to get tradition to serve unprecedented ends.

The organization of large shareholders' companies, on which the development of Western capitalism was founded, implied a distinctive hierarchy and gave shareholders the right to supervise the company's management. In contrast, traditional Chinese capitalism depended upon networks of personal relations and family and geographical systems of solidarity, favoring forms of lateral communication rather than vertical hierarchies, and mutual obligations rather than authority of an impersonal nature.

In the management of their business ventures, the greatest of the Chinese businessmen tried to adapt methods that had been tried and tested in the West. But in China, even in the concessions, they did not find the kinds of conditions that preserved the autonomy and stability of Western businesses. So, in the absence of an effective central government, unified banking and monetary systems, and legislation able to regulate the course of business affairs, these entrepreneurs continued to rely on the existing networks of traditional solidarities. The economic miracle of the 1920s was conditioned by the presence of those networks, as was society itself. Although many foreigners regarded them as archaic survivals and factors of paralysis, in truth those networks played an essential role in the acclimatization of modern capitalism to Shanghai and China generally.

The mixture of Western management techniques and traditional Chinese practices led to the formation of hybrid systems that varied according to the temperaments of the business leaders. Although they may not have compensated for all the institutional and political handicaps, such systems did allow some businesses to grow and prosper. The industrial empire of the Rong brothers and that of the Guo brothers present examples of those successes and illustrate the efficacy of what, in 1920, was not yet called "modernization in the Confucian manner." Guo Le (1874–1956) and Guo Quan (1878–1966) were natives of Guangdong but, like many of their compatriots, they started their careers in Australia where, at the turn of the century, they opened a shop selling fruit.[6] After making a certain amount of money and familiarizing themselves with the way distribution worked in Sydney, they created the Wing On Department Store in Hong Kong. The capital had been put together through the contributions of a dozen or so former Cantonese associates in Australia and a few friends from their own native village. In 1918, the Guo brothers decided to extend operations to Shanghai and to that end raised 2 million dollars in Hong Kong. The status of limited company (*youxian gongsi*) that they adopted for their firms entailed neither the sale of shares on the Stock Exchange (for they were always offered within the Guos' social circle and the networks of their promoters) nor any shareholders' meetings to supervise the managers. All the power was concentrated in the hands of the director general. The Guo brothers did, however, borrow from Western companies the idea of dividing the business into different departments. But in accordance with Chinese tradition, they continued to appoint the heads of those departments on the basis of kinship or geographical origin. When Guo Le opened the Wing On Department Store in Shanghai, he thus brought with him about fifty Cantonese whom he installed in posts of responsibility. On the other hand, when the Guo brothers set up a cotton mill in 1920, they had to turn to a Chinese engineer recruited for his skill, whom they

The Wing On Department Store on the Nanjing Road

employed until 1926, at which point two of their sons, trained in Great Britain, took over the technical direction of the family factories.

The business culture that the Guo brothers impressed upon their employees was deeply stamped with paternalism. Regulations accompanied by penalties for their infraction defined the organization of both professional activities and the employees' leisure. The company organized evening classes, a dramatic club, and sports teams. It also financed a fund for mutual aid. "The result seems to have been a rather successful blending of Chinese Confucian benevolent authoritarianism with English Victorian notions of self-help and of accepting responsibility for one's own action."[7] Attention has often been drawn to the extent to which the system of traditional solidarities weighed heavily on the lives of these firms. The Shanghai capitalism of the golden age did not escape the danger of nepotism. The company coffers frequently served to finance the personal expenditures of a vast circle of relatives, and family clashes would undermine the company management and cause the patrimony to split up. But the entrepreneurs learned to get around such inconveniences. The obvious need to survive and develop modified the practices of solidarity and limited the risks that they entailed. And even if membership in the clan conferred the right to live at the firm's expense, it certainly did not confer the right to direct it. The head of the family remained free to select those with the most aptitude from the vast pool of brothers, brothers-in-law, sons, sons-in-law, nephews, cousins, and other relatives by marriage.

The strategy that Rong Zongjing deployed as the head of the Shenxin textile mills testified to a similar flexibility. When he decided in 1915 to set up his first cotton mill in Shanghai, he had to give up the idea of having his family and in-laws finance him since, as natives of Wuxi, they were reluctant to extend family investments to the metropolis. Rong turned to Japanese banks that were willing to advance him large loans. At the same time, he chose to give his new firm the status of a company of unlimited liability, thereby restricting the number of shareholders and making it possible for himself to preserve a majority.[8] Although determined to transfer the activities of his family group to Shanghai and to concentrate authority in his own hands, Rong Zongjing did not ignore his obligations to his family and in-laws and involved them in the execution of his policies. In 1928, either Rong Zongjing himself or members of his family filled 84% of the posts of director in the flour and textile mills in his group of firms, the remainder going to men whom he trusted, all natives of Wuxi as he was.

THE BEGINNINGS OF A BUSINESS BOURGEOISIE

In reaction to the bureaucratic and corporatist practices of the traditional guilds, the new entrepreneurs conceived of the defense of their interests from the point of view of international capitalism. They created their own organizations but also strove to develop their influence within the existing merchant institutions.

Employers' federations appeared at the end of World War I as a result of united and spontaneous action. The Shanghai Bankers' Association was organized in 1917–1918 on the initiative of a few young modern Shanghai bankers. These men, led by Song Hanzhang and Zhang Jia'ao, had been trained abroad, for the most part in Japan, and all were keen to introduce modern banking methods into China. Although most of them were representatives of the Shanghai agencies of large official or semiofficial banks with central headquarters in Beijing, they enjoyed a very large measure of management autonomy and were critical of Beijing practices that were overinfluenced by officialdom and governmental interventions. Following their lead, other modern bankers' associations were created in the larger towns of China. In 1920, they united in the National Federation of Banking Associations within which the representatives of Shanghai played a leading role. The Association of Chinese Cotton Mill Owners was, from the start in 1918, organized on a national footing. Shanghai entrepreneurs, namely, Nie Yuntai, its founder and first president, and Mu Ouchu, its tireless organizer, dominated this association.

Within these new employers' federations, solidarity no longer stemmed from already acquired interests, as in the guilds, but rather from a perception of advantages yet to be won. The monopoly tradition gave way to an ideology of growth. With such preoccupations, these federations concerned themselves with the diffusion of economic information. They published professional reviews that described the new production and management techniques, analyzed external markets, and so forth. However, they did not supersede traditional organizations but tried their best to take over their leadership.

In 1920, the employers' federations made a veritable breakthrough at the head of the (Chinese) General Chamber of Commerce of Shanghai, the presidency of which passed from the comprador Zhu Baosan, then seventy-three years old, to the textile mill owner Nie Yuntai, who was thirty years younger. The bourgeoisie now became the dominant class in Shanghai society. The ancien régime elites formed a shifting coalition with the new entrepreneurs, based on particular networks of interests and personal relations. Despite frequent clashes, this alliance allowed the group of new employers to wield a far greater measure of social and political influence than their limited numbers might suggest.

The golden age of the Shanghai employers coincided with the reign of the warlords and political chaos. Since the death of Yuan Shikai, the president of the republic, in 1916, the entrepreneurs had distanced themselves from a discredited central government that was unable either to end the division between the north and south or to prevent the spread of civil wars. How could their priorities come to terms with an impotent state? The development of the modern sector called for reform, in particular monetary unification, fiscal reorganization, and customs autonomy, all of which should have devolved from state authorities. The economic growth that had stemmed from exceptionally favorable circumstances could not be sustained unless the international status and political institutions of China were transformed.

Forced to fall back on its own strengths, the Shanghai business bourgeoisie discovered within itself prodigious powers of adaptation. A return to customs autonomy was its primary objective. It was to this end that the entrepreneurs employed a well-tried weapon: boycotting. The earliest boycotts of the twentieth century—in 1905 against the Americans, in 1907 against the Japanese—were prompted by passionate and largely xenophobic reactions. But for many Shanghainese whose affairs were linked to import-export trade, those boycotts represented a double-edged weapon that struck at their own interests as well as those of the foreigners. For that reason, they inevitably mustered no more than fleeting support. From 1919 on, in contrast, the boom in national industries made it possible for Chinese entrepreneurs to make the most of the relative protection of the market afforded by the boycott. The anti-foreign protest movement was now backed by a project of economic construction. The boycotts became semipermanent and were boosted by vast campaigns in favor of national products, now known as "patriotic products" (*aiguo huo*). The movements of 1919–1921, directed against the Japanese in particular, were followed by that of 1923, which persisted into 1924 and then, in 1925–1926, became generalized. From that moment on, boycotting was no longer simply a measure of retaliation against this or that foreign power in the context of particular international rivalries; it was also a strategy in the service of economic development seen as a long-term method of reconquering the market. However, these new-style boycotts proved not much more effective than the earlier ones, for they were applied irregularly, tended to set merchants against one another, and also set them in opposition to radical students.

Unable to substitute their own methods for those of the state, the entrepreneurs now sought to reform the latter. They wished to break the vicious circle that for centuries had associated free enterprise with civil disturbance, and repression and exploitation with political and social order. They believed that they had found, in the federalist movement that enjoyed a brief burst of success in the early 1920s, a means of simultaneously satisfying their aspirations for both freedom and order. But the idea of provincial constitutions, whose creation they supported, simply remained a dead letter.

Would the businessmen of Shanghai lean toward revolution, as they had in 1911, when they supported Sun Yat-sen? Nationalism provided them with grounds for agreement with the radical intelligentsia and the activists who had sprung from various layers of the urban population, as has been shown by the high degree of mobilization in Shanghai on May 4, 1919.* However, the Shanghai bourgeoisie's commitment to the revolutionary movement remained sporadic and limited. The entrepreneurs no longer trusted Sun Yat-sen, and in 1923, when he drew closer to the Soviets, many distanced themselves from him. At a time and in a country in which political life was embodied by people rather than defined by policies, that disaffection from Sun Yat-sen estranged a large proportion of the Shanghai bourgeoisie from the Guomindang.

The problem of relations between the business bourgeoisie and the revolution was posed particularly acutely when the great nationalist movement of May 30, 1925, broke upon the scene.** The commercial organizations proceeded to provide support for the workers' unions and the strikers. They did so not so much because they sympathized with the revolutionary cause, however nationalistic it was, but rather because of their customary habit of compromising with a view to achieving a consensus and their profound desire for social stability and public order.

The economic miracle that coincided with the decline of state power marked Chinese society's boldest attempt to turn itself into a civil society. But what chance does a society have when it can find no interlocutors in the state institutions? How can its initiatives develop without the intervention of a political power capable of considering its many proposals? Until the mid-1920s, the great Shanghai entrepreneurs were constantly

---

* In May 1919, the students, merchants, and workers of large Chinese towns rose up in protest at the decision made at the Versailles peace conference to transfer to Japan the rights that Germany had acquired in Shandong Province.
** The movement of May 30, 1925, like that of May 4, 1919, was of a nationwide anti-imperialist nature. It started in Shanghai when security guards at a Japanese factory killed a worker.

demanding that a quasi-nonexistent "center" should issue directives and prohibitions and redress abuses. They nursed a veritable nostalgia for the state even as they continued to dread its arbitrary powers. When they rallied to Chiang Kai-shek in 1927, it was not purely in order to protect themselves from Communists and revolutionary violence. They were also hoping that the new regime would be able to block the progress of foreign interests and set up institutional frameworks essential for the modernization of the economy.

THE GUOMINDANG AND THE MODERNIZATION
OF ECONOMIC INSTITUTIONS (1927–1937)

After Chiang Kai-shek came to power in 1927, the international situation and the fluctuating value of silver on the world market continued to determine growth in the Shanghai modern sector. Foreign competition was still strong, with that of Japan taking the form of attempts to take over the Chinese market and of political and military interventions: in 1932, the Japanese army launched an attack on the Chinese industrial quarters to the north of Shanghai, as a result of which many businesses there were destroyed or ruined.* However, the fact that a central Nationalist government did now exist quite altered the situation. This government did manage to reestablish customs' autonomy, set about the reconquest of the foreign concessions, and worked hard to set in place the institutional and legal framework necessary for the development of a modern sector. Yet this policy, for which the entrepreneurs had themselves clamored, did not bring them the benefits that they expected. The Nationalist regime intended to take over the direction of the modernization of the economy itself, considering it to be an element of national power. It was hostile to the entrepreneurs, whom it proceeded to exploit in the most barefaced manner, advocating a state capitalism founded on the development of heavy industry, the production of military equipment, and the exploitation of the inland provinces, which were rich in mineral resources. As it happened, history afforded Chiang Kai-shek's government hardly any

---

* This military expedition was launched in response to the anti-Japanese boycott that followed the Japanese invasion of Manchuria in September 1931.

time to implement these ambitious projects; and no doubt it lacked the power to establish a truly state capitalism. The destiny of the modern sector between 1927 and 1937 has been the subject of a number of divergent diagnoses. Economic growth does seem to have continued, but it relied less and less on the action of the Shanghai capitalists who, as a group, were progressively stripped of their initiative and influence.

The Nanjing decade began with a period of prosperity for the modern sector.* Until 1931, banks, businesses, and industries in Shanghai continued to expand. This prosperity was brought about chiefly by a formidable depreciation of silver, which between 1928 and 1931 lost more than half its value on the world market, entailing a parallel decline for the tael. This de facto devaluation stimulated Chinese exports while slowing down imports, thereby affording the Chinese market a degree of protection that was not assured by customs dues, since these were too low. Nevertheless, imports of machinery increased as much as 50% over three years, stimulated as they were by demand from Chinese industries, which at this time were fast expanding: the Rong brothers increased the number of textile mills in the Shenxin group from six to nine, while the Guos increased those of the Wing On group from two to five.[9] Other new sectors were also prospering: cement works, cigarette factories, and mechanical and electrical industries.

The crisis came in 1932, heralding three years of depression. It was provoked by a combination of factors, in the first place a sudden recovery of the tael that discouraged exports, dried up foreign investments, drained the metal out of China, and made credit difficult to obtain in the Shanghai market.** At the same time, Japan's quasi annexation of Manchuria in 1931 led to the decline of the traditionally buoyant trade between Shanghai and that region, just when demand was falling in the Yangzi provinces, which were seriously struck by flooding, and the industrial suburbs of Shanghai

---

* This was the decade between Chiang Kai-shek's accession to power in 1927 and the start of the Sino-Japanese War in 1937. It is called the Nanjing decade because the capital was transferred from Beijing to Nanjing for this period.

** This rise of the tael was linked with the increased value of silver triggered by the Western powers' decisions, between 1931 and 1933, to abandon the gold standard and the American government's systematic buying policy, which was stipulated by the Silver Purchase Act of 1934.

were to a large extent demolished by the Japanese military expedition of January 1932.

The crisis hit the banking sector hard. Of Shanghai's seventy traditional qianzhuang at that time, seventeen went bankrupt. External trade fell sharply. The Shenxin Company was forced to close two of its textile mills, and its boss, Rong Zongjing, was not able to repay a loan of 2 million dollars contracted from the Hong Kong and Shanghai Bank. The flour mills were faring no better, and many silk factories ceased production. Between 1934 and 1935, the number of bankruptcies overall in Shanghai doubled from 510 to 1,065.[10] Business was just beginning to pick up when the Sino-Japanese War broke out in 1937.

During the Nanjing decade, as during the 1920s, the sudden oscillations in the situation revealed how heavily the modern sector depended on world markets. The economic instability that industrialized countries were experiencing spread to China through the effects of declining external trade. Moreover, for the Chinese entrepreneurs the instability of outlets was accompanied by the great uncertainty that surrounded rates of exchange, which were linked with the fluctuations in the value of silver.

At the beginning of the 1920s, the business bourgeoisie had struggled against foreign economic penetration by itself organizing wide boycotting movements. From 1927 on, the regime orchestrated such resistance: now the authorities promoted boycotting with the objective of abolishing the privileges that treaties granted to foreigners. Diplomatic negotiations and political and policing pressures were all designed to achieve the same ends.

The reconquest of Chinese national sovereignty was relatively successful, thanks partly to the determination of Chiang Kai-shek's government, but partly also to the spirit of compromise demonstrated by the foreign powers, which had become somewhat circumspect in response to the great wave of revolutionary insurrections in 1927. Between 1929 and 1934, China recovered the customs' autonomy on which protection of the national market depended: dues on imports rose from 4% to 25%. Furthermore, the abolition of the *lijin*, the internal transit tax, which was levied on Chinese merchandise only, seemed to herald the elimination of one important source of inequality between national firms and foreign ones.

In Shanghai itself, the regime of the concessions was increasingly threatened both de facto and legally. The new municipality of the Chinese town made use of the powers that the government had granted it in order to wage a veritable war of attrition against the foreigners and to impose an increasingly restrictive interpretation of the treaties. In this way, the regime of extraterritoriality began to be weakened. In the past, it had allowed the Chinese authorities the right to tax the foreigners and their businesses, but it had denied them the means to do so by preventing them from taking legal action against the foreigners. Some major foreign companies, such as the British and American Tobacco Company and the Standard Oil Company, taking a prudent and realistic line, now agreed to pay some large surtaxes.

The Nationalist government also embarked on a series of institutional reforms for which the chambers of commerce, the banking associations, and the employers' federations had long been campaigning. A modern mint had been created in Shanghai, paving the way for the abolition of the tael, which was decreed in 1933. The disappearance of this old currency unit simplified the monetary system, which was now based solely on the silver dollar. Monetary unification was completed in November 1935, when a worldwide increase in the price of silver forced China to abandon a metallic standard and adopt paper money, known as "legal money" (fabi), the printing of which was the exclusive privilege of four major government banks. The new regime also tried to tighten up the regulatory framework of economic activities by passing various laws that affected companies, trademarks, and so on.

Were the reforms of the Nanjing government going to sweep aside the obstacles that hampered the modern sector and the full flowering of capitalism? The Shanghai entrepreneurs were soon disenchanted, for the government was intent above all on filling the state coffers in order to finance military campaigns against Communist guerrilla fighters and intractable provincial authorities. The fact was that some reforms were never applied, whereas others gave rise to difficulties as great as those that they were supposed to remedy. The high import taxes made possible by the recovered Maritime Customs autonomy affected machinery as much as it did manufactured and luxury goods. In the zones where the lijin was abolished, that tax was immediately replaced by a group of taxes on production. The establishment of paper money opened the way for chronic inflation, since the government was now in a position to finance its deficit simply by printing more banknotes.

Thus, despite all the modernizing talk of Chiang Kai-shek's government, its reforms had less to do with the prosperity of 1928 to 1931 than did the international situation. In the years that followed, the perverse effects of those reforms aggravated the difficulties brought about by the depression. The government was interested in the modern sector only insofar as it could exploit it. The government was positively hostile toward national capitalism. Although recognizing the imperious need for economic modernization, the Guomindang regime had no intention of abandoning initiative and power to entrepreneurs whom it would be unable to control. But did it have the strength and the means to exercise such control?

STATE CAPITALISM AND
BUREAUCRATIC CAPITALISM

In their fear of revolution and their hope of seeing the establishment of a central government favorable to their aspirations, the Shanghai employers had at first extended a warm welcome to Chiang Kai-shek. Their financial aid, to the tune of 10 million dollars, had enabled the general to eliminate the Communists and take control of Shanghai on April 12, 1927. But that alliance was shattered a few weeks later when, in order to obtain a further 30 million dollars, Chiang Kai-shek unleashed a veritable reign of terror. Rong Zongjing and other major capitalists were arrested, and their children were kidnapped. Liberation could be obtained only upon the payment of large ransoms. The president of the General Chamber of Commerce opted to take flight. Soon the boycotting movements provided the local authorities with an opportunity to engage in veritable blackmail against the merchants, whom they accused, rightly or wrongly, of failing to apply the decreed boycotts. The concessions now offered no more than an illusory refuge to the merchants, who frequently fell victim to kidnapping raids organized by clandestine groups with menacing names such as the "Blood and Soul Traitor Extermination Corps."[11]

Once reestablished with all its prerogatives and authority, the new central government little by little stripped the Shanghai bourgeoisie of the political role that it had been playing since 1912. The Special Municipality of Greater Shanghai thus now found itself attributed responsibilities and powers that had until then belonged to the chambers of commerce and the guilds.* Through the intermediary of its Office of Social Affairs, it supervised the professional organizations, arbitrated in the event of labor clashes, collected economic statistics, provided for social aid and philanthropic works, and took over the maintenance of public health and town planning. Even if some entrepreneurs continued, as individuals, to be associated with the policies of local management, as a group they were ousted. Their professional organizations passed under official control and were required to demonstrate their submission to the Guomindang Party (*danghua*). On the pretext of unifying the representation of commercial interests, the General Chamber of Commerce was merged with the subsidiary chambers of the Chinese districts. By these means, the most important Chinese entrepreneurs of the international settlement, who had created the power and prestige of the chamber in the 1920s, were deprived of their majority.

Not only was the subordination of the Shanghai bourgeoisie the ploy of a dictatorial regime that regarded any form of social autonomy as a threat; it also reflected the ideological orientation of the Guomindang. The regime remained dominated by a distrust of private capitalism that it had derived from the doctrine of Sun Yat-sen and that the world crisis of 1929 simply reinforced. Operating at the heart of the party, T. V. Song, Chiang Kai-shek's brother-in-law and minister, did try hard to keep a dialogue going with the Shanghai group of employers, but the nationalist cadres and militants of Shanghai, most of whom had emerged from academic circles, opposed his influence.

During the 1930s, left-wing anticapitalism was overlaid by a right-wing anticapitalism enriched by Confucian precepts and Fascist axioms. Insofar as the Guomindang accepted modernization as an element indispensable for national power, it insisted that it should be modernization in the Ger-

---

* This special town council set up by the laws of 1927, 1928, and 1930 was placed under the direct control of the central government, and its authority extended to all the Chinese quarters of the town.

man or Italian style. This was certainly the position adopted by the Blue Shirts, an extreme right-wing organization whose disciplinary code classed "traitor-merchants" among the "rotten elements" that must be eliminated from society and that called for all main economic activities to be placed under direct state management.

The financial and economic crises through which the country passed between 1932 and 1935 made it possible for the Guomindang to take control of the banks and to step up its interventions in the industrial and commercial sectors. In the early years of the regime, relations between Chiang Kai-shek and the banks were good, for the banks had financed roughly one-fifth of governmental expenses at interest rates ranging from 12% to 25%. But faced with the crisis, the Shanghai bankers restricted their loans, and their leader, Zhang Jia'ao, was openly critical of the government's policy of maintaining a budgetary deficit. At this point, in its "coup of March 25, 1935," the government forced the Bank of China to buy new state bonds and incorporate them into its capital, thereby giving the government a majority on the board of directors and enabling it to oust the president, Zhang Jia'ao.* In the months that followed, the offensive continued, now targeting the principal commercial banks and the qianzhuang.

Control over banking capital made it easier for the Guomindang to intervene in the commercial and industrial domain. Moreover, with their backs to the wall as a result of the crisis, the Shanghai business community was itself asking for government aid. In June 1935, this was eventually forthcoming in the form of an overall loan of 20 million dollars. However, there was a price to pay: the committee responsible for distributing the loans favored those businessmen who proved themselves most docile at the political level. The commercial and industrial firms were not subjugated quite as brutally or as completely as the banks, but government representatives were increasingly recognized to be the real leaders of business circles.

Either the capitalists of the golden age became integrated into the administrative apparatus or they were reduced to a role of secondary importance.

---

* We should remember that, despite its official origins, the Bank of China was then owned by individual shareholders and managed as a private business.

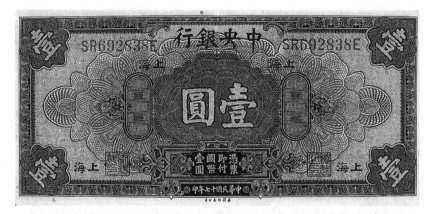

Chinese banknotes bearing the image of Sun Yat-sen (1935). The monetary reform of 1935 replaced silver dollars with paper money.

Many bankers, to whom the financial services of administration offered good career prospects, became officials: after being ousted from the Bank of China in the March 1935 coup, Zhang Jia'ao accepted the post of minister of railways. Some, now as representatives of the government, retained responsibilities in the very establishments that they had formerly managed as entrepreneurs. Such conversions were less common among traders and industrialists, who were less useful to the authorities and were therefore treated with less consideration.

The government's takeover of a number of firms and the migration of entrepreneurs into the bureaucracy opened the way for state capitalism. In 1936, the new Commission for Natural Resources, the main governmental organ responsible for development, launched a three-year plan.* Strongly influenced by the Soviet model, it envisaged the creation of bases of heavy industry in the provinces of the interior to cater to the needs of national defense. This strategy, which prefigured that of the First Five-Year Plan of 1953, turned its back on the Shanghai capitalism of the golden age; however, the Sino-Japanese War that broke out in 1937 allowed very little time for the development of the plan. Shanghai's modern private sector thus preserved its preeminence, but the increasing intervention of the Guomindang government altered the way that it functioned and favored the creation of a bureaucratic capitalism. It was no longer the bankers from Zhejiang or the great textile mill owners but high-ranking officials who were top dogs in the metropolis. Acting in either a private or an official capacity, the latter set up businesses for which they then arranged monopolies and tax exemptions, public funding, and access to confidential governmental information.

Unlike state capitalism, this bureaucratic capitalism was governed by no ideology, no preestablished plan. It was created by certain figures belonging to ruling circles in the political world, who used resources monopolized in the name of modernization simply to promote their own family wealth. By preferring to invest in the most immediately profitable sectors of commercial

---

* On the eve of the Sino-Japanese War, the Commission for National Resources, created by Chiang Kai-shek himself, supervised twenty-three units of industrial and mining production and employed 2,000 people—managers, technicians, and workers—whose wages were paid directly by the state.[12]

and financial speculation and light industry, they came into direct competition with the private entrepreneurs. The latter were reduced to seeking the cooperation and protection of these figures, so that they too might benefit from monopolies and privileges. Most of the firms set up by bureaucratic capitalism were thus mixed-business ventures. In some respects, their organization was reminiscent of the bureaucratic supervision and merchant management of the nineteenth century. But the bureaucrats of 1930 were quite unlike the mandarins of 1880. They enjoyed the support from central government that their predecessors had lacked. Furthermore, the most active of them had studied abroad, and their understanding of the industrial and financial techniques of the contemporary world was incomparably superior to that of their predecessors of the imperial age.

Chiang Kai-shek's two brothers-in-law, T. V. Song and H. H. Kung, were very close to power, and each in turn served as minister of finance.* They were the foremost players in this bureaucracy of would-be businessmen and modernizers. T. V. Song operated through the Bank of China, which, thanks to its seizure of mortgaged factories and machinery, had become an important force in the industrial domain. He also created private companies such as the China Development Finance Corporation and the China Cotton Company, which served as intermediaries between the market, the official banks that provided funding, and the governmental agencies that came up with the plans. In a private capacity, he acquired majority holdings in major Shanghai businesses such as the Nanyang brothers' tobacco company. In all cases, he placed his political influence at the service of the businesses of which he was patron, thereby ensuring their prosperity and making huge profits for himself. H. H. Kung depended on support from the Central Bank of China but left the management of the family's private investments to his wife and eldest son. They favored above all speculations (on merchandise, exchange rates, and shares) that could count on the insider information that Madame Kung obtained from her husband.

Communist historiography has decried the corruption inherent in bureaucratic capitalism and has pointed the finger at the "four great families"

---

* T. V. Song, the third child and eldest son of Charles Song, was the brother of Madame Chiang Kai-shek, born Song Meiling. H. H. Kung was Madame Chiang Kai-shek's brother-in-law, who had married her elder sister, Ai-ling.

that profited most from the system.* However, motives of personal or family interest did not always exclude higher-minded ambitions, for example, those of Wu Dingchang, a former banker and an influential member of financial circles in Shanghai, who, when he became minister of industry, launched a variety of modernization projects, the most successful of which was the creation of the Shanghai Central Fish Market.

As the evidence testifies, by and large the bureaucratic capitalism that developed in Shanghai and elsewhere in China during the 1930s represented a degraded form of state capitalism and, at the same time, a perversion of the market economy. Its appearance testifies to the fragility of the class of entrepreneurs, but it would be mistaken to regard it as a manifestation of state power. Despite its dictatorial character, the Guomindang regime remained dominated by the interplay of personal relations and was sometimes hard put to impose its authority even upon its own officials, who made use of it as much as or even more than they served it. After the capital's transfer to Nanjing in 1927, which brought Shanghai closer to the center of political power, the metropolis occupied an important place in the functioning of this bureaucratic capitalism. Shanghai was the seat of the headquarters of the modern banks that had become major actors in economic life. And most of the highly placed directors involved in official or semiofficial projects came from Shanghai business circles.

Those circles had lost much of the influence they had held in the 1920s. The power of the big bosses of industry paled in comparison to that of the politician-businessmen whose partners they had, willy-nilly, become. Now the initiative in modernization came from a central bureaucracy that was moved by national ambitions and no longer considered Shanghai to be the indispensable pivot of economic development. Nevertheless, the entrepreneurs who had created the prosperity of the golden age did not lose all their influence. Within the administrative apparatus into which many of them had passed, they tended to form a techno-structure that collaborated with the political system but did not identify with it. The bosses of industry who did remain at the head of their businesses still preserved credit

---

* These were the families of the principal leaders: those of Chiang Kai-shek, H. H. Kung, T. V. Song, and the Chen brothers, who controlled one of the most powerful Guomindang factions.

that stemmed from their experience and skills, and a power based on the extent of the machinery and staff that they controlled. Their relations with the authorities were the subject of endless negotiations in which they were not invariably the losers. The Guomindang government did not fulfill the hopes that the Shanghai entrepreneurs had placed in it. It had exploited the private capitalists and reduced their role, but it had not managed to oust them.

CHAPTER 8

The Revolutionary Center
(1919–1937)

IN THE 1920s, Shanghai was at the avant-garde of the Chinese revolutionary movement. The presence of a dynamic bourgeoisie and a relatively developed worker proletariat, together with the regime of the foreign concessions, favored the organization and activities of the opposition parties, the Guomindang and the Communist Party. This urban revolution, founded upon an anti-imperialist consensus, matured exceptionally rapidly and culminated in March 1927 in the establishment of the "Shanghai Commune," dominated by the Communists.* One month later, Chiang Kai-shek's April 12 coup shattered the alliance between the Guomindang and the Communists and stamped out the insurrection in a bloodbath. After this, the fate of Communism was to be played out from rural bases. Despite the setback to Communist activities in Shanghai, mass movements continued and even intensified, forcing Chiang Kai-shek into armed resistance to the Japanese aggression. Social and political demands accompanied patriotic mobilization. All this agitation was to contribute to a radical reorientation of government policy: in 1937, China entered into war against Japan, and Chiang Kai-shek committed himself once again to cooperation with the Communists.

THE RISE OF REVOLUTIONARY FORCES

It was six years before the anti-imperialist protest and the student demonstrations that had broken out in Beijing on May 4, 1919, turned into a mass revolutionary movement that combined nationalist ardor with socialist demands. Beijing, the center of the intelligentsia, was at the vanguard of this movement, but the parties that would structure the new forces were organized in Shanghai: the Guomindang, refounded in 1919,

---

* This was the name by which French diplomats and journalists of the time referred to the insurrectional town council that had emerged from the general strikes of February and March 1927.

and the Chinese Communist Party (CCP), created in 1921.* During this same period, Sun Yat-sen, the historic leader of the Guomindang who was now in Canton, set up a rival government to that of Beijing, along with a regional base that, with the help of emissaries from the Comintern, progressively turned into a revolutionary laboratory. So Shanghai was not the only revolutionary center. Nevertheless, it was the principal one. Thanks to its geographical position and the interprovincial nature of its society, it found itself more involved in the national destiny than Canton, situated on the edge of China, concerned above all with its relations with the neighboring colony of Hong Kong and always tempted to back off into regionalism even when it was a matter of revolutionary action.

The students who gathered in Beijing on May 4, 1919, were demanding the return to China of the German possessions and rights in Shandong that negotiators of the Versailles peace treaty intended to pass to Japan. This demonstration came in the wake of the New Culture movement, which since 1915 had been calling for rejection of traditional values and customs, the better to save the nation, and in which the University of Beijing and its elite groups had played an essential role. The movement spread to Shanghai but there changed its character, becoming a great campaign of nationalistic claims in which merchants and workers mobilized alongside the radical intelligentsia. For the first time, the various urban classes coordinated their action, and their claims met with some success: in June, three ministers, accused by public opinion of being pro-Japanese and of not defending national interests, were forced to resign. This mass mobilization served as a model for the many popular demonstrations that intensified throughout the 1920s. In that respect, it was one of the founding events of Chinese contemporary history.

Yet the modernity of this movement was still no more than relative. The native-place associations mobilized the merchants and coordinated the workers and their initiatives with those of the students. Those associations also diffused information; organized meetings, boycotts, and strikes;

---

* The Guomindang or Nationalist Party was created in 1912, taking over from the Revolutionary Alliance, on whose support Sun Yat-sen had depended when preparing for the 1911 Revolution. Subsequently, the Guomindang, while preserving a measure of influence, lost its institutional coherence.

and ensured maintenance of public order. Other organizations, such as the Union of Students and the Federation of Street Unions (which marshaled the merchants according to geographical sectors), were later to be more radical, but at this point the basic cells of these new organizations were still regionalist groups. The particular solidarities that were at the foundation of these groups, far from hampering, on the contrary encouraged nationalism.

In Shanghai, the merchants did not wait for the students to mobilize. As early as February, several native-place associations telegraphed Versailles, stating their opposition to the transfer of German rights to Japan. In March, the merchants formed an organization to coordinate resistance, the Federation of Commercial Organizations, which united fifty-three regionalist and professional guilds. When Shanghainese learned of the student demonstrations in Beijing and their repression, the federation organized many public protests and made contact with the University of Fudan and the Jiangsu Society of Provincial Education with the purpose of organizing a joint rally.* It took place on May 7 in West Gate Stadium, in the immediate neighborhood of the old Chinese town,** and it passed a decision to order a boycott of Japanese goods.

The center of student activism was the University of Fudan, many of whose young professors belonged to the Guomindang Party or supported it. The Chinese students of the foreign St. John's and Tongji universities took part in the movement,*** along with bands of Boy Scouts formed by the Young Men's Christian Association (YMCA) and a host of secondary school pupils and college students. The Students' Union, which came into being on May 11, represented the delegates of sixty-one establishments and claimed 20,000 members. Shanghai students followed in the footsteps

---

* The University of Fudan was founded in 1905, following a movement of dissidence involving both professors and students who left the Jesuit Aurora University. In 1919, it was based in Xujiahui in the suburbs of the French concession. Later it moved to the northeastern part of the town.
** This stadium, in the Chinese town but very close to the French concession, was built in 1917 upon the initiative of and funding from Chinese notables. It could accommodate between 20,000 and 50,000 people and in the 1920s was one of the main venues for popular gatherings and political demonstrations.[1]
*** St. John's University was created in 1879 by American Episcopalians. Tongji University was a secular German establishment.

of their Beijing comrades and decided upon a lecture strike, persuading the merchants likewise to decree a business strike.

On June 5, the workers joined these strikers. The Three Stoppages (*sanba*)—study, commerce, and production—soon paralyzed the town. Shanghai had experienced other strikes, but never on such a vast scale. The strike began in the Japanese textile mills, then spread to the shipyards, public utility services, and transport. Of the town's 300,000 workers, 60,000 ceased work, but the movement lacked cohesion and unity, as did the Shanghai working class itself. It was orchestrated by the native-place associations since, for the better-qualified workers—craftsmen and skilled workers*—geographical solidarities were just as important as they were among merchant communities. The two groups found themselves side by side in their native-place associations, and despite many tensions, they took part in the collective action together.

In 1919, the order of the day was not the class struggle. Consensus was founded on the nationalist cause. Worker militancy was born from patriotism—or xenophobia—and social solidarity. It was not fueled by ideology. Although long considered an obstacle to the formation of class consciousness, traditional solidarities in truth facilitated mobilization of the workers.[2] Among laborers and unskilled workers, those unable to join powerful regionalist guilds because of their own geographical origin followed the direct leadership of their respective foremen. These, who were responsible for recruiting and managing workers, maintained connections with the Green Gang secret society and had effective means of forcing stoppages in the workshops.** The workers' movement, with no real unity, was no more than a supportive force, the "rear-guard shield" of the merchants and students.

Despite the nationalist consensus and efforts at coordination on the part of the traditional organizations (guilds, secret societies, and so on) or other

---

* Many were natives of southern Jiangsu or other southern provinces.

** The Green Gang emerged out of a Buddhist sect that recruited its members from among Great Canal sailors. After the opening up of China, many of them, made jobless by the development of coastal navigation, converged upon Shanghai, where they earned a living from criminal activities or became labor entrepreneurs, providing firms with workers whom they controlled and organized in racketeering operations. The Green Gang was run as a traditional secret society: it had its own initiation rites, a hierarchy of masters and disciples, and a network of more or less autonomous lodges. It recruited from all levels of society, and its membership has been estimated to have been at least 20,000.

ad hoc institutions, the movement appeared very diverse in its methods of expression and operation. The merchants favored sending telegrams to the Beijing government and the Chinese negotiators of the Versailles treaty. They would alert the authorities and local elites who were natives of the same province as themselves, activate networks of their compatriots scattered in all four corners of China, make many declarations to the press, and resort to their ultimate weapon: boycotting.[3] The students proved equally inventive in their methods of organization. They copied the hierarchy of the imperial bureaucracy, appointing a plethora of presidents, vice-presidents, and officials. From the secret societies they borrowed the ritual of a collective oath, and foreign example inspired them to raise ceremonial flags and organize parades through the main thoroughfares of the town. They would make speeches at every crossroads and improvised a policing force to keep order at large meetings and to supervise the anti-Japanese boycotts.[4] The more highly skilled workers modeled their behavior on that of the merchants, displaying a similar flair for organization, discipline, and decorum. The unskilled laborers, freshly arrived from the countryside, brought to Shanghai the rites of peasant rebellion: they would gather in temples, armed with cudgels and banners, burn incense, and pray to their gods.[5] This did not really rate as a civil society, but it certainly was an urban society that was proving itself capable of general mobilization with a common goal. But beneath the consensus of the elites, the power of the masses was definitely perceptible. The lesson was not lost on the revolutionary parties.

THE REVOLUTIONARY PARTIES IN SHANGHAI

As brothers, before becoming enemy brothers, the Guomindang and the Communist Party set about trying to organize the newly emerged forces to their own advantage. In a country and a period in which parties were personified by men rather than programs, the visits that Sun Yat-sen, the main Nationalist leader, and Chen Duxiu, the Communist leader, made to Shanghai turned out to be determining factors in the location of political headquarters and the installment of institutions.

The Guomindang was the elder party. Born in the aftermath of the 1911 Revolution, it had been first subverted by opportunistic members, then banished by Yuan Shikai, the president-turned-dictator, after which it fell into a deep decline. Although many revolutionaries both inside and out-side China continued to identify with the Guomindang, it represented little more than the glorious tradition of republican revolution and attracted to Sun Yat-sen's side no more than a handful of prestigious figures, a mixed group of veterans, intellectuals, businessmen, former parliamentarians, journalists, military leaders, and provincial governors. It was thus after a long period in the wilderness that Sun Yat-sen at last made his political comeback, relying chiefly on the armed forces of the southern generals whom he had made his allies. Alerted by the mobilization of May 1919, he set about reorganizing the Guomindang. From his retreat at 26 rue Molière, in the French concession, the Nationalist leader gave his party new statutes that resurrected the Three Principles of the People and reaffirmed the supreme authority of its president (*zongli*). With funding from overseas, he was able to relaunch party propaganda. Among the many newspapers and periodicals that the Guomindang published in Shanghai, the *Reconstruction* (*Jianshe*) review included contributions from the party's most respected theoreticians. Sun Yat-sen himself contributed a series of articles, later collected under the title "The International Development of China," in which he sketched a grandiose picture of Chinese economic modernization and called for cooperation with the West, founded on mutual interest. He also advocated entente between employers and workers for the sake of the common good. But although Sun condemned imperialism, he did not condemn capitalism, which he hoped to place at the service of Chinese socialism, just as Deng Xiaoping was later to try to do.

Despite all efforts at reorganization, the structures of the Guomindang remained loose. The party continued to be embodied by Sun Yat-sen and his entourage. Whenever Sun returned to his Canton base, he took with him his entire general staff, leaving the party headquarters in Shanghai deserted. But when military reverses forced him into exile in Shanghai, the house in the rue Molière once again became "the Mecca of political leaders of all shades of opinion."[6] Although Sun Yat-sen claimed several hundred thousand members for the Guomindang, a membership count carried out in 1923, under the direction of Soviet advisers from the Comintern, found only about 20,000. Nevertheless, those limited numbers do not take into account the wide influence of the Guomindang, which was founded on a heroic tradition, the prestige of its leaders, and the charisma of Sun Yat-sen.

Beside the Guomindang, the Chinese Communist Party looked like a Tom Thumb. Its foundation has long been presented as the work of a group of intellectuals inspired by the message of the 1917 Revolution, stimulated by the rise of the workers' movement, and assisted by Comintern advisers. In reality, however, the first militants displayed considerable ideological uncertainty.[7] The beginnings of Communism in China were still steeped in the culture purveyed by the study societies that had sprung up in large numbers during the May Fourth Movement. Their object was to diffuse new ideas and encourage them to be applied in small communities, setting an example of a frugal life dedicated to both intellectual and manual work. But quite a range of diverse and fluctuating ideologies nurtured those study societies: liberalism, Marxism, and above all, anarchism. Among the young radicals who constituted the bulk of the societies' members, intellectual convictions carried less weight than geographical solidarities, personal friendships, and links between master and disciple. At the head of the informal network of the study societies were Beijing University and two of its prestigious professors, Li Dazhao and Chen Duxiu, under whose influence Marxism was beginning to be diffused in China.

Among the small proto-Communist groups that were now emerging in China, that of Shanghai displayed a dynamism that owed much to the leadership of Chen Duxiu. Chen was a professor of literature and the founder and editor of *La Jeunesse* review. In the May Fourth Movement, he had played a role that earned him several months of imprisonment in Beijing. His intellectual prestige and moral courage were matched by his great talent as an organizer. Having withdrawn to Shanghai for security reasons, he officially converted to Marxism in 1920, and with the assistance of Grigori Voitinsky, one of the first Comintern emissaries to China, he devoted himself to running the tiny local Communist group: he launched publications, organized a language school to prepare for the departure of young militants to Moscow, and created a section of the League of Socialist Youth.*

---

* Despite its name, this association was modeled on Soviet Russia's League of Communist Youth.

The first issue of La Jeunesse, *a mouthpiece of the New Culture movement and embraced by the Shanghai Communist group beginning in 1920*

THE COMMUNIST

共產黨

年一月大　七日出版

第一號　一九二〇年十一月七日　實價一個

短言

經濟的改造自然占人類改造之主要地位。吾人生產方法除資本主義及社會主義外，別無他途。資本主義在歐洲已經由勝利頂點上墜落下來了，在中國才開始發達，而他的性質上必然的罪惡照例扮演出來了。代繼而起的自然是社會主義的生產方法。俄羅斯正是這種方法最大的最新的試驗場。意大利的此社會主義的生產方法，也都想纔起開闢一個新的生產方法底試驗場。

中國勞動者布滿了全地球。一日夜二十四小時中太陽照著我們工作。但是我們的無論在本土或他國都沒一個獨立生產者，都是向資本家賣工。我們在外國的勞動者固然是他們資本家底奴隸，在本土的勞動者也都是本國資本家底奴隸或是外國資本家底直接的間接的奴隸。要想把我們的同胞從奴隸境遇中完全救出，非由生產勞動者全體結合起來，用革命的手段打倒本國外國一切資本階級，跟著俄國底共產黨一同試驗新的生產方法不可。什麼代議政體，都是些資本家為自己階級設立的，與勞動階級無關。什麼民主政治，什麼代議機關，都是些資本家裏去提出保護勞動者法案。這種話本是為資本家當走狗的議會議員替資本做說客裝幌勞動者的。因為向老虎討肉吃，向強盜商量走路是沒有的事。我們要選出奴隸的境遇，我們不可聽議會底說謊。我們只有用階級戰爭的手段，打倒一切資本階級從他們手裏奪來政權；擁護勞動者的國家以至於無國家，建設勞動者的國家。

無政府主義者諸君呀！你們本來也是反對資本主義反對私有財產制的。請你們不要靠可寶貴的自由濫給資本階級。一切權柄都歸勞動者執掌，就是我們的信條；你們生產工具都歸生產勞動者所有，一切權柄都歸勞動者所有。我們者者者甘心願意替能不肯從事生產勞動的資本家作嫁，也願該是你們的信條。

The first issue (November 7, 1920) of the Gongchandang (The Communist) review, published in Shanghai

The First Party Congress took place on July 23, 1921, in the French concession. Although this was a symbolic and founding event, its immediate importance was slight. The congress assembled thirteen delegates from six provinces and municipalities who represented fifty-nine members; two Comintern emissaries (Maring was one) were present.* Chen Duxiu was elected secretary-general of a Central Committee of three. The simultaneous creation of the Chinese Labor Secretariat, under the direction of Zhang Guotao, indicates that the young party, faithful to Marxism-Leninism, perceived itself right from the start as a proletarian party.**

In the first two years of its existence, the CCP succeeded in structuring the workers' movement in the northern and central provinces. In Shanghai, its influence at first clashed with that of the moderate organizations that supported the Guomindang and also with the domination that foremen and gangsters of the secret societies held over many workshops. But in 1924, the Guomindang and Communist parties committed themselves to collaboration. This united-front policy, which was negotiated in Shanghai and made official in January 1923 by a joint declaration from Sun Yat-sen and the Soviet minister, Adolf Joffé, was gradually put into operation in the revolutionary base in Canton. In Shanghai, the staff offices of both parties energetically resisted the alliance: the Guomindang side feared the danger of subversion, while the Communist side was anxious to proclaim its proletarian purity. The full authority of Sun Yat-sen and the Comintern, represented by Maring, had to be brought to bear in order to impose a partial fusion of the two parties in 1924. Activity now depended on a Canton-Shanghai axis. The importance of Canton stemmed from Sun Yat-sen's presence along with a strong team of Soviet advisers, as well as the creation of an armed revolutionary force there; that of Shanghai, meanwhile, resulted from its mobilization of the workers' world and the activism of its intellectuals and merchants, whose alliance endowed the movement of May 30, 1925, with its full force.

---

* Maring, alias Hendricus Sneevliet (1883–1942), was a Dutch revolutionary who worked in Java before becoming one of the foremost and most important representatives of the Comintern in China, where he helped form the United Front in 1924.
** Zhang Guotao (1897–1979) was one of the founders and earliest leaders of the CCP, within which he devoted himself to organizing a workers' movement. During the Long March, he clashed openly with Mao Zedong and in 1938 left the CCP.

THE MOVEMENT OF MAY 30, 1925

Like the movement of May 4, 1919, that of May 30, 1925, was an anti-imperialist movement of national proportions, in which all classes of urban society participated. But this time it began in Shanghai, not Beijing, and the workers were in the forefront rather than the background.

The strike that erupted on May 7, 1925, in the Japanese Naigai textile factories, the repression of which sparked off the movement, had been preceded by intense worker mobilization linked with the parallel or joint action of both revolutionary parties. The Guomindang, which laid emphasis on social harmony in the service of modernity, attracted the more highly skilled workers. The CCP strove to teach the most impoverished workers—dockers, rickshaw men, unskilled laborers working in the great cotton mills—about the class struggle. It tried to set up trade-unionist cells, and the students of the University of Shanghai (*Shangda*), came to its aid in the establishment of "leisure clubs" that facilitated contacts and provoked agitation in workers' circles.*

Foremen hostile to the Japanese managers' policy of direct staff recruitment organized the strike at the Naigai cotton mill in the western suburb of Shanghai. It was through the company's "leisure club" that the foremen made contact with some militant Communists. Further meetings were organized in the teahouses in the vicinity of the factory. The strike then spread to the quarter's other Japanese cotton mills. Thirty-five thousand workers stopped work, and the "leisure club" became a trade union. The anti-Japanese agitation intensified on May 15, when a factory guard killed a worker. It spread from the factories to the university and from the suburbs to the heart of the international settlement. On May 30, a procession of students in the Nanjing Road clashed with the British police force, resulting in thirteen deaths. A boycott accompanied the general strike that broke out after this tragic incident. The movement spread rapidly to other large Chinese towns and ended up again calling the presence of foreigners in China into question. Its relative success marked the rising power of the CCP in Shanghai and prefigured the revolution that was to break out two years later.

---

* Most of the professors of this university, created in 1922, belonged to the CCP and encouraged their students to combine the study of Marxism-Leninism with revolutionary activities.

The patriotic consensus that brought the bourgeoisie and the work-ers' world together now fueled nationalist demands. The Federation of Workers, Merchants, and Students, founded on June 4 to pilot the move-ment, put that alliance on a concrete basis. With the Communist leader Li Lisan as its president, it demanded not only the punishment of those responsible and compensation for the victims but also that the Mixed Court of the international settlement be restored to the Chinese authori-ties and that the right to strike be recognized.* The General Chamber of Commerce, the organ of the major Shanghai employers, did not join the federation but did cooperate with it and arranged for large subsidies to be handed out to the strikers. In the Thirteen Demands that it drew up, it seconded all the demands of the federation: these Thirteen Demands served as the basis for extremely laborious negotiations conducted simul-taneously in Beijing and Shanghai.

The gravity of the shootings, the anger that they aroused throughout the country, and the diplomatic complaints to which they led turned the Shanghai crisis into a national one that called for the mediation of the Chi-nese central government and the foreign legations in Beijing. But for the expatriates of Shanghai, Beijing was nothing more than "a dusty Mongol city," cut off from the realities of contemporary life, whereas the diplomatic corps, over which they (the expatriates) did not exert the same influence that they held over the local consular corps, was an intermediary that was not to be trusted. Meanwhile, the young Chinese radicals were equally wary of the warlords who controlled the Beijing government.

It was thus essentially in Shanghai and among Shanghai's residents that the crisis would be resolved by a series of compromises, the chief beneficiary of which was the Chinese bourgeoisie. In August, the Shang-hai Municipal Council accepted that the settlement's Chinese residents be represented and also, in principle, the return of the Mixed Court to Chinese sovereignty. At that point the alliance between the General

---

* The Mixed Court was created in 1864 to hear cases of the international concession's Chi-nese residents. The task was entrusted to an imperial magistrate. But in cases that involved foreign residents as well as Chinese, foreign assessors assisted this magistrate. The Mixed Court's powers were gradually eroded, and after the 1911 Revolution it fell under the au-thority of the Shanghai consular corps.

Chamber of Commerce and the Federation of Workers, Merchants, and Students collapsed. The entrepreneurs, who had obtained satisfaction for their demands thanks to the popular mobilization, were alarmed at the progress made by the workers' organizations, which were now headed by the Shanghai General Labor Union created on May 31 by the Communists, who were claiming an overall total of 200,000 members. Many of the employers were impatient for work to restart. So, too, were many strikers, for their aid reserves were now exhausted. The Green Gang was seeking to regain the territory that it had lost and was organizing attacks against the Shanghai General Labor Union. The radical wing of the movement was being undermined by factionalism and local militarists who forced the General Labor Union to close its doors. The strikes came to an end after pay increases had been granted, mostly for the foremen. But it was several weeks before the matter of the shooting episode in the Nanjing Road that had sparked off the movement was concluded with the sacking of the police officers responsible and compensation for the victims.

The return of peace was misleading, however. Embers were still glowing beneath the ashes. Fourteen months later they flared up again, and the fire that then engulfed the town changed the destiny of China.

NATIONALISTS AGAINST COMMUNISTS

The armed insurrection of March 22, 1927, which resulted in the strikers and Communist militants seizing control of Shanghai, was one of the high points in the revolutionary history of China. The bloody repression that followed three weeks later claimed several thousand victims and turned the episode into a tragedy.[8] Literature has conferred upon it the grandeur of myth: in the West, André Malraux's novel *La condition humaine*, which appeared in 1933, made a powerful contribution to the creation of the myth that became part of a worldwide revolutionary collective memory. Mythical it may be, but the entire event is still shrouded in obscurity. Too many forces were at work, too many interests at stake, for the accounts and interpretations of it not to prove fragmentary and contradictory. Many question marks still hover over the motives and responsibilities of the various actors involved: the local militarists, the Guomindang, the CCP, the Comintern, the trade unions, the foreign residents, the concessions' authorities, the consular corps, and so on.

The revolutionary strikes in the spring of 1927 occurred within the national political/military context of the Northern Expedition, or *Beifa*. After the death of Sun Yat-sen in 1925, Chiang Kai-shek proclaimed his authority over the Canton government and placed himself at the head of Beifa, whose objectives were to reconquer the provinces of central and northern China, overthrow the militarists, and unify the national territory. The expedition's successes during 1926 made it possible for the Canton government to transfer its capital from Canton to Wuhan, the geographical center of China. But conflict between the Wuhan government and General Chiang Kai-shek was brewing. In January 1927, the general decided to abandon the advance northward and deflect the march toward Shanghai, where he was hoping to obtain financial support from the local bourgeoisie and political support from the Guomindang right wing, which had always been hostile to cooperation with the Communists.

While Chiang Kai-shek's National Revolutionary Army was advancing toward the coast, a series of strikes and armed insurrections broke out in Shanghai. The strikers and the Guomindang soldiers had a common enemy: the warlord Sun Chuanfang, who reigned over both the town and the surrounding region. The successes of Beifa relaunched the workers' movement, producing the "Three Armed Uprisings" of October 1926 and February and March 1927.[9]

The first two enabled the General Labor Union and the Communist militants to perfect their tactics. As in 1925, the party depended on the activism of the skilled workers—for example, those of the Commercial Press and the Post Office*—and on mobilization of the dockers, the laborers, and workers of the great textile mills. This was achieved by renegotiating the alliance with the Green Gang. The Communist leader Wang Shouhua, at the head of the General Labor Union, adopted a strategy of alliance that, in the name of the struggle against militarism and the right to local self-government, was designed to unite the workers' forces

---

* The employees of the publishing house included four hundred Communists, 10% of its staff.

with those of the bourgeoisie and the secret societies. Just as hostility to imperialism had created a consensus in 1925, in the spring of 1927 the condemnation of militarism and the desire for national unity for a while brought together all the different layers of Shanghai society. But when General Sun Chuanfang had strikers and demonstrators beheaded in the streets, this violent repression prompted the General Labor Union to create combat units and arm the picketing strikers.

Forestalling the entry of the Nationalist troops, who were stationed in the suburbs, waiting for the local militarists to make a negotiated retreat,* on March 21 the General Labor Union launched an appeal for a general strike. Between 500,000 and 800,000 workers responded. Shanghai was transformed into a dead town. In conformity with the strategy of revolutionary strikes defined by Lenin, the General Labor Union then proceeded to organize an armed insurrection. Within thirty-six hours, "armed pickets" occupied the police stations and the main strategic points held by the militarists: on March 22, Sun Chuanfang's regime toppled. The strikers and the Communists were masters of the Chinese town. They showed considerable moderation as they exploited their military victory. They did not even consider setting up a soviet, as the revolutionaries in Petrograd had in 1917. Instead, in conformity with the program worked out in early March with the urban institutions—the chambers of commerce, guilds, and professional organizations—the provisional municipal government declared itself to represent all their various interests, and the Wuhan government confirmed its legitimacy.

The speed of this victory took the principal actors on the political stage by surprise. In the weeks that followed, many secret negotiations took place, old alliances were broken, new ones were adumbrated, and agreements were concluded. Over all these consultations hung the shadow of the foreigners and the implicit threat to the town that their troops and weapons implied. Would their rifles and cannons suffice to preserve their "bastion of imperialism"? Many were beginning to doubt that they would.

---

* Chiang Kai-shek was unwilling to order an attack on Shanghai because he feared not so much resistance from Sun Chuanfang and his allies (who were already much weakened) but the reactions of the foreigners, who were strongly entrenched inside their concessions.

THE FOREIGNERS' GREAT FEARS

Since the beginning of 1927, anxiety had been growing among the foreign residents of Shanghai. It was fueled by the news from Hankou, where on January 4 a crowd of demonstrators had invaded the British concession, forcing the residents to flee.* That scenario was repeated the following day at Jiujiang, a port situated further downstream on the Yangzi. Determined to avoid any armed retaliation that might provoke an all-out explosion of xenophobia, Britain had already agreed to return the British concessions of the mid-Yangzi ports to China. But such moderation could not be applied to Shanghai, the bridgehead for the foreign businesses and, indeed, the very foreign presence in China. Both the authorities and the residents were of the opinion that the concessions had to be defended against the double danger that threatened them: namely, external aggression by the Nationalist troops and internal subversion by the revolutionary trade unions.

Once the insurgents had seized control of the Chinese quarters on March 21 and the men of the National Revolutionary Army had entered the town on the following day, rumors were rife of an imminent armed picketers' attack on the concessions. The foreigners were not counting on any preventive intervention by the Nationalist soldiers, whom they regarded as Reds. The "Nanjing Incident" of March 24 had confirmed their worst fears and engendered panic. Nationalist troops had seized Nanjing and perpetrated many violent attacks against both the property and the persons of foreigners: six residents had been massacred, and the rest had saved their lives only by taking flight, protected by the firepower of gunboats on the Yangzi.

Amplified by rumors and the stories of hundreds of refugees who landed on the Bund, the misfortunes of Nanjing seemed to foreshadow the fate of Shanghai. In early January, military reinforcements had begun to arrive. The Foreign Office had decided to send in a division with the mission of protecting the property and lives of the residents and preventing Nationalist troops from entering the international settlement. The other powers

---

* Hankou was one of the three cities that made up the urban conglomeration of Wuhan, which the Nationalists had held since the autumn of 1926.

were slower to mobilize. But by the end of March, the volunteer corps and police forces of the concessions had been reinforced by 12,000 soldiers and marine fusiliers. Tanks and armored cars patrolled the streets. Machine guns protected strategic points, and barbed wire and sandbags closed off access roads, while on the Huangpu twenty-eight warships, sent in by seven nations, formed a line almost 2 kilometers long. This deployment of military might, orchestrated by Great Britain, reassured the residents, who unanimously praised the determination of the British.

The French residents indignantly contrasted that determination to the attitude of their own consul-general, Paul-Émile Naggiar. Dozens of telegrams sent to the Quai d'Orsay by the French firms, the elites, and the French Chamber of Commerce protested both the inadequacy of defensive measures and the official contacts made with officers of the National Revolutionary Army. It was quite true that in the French concession military reinforcements amounted to no more than one company of Annamite soldiers from Hanoi and 300 marine fusiliers from the *Jules Michelet* and *La Marne* vessels. Even including the combined forces of the police and volunteers, fighting men numbered fewer than 1,800. The consul had no choice but to resort to political means to ensure the safety of the concession. Possibly his own temperament predisposed him to prefer such means in any case, for Naggiar was an extremely skilled negotiator, a fact that observers sometimes attributed to his Middle Eastern origins: "He is the type of man who in Europe . . . is called . . . a Levantine. He knows Asia better than all the rest of us put together. He got the measure of it . . . by instinct."[10]

The consul now enjoyed considerable liberty of movement because in January, on the pretext of the crisis, he had replaced the (elected) municipal council by a provisional (selected) commission. Arguing on the grounds that he had been appointed by Aristide Briand, his opponents attributed Socialist or even Communist sympathies to him and suspected him of wishing to sell off the concession. In truth, he was defending it, but doing so by means of more or less secret maneuvers and negotiations. He was well served by the high quality of the information that the concession's police supplied him, and his pragmatism inclined him to make deals with those—whoever they might be—who held the real power. In working-class circles, the only force capable of counterbalancing the revolutionary trade unions were the secret-society gangsters. By February 1927, Naggiar had persuaded one of the Green Gang's chief leaders, Du Yuesheng, to intervene personally among the leaders of the principal guilds to prevent the strikes from spreading into the concession. In exchange, the consul apparently promised him 300 rifles and 100,000 cartridges as well as increased police protection for the opium and gaming rackets in the concession.*

Naggiar was the first diplomat to make contact with the agents of Chiang Kai-shek, whom the foreigners (and many Chinese) still regarded as a revolutionary. The French residents and notables were extremely worried about these "private negotiations with unqualified authorities."[12] But thanks to his contacts, the consul very soon sensed the possibility of an about-face on the part of Chiang Kai-shek and could see all the advantages that such a development might offer the foreigners. In a *pro domo* document of self-justification sent two months later to the French minister of foreign affairs, he defended his "discreet methods" and the collaboration that, with a view to maintaining order, he had set up with "the new Chinese authorities" and contrasted his behavior to that of the British, "who had remained out of contact with the Nationalists, in a position of hostility that, in a town crammed with armed troops and panicking foreigners, could at any moment provoke the gravest of incidents."[13] Although the French residents and other foreigners exalted the one line of behavior and condemned the other, in truth the French and the British strategies probably played complementary roles: the discreet contacts diminished the risks of confrontation, whereas the deployment of military force diminished those of a pure and simple capitulation.

Amid an apparent calm in Shanghai, the Nationalist troops, the armed pickets, and the foreign forces eyed one another. The French consul was not alone in entering into negotiations: on all sides, many more contacts were now made. Twenty or so days later, they would lead to a redistribution of the political forces.

---

* The existence of such a deal is suggested by Naggiar's telegram to the Ministry of Foreign Affairs on February 26, 1927, in which he wrote that "rifles and shells rapidly made available to our concession would allow us to make better use of certain local elements."[11]

CHIANG KAI-SHEK AND THE
COUP OF APRIL 12, 1927

Between the victorious insurrection of March 23 and the bloody purging of April 12, Shanghai was the scene of many secret deals. False rumors and maneuverings ran their course, while the forces in play argued over what strategies to adopt. Although the ups and downs of the drama were not always clear to observers, there could be no doubt of the importance of what was at stake. In Wuhan, in Moscow, and in the capitals of the West, all eyes were fixed on Shanghai.

The master of ceremonies was Chiang Kai-shek. The general was at this time forty years old, with a long revolutionary past already behind him. He was a native of Zhejiang and had been trained as an officer in Japan, where he had joined Sun Yat-sen's Revolutionary Alliance, and had then taken part in the 1911 Revolution both in the Shanghai region and in the town itself. That was when, through his protector Chen Qimei, he established his first contacts with business circles and with the metropolis's mafiosi.

When the revolution failed, he sank into gambling and debauchery, grasping at friendships with adventurer-politicians such as the millionaire Zhang Jingjiang, a leading member of the Guomindang who was also closely linked with the Green Gang. In the early 1920s, Chiang reappeared on the political scene in Canton as a member of the entourage of Sun Yat-sen, who made him his military adviser and sent him on a mission to Moscow. The young officer returned deeply suspicious of Soviet intentions in China. He nevertheless went through the motions of collaboration with the Comintern advisers, who helped him to organize the National Revolutionary Army. After Sun Yat-sen's death in 1925, Chiang put himself forward as Sun's successor, exploiting his authority over the military apparatus in order to begin distancing his rivals and to limit the influence of the Soviet advisers. However, he was careful to avoid any open break. With a mandate from the Guomindang and the Canton government, in 1926 he took command of the Northern Expedition with the objective of toppling the warlords and reunifying China.

When he arrived in Shanghai on March 26, 1927, three days after the Nationalist troops had entered the town, Chiang Kai-shek was fêted by the population. He did not seem to be about to launch himself into an armed coup, for with no more than 3,000 soldiers at his disposal, some of whom sympathized with the insurgents, he faced 2,000 armed pickets and also had to reckon with the 15,000 men held in reserve in the concessions. Moreover, part of the bourgeoisie had made common cause with the insurgents, and although the leaders of the Guomindang right wing had taken refuge in Shanghai, many local militants still favored cooperation with the Communists.

Chiang Kai-shek could not simply rely on force and abandon the policy of a united front; he needed to reassure the foreigners, rally the bourgeoisie, and neutralize the insurgents and their sympathizers. So he resorted to cunning, set about forging a new legitimacy for himself, and for the rest, relied on the good offices of the Green Gang, with which he had renewed contact even before his arrival in Shanghai. At the same time, as he repeatedly reassured the authorities and residents of the concessions, he was making advances to the Chinese capitalists, who agreed to lend him, in the first instance, 3 million dollars to facilitate an anti-Communist purge. Even as he reiterated his loyalty to the united-front policy, Chiang was negotiating with the leaders of the Guomindang's right wing, who were urging him to "protect the party and save the country," in other words, to exclude the Communists and eject the Soviet advisers. The input of several veterans, such as Wu Zhihui and Cai Yuanpei, provided him with valuable support.*

But the most delicate part of the operation fell to the underworld, namely, breaking up the unions and disarming the striking pickets. To weaken the Communists' control over the workers' organizations, Du Yuesheng had created the Shanghai General Labor Federation to compete with the General Labor Union and had supplied it with an armed

---

* Wu Zhihui (1864–1953), a scholar and educator, helped to start the revolutionary movement in Japan and Shanghai. He joined the Revolutionary Alliance as soon as it was founded in 1905. He was one of Sun Yat-sen's principal collaborators, but in 1924 he opposed the policy of a united front between the Guomindang and the CCP. He was a loyal supporter of Chiang Kai-shek and immigrated to Taiwan in 1949. Cai Yuanpei (1868–1940), who had won the highest grade in the mandarin examinations, devoted himself to modernizing teaching, which he regarded as an indispensable condition for all political reform. After the collapse of the Manchu dynasty, he became minister of education (in 1912) and president of Beijing University (1916 to 1926). In 1928, he helped to found the Academia Sinica and became its first president.

force known as the Chinese Mutual Progress Association. This association recruited its members from among the Green Gang thugs and those of other secret societies and was able to arm them from funds advanced by the Chinese merchants and the weapons provided by the authorities of the French concession.

Preparations were completed on April 11. That evening, Du Yuesheng invited Wang Shouhua, the Communist organizer of the General Labor Union, to dinner at his villa in the rue Wagner in the French concession and then had him abducted and strangled. All this was carried out in the style characteristic of settling scores among criminals. After the murder, the corpse was dumped on wasteland in the suburbs. Then Du Yuesheng needed to obtain a free pass for his henchmen from the authorities of the international settlement, for the Chinese Mutual Progress Association's headquarters happened to be situated in the French concession, and the armed pickets were dug in in Zhabei. The officially neutral territory of the international settlement separated the two sectors. To skirt it would have entailed a long detour through the western suburbs, which was incompatible with the desired element of surprise. During the night, Du Yuesheng received a visit from Stirling Fessender, the American president of the Shanghai Municipal Council. The head of the French police, Captain Étienne Fiori, had arranged the meeting. During the meeting, they reached an agreement.

At dawn on April 12, a clarion call from General Chiang Kai-shek's headquarters and the sirens of a Chinese gunboat signaled the attack. Disguised as workers, the better to spread confusion, men of the Green Gang attacked the headquarters of the General Labor Union and the main strongholds of the insurgents in Zhabei and other Chinese quarters. The assailants were supported by Nationalist soldiers who, pretending to intervene in order to calm things down, proceeded to disarm the pickets. In no more than a few hours, the latter had lost half their men and most of their weapons. The strike that the General Labor Union attempted to launch on April 13 collapsed; and the demonstration organized in Zhabei in protest at the violent coup ended in the Baoshan Street massacre, in which several hundred men, women, and children were mown down by the Nationalist machine guns or pursued and felled by rifle butts, bayonets, and swords in the neighboring streets. The "Shanghai Commune" had had its day. Now the White Terror took over, along with new institutions dominated by the Guomindang and the Green Gang.

The April 12 coup changed the course of contemporary Chinese history. It ended the united front between the Nationalists and Communists, brought Chiang Kai-shek to power, and established his Nationalist government in Nanjing. It also constituted a setback for the CCP, which proceeded to reorient its activities toward its rural bases; and it led to a considerably reduced foreign presence in China.

Although the insurrection of the spring of 1927 was crucial to the destiny of the nation as a whole, it had been deeply rooted in Shanghai circles. The unfolding of the insurrection depended on the interplay of local social forces as much as, or more than, on the imperatives of national policy and international revolution. The attitude of the insurgents following their victory of March 22 raises many questions. They appeared to hold numerous trump cards: they could rely on vast trade-unionist mobilization and a large armed force; they enjoyed the support of the revolutionary parties and most of the Shanghai population. So why did they impose upon themselves a moderation and legalism that eventually left them defenseless before their enemies?

This strange paralysis has been at the center of violent polemics. Stalin attributed it to the blindness and opportunism of the CCP, while the Trotskyites blamed the stubbornness of the Comintern and Stalin, claiming that they sacrificed the Shanghai insurrection to their own global strategy. But was the workers' movement really all that strong? Was not its power an illusion created by its temporary alliance with the Green Gang? Might the cause of the paralysis not have been, rather, the heterogeneous and relatively unstructured nature of the workers' world, a world subject to spasms of anger but incapable of making the transition to politics because, being insufficiently aware of its own interests, it readily turned to other social groups—students, local elites, gangsters, and so on—to defend its cause?[14]

Another point, highlighted by the history of the April coup, is the position of the Green Gang in Shanghai society. The mafia was not just an extra group with power, nor was it content simply to provide killers on demand; it lay at the very heart of Shanghai society and determined its history. By tipping the scales against its alliance with the Communist trade unions and toward the Nationalist general, the Green Gang sealed the fate of the revolution and succeeded in making its power, up until then secret, an official factor.

Those who made the deal with the Green Gang in March–April benefited greatly but were then obliged to share power with it. This was so in the case of the Guomindang, as we shall see in Chapter 9, and also in that of the French concession. The "pact with the devil" that Paul-Émile Naggiar made had, without doubt, saved the concession, which was in a very weak position,[15] but to make use of the mafia yet at the same time limit its power required a great deal of skill. After Naggiar's departure in 1928, his successors did not know how to establish a distance from their dangerous associates: either impotent or complicit, they stood by while Du Yuesheng and his men subverted the concession's institutions, until a tardy attempt by the French Ministry of Foreign Affairs to regain control eventually partially rectified the situation.

As seen from Shanghai, Chiang Kai-shek did not appear as the traitor whose dark portrait the Communists painted after the April coup: an enemy of the working class and a lackey of the bourgeoisie and the foreigners. His open hatred of the Communists did not lead to the workers' claims being crushed, for they regained a certain vigor in the late 1920s within a framework of official trade unions; it did not lead him to knuckle under to capitalist interests, for these received short shrift from the new regime, nor to underwrite the foreigners' privileges, which underwent a sharp decline. In the years following his seizure of power, Chiang Kai-shek did not perceive himself as the standard-bearer of reaction, nor was he so perceived by Shanghai public opinion. Rather, he was regarded as continuing in the footsteps of Sun Yat-sen, the defender of the Three Principles of the People and the creator of the national revolution.

FROM INSURRECTIONAL STRIKES TO URBAN TERRORISM:
THE DECLINE OF COMMUNIST INFLUENCE IN SHANGHAI

During the Nanjing decade—that is, the ten years of Chiang Kai-shek's Nationalist government in the southern capital—the Chinese revolutionary movement identified itself above all with the armed struggle that the Communists were waging from their rural bases. The apparatus of the CCP, forced underground and repressed by the authorities, soon deserted Shanghai, where only a dwindling group of militants continued to challenge the Guomindang police. Now deprived of their working-class bases and cut off from the bourgeois elite groups, these militants were reduced to commando actions and terrorist attacks. During the 1930s, the mass movements in Shanghai attracted just as many and as diverse participants as those of the preceding decade. But they took place in a political and ideological environment that had changed as a result of the metamorphosis of the central power and of the intensification of Japanese aggression.

Until 1927, the weakness of the Beijing government and its distance from Shanghai had enabled Shanghai leaders to preserve a measure of autonomy, passed on from the reforms of the beginning of the republican era. The local militarists would exercise their brutal power only intermittently: one warlord would eject another, and all of them could be bought off by subsidies. From 1927 on, when Chiang Kai-shek was installed in Nanjing, Shanghai became a kind of second capital. Ministers and high-ranking figures were constantly shuttling between the political capital and the economic metropolis. The Special Municipality of Greater Shanghai was led by a mayor appointed by the central authorities.* As a result of this and of the fact that once the Mixed Courts had been returned to Chinese sovereignty, the Nanjing government regained legal control over the Chinese residents of both concessions, the repression of Communist activities became much more effective.

Not only was the government closer and more active but it also changed in character, since the Guomindang derived its revolutionary legitimacy from the role it had played in the struggles of the first quarter of the century and from its loudly proclaimed loyalty to Sun Yat-sen and his doctrine. Party rhetoric represented the revolution as the symbol of progress. Subsequently, even when the military and authoritarian nature of the regime became more pronounced, that revolutionary rhetoric persisted. Such ambiguities were to act as a brake on mass movements, but without

---

* This municipal government, created in 1927–1928 by the Guomindang government with the aim of unifying the Shanghai administration, managed all the town's Chinese quarters (see Chapter 9).

paralyzing them altogether, and were to limit their scope, but without draining them of all subversive content.

The White Terror, which continued for two weeks following the coup of April 12, 1927, succeeded in breaking the Shanghai revolutionary wave: it claimed 5,000 victims, either shot or vanished, and wiped out the organized forces of revolutionary trade unionism. The CCP and the General Labor Union, proscribed by the Guomindang, went underground.

The lessons that the Comintern drew from this defeat were biased by the internal conflicts then tearing apart the Soviet Communist Party and setting Stalin in opposition first to Trotsky, then to Bukharin. To safeguard Stalin's prestige, the Comintern and, following suit, the CCP laid the blame for the failure on the secretary-general, Chen Duxiu, accusing him of having sinned "through right-wing opportunism."* Their strategy for winning back the Shanghai workers' world was based on the postulate that the coup of April 12, 1927, was just an incidental hiccup in the overall scheme, one that would make no major impact on the rising revolutionary tide and that the struggle should now be continued, relying exclusively on the proletariat. That postulate was erroneous, its strategy disastrous. Between 1928 and 1935, the Central Committee of the CCP implemented a radical policy, seeking to relaunch insurrectional strikes. But the Shanghai proletariat was not prepared to mobilize for another revolutionary adventure. It was not that the April coup had wiped out all working-class combativity: the strikes resumed as early as the autumn of 1927. However, the renascent workers' movement was quickly channeled into official trade unions that the Guomindang supported or tolerated.

This official trade unionism, often labeled "yellow" by Communist historians and accordingly reviled by them, nevertheless proved capable of defending the material interests of the workers and of preserving a modicum of autonomy.[16] At the heart of this new institution, the Seven Major Trade Unions—postmen, tramway workers, tobacco-factory workers, and so on—were not bogus creatures of the regime. They had appeared

---

* Chen Duxiu was accused of having all along pursued a dire policy of alliance with the Guomindang and Chiang Kai-shek. In truth, Stalin and the Comintern advocated and imposed that policy, against Chen's own views.

before or during the revolutionary wave of the spring of 1927. Despite the purge, they still preserved a working-class basis and combative leaders. Although kept under surveillance by the police and infiltrated by the secret societies, they were still able to make successful wage claims and to press for better working conditions.

The rise of this "precarious working-class strategy"[17] stands in contrast to the failure of the political strikes that militant Communists in the cotton mills of Pudong and Yangshupu and the British Tramway Company launched in the autumn of 1927. "Down with imperialism," "Down with the Guomindang," and "Long live the Soviet bases" were slogans backed by no mobilizing power. "The Shanghai workers' movement ceased to represent a chapter in the history of the Chinese Communist Party and instead became quite an important component in that of the Guomindang."[18]

The CCP was determined not to renew the alliances that it blamed officially for the catastrophe of April 1927. It now shunned the students, declaring them to be "bourgeois enemies," and also the elite bourgeois groups that it considered to have been "domesticated" by Chiang Kai-shek. Nor did it seek to exploit the anti-Japanese feeling that public opinion was manifesting more violently than ever. Its desire for ideological purity led it to ride alone, but its impotence was revealed by gestures as useless as they were spectacular. Every anniversary of national or international revolutionary history became a pretext for an impromptu demonstration in one of the main thoroughfares, preferably the Nanjing Road. Small groups of militants would suddenly swarm out of the crowd, yelling slogans and hurling tracts around before being swiftly carted away by the police. Such demonstrations, which made no impression on the public but did fuel the anti-Communist hysteria of both the foreign and Chinese authorities, exposed those who took part in them to severe reprisals: there were many arrests and executions.

In the face of police terror, the Communists organized terror of their own. Placed under the authority of Zhou Enlai, the party's special services, or Red Brigades, operated in the larger towns, liquidating not only denunciators and traitors but also any militants who proved recalcitrant to party discipline. Their leader in Shanghai was Gu Shunzhang. He was a mechanic working for the Nanyang Tobacco Company who had joined the party in 1924. He had served in Canton as bodyguard to the Comintern adviser Mikhail Borodin and had then taken a training course in the Gepeou (the Soviet security agency) in Vladivostok. In the Shanghai insurrections of the spring of 1927, he had been in command of a brigade of worker pickets. And now, disguised as a juggler, putting on conjuring shows in the Sincere Department Store and combining his skills as an illusionist with those of a strangler, he was setting up executions (as many as thirty were attributed to him in 1928–1929) and was infiltrating his agents into the Guomindang offices and those of the police forces of both concessions. In April 1931, he was sent to Wuhan with the mission of assassinating Chiang Kai-shek, but he was arrested and then went over to the enemy. Following his defection, thousands of militants were identified, arrested, and executed in the course of the "red days" of July. The Red Brigades abducted four members of the Gu family as reprisal. Their mutilated corpses were exhumed a few months later from under an alleyway in the French concession, as were thirty or so others buried in various sites in the concessions, all of them the remains of unidentified victims of the party's score settling. Although they were justified by the great writer and left-wing militant Lu Xun, who declared, "Bloodshed must be compensated by bloodshed,"[19] these acts of revenge horrified the public and led the concessions' authorities to strengthen their cooperation with the Guomindang in the hunt for Communists. The foreign authorities were also becoming increasingly alarmed at the Communist propaganda being diffused among their own police forces. The British feared a destabilization of the large Indian community in Shanghai, while the French were concerned that disturbances would spread to Indochina.

The Party ranks were decimated by arrests, executions, and defections. The number of its members slumped from 8,000 in April 1927 to 300 in 1934. Factionalism also caused ravages. In 1927, Chen Duxiu, seeking historical absolution, declared himself a Trotskyite, carrying with him a number of other militants, all of whom the Central Committee rapidly excluded.* Many local leading figures in their turn condemned the radical and dogmatic line imposed by the new cadres, Qu Qiubai and Li Lisan,

---

* Trotsky blamed Stalin and the Comintern for the 1927 failure.

and from 1931 onward, also by the Twenty-eight Bolsheviks.* These local men were faced every day by the impossible task of reviving the revolutionary ardor of Shanghai workers, who, under close police surveillance, were now organized by trade-unionist leaders and secret societies and were preoccupied by the defense of their own immediate economic interests. The leader of these "realists," He Mengxiong (1901–1931), favored the organization of economic strikes in cooperation with the official trade unions. Having been expelled from the party, He Mengxiong was preparing to set up a dissident central committee when he was arrested in January 1931 at a meeting held in the international settlement. He was handed over to the Guomindang authorities, who had him shot along with twenty-six of his followers. Whether this arrest was simply a result of the risks inherent in clandestine militancy or of a deliberate denunciation on the part of a party hoping to rid itself of all dangerous rivals was never discovered.

The Shanghai Communist militants became more and more isolated. In the rural bases, a new strategy was adopted. This was founded upon mobilizing the peasants, militarizing the revolutionary movement, setting up soviets, and establishing the party upon a state footing; meanwhile in Shanghai, the Central Committee was imposing a line more in conformity with Marxist-Leninist postulates but hardly suited to the realities of the economic and social situation. The Comintern, acting through this Central Committee, whose factional struggles it was able to manipulate, was holding the Shanghai Communists hostage.

At no time did the Comintern send out so many emissaries, couriers, spies, and money as during the early 1930s. Shanghai, increasingly out of touch with the destiny of Chinese Communism, became an important hub in the international revolutionary movement. Following a number of raids on its embassies in Beijing and London, the Soviet government was loath to involve its diplomatic outposts in liaison operations with local Communist movements. Rather, it decided to entrust most of the tasks of disseminating information and liaison to secret agents who adopted the

---

* This was the name given to a group of militants who had studied in Moscow. They made up the "internationalist faction" of the CCP, which was hostile to Mao and his peasant revolution. Thanks to the support of the Comintern, whose directives they submissively applied, from 1931 to 1935 this group dominated the CCP Political Bureau.

identities of businessmen, journalists, or professors. In Asia, these spying networks centered upon Shanghai where, among others, Richard Sorge and Hilaire Noulens operated.* The latter, at the head of the Comintern office for the Far East, was responsible for directing the action of a number of Asian Communist parties and financing them to the tune of 17 million francs per year.[20] Despite all his precautions—seven addresses, eight postal boxes, ten bank accounts, and countless pseudonyms—in 1933 the police of the international settlement arrested Noulens, and the courts of Nanjing condemned him to death.** That judgment was then commuted to a prison sentence thanks to the international mobilization of left-wing intellectuals organized by a committee headed by Henri Barbusse and activated in Shanghai itself by American journalists, such as Harold Isaacs and Edgar Snow, and a number of Chinese democrats. The many documents seized when Noulens was arrested enabled the police to identify other agents and to paralyze their networks. After this, relations between Shanghai and Moscow became increasingly strained, and in August 1934, when the Comintern's clandestine Shanghai radio station was discovered and destroyed, they broke down altogether.

By this time, the Central Committee had already transferred to the Jiangxi base, where it had been installed for the past eighteen months. That move put an end to direct contacts between the party leadership and the remnants of the Shanghai apparatus. When the Long March began in late 1934, the Shanghai Communists were left to themselves. The only circles in which they continued to exert influence were those of the left-wing intellectuals, alongside whom they worked within the Writers' and the Journalists' Leagues and that of the filmmakers. These organizations, known as the "red leagues" (*hongse minlian*), attracted not only a kernel of militants but also a more numerous group of sympathizers made up of

---

* Richard Sorge was a German citizen, born in Tiflis in 1895, and was a Comintern agent from 1924 on. He worked in Shanghai from 1930 to 1932, before moving to Tokyo where, seemingly spying for Germany, he kept the Soviet Union informed of developments. The Japanese discovered his double game and arrested him in October 1941. Noulens, whose real name was Yakov Rudnik, was of Ukrainian origin. After his arrest, he in vain claimed first Belgian, then Swiss nationality. So when he came to trial, he could not benefit from the privilege of extraterritoriality, which was reserved for citizens of the states linked to China by treaty.
** After five years, Noulens was released and thereafter disappeared, probably in a Stalinist gulag, where most Comintern agents and Soviet spies in East Asia ended up.

fellow travelers, patriots, and liberals hostile to Chiang Kai-shek's increasingly dictatorial regime. Although these leagues disseminated Communist propaganda, because of the renown and diversity of their members they were spared the harshest measures of repression. Thanks to them, the Shanghai Communists were able to break out of the ghetto where they had withdrawn and to establish some contacts with urban society. Their entirely spontaneous behavior foreshadowed the policy of a Second United Front that was officially adopted by the Comintern in 1935 and thereafter by the CCP. It was a policy that was to be applied particularly vigorously in Shanghai, on account of its population's fervent mobilization in support of the cause of National Salvation.

NATIONAL SALVATION AND
A NEW SURGE OF MASS MOVEMENTS

In the 1930s, extensive popular mobilization became increasingly intense in Shanghai. Public opinion was more inclined than ever to express itself, insisting that those with political power should satisfy its demands. What it expressed was its hostility to Japan; and what it demanded was armed resistance to the encroachments of this powerful neighbor of China. The struggle against imperialism in the 1920s gave way to a fight for National Salvation, a patriotic struggle against Japan, which was perpetrating more and more aggressions: in Manchuria in 1931, in Shanghai in 1932, and in the northern provinces between 1935 and 1937, at which point open warfare broke out.

For the authorities, the formidable consensus that fueled the passions of urban society represented both a trump card and a danger. Although deeply nationalistic himself, Chiang Kai-shek could not respond fully to popular feeling. Conscious as he was of the disproportion between the armed forces of China and Japan, he sought to temporize, to defer resistance to the invader, and to prioritize the modernization of the economy and the unification of the country, that is, the struggle against the Communist guerrillas. As a result, popular nationalism was in danger of moving into opposition against the government, and this became an essential element in the struggle for power between the Guomindang and the Communists. Given the eventual triumph of Communism, this has been the angle from which both Chinese and Western historians have mostly studied popular nationalism. However, the movement for National Salvation increasingly appeared as a major political force in itself, dominating the public life of Shanghai and other large towns in China. The structures that it created lacked the cohesion of those of the Guomindang and the CCP, but its influence pervaded every level of urban society and engendered a widespread consciousness of the Chinese national identity.

Shanghai was at the epicenter of the rising tide of mass nationalism that was to shape the country's history throughout the twentieth century and will no doubt continue to project its influence well into the twenty-first. The 1928 boycott, a retaliation to the intervention of Japanese troops in Jinan (Shandong),* presented the Guomindang authorities with their first opportunity to orchestrate public emotions, the better to harness them to their own ends. This entire experience proved extremely useful when large-scale anti-Japanese mobilization took place in 1931.

The Manchurian Incident sparked the movement for National Salvation. On September 18, 1931, Japanese forces took control of the region without encountering any resistance from Chinese forces. The students of Shanghai were the first to react. They organized lecture strikes, demonstrations, and marches and to this classic repertory added a new stratagem: they dispatched delegations to Nanjing, the capital, where the Guomindang leadership and Chiang Kai-shek personally endeavored to calm the young peoples' indignation with promises and soothing declarations delivered during interviews staged with considerable pomp.[21] The students were soon joined by the merchants, who relaunched the boycott; by the workers, who organized massive strikes in the Japanese factories of Shanghai; by journalists purveying inflammatory rhetoric; and even by female citizens, who decided to create a body of volunteers and take part in the nation's defense. Mobilization was encouraged by the local branch of the Guomindang, which at the same time tried to assume control by sponsoring an association of anti-Japanese salvation groups. This quasi-official phase of the movement culminated on September 26 in a Great Assembly

---

* The Japanese had intervened in an attempt to check the advance of Chiang Kai-shek's Nationalist forces toward the northern provinces, where the Japanese wished to impose their own influence.

of citizens (*shimin dahui*). In West Gate Stadium in the suburbs of the old Chinese town, tens of thousands of people—students, bourgeois, white-collar employees, and workers—roared out their hatred of Japan and called for the death penalty for anyone who failed to observe the boycott. The demonstration ended with a march through the main thoroughfares of the town under the benevolent gaze of the police.

Shanghai, the capital of boycotts and student protests, contained a community of 30,000 Japanese, who now feared for their interests and their lives and demanded protection from their government. Anxious to avoid any incident that might serve as a pretext for armed intervention, the Chinese municipal authorities adopted more repressive measures. Scuffles several times broke out at the Northern Railway Station between petitioning students demanding trains to carry them to Nanjing and the police, who were trying to prevent their departure. The most serious clash took place on December 9, when 15,000 students took the mayor hostage and organized a popular court to try the chief of police in absentia.

The Japanese, not without reason, nevertheless remained convinced that the Guomindang was orchestrating the boycott; and on January 28, 1932, their troops attacked the Chinese quarter of Zhabei, where for five weeks they fought against the desperate resistance mounted by the 19th Nationalist Army. Business premises, homes, soldiers, and civilians were crushed by shells, tanks, and incendiary bombs. It was in this densely populated quarter that, for the first time, the most modern and murderous weaponry was used, foreshadowing the deluges of fire and steel that were to destroy so many towns in Asia and Europe just a few years later.

If the Manchurian Incident struck at the patriotism of Shanghai, the Zhabei war wounded the town in its very fabric; but it did not overcome the activism of its citizens. Patriotic parades were replaced by support for the soldiers and aid for the wounded. Public opinion considered the truce negotiated through the League of Nations to be humiliating.* The *Life* (*Shenguo*) review, which appealed for the continuation of resistance, printed the greatest number of copies (150,000) ever produced by any

---

* Among other conditions, it prohibited the stationing of Chinese troops in Shanghai or within a 30-kilometer-wide band around the city. The prohibition remained in force until the Sino-Japanese War.

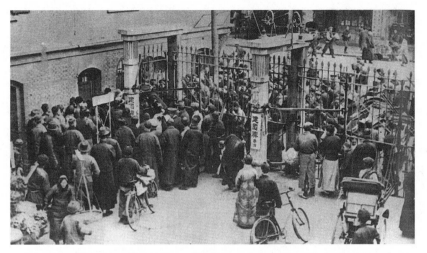

*Chinese refugees crowding around the entrance to the
international settlement in February 1932*

Shanghai or Chinese periodical. In the summer and autumn of 1932, the
boycott was vigorously resumed for brief periods. But now its principal
organizers were no longer the chambers of commerce, the guilds, and the
students but the secret societies. Persuasion gave way to intimidation;
parades were replaced by assassinations and bombs. It was as if, in the
violent and tragic atmosphere of Shanghai, any movement was fatally
destined to slip into terrorism.

The 1932 movement did not give rise to a cultural revolution, as that
of 1919 had, nor to a general strike, as that of 1925 had. But it was nevertheless important, even if its significance has often been underestimated by
Chinese historiography simply because the Communists played virtually
no part in it. Its importance, like that of earlier movements, lay in the extent of the mobilization and the active participation of every layer of the
population; its originality stemmed from the influence that it exerted upon
the central authorities through the factional struggle that it involved.

The opposition that Wang Jingwei, leader of the Guomindang left
wing, mounted against Chiang Kai-shek was a matter of personal rivalry
and regional separatism as much as ideological differences, a struggle
between rival generals as much as a political clash. The 1931 movement
nevertheless played a determining part in the success of Wang Jingwei and

his faction, which forced Chiang Kai-shek to withdraw temporarily from the government. The use of mass movements by leaders at the head of the state, fighting among themselves for power, was to remain one of the constant features of Chinese political life under the Guomindang, just as it was to be later under the Communist regime. However, the intrusion of the masses onto the political stage usually resulted in a change of personnel rather than a change of policies. That was already the case in 1931. The distancing of Chiang Kai-shek led not to China embarking on war but simply to a partial and fleeting change in the composition of teams of leaders:* Chiang Kai-shek himself soon recovered most of his powers as head of the government.

Between 1935 and 1937, the movement for National Salvation revived, more vigorous than ever. The source of this new spurt of popular nationalism was Japanese aggression in the northern provinces and plans to turn those provinces into "autonomous regions" withdrawn from Nanjing's authority and managed by puppets in the pay of Japan. Again students took the initiative in retaliating, this time in Beijing, where they mobilized on December 9, 1935. Their protest movement soon spread to Shanghai, where it was taken up by the population as a whole.

Of all the associations for National Salvation that re-formed at this point, the most active was that drawn from cultural circles, which included about 200 writers, journalists, and lawyers. In January 1936, all these associations formed a federation known as the All-Shanghai National Salvation Association League, which had 5,000 members and was capable of mobilizing between 20,000 and 30,000 demonstrators.[22] Four months later, delegates from all eighteen provinces set up the All-China League of National Salvation Associations. The leaders of these associations came from Shanghai elite groups. Most were well-known intellectuals, such as the journalist Zou Taofen (1895–1944), the banker and economist Zhang Naiqi (1897–1977), and the lawyer Shen Junru (1874–1963). On July 15, 1936, recognizing the CCP's declared desire to cooperate with the Guomindang, they published a manifesto acknowledging the failure of the

---

* In Shanghai, this renewal was important and brought more dynamic teams to power under the direction of the mayor, Wu Tiecheng (1883–1953).

policy to eradicate Communism, calling for an end to the civil war and for armed resistance to Japan and freedom of expression. This manifesto was greeted with great enthusiasm in Shanghai and other Chinese towns. However, it simply increased Chiang Kai-shek's distrust, for he regarded its publication as a CCP plot designed to manipulate the movement of National Salvation so as to achieve its own ends.[23] His suspicions were not entirely groundless. Since the adoption of the policy of a Second United Front in 1935, the Shanghai Communists had merged with the rising wave of popular nationalism. Breaking out of their social isolation, they had renewed their contacts with commercial and industrial elite groups and had infiltrated many associations for National Salvation.

All the same, mass nationalism had certainly been created by Japanese aggression, not by Communist machinations. The All-China League of National Salvation Associations acted as an autonomous organization when it financed and supported the 20,000 strikers who stopped work in the Japanese textile mills of Shanghai in November 1936. Impervious to this aspect of the situation, Chiang Kai-shek aroused the hostility of Shanghai society and the whole of urban China by disregarding all this hostility, pursuing his policy of appeasement with regard to Japan, and ordering the arrest of the seven principal leaders of the salvation movement. The imprisoned leaders, known as "the Seven Gentlemen," became national heroes;* meanwhile, the need for a policy of national reconciliation and armed resistance to Japan grew ever greater. Would this have made Chiang Kai-shek give in if the Xi'an Incident, one month later, had not forced him to do so?** We cannot be sure, for in China at that time, armed force invariably played a major part in the solution of political conflicts. However, through its widespread nature and its vigor, the movement for National Salvation certainly contributed to the creation of a political

---

* The term "gentleman" bore the very Confucian meaning of moral rectitude. "Honest man" or "virtuous man" would be closer to the meaning of the Chinese term than the time-honored translation "gentleman." The seven leaders were sentenced to prison and were released in 1937 after the outbreak of the Sino-Japanese War.
** In December 1936, Chiang Kai-shek was taken hostage in Xi'an (Shanxi) by Nationalist generals while he was on a tour of inspection in the northern provinces. After negotiations, the development and content of which remain obscure, he was released and agreed to rally to the united-front policy and armed resistance to Japan.

and psychological situation that made the Xi'an Incident and its astonishing outcome possible.

In the 1930s, the gravity of the national crisis and the imperative need to save the country caused demands for social justice, political participation, and the defense of human rights, which had been voiced in the wake of the May Fourth Movement of 1919, to be sidelined. It is true that a minority of intellectuals made the most of the nationalist mobilization to plead the cause of democracy. But those partisans of the Third Way, who sought to create a liberal and democratic option, were aspiring to improve rather than change the regime. Nevertheless, the intellectual effervescence and social agitation fueled by patriotic ardor did threaten to destabilize the Guomindang, as that party was well aware. If the mass movements of the 1930s did not lead to upheavals comparable to those of the previous decade, that was partly because the Nationalist government was on the watch. Conflating the preservation of public security and that of its own political monopoly, Chiang Kai-shek's government chose to make order its absolute priority and the mafia its preferred instrument.

CHAPTER 9

Order and Crime
(1927–1937)

U NLIKE THE COMMUNIST PARTY, which after 1949 was to endeavor to limit the role of Shanghai, the Nationalist government
established by Chiang Kai-shek in 1927 ascribed a particular importance
to the town. It is true that this government derived substantial resources
from the advances that Shanghai bankers allowed it. But it did not represent the interests of the local upper bourgeoisie, and its relations with
most of the major entrepreneurs were often conflictual. The reason Chiang
Kai-shek took such an interest in Shanghai and wanted to turn it into
a model city and a showcase for modern China was to demonstrate the
Chinese people's ability to ensure the development of the metropolis and
thereby to legitimate China's claims that the foreign concessions should
be returned to national sovereignty.

The challenge that the Nationalist government thus took on was considerable, for not only was Shanghai a bastion of imperialism, a hub of
economic modernization, and a revolutionary center but it had also become a veritable capital of crime. The restoration of public, moral, and
political order had been entrusted to a special municipality, but it clashed
with a criminal society that was competing with the administration for
control over the town's population and financial resources. Increasingly
close collaboration between the public authorities and the criminal organizations resolved this rivalry. Banditry became institutionalized and won
a measure of respectability, whereas the corrupted government fell under
the thumb of drug barons. The triumph of order, when imposed, was also
a triumph for crime.

THE MUNICIPALITY OF GREATER SHANGHAI

Right away, the national government declared its determination to take
on the twofold challenge represented by the shortage of urban equipment
and lack of security that prevailed in the Chinese quarters of Shanghai.

The efforts to improve the Chinese quarters at the end of the empire and the beginning of the republic had been abandoned in the 1920s when the warlords' regime had imposed a reign of arbitrary and violent behavior. Houses had been built in chaotic fashion that disregarded all safety regulations. The network of urban streets remained extremely poor, both in length and in quality, compared to that of the concessions. And, finally, public transport was inadequate: the Zhabei quarter had none at all, and the tram line that crossed the old walled town was not linked to those of the concessions.[1]

During this period, there was an explosion of crime. In 1927, the Chinese municipality recorded 5,000 crimes and offenses.[2] The rise of crime resulted partly from the rapid population increase. In 1930, Shanghai had about 3 million inhabitants, more or less equally divided between the concessions and the Chinese town. The lack of coordination between the police forces of the various sectors and the violence of the social upheavals that affected society during the 1920s aggravated the delinquency that usually accompanied industrialization and urbanization. All this was compounded by the spread of a popular culture from the foreign concessions that exalted gambling, sexuality, and wealth, however acquired. Disorder was also increased by the extreme disparity in wealth between a minority of well-to-do people with an opulent lifestyle and the wretchedly poor masses: in the early 1920s, the number of recent immigrants and vagrants (*liumang*) was estimated at 100,000, and this figure was increased by an indeterminate crowd of jobless people and refugees (*youmin*), whose numbers varied according to the ups and downs of economic and political circumstances.[3] Mendacity, racketeering, armed robbery, abductions, murders, and drug trafficking sustained an entire underground economy. The traditional strategies for maintaining order—such as merchant militia and the registration of homes (*baojia*)*—were unable to stem the rising tide of crime among these homeless and destitute people. The bureau of police, created in 1913 within the framework of Yuan Shikai's policies for municipal moderniza-

---

* This system of mutual responsibility dated from the tenth century. The population was divided into groups, each consisting of ten homes. Members of the group were together responsible for the respect of order and were expected to keep one another under surveillance. The local magistrate appointed group leaders.

tion, had subsequently been turned into an auxiliary in the service of the warlords, whose dirty work it carried out.

The Nationalist government wished to restore order in the town in the name of both the traditional ideas that it set out to support and the revolutionary ideal to which it was pledged. In imperial China, every new dynasty bent on establishing its power after the succession struggles had to be committed to the restoration of security and the consolidation of social stability and moral order. Chiang Kai-shek took over these objectives. As he saw it, crime and even permissive mores could lead only to political radicalism. The new regime therefore returned to a tradition in which cultural conformity was the condition and guarantee of social harmony, which was itself the ultimate aim of the exercise of authority.[4] Yet even as he adhered to this traditional morality, he proclaimed his loyalty to the teachings of Sun Yat-sen, for whom nationalism was the first of the Three Principles of the People. In the nineteenth century, the foreigners, in order to wrest privileges and concessions from the imperial government, had based their arguments on the backwardness and deficiencies of its administration. Now the time had come to put an end to all this. The restoration of order in the Chinese quarters and the modernization of public utilities and administrative services were supposed to provide proof that the Chinese were now capable of running the entire metropolis and that the presence of foreign municipalities, always undesirable, had now furthermore become unnecessary.

Chiang Kai-shek's government was thus led to set in place a municipal policy in Shanghai that combined a Confucian ideal of cultural conformity with a nationalistic plan for modernization. From 1927 on, the central government directly controlled this policy. In Shanghai, as in Nanjing, the new capital, Nationalist policy was founded above all on the principle of authority. Precisely to ensure that the exercise of that authority was effective and at the same time to modernize the local bureaucracy, as early as July 1927 the government created the Special Municipality of Shanghai. However, despite its authoritarian character, the regime was perfectly willing to involve local elite groups in its actions. This classic strategy, which had enabled the imperial authorities to overcome many moments of weakness, took a corporatist form throughout the Nanjing decade. Formally, the Shanghai elite groups lost the managerial role in public affairs that they had held since the end of the nineteenth century. Their institutions were now subordinated to the municipal authorities, and their margin of initiative was reduced. However, over the following years they did manage to preserve a degree of power within a number of semiofficial organizations because the government, with a view to promoting the penetration of the state apparatus into society, favored interactions and an interplay of mutual influences.

The powers of the new municipality extended to Greater Shanghai,* which incorporated not only the Chinese quarters of the town but also many of the neighboring villages and rural zones.[5] For the very first time, a single administration's authority extended to all the various sectors of the Chinese town: the walled town and its suburbs to the south, Zhabei to the north, the workers' suburbs to the west, and on the opposite bank of the Huangpu, the as-yet-scattered beginnings of Pudong.

The mayor, appointed by the Nanjing government, held extensive powers. He directed both the administrative services and those provided by the police and was also in command of the military units stationed in the town. He appointed and fired municipal officials and was responsible only to the central authorities. The new municipality enjoyed great freedom of action, the more so given that the Municipal Council, to which the law in theory entrusted a legislative role and controlling powers over the executive, was never elected. In its place, there was a council whose members were appointed by the mayor and whose role was purely consultative. In the early years, the local Guomindang apparatus, which was full of young radical militants, tried hard to intervene in municipal politics and force it to conform to the revolutionary ideal championed by the party, but it soon desisted. Thus, Nanjing, or sometimes even Chiang Kai-shek in person, dealt with any contentious situations that arose.

The modernization of the municipal administration resulted in improvements in its personnel, despite the role that clientism played in re-

---

* The concessions and the Chinese quarters occupied areas of 33 and 30 square kilometers, respectively, but the total area of the Municipality of Greater Shanghai covered as much as 572 square kilometers.

cruitment.[6] The thirty or so directors responsible for central services and the major departments all held diplomas of higher education acquired either in China or abroad. At a lower hierarchical level, graduates from local universities or secondary schools still made up half of a staff that was 1,500 strong. A typical figure in this new administration was the Cantonese Wu Tiecheng (1888–1953), who had been educated in a Baptist missionary school and at Meiji University in Tokyo. Since 1910, he had been associated with Sun Yat-sen's revolutionary activities and in the early 1920s had been director of the municipal police force of Canton.[*] In 1929, he became a member of the Central Executive Committee of the Guomindang, where he enjoyed a close relationship with Chiang Kai-shek. He was a man of considerable authority who brought both energy and diplomacy to the exercise of his responsibilities. The time that he spent in the Shanghai town hall, from 1932 to 1936, coincided with the period when major municipal changes were introduced.

Taxation was included in the modernization of the administration. In 1927, there were dozens of different taxes that produced very little revenue. First, the basis of direct taxation—essentially the tax on dwellings—was founded on out-of-date information that took no account of the steep rise in rents during the 1920s. Second, the collection of the many indirect taxes (on vehicles, boats, abattoirs, the sale of tobacco and alcohol, and so on) was customarily farmed out to the professional guilds, which endeavored to prevent taxes from rising and sometimes misappropriated them. In order to extract indispensable resources, the Municipal Finance Bureau began reforming this archaic system. It brought the basis of the tax on dwellings up to date and made the rate uniform, canceled all tax-farming contracts with the guilds, and entrusted the collection of indirect taxes to municipality agents. The taxpayers gave these reforms a cold reception because they resulted in higher levies in many cases and suddenly admitted numerous officials to domains that the guilds had always considered their own; the reforms upset long-established customs

---

[*] When Sun Yat-sen was trying to consolidate his revolutionary base in Guangdong, the municipal government of Canton was under the responsibility of a very keen team of young Guomindang cadres, mostly trained in the United States and under the leadership of Sun Yat-sen's son, Sun Fo.

and violated long-standing privileges. By resorting now to negotiation, now to police constraint, the municipal government managed to increase its fiscal revenue by about 25% per year, but even this was not enough to cover its expenses.

The modernization of the police force was another of the municipality's priorities. To this end, the Public Security Bureau (*Gong'an ju*) was set up. This held authority over 3,500 men, most of whom had served under the previous regime, led by young officers trained in the military academies of North China or in Japanese police colleges.[7] The objective was to create forces of law and order that were armed with modern weapons, disciplined, and imbued with a sense of mission and a professionalism that would repair the extremely low opinion of the Chinese police that the local population and foreign residents held. The Public Security Bureau introduced many new training courses, put together an arsenal of 4,000 firearms, and gave its agents a compulsory uniform and a quasi-military set of rules and regulations. It revised the geographical distribution and hierarchy of police stations and provided the latter with telephone equipment. Despite the heavy toll that these reforms placed on the municipal budget, they were relentlessly pushed through. The importance that the Shanghai authorities, like those of Nanjing, attached to them was reflected in the appointment of prestigious leaders such as General Cai Jingjun as head of the Public Security Bureau.*

The creation of a new civic center in Jiangwan in the outer northern suburbs (halfway between Shanghai and the port of Wusong on the Yangzi) was symbolic of the determination that drove the municipal government to modernize and to shake off foreign control. Town planning was inspired by American models but combined elements of national architecture. The town hall premises were first put into use in 1933, and most of the municipal services were progressively transferred there.** The New Life campaign was also orchestrated from Jiangwan, dubbed "a district model."

---

* This Cantonese, who held office from 1935 to 1937, had belonged to the first class of the Huangpu Military Academy, founded in Canton by Sun Yat-sen with the assistance of Soviet advisers. After completing his military training in Germany, Italy, and the USSR, in 1926–1927 Cai Jingjun took part in the National Revolutionary Army's Northern Expedition.
** Building in Jiangwan continued up until the start of the Sino-Japanese War in 1937.

MORAL ORDER AND SOCIAL CONTROL:
THE NEW LIFE

The imposition of cultural uniformity (*wenhua tongzhi*) upon Chinese society and the quest for an ideological consensus were aimed as much at moral values and social norms as at political opinions, everyday behavior, and militant activities. The authorities resorted to constraints: the 1928 law on counterrevolutionaries punished as a crime the diffusion of all doctrines that ran contrary to the Three Principles of the People, and the 1930 law relating to the press gave censors full powers to condemn the authors of publications hostile to the regime. But in line with the educative mission with which the state authorities in China had always believed themselves to be invested, the Guomindang regime was also keen to educate the people and rally hearts and minds. This was the goal of the New Life campaign that Chiang Kai-shek and a group of officers in his entourage launched in early 1934.

Much has been written about the nature of this movement to promote a national cultural renaissance. It was essentially conservative and condemned Western values—liberalism, individualism, democracy—that the intellectuals of the May Fourth Movement had tried to adapt to China. It called for the restoration of Confucian norms and extolled respect for morality and the social hierarchies and also the primacy of collective interests over those of individuals or particular social groups. However, the movement did not wish to be seen simply as a return to the past, and it condemned certain obscurantist practices. It claimed to be responding to the economic and social problems posed by modernization and derived part of its inspiration from Fascism, which Chiang Kai-shek greatly admired. The discourse of the New Life movement was replete with familiar themes of Hitlerian and Mussolinian rhetoric: it exalted the self-sacrifice of individuals and total loyalty to the leader and the nation. What has been labeled "Confucian Fascism" emerged from this combination of cultural reaction and conservative modernization.[8]

Within the Guomindang, the secret organization of the Blue Shirts, composed of an elite group of militants fanatically devoted to Chiang Kai-shek who operated through the mediation of a multitude of national and local associations, orchestrated the campaign for popular mobilization.

Official propaganda did not find such favorable terrain in Shanghai as in the interior provinces, but it was imbued with an intensity to match the challenge that the cosmopolitan and permissive culture of the metropolis represented to the regime. The campaign was launched in April 1934, with the active support of the Public Security Bureau and the municipality. Parades and huge meetings followed one another in quick succession. The Shanghai New Life Movement Acceleration Association had soon recruited 5,000 members.[9] The authorities seemed to particularly value professors as partners; many joined the movement, whether under professional pressure or to promote career ambitions. Their docility contrasted strongly with the general reserve or hostility of writers, filmmakers, and journalists, who were the main targets of the movement and its censorship.[10]

The Blue Shirts also infiltrated student circles, rallying many pupils in the major scientific schools to their cause. On campuses and in schools and colleges the militarization that the New Life advocated was most ostentatious: uniforms were sported, physical training and obedience were encouraged, and troops of Boy Scouts were formed. Aided by the police and the municipality, the supporters of the New Life endeavored to extend this discipline to the urban population and to implement a code of good conduct that was summed up in the Ninety-five Rules. Shanghainese were told not to drink, smoke, or dance; to be frugal, honest, and clean; not to spit on the sidewalks; to stand up straight; to button up their clothing meticulously, and so on. This civic catechism was no laughing matter, for it paved the way for the terror that the Blue Shirts would later wield against the "rotten elements" of society and other "traitors."

Dai Li (1895–1946), who also headed the Military Statistics Bureau (*Juntong*), directed the Blue Shirt special services.* The collaboration between Dai Li and the chief of the Shanghai police, Cai Jingjun, spawned a veritable state terrorism that targeted liberal intellectuals in particular. On November 14, 1934, Shi Liangcai, a member of the League for the Protection of Human Rights, editor of the major daily newspaper, *Shenbao*, and president of the council of the Chinese municipality, was struck down on a road close to Shanghai as he was returning from a holiday in

---

* The Military Statistics Bureau was one of the regime's main intelligence services.

his car with his wife and children. The complicity of the police enabled the assassins to escape. To calm the public indignation that followed, Chiang Kai-shek sent a telegram of condolence to the family of the victim, whom he himself had selected for the killers. Like many other mobilization campaigns imposed from above, the New Life campaign ran up against the skepticism of the population of Shanghai. As the months passed, its slogans became increasingly vacuous, and the movement turned into a pure formality before fading away entirely at the end of 1935.

THE INTERPENETRATION OF STATE AND SOCIETY

Chinese tradition erected no institutional barriers between state and society. The pressure that authorities exerted in order to penetrate and control society had varied from one period to another, but society and its elite groups had frequently rallied to the directives of those in power, embracing good government and social harmony as their ideal. What was involved was not so much cooperation but rather a phenomenon of porosity. Whereas in the West, historians tended to analyze relations between state and society in terms of confrontation, in China state and society interacted rather than clashed. Since the collapse of the empire, the situation had certainly evolved, particularly in Shanghai in the 1920s when new institutions—chambers of commerce, employers' associations, workers' trade unions—had all laid claim to autonomy and power. But from 1927 onward, these seeds of a civil society were smothered by the Guomindang, whose Fascist ideology prioritized an organic concept of society and placed the interests of the collectivity above those of individuals or particular social classes. As has been suggested previously, this produced a convergence between Confucianism and corporatism, but the ultimate objectives that those two assigned to the symbiosis between state and society were not the same: Confucianism sought harmony between human society and the natural order; corporatism was designed to increase the power of the national state.

However, Chinese society's propensity to allow itself to be penetrated by official power did not necessarily lead to more effective state control. Despite modernization and increasing interference from the municipal bureaucracy, and despite the propaganda campaigns and recourse to violence, Shanghai society managed to preserve some room for maneuver.

Even if it did not want or was unable to oppose official directives openly, it often succeeded in eluding or evading them, and when it did knuckle under, it did not do so without negotiating compromises and imposing conditions of its own.

Historians of imperial China have for many years analyzed this interplay of influences through the role played by scholar-elite groups that included both agents of the authorities in power and local elites who represented the interests of their respective communities. Such situations persisted in the republican period, even in Shanghai. But historians, being more interested in class struggles or the emergence of a civil society, have not bothered to examine them. The Seven Great Trade Unions officially recognized and controlled by the Shanghai Municipal Bureau of Social Affairs and the local branch of the Guomindang were for a long time labeled "yellow" because their activities were not part of the revolutionary proletarian struggle. The representativeness and combativeness that they demonstrated in the early years of the regime were completely ignored.[11] In similar fashion, no attention was paid to many Shanghai workers' support for the regime's nationalistic ideology and its paternalist policies, nor to the role played in the workers' struggles by traditional associations such as fraternities or mutual aid societies and so on.

Likewise, the new professional associations of bankers, professors, engineers, doctors, and lawyers did not inevitably become the main support of an emerging civil society, as some historians seek to suggest: they were coopted by the Guomindang, which integrated their patriotic and modernizing projects into its official programs. This astonishing combination of state penetration on the one hand and, on the other, the preservation of an autonomous community space or even the creation of a space for citizenship have recently been the subject of an illuminating study.[12] In order to strengthen their control over native-place associations, the authorities made it compulsory from 1928 on for the associations to register with the municipal government and the local branch of the Guomindang. The associations did not protest this requirement but deliberately responded to it slowly: by 1936, fewer than half (twenty-seven of the sixty-five associations in Shanghai) had complied with the law. Their inertia and discreet evasion of the directives enabled them to divert the impact of state power and find compromises. Officials and members of the police force undertook to keep the native-place associations, to which many of them belonged, under surveillance, but at the same time they defended the associations' cause to the authorities responsible for their supervision. The inroads that official interventions opened up within social organizations always allowed for communication in both directions. The Bureau of Social Affairs and the Guomindang insisted that the associations swear loyalty to the Three Principles of the People: dependence on the regime, designed to guarantee the docility of the social organizations, by the same token conferred upon them a greater legitimacy. The partially victorious resistance with which native-place associations and other social organizations opposed fiscal reforms testified to the limits of state authority.

During the Nanjing decade, the idiosyncratic nature of the loyalties upon which the existence of the native-place associations rested became less pronounced. The associations resorted to various strategies to create a veritable space for citizenship. They manipulated the official rhetoric, exploiting the theme of local autonomy, for example, so as to present themselves not only as institutions committed to the defense of corporate interests but also as elements on which to found the future constitutional state that Sun Yat-sen had envisaged.* They chose as their leaders figures in the public eye who would, they hoped, protect them and upon whom they in return conferred greater "face" and consequently greater influence. In some situations, they proved themselves skillful at mobilizing public opinion and organizing press campaigns and petitions. Whatever the circumstances, they always made use of the alibi of nationalism, basing the legitimacy of their claims not upon the defense of human rights but upon their duty to work for the salvation of the country.

The control that the Guomindang established over Shanghai society thus appears to have been less absolute than the absence of any opposition based on principles seems to suggest. Although that control became much tighter after the 1920s, when the declining power of the state had

---

* According to Sun Yat-sen, preparation for the acceptance of democratic processes had to be learned at a local level, within the framework of an autonomous regime, and the construction of a constitutional state was something that had to progress upward from the grass roots.

given up intervening in social institutions, it certainly came up against purely pragmatic limits, which suggests that the degree to which official authority was actually exercised is questionable.

AN UNEVEN BALANCE SHEET

Compared with its declared objectives—modernization, reestablishment of public order, reconquest of the foreign concessions—the achievements of this municipal management look somewhat slight. True, progress was made in the improvement of the urban space. The road network was extended, the system of public transport acquired a bus service to Zhabei, and the tram line from the old Chinese town was linked with the tram lines in the concessions. The treatment and supply of water as well as electricity production were improved. The municipality also scored a number of successes in the unification of the schooling system, introduction of hygienic practices, and development of sanitary infrastructures.

Another point in the municipal government's favor, in a domain strongly supported by the central government, was a certain decline in foreign influence in Shanghai. The status of the concessions was not reversed, but the Chinese authorities did manage to regain some rights they had lost through abusive practices. In 1930, the Mixed Court of the international settlement and that of the French concession gave way to local and provincial courts that were integrated into the Chinese judicial system. The municipality also succeeded in strengthening its control over External Roads, where it set up police stations and began to levy tolls.* It waged a war of attrition against the foreign concessions, encouraging incidents and difficulties and adopting an ever more restrictive interpretation of treaty clauses or sometimes pretending quite simply to be unaware of them. Realism and prudence dictated that the foreigners should avoid a showdown. But with every compromise made, their privileges were being whittled

---

* The Shanghai Municipal Council, to which the Chinese government had since 1898 denied the right to extend the territory of the international settlement, had adopted a policy of indirect extension by constructing to the north and the east of the settlement about 70 kilometers of roads and by assuming the right to police and collect taxes in the territory crossed by those roads. This sector of "External Roads" constituted an illegal extension of the concession's territory. Many fine villas had been built there and, before the war, served as residences for both Chinese elites and foreigners.

away. By these means, the Chinese authorities acquired a veritable right of surveillance over the concessions' affairs. In particular, they began to tax the large foreign companies and insist on the registration of missionary schools and colleges attended by Chinese pupils, as well as registration of Chinese and foreign newspapers.

Nevertheless, the achievements did not measure up to the proclaimed ambitions by any means. Poverty, unhealthy conditions, vice, and crime continued to reign, and the harassment inflicted on the concessions poisoned the lives of the foreign residents but had less effect on their economic interests and the bases of the foreign presence. Could the Chinese municipality have done better? Plenty of reasons can be found to explain the mediocre results obtained. It did not have time to implement the vast program it had set itself. Many of its actions were paralyzed by the internal divisions among those in power, by the rivalries between the municipal government and the local branch of the party, and by the struggles among various factions within the Guomindang, struggles in which a number of mayors became embroiled. The close links between Shanghai and Nanjing did not always serve local interests. By embracing Chiang Kai-shek's anti-Communist hysteria and incorporating into the local police force Dai Li's officers and counterespionage agents, the municipal government sacrificed the fight against crime to the hunt for the Reds.[13]

Above all, despite the regular increase in tax revenues and more and more loans, the municipality's financial resources were inadequate.[14] This was partly the municipal government's own fault, for its overstaffing (2,200 agents for the central services alone in 1935) was not justified by the needs of management but simply resulted from uncoordinated recruitment, which was carried out by each of the various offices on the basis of personal recommendations, with every office director intent on slotting in his own relatives and friends. However, the Nanjing government also had a hand in the financial difficulties of the municipality since it off-loaded onto it many missions that were the responsibility of the central authorities. Thus, the municipality was made to pay for the upkeep of the 3,000 men in the unit of peacekeepers whose task was to defend the town after the truce with the Japanese in 1932 had forbidden regular armed units to be stationed in Shanghai or its suburbs. Completely unaided by the central government, the municipality also had to cope with the grave crisis resulting from the Japanese aggression in Zhabei and the town's northern suburbs in 1932. It had to help the fighting men, tend the wounded, and look after the refugees, as thousands of homes and shops had been destroyed, hundreds of businesses and schools had disappeared, public equipment was ruined, and half a million workers had been reduced to unemployment. Despite the efforts of private initiatives, the tasks of reconstruction and helping to relaunch the economy constituted a heavy drain on municipal resources that had already been depleted by tax revenues lost as a result of the war destruction.

Such circumstances certainly suffice to explain the weakness of municipal action. But there was another, even more formidable obstacle, namely, the existence of an omnipresent criminal society that competed with the municipal government for control of the town, its economy, and its population.

THE TRIUMPH OF CRIME

Under the imperial regime, the state had never strictly controlled Chinese society. As a result of insufficient numbers of officials and the vastness of the territory, large gaps were left in the administrative network, and within those gaps not only lineages, religious communities, circles of scholars, and merchant guilds were left free to operate but so, too, were bands of brigands and secret societies, the refuges of social dropouts and outlaws. Shanghai, where repeated waves of immigrants driven by poverty from the countryside fed demographic growth, constituted an ambience particularly favorable to the formation of an urban underworld that ignored public authority and was a law unto itself. Not all the destitute became gangsters, but inevitably, without protection or under constraint, they provided the criminal gangs with their clients and auxiliaries. The number of gangsters belonging to secret societies in the 1920s has been calculated at about 100,000.

At the end of the 1920s and particularly in the 1930s, the criminal organizations of Shanghai infiltrated the political and administrative apparatus of the town, gaining ascendancy over the state authorities that they claimed to be serving. The Triads and the Society of Elder Brothers, which had actively supported the Taiping rebellion in the nineteenth century, continued to exercise their influence through the activities of the Red Gang. However, the latter, severely penalized by the central authorities because of the role that it had played in the revolutionary uprising of 1911, had lost considerable ground and, in the early years of the republic, had faced increasingly strong competition from the Green Gang.[15]

Although it portrayed itself as heir to the sects of sailors and smugglers of the Great Canal, the Green Gang had in truth appeared in Shanghai in the late nineteenth century. Its existence was founded on cooperation among several dozen "godfathers," each of whom dominated his own group of accomplices. Relations among the various centers of power represented by these little chieftains were unstable. At the beginning of the 1920s, the town was divided among three main groups. Gu Zhuxuan (1885–1956) operated in Zhabei and Hangkou, where he controlled teahouses and theaters, recruiting his members among the crowds of rickshaw men and other coolies, who were all natives of Subei (northern Jiangsu), as was Gu himself. The Big Eight Mob (*Da Ba gu dang*) controlled the opium trade, at that time centered in the international settlement. The French concession was the domain of Huang Jinrong (1868–1958), known as Huang-the-pockmarked because of the scars on his face left by a childhood bout of smallpox. Huang combined his protection activities and racketeering (opium dens, gambling houses, and prostitution) with detective work for the French police.

The Green Gang modeled its organization on that of the lineages and, like them, organized its staff on a generational basis. New members had to be recommended by older ones, and the initiation ceremony was inspired by Buddhist rites of purification. Members were required to respect the code of honor that, harking back to the tradition of knights errant, exalted courage, loyalty, and an imposed secrecy. Despite such borrowings from tradition, though, the Green Gang was a specifically Shanghai organization whose rise and success were linked to the urban context in which it developed.

The presence of three autonomous and rival courts of justice (respectively representing the two foreign concessions and the Chinese town) facilitated the activity of these criminal gangs, so that simply crossing a

An opium den circa 1900 (Shirmann Collection)

road was enough to move from one sector into another and elude police proceedings. Furthermore, the indirect imperialistic practices of the Western powers afforded the criminal organizations extra advantages. Both the British and the French used Chinese collaborators to maintain order: the former because they were determined to develop their economic interests while limiting their political investment and military commitments as much as possible; the latter because they dreamed of administering their concession just like a metropolitan *sous-prefecture* but did not have the means to do so.

Just as the great foreign companies subcontracted many commercial and financial operations to their compradors, the police of the international settlement and the French concession entrusted many of the tasks of public security to Chinese agents or detectives. And most of the Chinese police in the concessions belonged to the Green Gang, either because they were already members when they were recruited or because they joined later. If well managed, this double membership—of both the police and the mafia—was beneficial to their careers. They became well-informed connoisseurs of criminal circles and were therefore highly appreciated by their hierarchical superiors, while at the same time they acquired greater prestige in the eyes of their compatriots and were able to devote themselves to racketeering and extortion with perfect impunity.

OPIUM AND "PROSPERITY DERIVED FROM CRIME"

Like all mafias the world over, the secret societies of Shanghai lived off the exploitation of vice.[16] Smuggling, gambling, and prostitution were all illegal activities, but secret societies "protected" them; and as protectors, they claimed their dues. In the 1920s, however, they increasingly devoted themselves to opium trafficking, which provided huge financial profits. The Green Gang owed its rise to power and the consolidation of that power to its hold over opium trafficking.

At this time, opium played a role in Shanghai similar to that of alcohol in Chicago in the prohibition period. In both cases, the prohibition of a legal trade at a time when the demand from consumers was huge stimulated smuggling and allowed gangsters to gain control of a most lucrative market. The major opium-smuggling outfit in Shanghai went by the name of the Three Prosperities Company (Sanxin gongsi), a modest title, for what this smuggling showered upon those who engaged in it and directed it amounted to not just three, but a thousand and one prosperities.

Following the wars waged over the opening up of China, imports of opium, which were legalized in 1860, were until the end of the nineteenth century one of the principal stimulants to the commercial development of Shanghai. But little by little they were replaced by the production of opium in China itself. At the beginning of the twentieth century, the imperial government and the foreign powers reached an agreement to apply a policy of progressive suppression, which in 1919 culminated in total prohibition of the production and importation of the drug. That prohibition led to a fantastic rise in the price of contraband opium; trafficking in opium was monopolized by a coalition formed among the local militarists, merchants from Chaozhou (Guangdong), and secret societies. The militarists, first and foremost Lu Yongxiang, the Zhejiang warlord, ensured the drug's safe transport to Shanghai; the Chaozhou merchants were responsible for stocks and distribution; in the town itself, Green Gang henchmen protected deliveries from police interventions and attacks by rival gangs. The international settlement became the center of opium trafficking; the Big Eight Mob exploited its complicity with the concession's police force so as to establish its preeminence over the Green Gang's other centers of power. But the scale of what was financially at stake ignited envy and fueled conflicts among the warlords and rivalries within the Green Gang.

In 1924, the defeat of Lu Yongxiang and the vigorous campaign to eradicate opium trafficking waged by the authorities of the international settlement forced the smugglers to transfer their base to the French concession, in which the Chaozhou merchants now gathered. From then on, it was Huang Jinrong's turn to profit from his special relations with the foreign police and assert his power within the Green Gang.

The Three Prosperities Company now "protected" the twenty-one businesses devoted to the refining and distribution of opium that were established in the concession. Heading this company were Huang Jinrong himself and his lieutenants Zhang Xiaolin (1877–1946) and Du Yuesheng (1888–1951). The latter appears to have rapidly understood the importance of opium trafficking, upon which he proceeded to found his extraordinary career. This illiterate peasant from Pudong lived the life of a petty delinquent on the wharves of Shanghai before becoming involved with Huang Jinrong and his wife, whom he served as an odd-job man and to whom he addressed a filial devotion to the end of his days.* Du negotiated with the leaders of rival gangs and the French local police for the safety of opium deliveries in the concession. The jeweler's shop that he bought in the rue du Consulat became the smuggling headquarters. To reward him for his services, Huang Jinrong entrusted him with the protection of a number of gambling halls and opium dens also situated in the French concession. Zhang Xiaolin acted as a mediator with the Chinese politico-military authorities and maintained contacts with the new warlord, Sun Chuanfang.

---

* Madame Gui, formerly a brothel keeper, was very active in criminal circles, in which she was often called upon to represent her husband given that his functions within the French police force obliged him to observe a certain discretion. Madame Gui herself ran the garbage collection business in the French concession, thereby acquiring the title "Queen of the Shit" (fen dawang).

Du Yuesheng, head of the Green Gang (courtesy of Qian Zonghao)

Initially, the system set up by Huang Jinrong took over that instituted by the Big Eight Mob in the international settlement, and it functioned on the basis of the corruption of individuals. The enormous profits derived by the Three Prosperities Company (around 56 million Chinese dollars per year) made it possible to pay out large sweeteners to both the Chinese military and the French police.[17] The consul-general, Auguste Wilden, complained, "In 1922, I had to license the staff of an entire station (consisting of one sergeant and four agents), who were receiving from the opium merchants regular handouts varying from 500 to 1,000 dollars each month; in return, they were requested simply to turn a blind eye."[18] However, in 1925 the purchase of protection in the French concession took a quasi-institutional turn, when a deal was made to farm out the opium. Some of the concession's leaders had become convinced that the prohibition policy was doomed to failure and that it was simply encouraging smuggling and corruption. They invoked the warning issued by figures who were above all suspicion: "The inspector general of the [Maritime] Customs suggests purely and simply abolishing prohibition and setting up a state monopoly.

I am of the same opinion: as long as opium is produced in China as it is at present, . . . with the complicity of the officials themselves, prohibitions on consumption will be illusory."[19] They also referred to the example of Indochina, where state control of opium was able to feed the colonial budget. But the establishment of such a monopoly clashed with Chinese public opinion and with the campaigning of English and American Protestant missionaries in the international settlement.

The negotiations between the French municipality and the Three Prosperities Company thus retained an official air. As far as can be ascertained, the agreement confirmed the monopoly of the Three Prosperities Company, which obtained even greater protection from the French police in return for an annual payment estimated at 10 million dollars.[20] After this arrangement, Du Yuesheng's influence in the concession began to eclipse that of the group of Chinese Catholic elites from the old Shanghai families: as protégés of the missionaries, they had up to this point been councillors regularly heeded by the consuls and were the customary mediators between the municipal administration and the local population.

Two years later, the April 12 coup, in which Du Yuesheng played a decisive role, and the compromises upon which the authorities of the French concession now entered upset the existing equilibrium. The rise of Du Yuesheng gathered speed: his authority now ousted that of the Catholic notables and rivaled that of the French authorities.

THE GREEN GANG AND THE "FRENCH CONNECTION" (1927–1932)

The Green Gang's influence in the French concession peaked at the turn of the 1920s.[21] The reign of organized crime was facilitated by the lack of foresight and authority of the new consul-general, Edgar Koechlin, who had succeeded Naggiar in December 1928 and proved incapable of resisting the pressure applied by Du Yuesheng and his paid accomplices in the municipal administration and the police force.

Du Yuesheng was by now a well-known figure. Not only had he become the principal leader of the Green Gang, but Chiang Kai-shek, in recognition of services rendered, conferred upon him the honorary title of councillor, which gave him an aura of respectability. In the French concession, his power increasingly overrode that of the authorities whose obliging auxiliary he used to be. By dint of corruption and force, Du Yuesheng was now recruiting his allies among the concession's principal administrators and notables. He was a friend of Étienne Fiori, head of the Municipal Guard,* and also of Marcel Verdier, director of municipal services. His accomplices also included the lawyer Maurice Frédéric Armand Du Pac de Marsoulies. This refined and cultivated former colonial civil servant, who was popular with both his compatriots and other foreign residents in the concession, tarnished his reputation by engaging in dubious activities—organizing lotteries, trafficking in arms and opium, and speculating in property—that he claimed to be in the public interest. Since 1924, Du Pac had been waging a war of attrition against the consulate-general, from which he wished to wrest command of the Municipal Guard. He dreamed of a police force under the control of the easily influenced Municipal Council that he could use to serve his own interests. It was largely to thwart those ambitions that Naggiar had replaced the elected Municipal Council in 1927 by a provisional commission that he appointed, from which he took great care to exclude Du Pac.[22]

With the support of such influential friends, Du Yuesheng had no difficulty in getting his monopoly over the concession's opium trade renewed. By the end of the 1920s, the drug was being bought and sold openly. Only the resolute opposition of the British and the Americans prevented the French authorities from accepting further propositions from Du: for example, the increase and regularization of payments to the municipality and its principal leaders in exchange for nonapplication of anti-opium legislation by the concession's Mixed Court. The complicity that linked the municipality to the Green Gang continued. The protection pact eventually covered half a dozen large casinos and a multitude of smaller gambling joints.

But Du Yuesheng's strength did not lie solely in the distribution of bribes and sweeteners. His influence over the concession's merchant guilds and workers' trade unions ensured that he became the unavoidable mediator in all social conflicts, and he pacified or inflamed these strictly in accordance with his own interests. Social peace depended on him, and consequently, so did the prosperity of local businesses.

---

* This was the official name of the police force.

In 1926–1927, he had managed to prevent the revolutionary strikes from spreading to the concession. In the years that followed he remained Mr. Good-Guy, without whose intervention the slightest work stoppage was likely to degenerate into a major incident. The strikes that broke out in the French Tram Company in 1928 and 1930 spotlighted the importance of Du's mediation for the French authorities and businesses and the Green Gang's increasingly firm grip on the workers' organizations in the concession.[23]

The French Tramways and Electric Light Company, which supplied water and electricity as well as public transport (bus, trolley bus, and tram), was one of the concession's principal businesses. It employed 1,700 workers who, until the formation of a trade union in 1925, belonged to a multitude of fraternities that their foremen and the Green Gang manipulated. After the 1927 coup, that trade union was purged of most of its Communist members but remained active within the framework of the official reformism encouraged by the Shanghai branch of the Guomindang. This somewhat diminished the Green Gang's influence. However, as the years passed, the Chinese municipality began intervening in the social conflicts that continually set the trade union in opposition to the company, and this gave Du Yuesheng the chance to set up triangular mediations. In the eyes of the French employers and officials, Du Yuesheng appeared as an indispensable courtier, the comprador who could guarantee public order in the concession. Meanwhile, public opinion and the Guomindang regarded him as a patriotic notable. Thanks to his mediations, the municipal government of Greater Shanghai regained the right of surveillance over a territory that was formally placed outside its authority.

Soon, Du Yuesheng began to establish closer links with the Chinese municipality and the local apparatus of the Guomindang without, however, ceasing to make himself indispensable to the French authorities. This explains the complexity of his maneuvers at the time of the two great strikes that paralyzed the French Tramways and Electric Light Company in December 1928 and June 1930. The situation was certainly not an easy one to control. Encouraged by certain radical elements in the Guomindang and even more by the small Communist cell that had survived within the trade union, the strikers pushed for radical wage increases and improvements for the trade union that the French employers were not prepared to accept. The slightest clash between French employers and Chinese workers threatened to escalate into an anti-imperialist movement and to give rise to solidarities both within the concession (for example, at the time of the strike of municipal employees in 1930) and among workers in the international settlement and the Chinese town. In addition, factions within the Guomindang and internal squabbles were always prompt to exploit or, on occasion, ignite clashes in the French concession. Du Yuesheng used prudence and brokered compromises. When it was a matter of pacifying the workers' anger, he was not sparing with his dollars: he would finance strike funds and from time to time take the place of the French employers and pay out compensation money. But when the right moment came, he would shatter resistance by appealing to the French police, still packed with disciples of his former boss and loyal ally, Huang Jinrong, or to the henchmen of the Green Gang. Du Yuesheng was also clever at dividing the trade-union organization, the better to control it. He brought those who ran the trams—the conductors and ticket inspectors—under his control, abandoning the mechanics to the leadership of the Communist Xu Anmei, whose arrest he eventually secured in late 1931.[24]

By this time, Du Yuesheng's power in the concession was no longer a secret force: he was recognized by the Chinese residents, who regarded him as their leader, and also by the French authorities, who bestowed official titles and functions upon the bandit. To acquire this new respectability, he had had to oust the consulate's former advisers, the Catholic Chinese notables in whose eyes he remained nothing but a gangster and a dangerous disseminator of vice. To get what he wanted, Du Yuesheng would stop at nothing, including the abduction in 1929 of one of the most respected longtime advisers, Wu Tingrong. Yet that very year the consul-general showed no qualms about appointing him to the Provisional Municipal Commission. However, far from appearing to be a lackey of the colonial authorities, Du adopted the role of spokesman for a Chinese community whose Nationalist claims he embraced. To establish his legitimacy, he made use of the concession's Chinese Ratepayers' Association. He demanded and in 1930 obtained from the consul-general the association's right to elect Chinese members of the Provisional Municipal Commission.*

Master as he was of opium trafficking, controlling both the police and the underworld, capable of unleashing or calming the anger of workers, leader of the notables and respected by the Guomindang, Du Yuesheng seemed the man who really held the power in the French concession. The authorities of the international settlement and the British consulate-general were concerned at this crisis of authority, which made the French concession a weak link in Western imperialism in Shanghai. Paris was also alarmed at such a degeneration of republican institutions. Operations to regain the upper hand were facilitated by the state of emergency proclaimed in the concession at the time of the Japanese attack on Shanghai in January 1932. The authority of Rear-Admiral Herr, commander of the French fleet in the Far East, now replaced that of the civil administration, and new, experienced officials of probity were appointed: Jacques Meyrier as consul-general and Louis Fabre as chief of police.** In February, Du Yuesheng was invited to resign from the Provisional Municipal Commission, and the fight against opium was vigorously relaunched.

The French authorities' reconquest of the concession was not achieved without resistance. In early March, the friends of Du Yuesheng who had not managed to protect him, the former consul-general Edgard Koechlin and the lawyer Du Pac de Marsoulies, both died within a few days, struck down by illnesses as sudden as they were mysterious. An unexpected strike suddenly broke out in the French Tramways and Electric Light Company on the eve of the national festival of July 14. The new authorities were forced to compromise, and Du Yuesheng departed in glory. He was obliged to move his Three Prosperities Company out of the concession, but the French police protected the transfer of his stocks of opium to the old Chinese town.

---

* The consul-general continued to appoint the other French and foreign (but not the Chinese) members of the commission.
** Both had already served in similar roles in the French concession of Tianjin. Meyrier was familiar with the situation in the Shanghai concession, where he had served first as consul, then as acting consul-general.

THE TAKEOVER OF THE CHINESE TOWN

Du Yuesheng now concentrated his operations in the Chinese town, and he did so with the active support of the municipality and the Guomindang. Cooperation between the Green Gang and the authorities was now so close that it had the air of a veritable symbiosis at the local level and, to a certain degree, at the national level. Du and the regime shared the revenue from the opium trafficking. This revenue made it possible to finance the struggle against Communist guerrillas, which was Chiang Kai-shek's first priority. Du Yuesheng used the money to take control of the town by buying himself social and political respectability. His transfiguration into a great Shanghai elite and a luminary of the regime reflected the growing discrepancy between discourse and reality. Moral order, so actively promoted by the regime, was embodied by a gangster, while the offices responsible for suppressing opium facilitated the sale of the drug. The respectable bandit and the criminal government fought side by side in defense of their own respective interests.

From 1932 on, the "French connection" was thus replaced by the Guomindang's and Du Yuesheng's co-management of an official monopoly over the distribution of opium. In theory, the political prohibition remained in effect (it dated from 1919); indeed, it was even tightened under the influence of certain members of the government such as T. V. Song. Officially, the purpose of the governmental monopoly that accompanied prohibition was to regulate the consumption of the drug, the better to reduce it. In reality, however, the government exploited that monopoly so as to preserve its exclusive access to the profits from all opium trafficking. In Shanghai, this monopoly was farmed out to Du Yuesheng in exchange for a monthly payment of 3 million dollars to the Ministry of Finances.[25] The protection costs paid over and above this to local authorities (the town hall, the police, and the garrison) were valued at hundreds of thousands of dollars per month, but profits more than compensated for that outlay.

Shanghai was now one of the main opium markets in Asia and, indeed, the world. Every month, the town imported 130,000 pounds of Indian and Persian opium, which were augmented by large deliveries of Chinese opium from Yunnan and Sichuan. This opium was treated in a dozen or so refineries, most of them situated on the Chinese Bund. The product was partly exported, partly leaked onto the local market, which served 100,000 habitual consumers.[26] Thanks to his leasing contract from the government, Du Yuesheng could now pursue his activities without constraint. His dealers held official licenses and enjoyed police protection against rival gangsters. The Customs Office and the Shanghai Municipal Opium Suppression Committee, to which Du Yuesheng belonged, could thus reintroduce into the authorized market circuit all the stocks of contraband that they had confiscated. The government's fight against the nonofficial opium strengthened Du Yuesheng's control. The resources derived from opium were as vitally important to the regime as they were to the Green Gang, and although splitting them between the two sometimes ran into difficulties, it established a deep complicity between the government and the criminals. On occasion, this friendship was helped along by little gifts: for instance, Du Yuesheng presented Chiang Kai-shek with a complete aircraft squadron as his contribution to national defense.[27]

The Guomindang's recognition of the big drug baron's contributions made it possible for the latter to impose his authority on many of the organizations of Shanghai society, ranging from the trade unions to the chambers of commerce and from philanthropic and patriotic associations to the municipal council. By the same token, his activities within those organizations marked him out as a representative or even a defender of society. The legitimacy derived from his association with the authorities was reinforced by that afforded him by social activism. The head of the Green Gang was to be found at every turn in the economic, social, and political life of the metropolis, in which he was omnipresent and omnipotent. His power became increasingly institutionalized as the regime appointed him to multiple official posts: director of the Shanghai Municipal Opium Suppression Committee, member of the Board of Directors of the Chamber of Commerce, president of the Municipal Council, and so on. Du also maintained relations with the CC faction of the Guomindang and regularly met with Chiang Kai-shek whenever the general visited Shanghai.*

---

* This faction, gathered around the brothers Chen Lifu and Chen Guofu, worked to strengthen Chiang Kai-shek's power over the Guomindang. Its representatives in Shanghai were leaders such as Wu Kaixian and Pan Gongzhan, and it dominated the political life of the metropolis from 1932 to 1936.

Where workers were concerned, Du Yuesheng was no longer content simply to manipulate foremen and brotherhoods or to act from time to time as a mediator. Exploiting the strength that he had acquired in the French concession, he assumed control of the largest of the Seven Great Trade Unions, that of the Postal Service, whose principal leaders, Lu Jingshi and Zhu Xuefan, became his disciples. At the same time, standing alongside the Municipal Bureau of Social Affairs and local representatives of the Guomindang, he had a hand in the regulation of all industrial conflicts. Mr. Good-Guy had become an official mediator, an essential part of the corporatist system constructed by the Nanjing government.

By 1929, Du had secured the collaboration of a number of respectable Shanghai entrepreneurs in founding the Zhonghui Bank. While some of them, such as the great banker Qian Yongming, had willingly accepted the collaboration of the head of the Green Gang, others did so as the result of intimidation and blackmail.[28] The new bank, whose role was to launder the proceeds from drugs, gambling, and prostitution by reinvesting them in legal businesses, was set up on Edward VII Avenue in an opulent building that Du had commissioned one of the best firms of architects, Léonard and Veysseyre, to construct.* From his vast office on the second floor, Du Yuesheng projected his power onto the Shanghai business world. From 1932 on, Du depended on this bank to accumulate more shareholdings and to extend his control over the sector of modern finance. The regime's nationalization policy soon ensured his entry onto the boards of directors of the most venerable Shanghai firms, such as the local branch of the Bank of China and the China Merchants' Steam Navigation Company, and on this basis, associated him with the realization of pilot projects such as the creation of the Central Fish Market.

Thanks to his show of philanthropic and patriotic zeal, Du was able to infiltrate the circle of major Shanghai entrepreneurs and notables. In the winter of 1931–1932, when factional struggles within the Guomindang were paralyzing the municipality of Greater Shanghai and preventing it from taking the measures necessary to quell the Japanese aggression, he

---

* After the 1949 Revolution and thereafter for almost half a century, this building housed the Shanghai Museum. When a new museum was opened on the People's Square in 1994, it reverted to its original function and was used for offices.

distinguished himself by his efforts to promote the boycott and provide aid for the Chinese forces, the refugees, and the wounded. He came up with generous funding for the Shanghai Citizens' Maintenance Association (*Shanghai shimin difang weichihui*), an organization set up by Shanghai elite groups that he now headed alongside Shi Liangcai, editor of the major newspaper, *Shenbao*, and Wang Xiaolai, president of the General Chamber of Commerce. Subsequently, he continued to support the Shanghai Civic Association (*Shanghai shi difang xiehui*), which, following mobilization at the time of the crisis, presented itself as representing the interests of the local bourgeoisie and as a favored interlocutor with the authorities. To ensure publicity for his good works, he bought newspapers and journalists: in 1935, he acquired control over a group of newspapers composed of three dailies and one press agency. There was no stopping Du Yuesheng. In 1936, he tried to infiltrate missionary and Christian circles by having himself baptized, and some observers even expected to see him awarded a high position in the ecclesiastical hierarchy.[29] Had it not been for the Sino-Japanese War, Du would probably have become mayor of Shanghai. That was certainly a project close to his heart and one to which Chiang Kai-shek had given his approval.[30]

The Endurance Club (*Heng she*), created in 1932, whose members were required to qualify by meeting certain standards of wealth and honorability, became the instrument of Du Yuesheng's further ambitions. Its few hundred members—entrepreneurs, politicians, journalists, and lawyers—ensured Du's contacts with Shanghai high society. The club was the public face of power, the hidden face of which was represented by the Green Gang and its bandits. These two symmetrical and complementary organizations ensnared the whole of Shanghai society in their networks. In 1931, the dedication of the ancestral temple of Du Yuesheng in Pudong had already been an occasion when solemn homage was offered to the man who possessed both secret power and public authority. During the three-day-long celebrations, 80,000 Shanghainese came to offer their congratulations to Du Yuesheng. In the list of the ceremony's organizing committee, the names of the town's greatest entrepreneurs—Yu Xiaqing and Wang Xiaolai—stood alongside those of the leaders of the Green Gang. In the huge procession that paraded along the streets of the French concession before crossing to Pudong, officials mingled with gangsters, policemen with merchants. Messages of congratulation poured in from Chiang Kai-shek and his ministers, the municipality of Greater Shanghai, the authorities of the French concession, and foreign merchants. The tablet dedicated to Du's ancestors was adorned by the calligraphy of the great scholar Zhang Binglin. This ancestral temple was soon to house the largest morphine refinery in Shanghai.[31]

Would the apotheosis of such a hero have been conceivable anywhere else but Shanghai? The destiny of this former tramp-turned-millionaire, petty trafficker–turned–patriotic elite and philanthropist, drug baron promoted to the foremost ranks of the nation was intermeshed with that of a town swept along in a whirlwind of uncontrollable modernization.

CHAPTER 10

Haipai and the Ideal of Modernity

THE KEY TO THE SINGULARITY OF SHANGHAI lay in the rise of *Haipai* as much as it did in the town's economic success and social transformations. *Haipai*, or "the Shanghai style," was the very expression of the commercial and cosmopolitan culture of modern China. Initially, the term designated a regional genre of opera, but at the beginning of the twentieth century, it took on a more general sense and was applied as much to the practices of daily life as to forms of literary and artistic expression.[1]

Haipai was often denigrated by the champions of the high Chinese culture of the Confucian scholar-elites who continued to regard trade as a source of moral degradation and intellectual vulgarity.[2] In their eyes, Haipai represented nothing but a degenerate culture contaminated by foreign influences and subordinated to commercial interests. The distaste of many members of elite groups reflected the general hostility that they felt toward the new China that was blossoming along the coast and symbolized by Shanghai. Against the culture of the scholar-mandarins, who held power, Shanghai set that of the merchants, who possessed wealth. In opposition to the traditions of the north, it set those of the south; it preferred foreign models to the rigidity of the old norms, and the fashions and tastes of the masses to the esotericism of the literati. Its rejection of *Jingpai*, "the Beijing style," which perpetuated the inertia of the past, was Shanghai's riposte to those who rejected Haipai.

However, the definition of Haipai cannot be reduced to the simplistic declarations of its detractors. Even if the westernization of Shanghai culture went hand in hand with its commercialization, Haipai represented far more than a mere imitation of lifestyles and modes of expression from elsewhere. No trend, whether in the practices of daily life or in literary and artistic disciplines, could have become established unless it had the approval of the Chinese public. The adoption of foreign models was accompanied by their adaptation, and the latter was governed as much by long-established habits as by the constraints and aspirations produced by a new kind of urban environment. Haipai culture was rooted in the daily life of the urban population. Its detractors between 1920 and 1930 were quite correct when they declared Shanghai culture to be no longer Chinese and not yet Western. But they were mistaken in seeing it simply as a double betrayal at once of traditional culture and its foreign models: the richness of Shanghai culture stemmed from its fertilization through its cross-cultural influences.

The preponderance of borrowings from the West in the elaboration of Haipai naturally raised the problem of imperialism. At the time, there were many—xenophobic conservatives, nationalist militants, radical intellectuals—who condemned the colonization of peoples' minds. After the 1949 Revolution, Chinese historians, along with many of their European and American colleagues, also deplored the unfortunate consequences of foreign influences. But the Shanghainese of 1920 to 1930 were also receptive to the modernity of Western culture. It was not by chance that the term *modeng*, a transliteration of "modern," first appeared in Shanghai, designating all that was new and fashionable. The widely shared desire for modernity legitimized those foreign borrowings and even made them seem an expression of nationalism. Making China modern would surely help to return power and influence to it! And in contrast to the reformists of the preceding century, Shanghainese now no longer limited modernity to factories and banks, or even political institutions. For them, modernity also applied to new lifestyles and new kinds of intellectual and artistic creation.

SHANGHAI'S NEW FACE

The emergence of Haipai was linked to the changes in urban development that were to turn Shanghai into a great modern city bearing comparison with the metropolises of the West. Despite the persistence of separate municipal administrations (for the Chinese quarter, the international settlement, and the French concession), in the twentieth century the city acquired a physical unity.[3] In 1912, the walls that isolated the old Chinese town were torn down and replaced by a circular boulevard. In 1914, the Yangjingbang canal that separated the international settlement and the French concession was filled in. The city expanded considerably with extensions to the west of the international settlement in 1900 and the French concession in 1914, and the creation in 1927 of a special Chinese municipality governing seventeen sectors. Bounded on the east by the Huangpu and to the west by the sweeping arc of the railway, the urban territory was relatively homogeneous. Its division into different quarters was no longer ruled by political and administrative criteria; as in all modern metropolises, it had become functional, reflecting the distribution of various activities.

The business quarter was situated in the central district (*Zhongqu*) of the international settlement, along the Bund and behind it, where banks, real estate companies, insurance companies, and luxury shops were located. The Nanjing Road, flanked by over two hundred shops, was Shanghai's busiest commercial thoroughfare. In this quarter devoted to finance and services, where by 1900 density was already over 60,000 inhabitants per square kilometer, the population had ceased to grow, but land prices continued to soar. Along its avenues, stone or concrete buildings testified to the wealth and power of the great companies.

The financial and commercial concentration in this central sector stood in contrast to the relative dispersion of industrial firms in the northern and western quarters, in the vicinity of the outlying quarters of Nanshi, to the south of the old Chinese town, and in Pudong. The specialization and segregation of industry were still incomplete. Factories were closely linked with commerce, and many were interwoven into the urban fabric; they were to be found everywhere in Shanghai. The extension of the concessions had encouraged bourgeois homes to transfer toward the west, which was less densely populated and where, on larger plots of land, it was possible to build villas surrounded by private gardens and apartment blocks in landscaped parks. The number of inhabitants in the French concession, which was the most sought-after area because of its calm, green spaces, increased from 116,000 to 300,000 between 1910 and 1927.[4] Avenue Joffre, bordered by restaurants, cafés, and fashion boutiques, was the most elegant in the city and was known as the Champs-Élysées of Shanghai.

As in large European and American towns, the workers' quarters were relegated to the periphery: to the north and east toward Zhabei and Yangshupu; to the west toward Jessfield Park, on the borders of the international settlement, and in the Chinese quarter of Caojiadu; and to the south in the suburbs of Nanshi. Industrial firms constructed special housing estates and dormitories for their staff. But many unskilled workers and laborers arriving from the countryside had to make do with more precarious lodgings. They would live on the junks that had brought them to Shanghai, which they anchored along the Suzhou River or the Huangpu toward Pudong, or hauled onto the bank and perched upside down on poles to provide a roof. Others elected to live in one of the shantytowns, a mass of reed huts that sprawled among the wastelands bordering the railway line or close to the wharves and factories. With no facilities, regularly ravaged by fires, destroyed in police raids, yet ever springing up again, these clusters of huts constituted "the last circle in the Inferno of the poor."[5] Shanghai's shantytowns, which in the early 1930s, were home to 150,000 inhabitants, were as wretched as any to be found around the sprawling cities of Asia and Latin America.

To discover the Western and modern face of the town, we must turn toward the business districts and residential zones. The evolution of construction techniques shaped Shanghai architecture at the beginning of the twentieth century. The arrival of new materials on the market—steel beams, cement, and concrete—helped to overcome the contradictory constraints imposed by a marshy and unstable subsoil and the high price of land, which encouraged landowners to build high. In 1916, a new process made it possible to sink piles into the subsoil by constructing a slab of reinforced concrete, a kind of floating bed plate upon which the weight of the building could be distributed. Thanks to this process, the height of buildings could be increased; and it was not long before skyscrapers were being erected.

The reconstruction of the Bund between 1920 and 1930 fixed the famous view. Its majestic buildings testified to the talent of the engineers and architects of Shanghai, who rebuilt on the same sites and acquired more space by building higher. Apartment blocks also had to meet new requirements of comfort and security. The most long-established of the British firms, Jardine and Matheson, led the way. In 1920 it built a new head office: a building 25 meters high in the neoclassical style, adorned with colonnades. Its five stories were served by the first elevators to appear in Shanghai. The edifices of the *North-China Daily News*, the Glenn Line

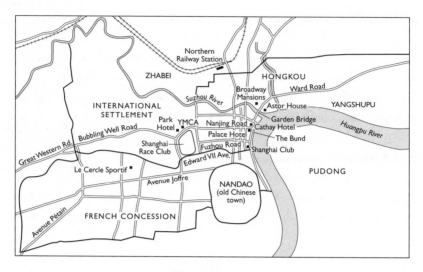

Shanghai in 1932

Building, and the Chartered Bank, all constructed between 1920 and 1930, still boasted their colonnades, pediments, and clocktowers. Because techniques were being perfected in constructing foundations, buildings were rising ever higher. On this neoclassical parade known as the Bund, the highest accolade went to the headquarters of the Hong Kong and Shanghai Bank, erected in 1923. With its 91-meter-long facade and crowned by a dome 54 meters high, the bank dominated the Bund just as it did the Shanghai and Chinese financial world.

From 1925 on, this early modernism deeply stamped by European influences began to give way to the vertiginous, pure lines of skyscrapers with exuberant art deco ornamentation. This dynamic style, inspired by the New World, was nicely in keeping with Shanghai's vitality. The new Customs House marked the transition. It preserved a Doric doorway, but its clocktower, a replica of London's Big Ben, rose to a height of 85 meters. One year later, Sassoon House (now the Peace Hotel) topped its twelve stories with a pyramid-shaped roof, the predominant landmark of the Bund. That roof sheltered the Cathay Hotel, the haunt of the cream of local society and rich tourists, and also the private apartment of its proprietor, the most flamboyant of the Shanghai capitalists, Sir Victor Sassoon.

Within one decade all the buildings along the Bund were reconstructed. The absence of any spare space prevented the addition of any new ones, except the Bank of China, which managed to squeeze in in 1937. From then on, the modern architecture of Shanghai developed only inside the concessions. Here, it was not a matter of the headquarters of companies or administrative offices but of buildings that answered the requirements of society: residences, hotels, shops, places for leisure diversions and amusement. Most of the residential blocks (*gongyu*) were erected in the western

The Customs House, built in 1927, proclaiming the
triumph of modernism and art deco on the Bund

The Cathay, at the top of Sassoon House, one of the most luxurious hotels in Shanghai; now the Peace Hotel

part of the French concession, where land was cheaper. They were built between 1931 and 1937 by Swiss or French architects and bore the names of French provinces: Dauphiné, Béarn, Gascony, Picardy, Normandy, and so on. At ten stories tall, they soared above the flat vista of Chinese roofs. Their pure lines, the vertical or horizontal patterns of their window frames, and their ceramic tiling conferred upon them an elegance to rival that of contemporary constructions in Europe and America.

The major hotels—Broadway Mansions in the international settlement and the Cathay Mansion (the oldest wing of what is now the Jingjiang Hotel) in the French concession—were inspired by the same aesthetics. The most remarkable was the Park Hotel, built by the Austro-Hungarian architect Ladislas Hudec, opposite the racecourse. The Park Hotel, 86 meters high, was the first true skyscraper in China and East Asia. The fine restaurants and ballrooms of these luxury hotels were mostly to be found on their top floors. But the most elegant meeting place of Shanghai's high society was without a doubt the French Sporting Club, built in 1926 by the architects Léonard and Veysseyre. Until it was replaced by a Japanese

The Park Hotel, Shanghai's first skyscraper (1933), on the Nanjing Road opposite the racecourse

hotel in the 1990s, it was an object of admiration, with its long facade opening onto gardens, semicircular central frontage, towering succession of French windows, colonnades, and urn-crowned balustrade.

The big department stores established from 1917 on were all situated along the Nanjing Road. Their proprietors went to great lengths to adorn these cathedrals of material culture. The Sincere and the Wing On stores, located opposite each other, boasted a multitude of columns and pinnacles typical of the beaux arts style. The design of the recreation and leisure centers that sprang up throughout the concessions provided architects with further opportunities to show off their skills. In 1920, a massive six-story building was built on the northern side of the racecourse and topped by a clocktower that soon became one of the major landmarks on the Shanghai horizon.* The dog-racing stadium in the French concession, part of a vast complex of recreational establishments that opened in 1928, included 7 hectares of greyhound-racing tracks, dance halls, and restaurants. The Haï-alaï Hall, or Basque pelota, opened a few years later by the same entrepreneur, a Burgundian named Félix Bouvier, boasted five levels of air-conditioned spectator stands.

At the corner of Tibet Street and Edward VII Avenue (now Yan'an Street), the Great World (*Da Shijie*) complex, which consisted of restaurants, dance floors, theaters, and casinos, was one of the best-known leisure centers in Shanghai. After reconstruction in 1924, it was dominated by a turret with ornamental apertures that was said frequently to serve as the launching point for unlucky gamblers bent on suicide. Of the thirty or so cinemas that were Shanghai's pride and joy, the finest was the Grand Theatre (*Da Guangming*), erected in 1933 on the Nanjing Road, which could accommodate 2,000 spectators.

All these modern buildings sprang up in the midst of Chinese houses built of wood and bricks, no more than one or two stories high. The "great magic buildings soaring skyward" (*motian dalou*) fascinated the Chinese. But some mocked the "great towers built so as to withstand the rising wa-

---

* After the 1949 Revolution until 1996, the Shanghai Race Club served as a municipal library. A number of foreign researchers, including the author of the present work, were allowed access to it and were thus able to admire the recurrent decorative theme of a horse's head, which even adorned the columns of the banisters.

*Greyhound racing and Basque pelota, popular sports
among Shanghai's public and punters*

ters of the Huangpu," while others remained indifferent: "Those places
have nothing to do with us Chinese," a guidebook of the time states.[6] And
true enough, the Chinese had little access to those temples of modernity.
For the great majority of them, the banks, the great hotels, and the luxury
residences were so many "unknown places." On the other hand, the new
public places created for general use and enjoyment were assiduously frequented by rich and poor alike, the lower middle class (*xiao shimin*), and
literary and artistic bohemia.

THE EXALTATION OF CONSUMERISM

The rise of the Shanghai commercial culture can conveniently be dated to the installation of the first Chinese department stores in 1917–1918. Of course, China had long been involved in trading. The opulence of its great merchants had frequently been reflected in the refinements of their material lives, but Confucian ideology merely tolerated, rather than encouraged, the display of luxury. At the beginning of the twentieth century, things changed in Shanghai. The more fully recognized contribution that trade and industry made to the power of nations, the more respected status of merchants and entrepreneurs, and the attraction of the material goods to be seen in the foreign concessions conferred a new positive value upon consumerism. It became a criterion of modernity and, by the same token, of social distinction.

Such changes were stimulated by the new modes of distributing merchandise.[7] Ma Yingbiao, founder of the Sincere Department Store, and the Guo brothers, founders of Wing On, were Cantonese who had traded in Australia and Hong Kong before settling in Shanghai. Inspired by the sales methods they had seen practiced in Australia, these pioneers devoted the greatest care to the construction of vast modern, functional premises; they did away with bargaining and haggling by labeling their goods with fixed prices, organized public displays of their products in shop windows facing the street, and introduced special counters selling particular items that ranged from general foods to confectionary and from household goods to jewelry and perfumes. Their clients, treated like royalty, were served by hundreds of employees trained to be courteous. In 1920, purchase by correspondence and home deliveries were introduced, followed by bargain sales, special promotions, and the popular sales vouchers. Their objective was at once to facilitate and to legitimate the act of acquisition and to make the consumption of luxury or simply practical products in good taste to appear as a manifestation of progress. Some of the merchandise on offer was imported directly from Paris, London, or New York; some was manufactured in Chinese factories, in many cases copied from foreign models. To both the public and wholesalers, the creators of these department stores appeared as initiators. They turned the Nanjing Road into China's shopping mecca and a national model.

To attract regular customers, familiarize them with the use of imported products, and create new needs, these department stores resorted to publicity. This first appeared in Shanghai as early as 1905, on the initiative of the British-American Tobacco Company (BAT), which imported sophisticated printing machinery and hired Chinese artists to produce images that would capture the imagination of their compatriots. At this time, calendars were the principal means for advertising. First in Shanghai, then throughout China, they were distributed to companies, restaurants, and private individuals and enjoyed great success that stimulated BAT's sales.[8] Other foreign and Chinese businesses were quick to follow this example, and various types of advertisement were soon to be seen. Newspaper pages

Publicity for Menier chocolate (Beudin collection)

were full of illustrated publicity items and commentaries. Posters plastered the walls and the sides of trams, and dancing neon lights made the heads of passersby dizzy: "Dancing neon light . . . multicolored waves . . . a sky mad with color, a sky filled with wine, cigarettes. . . . Try White Horse whiskey! Marlboros soothe the smoker's throat!"[9]

In the 1930s, the radio, too, broadcast advertisements. There were over thirty radio stations, some public, others private. Because few homes were equipped with receivers, various stations strove to increase the numbers of their listeners and the efficacy of their publicity announcements by financing broadcasts in public places, theaters, teahouses, and so on. The most popular of these broadcasts were hosted by tellers of *tanci*, a traditional genre in which a story was preceded by a sung introduction (*kaipian*) that was skillfully syncopated and much appreciated by connoisseurs. Beneath their formal elegance, these radio kaipian extolled the joys of consumerism and sang the praises of the female clients hurrying to make new purchases:

> [There are] young married women in powder and rouge
> Who invite one another to try on new clothes.
> [There are] modern women with fluffy perms,
> Twittering bird-like, each with a view of her own.[10]

Such advertisements that shaped collective awareness constituted a veritable semiotics of material culture. Even if the objects and models to which they drew attention remained beyond the means of most Shanghainese, they were part of an imaginary world full of fascination and inspiration. This consumerist ideology remained impervious to the attacks that the conservative Guomindang politicians launched at it during the New Life movement in 1934. Borrowing the weapons of their opponents, the Nationalist authorities used the official radio to broadcast kaipian that criticized the luxury paraded in the concessions and the laziness of the "modern girls": "All day long they won't do a thing / But deck themselves out in the latest fashions."[11] The advocates of the New Life represented luxury consumerism as a kind of enslavement to foreign influences. However, the Shanghai entrepreneurs, and the storytellers and pamphleteers whose services they hired, soon reversed their arguments. They became ardent supporters of "national merchandise" (*guohuo*) that would be further promoted by rising consumer demand: "When shopping, always demand Chinese goods / Resolutely save the nation and carry on the resistance / By cutting the outflow of currency to Japan."[12]

Although condemned in the name of patriotism, consumerism was rehabilitated in the name of that same patriotism. The elegant young woman

A bar hostess and her client

255

buying silken articles in the Nanjing Road was doing her bit to strengthen the economy and, thereby, the Chinese nation. The commercial culture based on a desire for modernity of Western inspiration that was prospering in Shanghai in no way implied a rejection of pride in being Chinese. In Shanghai, cosmopolitanism and nationalism were by no means exclusive. Quite the contrary.

OPENING UP TO FOREIGN INFLUENCES

The impact of foreign influences on Shanghai culture prompted criticism from purists, conservatives, and nationalists as well as from anti-imperialist revolutionaries. In his parody *The Travels of Alice in China (Ailisu Zhongguo Youji)*, the Hunanese writer Shen Congwen made fun of the strange allure of the buildings, window displays, and passersby in the streets of the concessions. "Modern" China was a favorite target for satirists: "She must wear . . . high-heeled shoes, flesh-colored silk stockings, with her hair given a permanent wave. . . . Unfortunately, her breasts are not big, her hair is not blonde, and her nose not high."[13]

The unusual spectacle that the concessions offered to Chinese eyes often engendered feelings of alienation and hatred. But equally important were the process of imitation and the appropriation of foreign models. Although the enemies of imperialism and their postmodernist heirs fiercely condemned that acculturation as a form of enslavement, Shanghainese seem to have welcomed it as a necessary stage in their quest for modernity. The years 1927 to 1937, when Shanghai cosmopolitanism was triumphant, were also a period when nationalism was more vigorously assertive than ever. For many intellectuals the implantation of foreign disciplines, norms, and practices in Shanghai society was an indispensable stage in the nation's renaissance. The diffusion of new knowledge (*xinzhi*) in all domains—the sciences, economics, the arts, technology, and philosophy—was carried out with an intensity reminiscent of the French eighteenth-century *encyclopédistes'* adventure. In fact, the Chinese used the term "enlightenment" (*qimeng*) to refer to this huge operation of popularization.

To bring this "new knowledge" to the urban public, the Chinese intellectuals relied above all on the printing press or, as the historian Daniel Roche put it, "the strength of the written word." On the eve of the Sino-

Japanese War, 86% of the publishers in China were concentrated in Shanghai. Their development coincided with the growing success of a varied newspaper press that was abreast of what was going on and adapted to various sectors of the public. Every publishing company, whether large or small, brought out one or more items. In 1933, over two hundred magazines—that is, almost all the magazines in China—were published in Shanghai. One example was the *Eastern Miscellany Magazine* (*Dongfang Zazhi*), published by the Commercial Press, which was a twice-monthly informative paper containing articles on international news, evolutionary and Freudian theories, and many of the inventions that were turning daily life upside down—motor cars, the gramophone, the cinema, and so on.

Many of the larger papers produced supplements or special issues to complement these magazines. There were about a dozen such newspapers in Shanghai, such as *The Shanghai Daily* (*Shenbao*), *The Times* (*Shibao*), and *The News* (*Xinwenbao*). In 1935, the various supplements produced by *Shenbao* regularly addressed subjects such as the economy, national goods, the railways, the construction industries, the telegraph system, libraries, literature, and so on. There was also a local supplement devoted to Shanghai shows, society gossip, and commercial novelties.[14]

The diffusion of enlightenment was also served by the creation of libraries. The major publishing house, the Commercial Press, took part in this movement, making its own collections that in the early 1930s consisted of 463,000 volumes (80,000 of them written in foreign languages) available to the public. By way of comparison, it is worth noting that the National Library of Beijing could at this time boast only 371,750 volumes.[15] As well as the creation of libraries, the Commercial Press launched itself into the publication of large encyclopedias, in the form of cheap books accessible to all readers, to provide reference texts and items of knowledge considered indispensable to the modern Chinese citizen. The largest of these encyclopedias, *The Complete Library* (*Wanyou wenku*), appeared between 1929 and 1934 and consisted of 2,000 volumes.* The existence of such collections facilitated the opening of some 2,000 popular libraries, set up by buying

---

* The publication of such encyclopedias continued and renewed the tradition of *congshu*, collections that contained the works of a variety of authors on a variety of subjects. These included as many as several hundred titles and several thousand volumes.

thousands of volumes all at the same time. Despite its limitations—its exclusively urban orientation, pragmatic considerations, and a questionable selection of the "classic" and "modern" problems to be illuminated—there was a certain grandeur to the project. In its determination to identify and diffuse indispensable knowledge essential for society's development, it was certainly akin to the spirit of the French *encyclopédistes.*

In the interwar period, more and more Chinese students were trained abroad. When they returned home, they influenced Shanghai society. While some, particularly those who had been in France or Soviet Russia, set out along a revolutionary path, most decided to place their skills at the service of both their own careers and the project of national modernization as conceived in a pragmatic fashion. Chinese engineers and architects played a crucial role in the adaptation of the technical and aesthetic norms that molded the new face of Shanghai. The first generation of these experts was trained in the early years of the century in English or German universities. After 1914, American universities took over. During the 1920s, training in the skills necessary in the construction of buildings became available in China. The Dah Sun, the last of the Nanjing Road's great department stores and, with its modern, uncluttered lines, probably the most elegant of all, was entirely designed and built by a Chinese architect and Chinese contractors.

Writers who had lived abroad also had a part to play in the Shanghai and national literary scenes. Their time abroad, for many in their late adolescence, was of an initiatory nature. As they studied and wandered around Europe, Japan, or the United States, these young Chinese discovered new literary forms, met fashionable authors or their interpreters, entered upon exotic friendships and love affairs, and no doubt suffered a few humiliations. Their intellectual and sentimental educations ran along parallel lines. Their experiences created new attitudes toward life and society. Although some proved, upon their return, to be "pretentious dried fruits,"[16] others became guides and models. The poets Yu Dafu (1896–1945) and Guo Moruo (1892–1978), who both returned from Japan in 1921, brought with them a solid familiarity with contemporary Japanese literature and, through this, with the European Romantics, particularly the Germans, and they published numerous translations of these foreign works. Four years later,

Liu Na'ou (1900–1939) also settled in Shanghai, having studied at Tokyo University, and offered his friends the use of his extensive library.[17]

The influence of French culture owed much to Dai Wangshu (1905–1950), a symbolist poet and prolific translator. In 1932, this former student at Aurora University embarked for France, where in the course of the next few years he received encouragement from Louis Aragon and André Malraux and also help from René Étiemble. During that period, he sent many reports back to Shanghai magazines. He returned to Shanghai with thousands of volumes in his luggage. Another figure who shone in Shanghai was the dandy, poet, and essayist Shao Xunmei (1906–1968).[18] This scion of a wealthy Shanghai family, who had studied at Cambridge University, led a trendy life, collected Western works of art and books, and organized literary salons in the residence of his mistress, the American journalist Emily Hahn.

These transmitters of culture from elite groups addressed themselves and their avant-garde articles to a somewhat limited public. But the refined cosmopolitanism of such intellectuals and artists was backed up by a mass cosmopolitanism that conveyed the essence of Hollywood movies. In the 1920s and especially the 1930s, the cinema became an essential medium of cultural consumption. The number of cinema halls that sprang up testified to the popularity of this new form of entertainment. The first cinema was built as early as 1908. By 1937, Shanghai boasted thirty-six.[19] The movie palaces in the concessions—the Odeon, the Paris, the Isis, and the Grand Theatre—projected foreign films, 90% of which were American, as soon as they were released. The optimism of these imported films, with their happy endings and their Manicheism, was in tune with local taste, formed by Chinese opera and popular novels. In the foyers of cinemas showing these films, the spectators were handed pamphlets in which the film scenario was translated, or rather, adapted: more or less explicit references to Chinese tradition were introduced to make these stories from another world more familiar and to make it easier to understand these cinematographic myths.[20] In the dream factories that the dark cinema halls represented, Shanghainese were initiated into Western civilization, or at least into its reflection in Hollywood productions. And as they got to know the heroes of the silver screen, spectators also discovered the environment in which those heroes lived, the cars that they drove, and the manner in which they coped with the great and small problems of life. Hollywood movies furthermore showed the Chinese public the beauty of the female body in a new light. They dispelled traditional taboos against nudity and sexual relations. The kiss, so alien to Chinese mores, spread from the screen to the streets, or at least into dreams, as did high heels, silk stockings, and other elements and strategies of sex appeal.

The impact of such images on Chinese minds and their efficacy in the diffusion of Western customs alarmed the Nationalist government, which in the early 1930s was setting up a string of censorship committees. But how to separate modernity, as defined by Chiang Kai-shek's regime, from the harmful influences that that modernity brought with it? The censors banned erotic nudes but exalted athletic ones, the symbols and harbingers of a national renaissance. However, the Shanghai public recognized no such distinction. The government was no more successful in banning the taste for eroticism than in discrediting consumerism. Promotion of the sporting ideal—a pretext for showing pretty girls clad in swimsuits—made it possible to get around the prohibitions, just as embracing the defense of "national goods" encouraged people to shop.

The force of Shanghai's cosmopolitanism stemmed from the support—either carefully considered or spontaneous—of much of the urban population. Foreign influences, recognized by society to be conveyers of modernity, combined with the local culture and were adapted to it. The impact of Haipai on daily life is still hard to assess, as the movement remained relatively ignored by Chinese historiography, principally intent on deploring imperialism and its damaging effects. One senses, however, that the economic and financial difficulties that beset Shanghai from 1932 on can hardly have helped to diminish the gap that separated the dreams that burgeoned in the Nanjing Road or in the dark cinema halls from an often frustrating reality. It would be most imprudent to conclude that the exaltation of consumerism led to the creation of a consumer society, or that the vogue for Hollywood movies brought about an Americanization of Shanghai culture. Nevertheless, there can be no doubt that that culture was changing. However wrong it may be to identify it with the Western model that it had adopted, already it was not quite the same as that of the rest of China.

TRANSFORMATIONS IN SOCIAL TIME

The new culture affected the well-to-do classes that lived in contact with the foreigners. But what about the rest? Alongside the great avenues, in the residential enclosures (lilong), where the xiao shimin lived in cramped conditions, life certainly did not seem "modern."[21] They cooked on charcoal stoves, washed their clothes in bowls on the doorstep, and moved around in wheelbarrows, rickshaws, or by the "number 11 bus" (that is, on their own two legs). For the workers crammed together in outlying quarters or the wretched inhabitants of the shantytowns, the main problem was simply survival. Yet even those who were the most impoverished felt a sense that urban civilization was superior to and quite different from the traditions of rural elite groups: however inhuman their conditions of survival in the city, they seemed more bearable than poverty in the countryside. A hint of the arrogance of Shanghai elite groups was even to be found among the freshly installed immigrants who mocked the clumsiness of newer arrivals. The idea that peasants from Jiangbei (the northern part of Jiangsu) were uncouth louts incapable of adapting to the Shanghai way of life—not that of the elite groups, of course, but that of the ordinary people—was a modern version of long-standing ethnic prejudice.

The inroads made by Haipai varied according to the economic levels of the various groups. But modernity was not completely identifiable with wealth or education. Its pressure affected the whole of society: it was what kept the melting pot of Shanghai going. The rapid rhythm of Shanghai life—high heels tripping along the sidewalks, cars whizzing down the wide avenues, elevators shooting down the skyscrapers in twenty or so seconds—testified to the way that social time had changed. At the end of the nineteenth century, already reformists were embracing the idea of linear time, rejecting the traditional notion of cyclical time linked to the rise and decline of imperial dynasties, and rallying to the Darwinian schema of selective evolution. A few decades later, with the May Fourth Movement abetting, the philosophy of the struggle for life was largely accepted in urban society. In business circles, "time was money." Religious and cosmic references gave way to commercial objectives. Natural time, the time of the cycles of day and night and the changing seasons, competed with the time regulated by clocks.[22] In the international settlement, clocks were omnipresent, soaring above its principal monuments. The Customs House clock on the Bund was complemented to the west by the racecourse clock. Employees had to abide by strict office hours; workers were summoned to work at 4:40 in the morning by the textile mill sirens; the fortunes and fates of speculating capitalists fluctuated feverishly in rhythm with movements on the Stock Exchange.

The economic discipline linked with this new concept of time did meet with a certain resistance, for the power of the clocks clashed with Chinese customs and beliefs. Although the Western (solar) calendar was adopted, the periodicities of the lunar calendar did not disappear, for they marked out all the religious and family festivals. The Western calendar did not wipe out the propitious and unpropitious days for marrying, burying a relative, setting off on a journey, or building a house. And businessmen continued to balance their accounts and pay off their debts at the time of the Dragon Festival (in early June) or the Full Moon Festival (in October). This overlap of homogeneous industrial time and time structured by rites and predictions was reflected in calendars that, while observing the Western division of time into months and weeks, also indicated all the dates of the traditional festivals.

THE CULT OF THE BODY AND
PHYSICAL APPEARANCE

As new attitudes to time developed, so too did new attitudes to the body. In Confucianism and Daoism, the preservation of health was conceived as a battle for longevity, a preoccupation of the elderly. In Shanghai, the new discourse on health laid the emphasis on physical vigor and embraced the entire family.[23] Popular magazines were invaded by chubby, round-cheeked babies. There were even beauty contests for tiny tots.

Family hygiene and healthy eating were presented as the keys to physical well-being. Advertisements taught the public the use of toothpaste and detergents and encouraged the consumption of "modern and scientific" foodstuffs, that is, those taken from Western diets. Milk, indigestible for most Chinese stomachs, was recommended as a key factor in the Darwinian struggle for life. Sport was another means of developing a robust body, desirable both in itself and for the good of the country. Nationalist propaganda in the 1930s declared that national regeneration depended on the individual vigor of every citizen. In Shanghai, football and basketball were part of the curriculum in both Chinese and foreign universities. The executives and clerks of the Bank of China, whose activities even outside working hours were organized by the firm, were expected to play tennis or engage in some other sport.[24] Popular magazines encouraged women to take exercise by displaying photographs of stars in swimsuits or busy pumping up their bicycle tires.

The cult of physical appearance as a criterion of modernity established the reign of fashion. Women's magazines, Hollywood films, and the shops of Avenue Joffre informed the public of the latest trends of the Western collections. High society, movie circles, and literary dandies set the tone. The sequined dress worn in 1925 by one of the top Chinese stars, Yang Naimei, was copied in no time at all by all Shanghai's socialites.[25] The young women of the best society were certainly not averse to running a fashionable boutique.

The combination of Western influences and Chinese customs was particularly striking where clothing was concerned. Although dandies would parade in a complete Western suit, most modern Shanghai men were content to wear Western trousers beneath a scholar's robe. Elegant Shanghai women favored permed hair, high-heeled shoes, and a *qipao*, a figure-hugging dress derived from the old Manchu costume that revealed the legs through a slit skirt and was closed at the neck by a high collar. Short, straight hair, a flat chest, and a black skirt signaled a young, emancipated, intellectual woman, a supporter of the New Culture and an emulator of Henrik Ibsen's Nora.

The fashions of high society were also those of the demimonde: a permed hairstyle, lipstick, and a pair of silk stockings were all that were needed to turn a young country lass into a bar hostess. Hoodlums treated themselves to a presentable look by slipping their feet into leather shoes and clapping a soft hat on their heads. In the working-class suburbs, girls would dream of swapping their trousers and jackets—the uniform of poor and country people—for a figure-hugging qipao. Those who were factory workers living in the family home sometimes managed to satisfy those desires by saving money from wages that they refrained from handing over in full to their families.

THE "MODERN WOMAN"

"Haipai is like a modern girl," one contemporary observer remarked.[26] His words could be interpreted as a comment on a number of aspects of the situation: the increasingly important role women played in social and political life, literature and the arts, and the availability of modern products and services. But they seem above all to refer to the role that women played as the agents par excellence of modernization, that is, as consumers.

Women were the principal targets of advertisers. The magazine photographs of elegant women in their refined homes promoted the sale of many items besides cosmetics and clothes. "Modern women" continued to assume the responsibilities that traditionally fell to them within the home, but now they did so within a context that had been transformed by the arrival of purchasable items designed to increase comfort. Whether they were in a position to acquire all these new items or were obliged simply to window-shop longingly on the Nanjing Road, modern women were the preeminent mediators between society and a world full of technical innovations.

In Shanghai, as in many places the world over, the consumer culture was oriented by the desires of women, and the quest for modernity included a domestic version of it that involved a reordering of private space. The upper bourgeoisie spearheaded the movement. In the villa that Charlie Song had built for himself in Hongkou in the early years of the twentieth century, bathrooms were as numerous as pianos.* In a modest fashion, allowing for the difference in financial means, the trend was carried on in the lilong. The houses in these residential enclaves, now smaller and reduced to a single block, no longer accommodated a "public" space reserved for the ancestors' altar and for receiving guests. The hierarchy of a house's rooms was now based purely on size, lighting, and the comfort that they provided for private life.

If women became the principal props of cultural change, this was also partly due to their position and role in the transformations that were bringing Shanghai society up to date. In the days when wives stayed at

---

* Charlie Song was a Shanghai businessman with many connections to Protestant missionary circles. One of his daughters married Sun Yat-sen, another Chiang Kai-shek, and one of his sons, T. V. Song, became a minister in the Nationalist government.

home and the favorite distraction for scholars was visiting courtesans, marital relations were hardly ever mentioned except to remind wives of their subordination to their husbands. Within the family, in many cases a young wife's fate had depended more on the personality of her mother-in-law than on that of her husband. In Shanghai, women's access to jobs, education, and shops now offered them a certain degree of emancipation. At the same time, the predominance of families of a nuclear type, which was in many cases imposed by the circumstances of immigration and by housing conditions, had the effect of readjusting the balance in intrafamily relations. The importance of a couple's conjugal relations increased. Men tended now not to content themselves with a wife chosen by the family, with a view to perpetuating the ancestral lineage. A man wanted a real partner. As Sun Yat-sen explained on the occasion of his second marriage, to Song Qingling in 1915, he wished to have at his side "a companion and collaborator." Concubinage was no longer a satisfactory solution, for "modern" girls were less and less inclined to settle for the position of a secondary wife.

In artistic, bohemian, and revolutionary circles, free love was common. Such emancipation gave a modern woman an aspect that was sometimes threatening, that of a cynical seductress, a man-eater as portrayed by the novelist Liu Na'ou: "Who tells you to be so awkward and stupid, with all this nonsense of eating ice cream and taking a walk? Don't you know that lovemaking should be done in an automobile racing with the wind?" says one of his heroines, exasperated by her suitor's politeness.[27] In polite society, family-arranged marriages continued to be the rule. But the young people involved were now consulted and had a chance to get to know each other before coming to a decision: they would go for walks together in the parks and to teashops and cinemas. The wedding ceremony itself underwent changes. The white dress and veil began to replace the red tunic and diadem. And a banquet in one of the concessions' fine hotels now either supplanted or complemented the old rituals. On the occasion of his wedding in 1927 to Song Meiling, Charlie Song's youngest daughter, Chiang Kai-shek opted to host a great ball in the Majestic Hotel.

Nor was the initiative in a marriage left to the young people themselves in popular circles. Despite the conviviality of the lilong alleys, they were not conducive to romantic idylls leading to marriage. In many cases a girl would even be sent temporarily back to the family's native village to find a suitable husband and go through the marriage rituals with him there. Free unions and the family breakups that they implied represented an alternative that was full of risks in the brutal world of the Shanghai proletariat; so marriage in its traditional form persisted. But for young working-class women it often came about at a relatively advanced age, around twenty-five or thirty. The reason for this was the wage that the girl would bring home to the house where she lived with her parents, who were anxious to hang on to that money for as long as possible.[28] This afforded the daughter a respite of roughly ten years of working life, with all the attendant companionship of fellow workers, possibly some social activism, and above all, flirting and having fun before the constraints of maternity and domestic duties brought a temporary or permanent end to factory work and withdrawal into the home.

NEW LEISURE ACTIVITIES

With the appearance of public recreation spaces in the concessions—dance halls, bars, cinemas, and so on—the old contrast between the leisure activities of the educated and popular amusements was blurred. The world of teahouses and receptions held by courtesans was juxtaposed to and eventually superseded by mass entertainments borrowed from the West. The vogue for these was not confined to the upper bourgeoisie, gilded youth, and bohemian artists. For many clerks, low-ranking officials, and students living in the lilong, frequenting places designed for leisure and entertainment provided their main chance of entering into contact with the Western world of the concessions. From 1927, even public parks were opened to the Chinese. Only foreign clubs continued to bar their doors to them. Elsewhere, everything was just a matter of money.

Strolling in the park was a British custom that satisfied a desire for both healthy exercise and the pleasures of a family outing. Once admitted, even though there was an entrance charge, the Chinese public flocked to the concession gardens. What the Chinese were after was more than just a breath of fresh air; taking a disinterested stroll was hardly a Shanghai custom. However, quite apart from constituting excellent places for ro-

Strollers on the Bund in front of the Cathay Hotel

mantic meetings, whether or not legitimate, many of these public gardens contained leisure complexes and amusement parks. In the shade of the trees by the lakes and ponds were restaurants and bars that possessed an exotic charm that one of Mao Dun's heroes associated with that of the *guinguettes* (little bars with dancing and music) on the banks of the Seine.[29]

The craze for cafés illustrates the degree to which people's imaginations and taste for exoticism fueled the success of the new leisure activities.[30] Like the cinema and the car, the café was a symbol of modernity, but modernity of a refined nature, bathed in the prestige of French literature. Around 1930, emulators of Théophile Gautier or Henri de Régnier would regularly be found gathered in the Federal Café in the international settlement, or the Renaissance or other less smart establishments on the Avenue Joffre. Café life, exalted by writers returning from Japan, where it was already widespread, was celebrated in works such as *Café Conversations* (*Kafei Zuotan*) or *A Night in a Café* (*Kafei guan de yiye*).[31] For young intellectuals, the café superseded the teahouse. But in the old Chinese town, the workers' suburbs, and even the concessions themselves, the teahouse remained the preeminent popular place of conviviality: merchants would meet there to talk business, workers to plan their strikes, and the elderly simply to chat together.

Sporting events such as horse racing, greyhound racing, and Basque pelota matches attracted a large public less interested in the performances than in the financial stakes involved. Bets were laid on horses, dogs, and pelota players. The Chinese passion for gambling found a legal outlet here, and the organizers of these sporting events made large profits out of the wagers laid, on which they charged a commission. After 1949, the new regime frowned upon and banned such means of enrichment as a form of imperialist exploitation.

As mentioned previously, in the 1920s the cinema became one of the most popular forms of amusement. Shanghainese were avid moviegoers. The cinema programs changed almost weekly. In 1935, Shanghai imported 350 films, and local companies produced 72.[32] The cult of movie stars financed a special press that took as great an interest in the stars' private

Behind the racecourse grandstands

lives as in their careers as artists. The suicide of one of the most beautiful and popular of these actresses, Ruan Lingyu, who, caught between two unfaithful lovers, killed herself in March 1935 at the age of twenty-five, desolated Shanghainese: tens of thousands lined the streets to pay their respects to the funeral procession. But what above all made Shanghai "the Paris of the East" was its dazzling nightlife. When World War I came to an end, the great avenues, with neon signs blazing, began to proliferate with dance halls, nightclubs, and bars with jazz bands, singers, dancing girls, and hostesses. In most of these establishments, the amusements on offer were a prelude to prostitution.

After World War I, dancing, long considered by the Chinese to be an indecent and ridiculous exercise, became one of the favorite pastimes of Shanghai society.[33] The slightest excuse—charity fairs, private or public functions of every kind—would serve for people to let themselves go to the rhythms of the tango or the fox-trot. An ever-growing public frequented the dance halls. In the great hotels, such as the Park and the Cathay, the ballrooms were constantly booked for dances and smart parties. There, the top Western taipans rubbed shoulders with Chinese business-world figures and underworld bosses. Evening dress was de rigueur. In less noted establishments, such as the Saint-George, the Del Monte, or the Casanova, patronized by the middle classes, and in the countless cafés, restaurants, and bars that provided a dance floor, what the clients wanted above all was the pleasure of physical proximity and possibly a sexual relationship with one of the hostesses. There were several thousand of these in Shanghai, of various nationalities and races, most of them under twenty-five years old. Little Chinese peasant girls transformed by the magic of a qipao, Russian and European drifters, Japanese and Korean girls—all working as professional dancers—were on offer to clients when they purchased at the door a booklet of tickets entitling them to a few turns on the floor.

These hostesses or "locomotives" (longtou) thronged the Shanghai darkness, bestowing upon it the allure of their youth and elegance. They also filled the pages of the local press, which devoted articles to them, the source of inspiration for many a novelist or filmmaker. Those who entered into prostitution retained a certain freedom of choice and bargaining power with their clients and in that respect may appear as heirs to the courtesans of the past. But in this culture governed by material interests and the immediate gratification of desires, their popularity coincided with a profound change in the forms that prostitution took.

In the years following World War I, the emergence of westernized elite groups, the accessibility of new public spaces—parks, shops, tearooms, cinemas, dance halls—to women, and their increasing participation in active life rendered obsolete the role of courtesans, formerly the providers of titillating conversation and artistic entertainment. Gilded youth and literary Bohemia, having supplanted the scholars of the past, sought the company not of flower-women but of female students and well-brought-up girls whose courtship involved frequent recourse to words such as *Miss* (*misi*) and *darling* (*daling*). Prostitutes were now invariably approached solely for their sexual services, and the standing of the profession was accordingly considerably depreciated. It was now dominated by hookers known as "wild chickens" (*yeji*), formerly regarded very much as an inferior category.

Under pressure from the Protestant associations, between 1920 and 1925 the Shanghai Municipal Council endeavored to close down the international settlement's 1,700 brothels. But this abolitionist movement simply forced such establishments underground or prompted them to move to the French concession, where the authorities practiced a policy of tolerance combined with a measure of control.[34] So the prostitutes carried on with their trade. Their numbers continued to rise: from 1,500 in the 1920s, it had doubled by one decade later. The "golden circle of prostitution" was situated in the very heart of the concessions,[35] to the south of the racecourse and set back from the Bund and out toward Hongkou. Although omnipresent, the prostitutes were not always visible. Their hotels and brothels were hidden away in the alleys of the lilong, those residential enclosures so close to yet apart from the town's great avenues.

Prostitution constituted the constant link between vice and crime. It led to pimping, and pimping led to gangster protectors who set up a sinister network of racketeering, kidnapping, abduction, violence, and suffering. Behind the neon lights blazing in the Shanghai night and all its festive excitement could be glimpsed a world of terrifying or pitiful shadows.

LITERATURE ABOUT AND IN SHANGHAI

Shanghai certainly had its shops, cafés, and dancing girls, just as did Paris, to which it was frequently compared. But can the comparison be pushed any further? From the point of view of Chinese literary and artistic creativity in the early twentieth century, did Shanghai play the same role as Paris did in French culture: the Paris without which, Flaubert claimed, France would have "no heart, no center, . . . no spark"?[36] A distinction should at once be drawn between, on the one hand, the literary domain, strong in its long tradition of regional variants but nevertheless centered on Beijing, where the cream of the literary elite was to be found, and on the other, new artistic media such as cinema, in which traditions were yet to be created and which looked to the West for inspiration.

In 1926–1927, the political chaos and violence that warlords brought to Beijing forced writers and intellectuals to leave the capital and seek refuge in the concessions of Shanghai. As a result, the center of literary life shifted. But the nexus of talent in the metropolis was broken up at the end of 1937 when the Japanese invasion led to more migrations, dispersing the literary circles of Shanghai. During that decade, the time spent in the concessions had made it possible for poets, novelists, and essayists to pursue creative activities that, however, for the most part ignored or despised the local cultural context.

Alongside the writers who had fled to Shanghai for reasons of security were Shanghainese writers. Most were not actually born in the city, but they all contributed to the urban culture that influenced their lifestyle and governed their literary production. Because of the public they addressed, the themes they tackled, the procedures to which they resorted, and the fantasies that fueled them, the works that these writers produced seemed specifically Shanghainese. In the eyes of the writers from Beijing, they bore the stigma of Haipai: mercantilism, vulgarity, cosmopolitanism. The great quarrel that raged from 1933 to 1935 between the Shanghai school (*Haipai*) and the Beijing school (*Jingpai*) illuminates their differences and opposition.

In the last years of the empire, Shanghai had seen the appearance of a literary trend that the intellectuals of the May Fourth Movement mockingly dubbed the School of Mandarin Ducks and Butterflies (*Yuanhuang hudiepai*).[37] Those ducks and butterflies symbolized the pairs of lovers whose checkered destinies provided one of the favorite themes of popular novels. The genre was despised by elite groups but enjoyed by the xiao shimin and continued to flourish until the early 1930s. As in the cases of Samuel Richardson's *Clarissa* in England and Alexandre Dumas the Younger's *La dame aux camélias* in France, this literature coincided with the rise of an urban bourgeoisie and a transformation in the social status of writers. Denied the opportunities offered to their elders by the imperial examinations (suppressed in 1905) and careers as mandarins, many educated young people now relied on their pens to earn a living.

At this point of transition, between the empire and the republic, authors began to be paid for what they wrote. Shanghai was deluged by a wave of talented young writers from the provinces of the lower Yangzi, who were attracted more by the prospect of money and the pleasures of a bohemian life than by the hope of literary glory. Drawing their inspiration from the popular novel and from foreign literature, these authors wrote in a simple classical style on a variety of subjects, producing adventures of knights errant, crime stories, novels with social themes, and especially love stories. They updated stereotypical idylls in which the hero was a sensitive and unrecognized genius, the heroine a fragile beauty. In *The Jade Pear Spirit* (*Yuli hun*), a prototype of the genre from the writer Xu Zhenya, a young widow educated in the traditional manner becomes the rival of a female student with advanced ideas, both girls being in love with the same man. The one is as gentle as the petals of a pear blossom, the other as dazzling as a bright camellia. Usually, tradition wins the day, and after savoring the seduction of novelty, the reader finds himself or herself once more on familiar ground. Such ambiguities, which reflected those of a society in transition, served the commercial interests of both the publishers and the authors. It was from this literature that the young Chinese cinema industry of the 1920s was to inherit its taste for melodrama and sentimentality.

In the meantime, the Shanghai literary scene was turned upside down by the eruption of the New Literature, whose reign was established by the May Fourth Movement. The impetus for cultural change had originated in 1915 in Beijing's university and intellectual circles. Shanghai had simply made the columns of its newspapers accessible to lambasters of the scholarly tradition and advocates of the vernacular language, science, and democracy. But the Shanghai literary scene was by no means impervious to the influence of the new movement. In 1921, a group of young writers trained in Japan and led by Guo Moruo and Yu Dafu founded the Creation Society (*Chuangzao she*).* These children of May 4 shared the romanticism and rebellious instincts of the rest of their generation. Borrowing their themes and techniques from Western poetry, they positioned the individual at the center of the universe: "I am the splendor of the moon, / I am the splendor of the sun," proclaimed Guo Moruo.[38] Yu Dafu, in both his writing and his life, cultivated the despair, self-disgust, and self-pity that befitted a *poète maudit*. The success of these two writers projected the "Creationists" onto the national literary stage. They entered into dialogue with Beijing literary circles. Their Shanghai roots did not confer any specific character upon them but were enough to discredit them in the eyes of Beijing scholars such as Lu Xun, who dismissed them as "dilettantes and rogues" addicted to women and wine.[39]

Did the urban civilization that flowered in Shanghai really leave no trace in the high Chinese literature of the twentieth century? Did it not produce works depicting city life, either glorifying its modernity or deploring the alienation that this modernity brought with it, just as Paris and London did? That is certainly what was repeatedly asserted both before and after 1949 by those obsessed with political orthodoxy. In the name of nationalism and proletarian values, the role played by the modernists was swept under the carpet. Only now are we beginning to rediscover works conveying aesthetics that, while not rejecting the commercialism and cosmopolitanism of Haipai, transcended them and expressed them in a purified, very original manner. In truth, the Shanghai modernists were

---

* Guo Moruo, born in 1892 in Sichuan, was one of the most productive Chinese authors of the twentieth century, at once a poet, novelist, dramatist, and revolutionary propagandist. From the time of the May Fourth Movement to the 1960s, he remained in the forefront of the literary scene. Yu Dafu (1896–1945) was a native of Zhejiang who won early fame through his stories about the neurotic heroes of a decadent China. When he became friendly with Lu Xun, he was influenced by proletarian literature. During the Japanese occupation, he took refuge first in Singapore, then Indonesia, where he died under mysterious circumstances.

faithful bards of their city.[40]

This group of modernists was formed in 1925 when a few students, eager for novelty and curious about the most contemporary Western trends, met at Aurora University. What distinguished them from the writers of the New Literature were the close attention they paid to the urban environment and the bold nature of their stylistic experiments. They were influenced by the neosensationist group that flourished in Japan in the early 1920s and, either via that school or directly, by the avant-garde European currents of expressionism, Freudianism, Dadaism, and so on.*

The founder of the Shanghai group of modernists was Liu Na'ou, from a rich family in Taiwan (then a Japanese colony), who had studied English literature in Tokyo. He was joined by three friends from Hangzhou, Dai Wangshu (1905–1950), Shi Zhicun (1905–2003), and Du Heng (1907–1964). These were gifted boys who at the age of twenty felt frustrated by the limitations that the Jesuit fathers tried to place on their exploration of French literature. Liu Na'ou, who benefited from both a cosmopolitan education and wealth, helped his friends to discover the latest developments in international literature and to finance their first publications. The last member of the group, Mu Shiying (1912–1940), was the youngest and also the most brilliant. The *Xiandai* (*Les Contemporains*) review, which from 1932 to 1935 served as the mouthpiece of the modernists, was one of the most influential literary reviews of the time. Abandoning the didactic preoccupations of the literature of the May Fourth Movement, it aimed to rejuvenate poetic and Romantic forms of expression, following the example of contemporary Western authors, and it published many translations of those works.

But the originality of the modernists stemmed more from their total immersion in city life than from their cosmopolitan and avant-garde attitude. Their way of life, their inspiration, their literary methods—everything about them related to their urban environment. Their Bohemia was not that of gilded youth, for most of them were "writers from a pavilion room" (the

---

* These writers, who included Kawabata Yasunari (1899–1972), resorted to metaphor to describe the psychological confusion and moral malaise of the individual amid the capitalist society that was emerging in Japan. They particularly influenced Liu Na'ou and Mu Shiying.

equivalent of French artists "starving in their garrets").* But they did like
to discuss matters together around a café table and enjoyed the cinemas and
dance halls in the concessions. Their experiences there allowed them to make
contact, real or imagined, with the Western world: "Late in the afternoon,
when I stroll over the tightly knit shadows of the tree-lined walk, the tragic
scenarios of *Le Cid* and *Horace* unfold on my left, vis-à-vis the rue Cor-
neille. And on my right, from the direction of the rue de Molière, the cynical
laughter of *Tartuffe* and the *Misanthrope* seems to enter my ears."[42]

However, in a Parisian garret the creative relationship between writer
and city was not the same as in a Shanghai pavilion. Whereas the Parisian
wandering through the city streets felt marginalized by his modern surroundings and Baudelaire lamented that "the form of a town / Changes
faster, alas, than a human heart," the spectacle of neon lighting, cars, fes-
tivity, and vice exalted the modernist of Shanghai: "Is it possible that there
is no beauty in modern life? No, there still is, but its form has changed. We
have no romance . . . nevertheless we do have thrills and carnal intoxica-
tion."[43] Whether humdrum or fantastic, it was the urban landscape that
provided these writers with their principal source of inspiration, the very
stuff of their novels. Mu Shiying described his work as a "tour of inspection through the city,"[44] and Liu Na'ou titled his collection of stories *City
Skylines (Dushi fengjingxian)*.

It was as visionaries that the modernists described their city. Under
the pen of Liu Na'ou, the racecourse vibrates to the tensions of the punters crammed into the spectator stands.[45] For Mu Shiying, the express
train hurtling on its way, with its arc lamps piercing the darkness, is "a
dragon gripping a luminous pearl between its teeth."[46] The night is dizzy
with intoxicating delights: "On Saturday evening, the world spins on the
axis of jazz . . . just as quick, just as crazed; gravity's gone, buildings are
thrown skyward."[47] The brightly lit streets, the sound from the dance
halls, the complicit darkness of the cinemas, along with high heels, silky

---

* In Shanghai literary life, these "pavilions" played a similar role to that of the garrets of
French Romanticism and post-Romanticism. In residential enclaves, the houses would include
above the kitchen a small room (of 10 or so square meters) that could be rented cheaply and
was provided with independent access. These pavilions became the lodgings par excellence
of young bachelors and artists struggling for literary or other kinds of success.[41]

legs, and painted lips all share in the same erotic fever. Woman, seductive and provocative, is omnipresent. Her body merges with that of the city. The prostitute's parted thighs represent the wharves along which one imagines "the majestic posture of a big steamship entering the harbor."[48] The female vamp and the elusive city, two equally powerful symbols of modernity, exert the same fascination and arouse the same frustration. "Shanghai, a paradise built on top of a hell!"[49] exclaims Mu Shiying. But Shanghai modernity wins out by virtue of the creative energy that it carries, propelling China into the future.

To do justice to this dynamic view, the modernists employed a radically new literary technique and style. In place of a narrative form and psychological analysis, they borrowed from the cinema its manner of cutting abruptly from one frame to another. Their elliptic phrases and disjointed syntax reflect the vibrations of urban life. Let us follow Mu Shiying into a dance hall: "On the gleaming dance floor, swirling skirts, swirling dresses, stiletto heels, heels, heels, heels. Bouffant hairstyles, masculine faces . . . whiffs of alcohol, whiffs of perfume."[50] From cinematographic techniques the modernists also borrowed close-ups that zoomed in on feminine beauty or expressive distortions: "A blaring saxophone, . . . a craning neck . . . a gaping mouth."[51] From the Japanese neosensationists they learned to resort constantly to metaphors to convey their impressions. Emulating Western novelists, they tried out internal monologues, scorning all punctuation.

To describe this new civilization, the modernists created a new technique of the novel that broke not only with traditional genres but also with the literature of the May Fourth Movement. But their practice of art for art's sake and their predilection for exploring impressions and seeking new forms of expression aroused the hostility of many writers who remained loyal to the moral commitment that tradition assigned to intellectuals. By the mid-1930s, the modernist current was already swamped by the rising tide of literature of political commitment; and subsequently it was discredited by the fact that its principal representatives, Liu Na'ou and Mu Shiying, collaborated with the Japanese.

Polemics raged in Shanghai throughout the decade of 1927 to 1937. What was the writer's role, and what was the function of literature? The adoption of ideological and political positions produced clashes. The town's role as a source of inspiration slipped away, but even so the Shanghai environment continue to affect the literary battles of this period. The relative safety of the concessions rendered these battles possible. The police pressure exerted by the Guomindang and the imperialist presence exacerbated them, and their relevance was emphasized by the movement to mobilize the population in the interests of national salvation.

Guo Moruo's conversion to Marxism and the radicalization of the Creationist group prompted the switch from a "literary revolution" to "revolutionary literature." After the 1927 coup, Chiang Kai-shek's accession to power, and the start of the White Terror in Shanghai, this movement gained momentum and eventually, in 1930, resulted in the formation of the League of Left-Wing Writers (*Zuolian*).[52] Apart from a few of the Creationists such as Lu Xun and Mao Dun and a number of talented theorists and polemicists such as Qu Qiubai, Hu Feng, and Feng Xuefeng, the league consisted mostly of young activists, militants from the CCP and its mass organizations. It was one of the "red mass leagues" (*hongse minlian*) in which Communists, fellow travelers, democrats, and patriots all collaborated, thereby enabling the Communist Party to preserve a measure of influence despite the Guomindang's domination in the metropolis. The league aimed to develop a proletarian spirit in literature and to encourage the creation of works of a kind to raise the class consciousness of the Chinese people. When it was banned by the Guomindang, it continued to exist in a semiclandestine fashion. Its members suffered persecution, and in 1931 five of them were executed.

Bathed in the aura of the prestige of its president, Lu Xun, and the glory of its martyrs, the league endeavored to establish its control over the literary scene, producing a spate of polemics and personal attacks directed against pro-Guomindang and independent writers. In 1932, the battle over the "Third Category" brought the league into opposition with the defenders of freedom in literary and artistic creation, in particular the modernists.* In response to an article by the modernist Du Heng, titled "Hands Off Literature" (*Wu qinglue wenyi*), the league attacked imitators

---

* The term "Third Category" designated writers who refused to commit themselves either to the CCP or to the Guomindang.

of foreign writing who paid no heed to their duties and more attention to urban unrest than to life in the countryside, where the true Chinese civilization lived on. Despite all Lu Xun's efforts, the league gradually fell under the control of the Communist cadres, among whom Zhou Yang was conspicuous for his lack of literary talent and his determination to smother that of others in the name of Marxist orthodoxy.

Midnight (*Ziye*), which appeared in 1933 and is regarded as Mao Dun's masterpiece, bore the marks of the ideological and political commitment of its author. His description of the Shanghai environment, the industrial areas and their workers, the extravagancies of the bourgeoisie, and speculation, corruption, and crime provided the foundation for his condemnation of modernization as carried out in the capitalist manner and under the direction of foreigners. The creative power and sensitivity of the writer often transcended the dogmatism of the militant. The first chapter of the novel describes Shanghai as discovered by an old rural notable, as he is driven by night through the city, and offers a magnificent description of the urban scene. All the symbols of modernity extolled by the modernists reappear but here carry a different message, one not of progress but of destruction and death. The automobiles are so many menacing monsters, and the sight of bared female legs, arms, and breasts brings on a heart attack that carries off the old man. But all too often, in the characterization of his subjects and the dramatization of various episodes in the story, Mao Dun falls into the trap of stereotypes of a doctrinaire naturalism in the manner of Zola or inspired by his own Marxist view of society.*

SHANGHAI AND THE NEW ARTS

In the domain of artistic practices, as in many others, Shanghai stands out because of the speed and success with which it appropriated Western models. The presence of the concessions and the foreign communities also facilitated the processes of transmission. But in truth the particular character of the city was so favorable to the reception of foreign models that it is tempting to speak in terms of synchronicity rather than imitation.

The importation of new artistic models that, with a delay of one or two

---

* Émile Zola's novel *Money* (*L'Argent*) served as Mao Dun's model.

decades, followed that of literary models, coincided with a large proportion of the public's realization that modernization was not only inevitable
but desirable. Like the Western art deco, to which it owed so much, the
"Shanghai style" that triumphed in the applied arts celebrated industrial
and commercial culture. The bourgeoisie felt at home with this style and
with the notion that the industrialization of art (*gongyihua*) constituted a
response to the needs of society and the country as a whole. The success
of Shanghai "modernism" rested upon a remarkable alliance between artists, writers, entrepreneurs, and technicians.

There also existed a margin unaffected by such economic and political preoccupations within which a number of artists who had opted for
Western practices worked on their own. In the 1920s these were quite
numerous in Shanghai, where one could find a dozen or so painters who
were familiar with Parisian trends and where White Russians, later joined
by Jewish refugees from Germany and central Europe, provided a solid
musical grounding for both amateur and professional pupils. Following
the example of the literary avant-garde, these artists organized themselves
around institutions such as the Academy of Fine Arts and the Conservatory
of Music (created in 1927, following the German model) and organizations
such as the "Two Worlds" and the "Tempest" societies. However, in domains that stemmed from the classical Western tradition—for example, oil
painting and classical music—Shanghai's contribution was but one among
those of other, equally active centers: Canton, where the Lingnan School
was the first to be receptive to Western painting; Hangzhou, where the
Western Lake Academy won considerable influence; and Beijing.

The influence on Haipai culture of painters and musicians trained in
the West was no more than marginal. If they practiced their art as purists,
they could expect only a limited public. Lin Feng-mian (1900–1991) exhibited his paintings at the Alliance française and sold some to residents
of the French concession. Others, for example, the slightly later painter
Zao Wou-ki (born in 1921), who took French nationality, chose to remain in or return to Europe or the United States to continue their careers
there. At that point, they became part of the current of Western art, which
they enriched with new elements stemming from Chinese aesthetics and
perceptions. But to the extent that some of these artists devoted their tal-

ents to mercantile activities—that doctrinaires would call inferior—they did help to shape and develop Shanghai's culture.

A movement that encouraged the applied arts began in the early years of the republic.[53] It found expression in a number of magazines, the most influential of which, *Art and Life* (*Meishu shenghuo*), was published from 1934 to 1937 with contributions from the principal artists of the day. This movement, supported by specialized departments in the Academies of Fine Art in Shanghai and Hangzhou, embraced a vast field incorporating architecture, furniture, decorative arts, porcelain, posters, advertisements, and graphic arts. It aimed to bridge the gap separating the fine arts and socioeconomic realities. It rejected the specialist tradition that a work of art could not be of any practical use or commercial value. It sought to destroy the barriers that social prejudice had raised between artists and craftsmen. The industrialization of art had to reinvigorate traditional craftsmanship, democratize aesthetic values, and respond to the needs of not only consumers but also producers and traders.

In Shanghai, where the capitalism of the golden age had been based on the development of light industry and the production of consumer goods, the previous argument was particularly pertinent, and artists and entrepreneurs alike promoted fine design. Among the founders of specialist reviews were the Gao brothers, pioneers of the Lingnan School of painters, and Wu Liande, a capitalist with connections to the networks of overseas Chinese. Meanwhile, *Art and Life* had no qualms about publishing photographs of objects produced by this or that Shanghai factory.

Among the applied arts, publicity held a place of particular importance. It first appeared upon the scene at the beginning of the twentieth century, when advertising calendars began to be produced; and in the 1920s and 1930s, it really took off. Initially, the use of imported modern techniques (lithography, polychrome printing) and the representation of contemporary scenes and figures went along with the persisting vogue for backgrounds featuring flowers and ribbons, copied from the tradition of the New Year (*nianhua*) painters. Following World War I, Western influences became ever stronger. In its own interests, the Commercial Press, which devoted much space to publicity in its newspapers and magazines, hired foreign painters to train an entire group of young artists. Some rapidly became sufficiently well known to go off on their own and found independent advertising agencies. A few years later, in specialized departments of the academies of Shanghai and Hangzhou future advertising artists became acquainted with the geometric forms, flat spaces, and curvilinear shapes that constituted the hallmark of both the Shanghai style and art deco. In the 1930s, publicity became an important branch of the Shanghai economy. The works of its creators were to be found everywhere, in the street, in newspapers, and in specialist magazines. Their forms and designs permeated the atmosphere of the time.

Although the objects dreamed up by these stylists were, because of their high prices, reserved as in the West for only a small elite group, they, too, contributed to the rapid rise of design. Conceived along the untrammeled lines advocated by the Weimar Bauhaus School, the items of furniture designed by Zhang Derong were reproduced in photographs in *Art and Life*, as were the plans of luxury villas. But the quest for forms at once aesthetic and functional also concerned the cups, thermos flasks, and mirrors that local factories produced. Magazines of the applied arts also covered architecture and published photographs that focused on the lines and decorative features of large modern buildings: wrought iron, stained glass, and mosaics.

Among the graphic arts, caricatures brought to critical social commentary the same purity of line and economy of means. The portrayal of dancing couples—with slim women clinging to the pretentious dandies or corpulent bourgeois who were their partners—was a recurrent theme on which artists dreamed up many variations, some cruel, others poetic.

Shanghai was the center of patriotic feeling and revolutionary thought. Progressive intellectuals there wished to place the new arts at the service of the revolution and turn them, like literature, into instruments of propaganda and mobilization. Wood engraving owed its development to such militancy, for it set out to be a resolutely proletarian art.[54] Under the influence of contemporary Soviet and German schools, it favored tormented designs with violent black-and-white contrasts to create realistic images that drew attention to capitalist and imperialist oppression. Although rooted in the popular tradition of New Year prints, woodcuts thus enjoyed a completely new lease on life, thanks in particular to the promotional efforts of Lu Xun, who regarded this as the preeminent art of the masses, accessible to all and easy and cheap to produce.

CHINESE CINEMA'S FIRST GOLDEN AGE

The first Chinese feature-length films to appear in Shanghai, in the 1920s, were influenced by both the shadow-theater tradition (*Piyingxi*) and popular theater with spoken dialogue (*wenmingxi*) and by imitation of Western films.* The pioneers of the genre worked for the Mingxing Company. Within a few years they turned out sixty or so adventure, sentimental, and erotic films in rapid succession. Their themes were for the most part borrowed from the literature of "mandarin ducks." Bao Tianxiao (1876–1973), who made his reputation with this kind of literature, was one of the suppliers of scenarios for the Mingxing Company. Also on offer to the public were plagiarisms of American films, for example, a "Charlie Chaplin in Shanghai" titled *The King of Clowns Visits China*, and martial arts films that were all the rage about 1928.[56]

But the Japanese invasion of Manchuria in 1931 and the attack on Shanghai in January 1932 changed the public's mood and expectations. Swept along by public mobilization, left-wing intellectuals took over cinematographic production. Their reign coincided with the first golden age of Chinese cinema. Either at the invitation of the Mingxing Company or working for companies directly controlled by the Communist Party, progressive producers and directors focused in particular on the content of films designed to reflect social realities and encourage anti-imperialist and anticapitalist resistance. They paid scant attention to technological progress and formal experimentation. Although American "talkies" invaded the Shanghai market from 1929 onward, up until 1935 Chinese studios continued to produce mainly silent movies.

With very few exceptions (one of which was the famous *Spring Silk-*

---

* In shadow theater, silhouettes cut from leather were manipulated behind an illuminated silk screen to illustrate a story told by a narrator to the accompaniment of an orchestra. The repertory of such theaters was borrowed from operas, folktales, and religious legends.[55] Spoken theater was imported from the West via Japan at the beginning of the twentieth century. Although singing was replaced by spoken dialogue, in the manner of Western plays, it retained many of the features of ancient opera. It was intended for a popular, rather than an elite, public.

worm, made in 1933 and based on a story by Mao Dun), the scenarios were set in an urban context, with the countryside merely providing an idyllic and nostalgic counterpoint to the realities of the city. These films tended to paint a somber picture. The corruption and culpable unconcern of the wealthy were set in contrast to the distress of humble folk driven into unemployment and poverty. The only notes of hope were struck by the disinterested behavior of patriots and the courage of militants.

Despite the stereotypes that they purveyed, the films of the 1930s portrayed a vibrant and complex society.[57] *The New Year Coin* (*Yasui qian*), a film with a soundtrack, made in 1937 from a scenario by Xia Yan, returned to themes of Shanghai modernity and evoked the nightlife of the bars, the emancipation and charms of women, and the frantic pace of modern life. The lucky coin given by a grandfather to his granddaughter as a New Year gift passes from hand to hand, and its progress serves as a device to explore society and its underworld. Beneath the author's patriotic and revolutionary rhetoric, one detects a deep distrust of modernization and, more particularly, female emancipation. Even as they promoted the struggle against arranged marriages and the tyranny of the patriarchal order and expressed commiseration with innocent young girls forced by poverty into prostitution and decadence, the progressive filmmakers of the 1930s could envisage no solution to the situation apart from a return to their roles as wives and mothers and commitment to a patriotic and revolutionary ideal.

This was the moral of *Wild Flower* (*Yecao xianhua*), a silent film made in 1930 by Sun Yu (1900–1990), in which the heroine, a young singing star, finds her salvation by returning to her fiancé and sacrificing her voice. The moral of *The Goddess* (*Shennü*), by Wu Yonggang, also a silent film and dating from 1934, is spelled out even more clearly.[58] The mother, forced against her will into crime and prostitution, is sent to prison, while the young son for whom she sacrifices everything is adopted by a generous-hearted school headmaster. Society is thereby preserved from contamination, and the patriarchal order is restored. For Tian Han, who wrote the scenario of *Three Modern Women* (*San ge modeng nüxing*), also released in 1934, the genuine "modern woman" is neither a sentimental young bourgeoise nor a femme fatale but an androgynous and ascetic militant.

If advocated at all, feminine emancipation was identified with the revolutionary and patriotic projects of men.

The rise of Shanghai cinema in this first golden age constituted one of the most successful attempts to appropriate an imported mode of artistic expression. The situation of Shanghai and China generally in the 1930s prompted an elite group of intellectuals to use cinema as a weapon in the patriotic struggle and ideological mobilization. Films were no longer simply "ice creams for the eye,"[59] a source of immediate pleasure for the spectator. When they began to reflect social reality and purvey a message, they lost their exotic character, became truly Chinese, and thereby acquired an originality that afforded the Shanghai school a place in the history of the seventh art.

Shanghai and, through it, coastal China did not manage to establish themselves as an institutionalized political and ideological force able to stand up to internal, rural, and bureaucratic China, but the city did assert its cultural originality with vigor. Compared to other regional Chinese cultures, Haipai was particularly important in that it presented a model of a new national identity. In this respect, the Shanghai experience differed from those of Hong Kong and Singapore where, in the second half of the twentieth century, economic success and westernization were accompanied by no more than a tardy and uncertain cultural redefinition. In Shanghai, the golden age of capitalism between 1917 and 1927 constituted a direct prelude to the peak of the "Belle Époque" of the 1930s.

PART THREE

The End of a World
(1937–1952)

CHAPTER 11

The War, the Occupation,
and the End of International Status

S HANGHAI, BRUISED AND HUMILIATED, as Paris was to be, was
now plunged into war. The neon lights went out. The Sino-Japanese
War broke out in July 1937, two years before World War II. One month
later, Shanghai was in the thick of it. The fate of the city, shattered by
bombs and shells and with every ruined building the object of a desperate hand-to-hand battle, prefigured that of many European and Japanese
towns to be swept away a few years later by the destructive impact of total
war. The West, however, was oblivious to this warning. The sole mission
of the Havas Agency, for which the journalist Robert Guillain worked,
was to inform local residents of the latest events in Europe and the United
States. The war in Shanghai was one between Asians in which the foreigners and their concessions were not—at least not yet—involved. Two
years later, however, the Sino-Japanese War merged with World War II.
Shanghai played no part in this but did not escape the consequences of
the planetwide clash. When the concessions disappeared, so too did the
international status that had made it a modern metropolis. Shanghai, like
so many other cities, was occupied, ravaged by poverty, and lived through
all the dramas of resistance and collaboration, along with the many compromises imposed by the simple will to survive.

For eight years, Shanghai was dominated by a string of armed conflicts,
some in the immediate vicinity, some more distant: the Japanese invasion
in 1937, the early World War II battles in Europe two years later, and then,
after the Japanese attack on Pearl Harbor on December 7, 1941, the battles
in the Pacific. At every stage in the conflagration, the situation deteriorated.
The battle for Shanghai, which raged from August to November 1937, was
the most savage of the Sino-Japanese War and culminated in the defeat of
the Nationalist troops, followed by the Japanese occupation of the city's
Chinese quarters. For a while, the foreign concessions, protected by their
international status, were spared invasion. They constituted an island of

relative prosperity and freedom, but it was a "solitary island" (*gudao*), cut off from and increasingly neglected by the European metropolises that were busy trying to avoid war in Europe or prepare for it.

By the time this eventually broke out in September 1939, the microcosm of the Shanghai gudao, deprived of the political and military support of Western imperialism and weakened by the local repercussions of the conflict between the democracies and the Axis powers, was no longer in a position to mount any opposition to the growing pressure exerted by Japan. As compromises gave way to concessions, the autonomy of the gudao was whittled away. With the invasion of the international settlement, a few hours after the attack on Pearl Harbor, the respite that its international status had afforded it expired. Although the French concession continued to enjoy a semblance of autonomy until its official restitution to China in July 1943, Shanghai was now subject to the will of the Japanese and their Chinese collaborators. The suppression of the concessions that was to have crowned the modernizing policies of the Guomindang and fulfilled popular patriotic demands came about simply as a result of the turn taken by the war, the initiative of the Japanese, and the constraints they imposed. It speeded up the city's descent into hell. The Shanghai of a thousand neon lights became a "world of darkness" (*heian shijie*).

THE BATTLE FOR SHANGHAI AND THE OCCUPATION OF THE CHINESE TOWN (1937)

The battle, which began on August 13, 1937, with the Nationalists' attack on the Japanese garrison, did not result from local dissensions, as the 1932 battle had. The Japanese presence in the city was certainly now much stronger. In the international settlement, the Japanese community, composed of 30,000 residents, was three times as large as the British community. It was located to the north of the Suzhou River in the Hongkou quarter known as "Little Tokyo." Since the 1932 intervention of the Japanese army, the concession's authorities had de facto lost control over this quarter, where 2,000 Japanese soldiers equipped with tanks and armored cars were stationed. The steady growth of the Japanese community had alarmed the British and American authorities, and they had adamantly refused to increase the number of Japanese councillors on the Shanghai

Municipal Council.*[1] It had also affronted the Chinese residents, who targeted most of their anti-imperialist boycotts and demonstrations against the Japanese. However, this mutual animosity was not the direct cause of the attack launched on the Japanese garrison. Chiang Kai-shek himself made the decision to extend the hostilities that had been engaged in northern China on July 7, 1937. In Shanghai, the local relationship with armed forces looked more favorable than in the north, and above all, the foreign presence seemed likely to give the conflict an international dimension from which the Nanjing government hoped to profit.

The fighting that broke out in the quarters of the international settlement situated to the north of the Suzhou River, in Hongkou and Yangshupu, was to last three months. At first, the numerical superiority of the Chinese troops gave them the advantage, and reinforced by two crack divisions from Nanjing, they pushed the Japanese back to the banks of the Huangpu. But when they came under fire from the enemy cannons of thirty ships at anchor in the river, the attackers were forced to beat a retreat. Soon the landing of an expeditionary force of 90,000 men enabled the Japanese to regain the upper hand and undertake a strategy of encirclement.

In spite of the superiority of the Japanese weaponry and their complete domination in the sky, it was several weeks before their troops conquered the quarters situated to the north of the Suzhou River. As more and more houses were flattened, hand-to-hand fighting continued until the end of October, at which point the few hundred heroes of the Lone Battalion (*Gujun*), holed up in a warehouse on the riverbank, abandoned all resistance. The Japanese were then able to take over the city, attacking the Nanshi suburbs and the Chinese town from the south. Threatened with encirclement, the Nationalist troops fled westward or took refuge in the French concession, where they were disarmed and interned. On November 11, the Japanese celebrated their victory and took possession of the Chinese town and the northern sector of the international settlement, Hongkou, and Yangshupu.

This terrible battle killed between 100,000 and 200,000 Chinese and reduced much of the town to rubble. In Zhabei, everything was "literally

---

* Japan had a right to two seats, which had been allotted to it after World War I.

riddled with holes, eaten away by a deluge of iron," the journalist Robert Guillain reported. In the western outskirts, to which the Japanese pursued the routed Nationalists, "Bombs rained down on the mud and bamboo huts of the smallest villages, and some sectors [were] as full of craters as the Verdun battlefield."[2] When the fighting broke out, the inhabitants of Zhabei, Hongkou, and Yangshupu, fleeing the battlefield that their quarters had become, tried to take shelter in the international settlement by crossing to the other side of the Suzhou River. The Garden Bridge, also known as "The Bridge of Life," now became a bridge of death. "Half a dozen times I know I was walking on children or old people sucked under by the torrent, trampled flat by countless feet."[3] A few weeks later, people from the Chinese town and the southern suburbs were jostling for access in front of the gates leading to the French concession.

For the residents of the concessions, the war was simply a spectacle to be watched from their rooftops and upper terraces. For weeks they saw those fighting "killing one another no more than 500 meters away." In the evening, "on leaving some elegant reception," the diners, "in dinner jackets and evening dresses," felt no qualms about climbing to the top of an eight-story warehouse, taking care that their "gleaming shoes" did not step on the bodies of coolies sleeping on the bare ground, to watch "the blood-red, flaming night."[4] However, the concessions were not completely spared. Their Black Sunday came on August 14, when Chinese planes carrying bombs intended for the Japanese ships at anchor on the Huangpu dropped them instead on the crowds thronging the Bund and Edward VII Avenue. More than 3,000 corpses were found.* "The gutters ran with blood."[5]

Soon the concessions had to cope with an influx of refugees that increased their population from 1.7 to 4.5 million within a few weeks. The municipal administrations, religious institutions, and charitable and humanitarian organizations, both Chinese and foreign or international, combined efforts to set up about two hundred reception centers. Schools, hospitals, theaters, pagodas, and universities all took in refugees. But

---

* This bombing raid was officially attributed to Nationalist forces in distress, but at the time some observers believed that Chiang Kai-shek himself, wishing to explode the myth of the invulnerability of the concessions and drag the United States into the war against Japan, was responsible for them.[6]

most had to camp out in the streets, in doorways, or on waste land. On the initiative of a Jesuit father, Jacquinot de Basenge, a disabled World War I veteran who combined remarkable organizational and diplomatic skills with an eminently military forcefulness, a safe zone was created in the old Chinese town itself in November. This took in 250,000 refugees whom the concessions could not accommodate without being completely overwhelmed. Both the Chinese and the Japanese military respected the neutrality of the "Jacquinot zone" for the time that it took gradually to disperse the refugees in the course of 1938.

The war had cut the international settlement off from the part of its territory situated to the north of the Suzhou River. Passage from the occupied zone to the free one was now extremely difficult. The Garden Bridge was turned into a frontier checkpoint, where the guards insisted on passes, a show of obedience, and tips from all those seeking to cross, whether they were residents or workers, Chinese or foreigners, on foot or in cars.

While most of the Japanese troops plunged into the interior of the country, in the occupied quarters of Shanghai the special services (*tokumu bu*) of the Japanese Imperial Army, responsible for civil affairs, set in place institutions designed to regulate relations with the local population. In December 1937, these services, on the strength of experience acquired in northern China, encouraged the creation of an Association of Shanghai Citizens (*Shanghai shimin xiehui*) consisting of several dozen major entrepreneurs whose role was to support the actions of the new "Great Way" (*Dadao*) collaborationist municipal government.

The Great Way was headed by a mayor imported from Taiwan, at that date still a Japanese colony, and was composed of a team of petty gangsters. It did not succeed in imposing its authority and was followed by a special municipality, headed by an authentic Shanghai banker, Fu Xiao'an, long hostile to Chiang Kai-shek. From 1940 on, this municipality functioned under the authority of the new central government in Nanjing,* which set at its head Chen Gongbo, formerly a high-ranking leader of the Guomindang but now an eminent collaborator.

---

* This government, set up in March 1940 and headed by Wang Jingwei as a rival to Chiang Kai-shek's Chongqing government, may be considered equivalent to the Vichy government in France.

Despite support from the Japanese special services, the new municipal institutions had a hard time establishing their authority. Eventually resorting to violence, they turned to gangsters, asking them to create a secret police and espionage service, known as Number 76 (a reference to the address of its headquarters at 76 Jessfield Road). These municipal institutions were financed by the protection racket, which, with Japanese assistance, they applied to gambling establishments, houses of prostitution, and opium dens. In this way, they ended up encouraging vice and crime, particularly in the outer western suburbs (Huxi). This quarter, formerly under the control of the international settlement's police force, now became a zone of lawlessness that the press of this period called "the Badlands" (*Daitu*).

THE SOLITARY ISLAND (1938–1941)

In sharp contrast to the desolate landscape and hardships of the Chinese quarters, the concessions to the south of the Suzhou River continued with their frenetic lifestyle of business and pleasure. However, international Shanghai was now a town living on borrowed time, "conquered but not yet occupied by its conquerors." Holed up in the gloomy quarters of Little Tokyo and the "lunar deserts" of Zhabei, the real masters of Shanghai lay in wait for their prey. In the concessions, "the mechanism of the old life [was] still ticking, but [seemed] doomed to stop, like a watch dropped in the desert."[7]

The ephemeral economic prosperity of 1938 and 1939 could not disguise the concessions' vulnerability. As early as 1937, military operations had slowed down economic activity in Shanghai. The Japanese blockade of the Chinese coastline that year and, in the following year, the ban preventing foreign ships from sailing up the Yangzi cut the city off from its inland markets. Between June 1937 and June 1939, the tonnage of ships entering Shanghai from all Chinese ports fell from 649,000 to 281,000 tons.[8] Half the industrial equipment of the city had been destroyed, and the Japanese had confiscated Chinese factories in the occupied quarters.

Very soon, however, activity resumed in the concessions, where the influx of refugees increased demands on the local market: the banks held large sums of money, for capital too had found its way there in search of security. Raw materials were imported. Jewish refugees from central Europe provided a large supply of executives and technicians. To elude Japanese control, Chinese entrepreneurs moved south of the Suzhou River, shifting the city's industrial center to the heart of the concessions. Industrial firms scaled down in size and diversified their products. Workshops set up in former private dwellings manufactured all kinds of consumer goods: soap, glue, toys, furniture, lightbulbs, pens, millinery, and mechanical and electrical equipment.

These industries supplied the French and British colonial territories of Southeast Asia, where the diminishing role played by their metropolises opened up the field to new suppliers. They also worked for regions still controlled by the Guomindang in the southwest and for Communist bases in the north that were supplied through many smuggling networks. Supplies were sent to the provinces of central China under the supervision of monopoly-holding Japanese companies, and above all, for the local market and the 5 million inhabitants now gathered in Shanghai. By 1939, production reached a level comparable to that of the prewar period or even higher, and the firms of Shanghai were making large profits.[9]

However, this was a fragile prosperity under threat from the increasingly rigid maritime blockade imposed by Japan and from inflation and monetary confusion aggravated by the issue of banknotes printed by Wang Jingwei's collaborationist government and the Japanese forces of occupation. After September 1939, the combination of the Sino-Japanese War and World War II reduced Shanghai's importance within what was now a multilateral conflict. Though cut off from the world and forgotten by it, the city still suffered the vagaries of the international situation. The war, which led to the collapse of the European colonial empires of East Asia, hastened the decline of the concessions, which suddenly found themselves without foreign protectors. It also upset relations among the various national communities present in the concessions and undermined the united front upon which the strength of the "Whites" there had rested for the past century.

THE WIND BLOWING FROM MUNICH AND VICHY

Until this point the military strength of the Western powers that were signatories to the opening-up treaties had always guaranteed the security of the concessions. In normal times, the symbolic presence of a few gunboats at anchor on the Yangzi had sufficed to maintain the established order. Whenever a crisis arose, the various governments involved would send in expeditionary troops to reinforce the local units of police and volunteers, such military responsibilities being mainly assumed by Great Britain, the de facto if not de jure dominant power in the international settlement.

At the outbreak of the Sino-Japanese War in July 1937, the great Western powers had local garrisons of no more than 1,000 to 2,500 men. They possessed neither the means nor the will to defend the concessions. The military reverses suffered by France and Britain in 1939–1940 destroyed their prestige once and for all, along with the foundations upon which Western imperialism in China and Asia rested.

Faced with pressure from the Japanese, the authorities of the international settlement could only adopt a policy of appeasement if they were to avoid any incident liable to bring Japan into the war alongside Germany.*
As negotiation degenerated into compromise, the authority of the Shanghai Municipal Council diminished and the neutrality of the international settlement was whittled away. The Japanese took over institutions set up by the Guomindang government on the concession's territory—telegraph, postal services, and radio. The National Salvation Associations were banned, and Nationalist resistance militants who continued to operate in the settlement were handed over to the Japanese Military Police. However, the council did manage to retain a measure of press freedom and, through technically legal but morally fraudulent maneuvers, prevented any increase in the number of Japanese representatives in the municipal elections held in April 1940.

This war of attrition in which the British, with their usual tenacity, endeavored to counter Japanese maneuvers and pressures, could achieve no more than a somewhat prolonged period of respite. In August 1940, the British government withdrew its last troops from Shanghai to spare them the humiliation of an inevitable defeat in the impending battle. In September, Japan entered World War II alongside Germany and Italy, and this increased the precarious nature of the situation. In April 1941, the

---

* Japan did not enter the war on the side of the Axis powers until September 1940, when the Tripartite Pact was signed.

Japanese, wishing to avoid the risk of further rigged elections, replaced the Shanghai Municipal Council by a nominated commission in which the British and Americans no longer commanded a majority.

Since the defeat of June 1940, the establishment of the Vichy government, and Japan's seizure of Indochina in August, the margin of maneuver possessed by the French concession was even more reduced than that of the neighboring international settlement. In the agreements of August 30, 1940, the French concession's authorities undertook to hand over to the Japanese all Chinese activists suspected of Nationalist sympathies, to oppose propaganda hostile to Japan and the collaborationist government of Wang Jingwei, and to foster cooperation between the municipal and the Japanese police forces. It was left to Roland de Margerie, the new consul-general appointed by Vichy who took up his post in October 1940, to put this policy of collaboration into operation. The French authorities then agreed to hand over to Wang Jingwei's government the arms seized when the routed Nationalist troops were interned in November 1937. However, they did refuse to relinquish the 250 crates of archives entrusted to the French concession by Chiang Kai-shek's government at the beginning of the war and also to admit Japanese to the concession's municipal commission and police force.[10]

The weakening of the European metropolises led to that of the Shanghai concessions. While France was invaded and London was bombed, their expatriates in Shanghai were left defenseless. Yet Shanghai was no ordinary colony. The Western elite groups there flattered themselves that they had, with their own bare hands, built up a society that was akin to that of the old Europe, but more dynamic, more cosmopolitan, and more autonomous. Did that "Shanghai spirit" of which the longtime residents were so proud desert them in the midst of all this turmoil?

WHATEVER BECAME OF THAT "SHANGHAI SPIRIT"?

Since the nineteenth century, the disruptions within Europe had reverberated, often with a deformed echo, within the microcosm of the foreign concessions. The various national communities that together made up Western society in Shanghai had not lost their sense of patriotism, but their interlocked economic interests, their common racism, and the privileges that they all enjoyed had created a solidarity upon which the interplay of diplomatic alliances made little impression. Yet when World War II broke out, the Shanghai spirit could not withstand the internal rifts that appeared. In September 1939, after the Germans hoisted the swastika flag in front of their sports club, which, like every other foreign sports club, was situated within the racecourse perimeter, the other foreign communities entered into a veritable flag war so disruptive that the Shanghai Municipal Council eventually banned the display of all national emblems.

The foreign society of Shanghai, less wealthy, less elitist, and far less homogeneous since the arrival of new waves of White Russians and Jews from central Europe, had long since lost its initial cohesion. The first great rift in this colonial society had appeared in the early 1920s, with the arrival of Russians ejected from their country by the civil war and the revolution. This wave of immigrants, made up chiefly of survivors from the White Russian armies, was followed ten years later by a flood of Russian colonists from Manchuria, fleeing from the Japanese invasion. A total of roughly 23,000 refugees settled in the northern quarters of the international settlement and in the French concession. However, this community did not become well integrated into the colonial Shanghai world, despite the contribution of technicians, managers, and military men that it made to the administration of the concessions, linguists to the intelligence services, and artists to local cultural life, and also despite the success of Ashkenazi Jewish small-scale entrepreneurs who set up cafés, restaurants, and jewelry shops. Exiled and stripped of their resources, many Russians were reduced to competing with Chinese laborers for unskilled jobs. Many of the men sank into delinquency; many of the women, into prostitution. The Russian émigrés were widely despised by both the Chinese population and Western elite groups, who resented them for having "devalued the image of the White Man" in the eyes of the Asians. In order to survive, they clung to their own cultural and religious practices and kept themselves to themselves. The Shanghai spirit meant nothing to them.[11]

The same applied to the Jewish community: not that of the great merchants who had arrived from Baghdad and Bombay in the nineteenth century—the Sassoon, Ezra, and Silas families—all of whom became part of the oligarchy of the international settlement, but that of the 25,000 émigrés ejected from Germany and neighboring Nazi countries who, from 1938 onward, landed in the concessions, the only refuge where they were still admitted without visas.* The short-lived prosperity of 1938–1939 had made it possible for the Shanghai economy to absorb some of the skills brought in by technicians, engineers, intellectuals, and entrepreneurs from central Europe. But many were forced to settle in the refugee camps to the north of the international settlement, where they survived thanks only to the aid provided by local or international Jewish organizations. Although this community was 18,000 strong, it remained on both the geographical and social peripheries of the concessions, more preoccupied with its own fate than with that of its host town.[12]

The White Russians and Jews from central Europe never became part of Shanghailander society; and the Germans were excluded from it at the time of World War I. Their businessmen had been expelled, and their membership in the Shanghai Municipal Council withdrawn; meanwhile, China, which had entered the war on the side of the Allies, had ceased to grant them the privilege of extraterritoriality. Subsequently, in the early 1930s, the German community regained its strength, with 2,000 members, but it continued to be held at a distance.[13] Its consequent resentment possibly explains the relatively warm welcome that it extended to the local branch of the National Socialist Party and its auxiliary organizations (centered on German youth and German culture). After 1939, the influx into Shanghai of a large number of Nazi leaders resulted in German residents being increasingly dominated by Berlin policies and, by the same token, weakened the implicit alliance between all old Shanghailanders in the face of anything from the outside that threatened the smooth running of their business affairs and their way of life. The Park Hotel, in the Nanjing Road opposite the racecourse, became the headquarters of the Abwehr's information services, the espionage service of the German armed forces, and the Gestapo, with a propaganda office and a group of secret agents operating under a variety of identities. The SS was also represented there,

---

* The Western democracies had limited the entry of Jewish refugees to their territories. The foreign concessions did likewise from August 1939 onward.

in the person of Josef Meisinger, "the Butcher of Warsaw."* Despite the misgivings of some of its members—diplomats and businessmen—the German community was swept along in the wake of Nazi policies. However, the distancing of the Germans from the other Westerners did not bring them much closer to their Japanese allies, with whom they maintained cool and frequently strained relations. Mutual distrust increased when the Japanese arrested Richard Sorge in October 1941. But racism no longer sufficed to weld together the common front of the concessions' foreign residents. Undermined by difficulties and clashes that had originated in Europe, Shanghai's foreign society lost the self-confidence that had been the source of its strength in earlier crises.

A WORLD OF DARKNESS (1941–1945)

The Pacific War, which broke out on December 8, 1941, sparked by the Japanese attacks on Pearl Harbor, led to the disappearance of the concessions:** the international settlement immediately and then, in July 1943, the French concession. This elimination of the foreign enclaves, for which the diplomacy of the Guomindang and the popular Chinese masses had striven so ardently, in the end resulted from the relation of forces in a worldwide context: not between the Western powers and China but between the Western powers and Japan. The direct cause was no doubt the French and British setbacks in Europe and those that America suffered at the beginning of the Pacific War. Far from fulfilling the hopes of Chinese patriots and heralding China's rebirth as a modern and sovereign great power, the demise of the concessions confirmed the power of Japanese militarism. It marked the beginning of an era of deprivations and humiliations for the foreign residents and, at the same time, increased the sufferings of the Chinese population, depriving it of an imperfect but nevertheless precious refuge from the brutalities of the Japanese occupation.

---

* Meisinger, born in Munich in 1899, was a longtime Nazi. After serving as adjutant to Heinrich Himmler, in September 1939 he was sent to Warsaw to head the Gestapo services there. He arrived in Shanghai in April 1941.[14]
** In calculating this date, it is necessary to take into account the difference in the hour between the east and the west coasts of the Pacific Ocean.

The Japanese forces took control of the international settlement a few hours after the attack on Pearl Harbor. At dawn on December 8, 1941, the Japanese ships opened fire on the last British gunboat still at anchor on the Huangpu, the *Petrel*. After a resistance as brief as it was heroic, the crew of the doomed ship tried to swim to the shore, under Japanese fire but with the assistance of the British guests of the great hotels lining the Bund who, still clad in evening dress, struggled through the muddy river water to reach them.[15] This was the only battle that took place in Shanghai during the entire Pacific War.

Japanese soldiers took over the buildings along the Bund without meeting any resistance. They ejected the diplomats and confiscated or took control of the businesses of the British and American nationals. The settlement was now liberated from Western domination, only to fall into the hands of the Japanese. The latter then ran it until August 2, 1943, at which point they handed the former settlement over to Wang Jingwei's government in a symbolic gesture that in no way reduced the control that they exercised over this sector and the rest of the city.

Once occupied, the former international settlement gradually turned into "a sort of concentration camp," as a Japanese military spokesman put it.[16] Day-to-day affairs continued to be handled by a municipal council, but it was now purged of all its British and American members and headed by a Japanese president. Most municipal officials, including those who were British, remained in their posts for several months or even a year to facilitate the handover. Under a regime of martial law and a curfew, established in that very December of 1941, the population was kept under strict surveillance. All commercial establishments, including nightclubs, had to close by nine P.M. The streets bristled with barbed-wire barriers guarded by sentries who insisted on identity papers accompanied by respectful bows. British and American residents were required to wear red armbands indicating that they were "nationals of enemy powers." The Japanese extended to the former concession the obligation to register all homes (*baojia*) that had already been imposed in the Chinese quarters. This system of mutual responsibility, a legacy of imperial China, was accompanied by a general census and the issue of individual identity cards and certificates to be displayed at the entrance of every home. The arrangement proved very effective in the struggle against terrorism.* In the event of an attack, the quarter involved was cordoned off. The blockade might last several days or several weeks, until such time as those guilty were arrested, even if this endangered the lives of residents left without supplies or medical care.[17]

At the end of 1942, the Japanese began to intern residents who were nationals of enemy powers. In one year, 8,000 British and several hundred Americans were dispersed to half a dozen or so camps, mostly situated on the city's periphery. The initiatives taken by certain people such as Hugh Collar, the ex-president of the former Association of British Residents, helped the prisoners to organize themselves, the better to cope with the privations, humiliations, and promiscuity of these camps.[18]

In February 1943, the Japanese also herded all "displaced refugees from central Europe" into a "designated zone" in the Hongkou quarter. Many Jews were already living there, and the rest were ordered to move in. In this rather singular ghetto, 16,000 Jews had to live on 2.5 square kilometers along with 100,000 Chinese. Living conditions in the ghetto were no better than those in the camps, nor were they worse.

The French community had remained sheltered in a concession that had been spared occupation by the Japanese, thanks to its connection with the Vichy government. But in 1943 it, too, lost the relative protection that the French concession had afforded it. Immediately after the occupation of the international settlement, the French consul-general, Roland de Margerie, had noted: "All is calm in the French concession," adding that the Japanese authorities had decided "to respect the neutrality of the concession . . . within the framework . . . of the de facto collaboration that has been established." However, in the months that followed, Japanese pressure mounted. In April 1942, the authorities of the French concession had to agree to accommodate a detachment consisting of one hundred or so Japanese police instructed to help the French police to "fight against terrorism" and to ensure "the surveillance of nationals hostile to Japan and the disposal of their possessions." The authorities were also forced to agree to collaborate in drawing up an inventory of French firms backed

---

* It was so effective that it was taken over, with very few changes, by the Guomindang after 1945 and by the Communists after 1949.

by British or American capital. Acting on their own initiative, the French authorities extended to their own concession the system of registration of homes that the Japanese had already introduced in the Chinese quarters and the former international settlement.[19]

In January 1943, the Nanjing government's entry into the war against the Allies prompted Japan to promise Wang Jingwei that it would restore all the foreign concessions to the Chinese. In February, the Vichy government was obliged to accept the return of the French concession to Chinese sovereignty. The dissolution of an administration that employed 400 French, 1,000 Annamites (in the police force), and several thousand Chinese raised problems that were all the more acute given that naval warfare had cut communications and prevented repatriation to France and to Indochina. Wang Jingwei's government undertook to reemploy all the Chinese and some of the French staff. Other employees were incorporated into the consular service or placed at the disposal of a rapidly set-up French center. The Annamite policemen were absorbed by the army and attached to the small French garrison whose existence the Japanese tolerated. The consulate-general's secret finances made it possible to effect these changes and, in the short term, to provide subsidies for various cultural and social institutions—hospitals, schools, the Pasteur Institute—and the vital needs of French residents who now found themselves without resources.* They also facilitated the consulate-general's purchase of a number of municipal properties, thereby converting them into possessions of the French State that could not be ceded to the Chinese when the ex-French concession was restored to China. As the ambassador, Henri Cosme, saw it, the liquidation of the French concession was carried out in the best conditions possible.[21]

All that remained to be done was to strike the flag and hand over the town hall keys to the mayor, Chen Gongbo. This happened on July 30 during a ceremony that was not attended by Ambassador Cosme, who, being accredited to the government of Chiang Kai-shek, could not enter into official contact with the representatives of Nanjing. Two days

---

* These funds came from the consulate-general's mutual aid fund, which was fed in particular by the taxes levied on greyhound racing. At the time of the retrocession of the French concession, the monthly income paid into the account totaled around 2 million francs.[20]

THE END OF A WORLD

later, the city was administratively reunited when the Japanese handed the ex–international settlement over to the Chinese. This became the first arrondissement in the Special Municipality of Shanghai, and the former French concession became the eighth arrondissement.

The decline of the French presence in Shanghai did not end with the restitution of the French concession. In March 1945, following the German defeats in Europe and the fall of the Vichy regime in France, the Japanese decided to take direct control of the administration of French Indochina, to break off diplomatic relations with the French consular representation in Shanghai, and to disarm the small garrison (1,400 men, 880 of whom were Annamites) that had survived the demise of the concession. Resistance was futile, but surrendering without a fight was nevertheless perceived as dishonorable, in particular by the garrison commander, who committed suicide a few months later.[22] The submission of the Shanghai garrison stood in contrast to the resistance put up by the French units of Indochina, which were more numerous but every bit as powerless. One last trial was in store for the French community: in July 1945, 723 Annamite guards rebelled against the French officers who still commanded them in the barracks where they were all interned together. Declaring themselves supporters of the Vietnamese revolutionary movement, the guards placed themselves under the protection of the Japanese military authorities.[23]

The retrocession of the concessions presents many ambiguities, both legal and diplomatic. In the case of the French concession, for example, the validity of the agreement signed between the collaborationist governments of Vichy and Nanjing was questionable. The two governments did not recognize each other and would both disappear at the end of the war when their actions were repudiated by their respective successors.* Nevertheless, despite the circumstances in which it took place, the retrocession of the foreign concessions certainly marked an essential turning point in

---

* Following the Japanese capitulation, some of the French in Shanghai, including the new consul-general, Jean Filliol, argued on the basis of these ambiguities that the 1943 restitution treaty was null and void. However, in February 1946, France, more concerned about reestablishing its presence in Indochina than saving a condemned concession, confirmed the retrocession, obtaining from Chiang Kai-shek the withdrawal of the Guomindang troops that had occupied northern Indochina in accordance with the Potsdam Agreement.

the history of Shanghai: its importance became fully clear two years later when, following the Japanese capitulation, the Guomindang set up the municipal government of a city now both free and reunified.

SHANGHAI UNDER THE OCCUPATION

In China, as in France, the history of the occupation was written to suit the ideologies and policies predominant in the postwar period. But in China, the myth of heroic members of the resistance clashing with collaborationist profiteers continues to impose its Manichean perspectives, leaving in the shadows the many ambiguities of resistance and collaboration alike, along with the predominance of patterns of behavior that were opportunistic or simply cautious.[24] Memories of the occupation were eclipsed by the epic and tragedies of the revolution that erupted in the wake of the war. All that the collective Chinese memory retained of those "dark days" was the culpability of Japan, the heroism of the Communist guerrillas, and the misfortunes of the people. What was at stake in the conflicts that set the Chinese in opposition to one another is something that is largely covered up. From the point of view of triumphant Communism, a Nationalist resistance fighter was hardly better than a Nationalist collaborator: both were reactionaries, and even a cadre who had pursued his clandestine activities in a "white zone" was already a potential traitor.

The situation of China after its defeat by Japan in 1937 in some respects calls to mind that of France three years later: the partial occupation of the national territory by enemy forces; the rivalry between the government of free China—that of Chiang Kai-shek, holed up in Chongqing, in the distant province of Sichuan—and the collaborating government of Wang Jingwei, established in Nanjing in 1940; the rapid spread of Communist influence carried forward by a surge of national resistance and, despite the united-front policy that linked Chiang Kai-shek to the Communist leaders in Yan'an, regarded as threatening by both governments. Shanghai, like Paris but even more so, suffered from rationing and a black market, the insulting luxury of profiteers, violence, denunciations, arrests, and torture.

But Shanghai's occupation was also characterized by certain specific features connected with the history and culture of East Asia. Japanese militarism had neither the same ideological bases nor the same ambitions as German Nazism. The presence of even a waning Western imperialism complicated the political choices of Chinese patriots. The rising strength of Communism and the fears that this inspired encouraged secret relations between Chongqing and Nanjing and even directly between Chongqing and the Japanese. In France, the ambiguities of the Vichy version of "re-sistance" did not prevent the emergence of a relatively clear picture of the commitment of the various parties.* In Shanghai, the idea that one could "save the nation by devious means" (*quxian jiuguo*) lent legitimacy to general recourse to a double or triple strategy, governed by political rather than ideological considerations and in many cases prompted by personal friendships or interests. Shanghai, the triumph of opportunism? But even opportunism surely presupposes a certain activism. In Shanghai, the vast majority of the population endeavored simply to survive in material and moral conditions that became increasingly difficult. But this apparent submission to the law of the strongest did not amount to collaboration. While putting private interests (of an individual or, more often, a family) before the national interest, it did not exclude sentiments of indignation and revolt, even if it did limit their expression to private areas and am-biguous statements.

RESISTANCE

The Japanese occupation relegated Shanghai to the margins of national resistance. Until 1937, this was where the nation's heartbeat had been located, the center of all the patriotic demonstrations and anti-Japanese movements. Yet now, from one day to the next, the city lost its influence. It was seen as a suspect refuge for the weak, egoists, and hedonists. All others had deserted it. They had set out westward, making for free China, or had rallied to the Communist base in Yan'an, or had taken refuge in Hong Kong to avoid all contact with the enemy.

Yet by the autumn of 1937, in the wake of the great patriotic mobili-zation that had accompanied the armed clashes of the preceding months,

* The concept of *resistantialisme*, forged by the French Right, meant, as opposed to "a left-wing resistance, infiltrated by Communists, which was somewhat suspect, in fact, 'revolution-ary,' . . . a right-wing and to a large extent anti-Gaullist resistance, closer to Pétain."[25]

militants and agents of the Guomindang and the Communist Party, members of secret societies, intellectuals, and journalists were already organizing resistance. For four years, these men were to wage a campaign of propaganda and harassment against the Japanese and their collaborators. The reiterated complaints of the occupier and the reprisals taken give one some idea of the efficacy of this resistance. It owed much to the support of the foreigners holed up in the gudao.

Once again—but for the last time—the presence of the concessions facilitated the action of Chinese hostile to the political institutions of their country. The foreign enclaves served them as a base from which to organize guerrilla warfare in the suburbs and launch terrorist strikes in the city; it provided them with a rostrum from which to heckle the Japanese and their collaborators and a refuge in which figures under threat could hide and to which clandestine organizations could withdraw. Despite its description as a solitary island, the gudao once again found itself the hub of many resistance networks whose operations it protected until they disappeared in 1942–1943, when the Japanese and their collaborators extended their control to the entire city.

Guerrilla warfare in and around the city prolonged the fighting of 1937. Survivors of the Nationalist armies, men of the New 4th Army based in Anhui, caused insecurity to reign as they sabotaged the railways that served Shanghai;* until 1939, the Japanese were constantly obliged to send in soldiers and tanks to restore order. However, the city itself was the principal battlefield, and its main weapons of resistance were terrorism and propaganda. Among the clandestine organizations that the concessions sheltered, a role of prime importance fell to the Guomindang Intelligence Service (*Juntong*), directed from Chongqing by Dai Li. This service employed a thousand agents headed by cadres from the lesser provincial gentry, the products of a traditional education that had filled their heads with heroic legends.[26] The Juntong's main objective was to foil Japanese

---

* In 1938, the 4th New Army (Communist) consisted of about 10,000 survivors of the Long March who had been abandoned in the lower Yangzi region in 1934. This army, which took in fugitives from Nanjing and Shanghai, increasingly carried out operations in a zone that had been under Guomindang influence before the war. In January 1941, Chiang Kai-shek ordered Nationalist forces to attack and disarm some of its units, thereby provoking the quasi breakdown of the Second United Front of the Guomindang and the CCP.

attempts to set up collaborationist municipal and central governments, and its tactics involved assassinating all Chinese disposed to fall in with such plans. Between September 1937 and October 1941, the Juntong organized 150 executions.

The settings for these assassinations impressed public opinion as much as did the notoriety of their victims. In September 1938, Tang Shaoyi was struck down. This former minister and ambassador was a candidate for the post of head of the central government that the Japanese were planning to create. He was an antiques specialist and a collector of artistic objects; he was assassinated as he admired an ancient vase in which his killers, disguised as antiquarians, had concealed a sharp knife. In February 1939, it was the turn of Chen Lu, a former ambassador to France. He was shot while celebrating the New Year, seated on a sofa in the midst of his guests. Fu Xiao'an, the mayor of the collaborationist Shanghai municipality, on an October night in 1940 was killed by his cook, armed with a butcher's cleaver.[27]

Alongside this terrorism, an intense propaganda program was developing, carried forward by an unprecedented wave of activity on the part of the Chinese press based in the international settlement. At the end of 1937, the Japanese had predictably insisted, in the name of neutrality, that the municipal authorities close down a dozen or so Chinese newspapers. About thirty others scuttled themselves. However, by virtue of the concession's extraterritoriality, foreign publications eluded this censorship. Some were extremely hostile to Japan. One example was *The China Weekly Review*, whose editor-in-chief, the American J. B. Powell, subsequently paid dearly for the position that he adopted. However, anti-Japanese propaganda, which intensified in 1938, was in the main produced by "the Chinese press under foreign management" (*yangshangbao*). This consisted of newspapers produced by Chinese but registered in a consulate as the property of foreigners and therefore not subject to Japanese controls. These papers spoke for the Chongqing government and the Communist authorities of Yan'an, whose communiqués and directives they diffused. The Japanese, who were powerless to halt these publications, did their best to curtail their circulation outside the concessions.

Patriotic theater was another form of resistance that began to develop in 1938, particularly in the French concession. The movement was run by clandestine Communist cadres who, in accordance with the united-front policy, joined forces with intellectuals who were moved especially by a sense of honor and moral integrity. One of these was Li Jianwu (1906–1982), a specialist in French literature. Thanks to the good relations that this translator and admirer of Flaubert maintained with the French authorities, many performances of a patriotic nature were put on. The most popular portrayed historic episodes in order to convey their resistance message; one such was *Flower of Blood (Bixuehua)*, which retraced the destiny of a group of scholars at the end of the Ming dynasty.[28]

The best-known left-wing intellectuals, such as Guo Moruo and Mao Dun, had already left Shanghai by the autumn of 1937. Others, less militant or subject to more family or financial constraints, remained. In order to avoid contact with the occupiers as much as possible, many of these moved into the concessions. There, in relative safety, they pursued their usual activities and developed social networks that were rebellious rather than positively resistant and thrived on meetings in cafés, public baths, mah-jongg contests hosted by friends, and wedding receptions: all provided opportunities to exchange news, foster hatred of the Japanese, and keep alive hopes of liberation.[29] Such patterns of behavior, which reflected at once impotence and a rejection of resignation, were also common in Europe, where in the company of friends people told jokes that ridiculed the occupying power, and also in Stalin's USSR, where dissidents would gather in one another's homes in the intimacy of their kitchens.

Apart from one or two journalists such as the American J. B. Powell and the British H. G. W. Woodhead, the foreign residents hardly involved themselves at all in a fight that should have been in the forefront of their preoccupations once war had broken out in Europe and Japan had thrown in its lot with the Axis powers. This was partly because of a persistent sense of racial separation and partly because, understandably enough, some foreign communities simply had no patriotic reactions at all.

The White Russians and the Jewish refugees from central Europe had been stripped of their nationalities. They were not affected by patriotic motivations, and their preoccupations as members of a community stemmed from an opportunistic strategy that varied according to day-to-day circumstances.* The few British residents who engaged in resistance operated under the direction of the Special Operations Executive, a body that Churchill had created in 1940 to organize resistance and sabotage in the occupied countries of Europe. A tiny Shanghai cell, which included no Chinese members, remained ineffectual and was dismantled by the Japanese as soon as they occupied the international settlement in December 1941.

In the French concession, a handful of Gaullists, spurred on by a local trader, Roderick Egal, created the "France Quand même" group in August 1940 and recruited sixty or so volunteers to go fight with the Free French forces.[30] In April 1941, after the arrest of Egal, who was accused by Consul-General de Margerie of having incited French marines to desert, the French concession's Gaullists regrouped around the inspector of education, Charles Grosbois, and the former consular judge, Horace Kaufman, who had been relieved of his duties in accordance with Vichy's anti-Semitic laws. But their activities were hampered by what one of them described as "the particularly difficult" situation created by "the existence of a large Vichy party" and the need not to "further deepen the gulf that already separated the French of Shanghai."[31] Although these Gaullists were in contact with Chongqing, they do not seem to have cooperated with the local Nationalist networks. The most determined of the French concession's resistance activists went off to fight in Africa, Italy, and France. Their history merges only temporarily with that of Shanghai.

COLLABORATION

Collaboration took many forms in Shanghai. If active, it implied support for the objectives of the enemy and a desire to help the latter to dominate the population and exploit local resources. If passive, it presupposed a more or less constrained acceptance of the status quo and participation in the management of day-to-day affairs within the framework of former responsibilities and duties. It is sometimes hard to distinguish between the

---

* Some of the White Russians, shocked by the German invasion of the USSR, put their love of their country before their hatred of Stalinist Communism. Soviet agents, who were still operating in Shanghai, were to exploit this surge of patriotism.

two, as became very clear in the courts appointed after the war to carry out the process of purgation. Passive collaboration sometimes sprang from opportunistic calculation, sometimes simply from a survival instinct, and to some extent became confused with strategies of accommodation.

Collaboration was one response to Japanese demands that were formulated in a variety of ways, depending on which cliques were dominant in Tokyo and in the Imperial Army and also on which Chinese regions were involved and how the war was going. In the early days of the occupation, the Japanese ascribed only a secondary importance to Shanghai and the provinces of central China, since they were not yet interested in attaching them (unlike the northern provinces) to the Japanese Empire. But in 1939, Japanese policy took a new turn: it now aimed to institutionalize and legitimize collaboration that eventually, under supervision from Tokyo, could take over the management of the coastal zone and compete with Chiang Kai-shek's Chongqing government. However, as this policy met with little success, the Japanese decided to harden the nature of their occupation.

At the end of 1937, in a Shanghai deserted by most members of its intellectual and political elite groups, the Japanese were having difficulty finding their first collaborators. Their special services responsible for civil affairs in the occupied territories were obliged to turn to Taiwan to find a few gangsters to man a municipal government. In Shanghai itself, they approached a score of captains of industry and commerce in their search for leaders to head the Association of Shanghai Citizens (*Shanghai shimin xiehui*), whose purpose was supposed to be to relaunch political activity. But the Guomindang's assassination of one of those entrepreneurs scared off the rest, and the project came to nothing. The fact was that the Japanese could count on cooperation only from a few aged politicians, has-beens from the warlord period, people with little prestige or authority who had been sidelined from Chinese political life once the Guomindang came to power in 1927. In the collaborationist municipal council of 1938, the only Shanghai figure of any note was Fu Xiao'an, a banker and former president of the General Chamber of Commerce. Since 1927 he had been living in Manchuria, forced out of Shanghai by Chiang Kai-shek's hostility; but now he had returned, part of the Japanese army's baggage.

In 1939, Wang Jingwei left Chongqing, where he had retreated with Chiang Kai-shek, and joined the Japanese. This rallying of one of the principal leaders of the Guomindang helped to impart some luster to the collaborationist standard. Although Wang Jingwei (1883–1944) was not regarded as a hero, as Marshal Philippe Pétain was in France, he was bathed in an aura that resulted from his extremely long revolutionary record, his comradeship with Sun Yat-sen, and his stormy partnership with Chiang Kai-shek, whose authority he had frequently defied, supported by the left-wing faction of the Guomindang. Picked by the Japanese to head the central government that they were trying to form, Wang Jingwei thus arrived in Shanghai in May 1939.* He brought with him two of his political allies, Zhou Fuhai (1897–1948), one of the founding members of the Chinese Communist Party, who later rallied to Chiang Kai-shek and became one of the principal theoreticians of the Guomindang,[32] and Chen Gongbo (1892–1946), another early Communist leader, who subsequently rallied to the Guomindang and was a former member of Chiang Kai-shek's government. In November 1940, Chen Gongbo became mayor of Shanghai, a post that he retained for four years, eventually to be replaced by Zhou Fuhai.

Despite their political and intellectual stature, the Chongqing defectors attracted few followers in Shanghai. But in September 1938, they were joined by Chu Minyi (1884–1946), who, after studying medicine in France, had entered upon a career within the Guomindang under the protection of Wang Jingwei, who was his brother-in-law. Chu Minyi became minister for foreign affairs in the Nanjing government and in 1943 negotiated for the retrocession of the French concession with the French authorities, by whom he was well known and highly respected.

The limited number of elite figures who rallied to the new regime led collaborators and their Japanese protectors to turn to adventurers and to recruit their associates and auxiliaries among secret societies and criminal gangs. These gangsters packed the administration, the "grassroots" collaborating self-government committees, and the political police force of Number 76. Du Yuesheng's departure for Hong Kong had weakened the

---

* He was to remain there until March 1940, when the new central government was installed in Nanjing.

old chief's authority over the Green Gang and left the field free for new godfathers, many of whom operated in the pay of the Japanese. Although the secret society had previously espoused the cause of nationalism, it was now increasingly won over by collaboration. This development provides a telling illustration of "the capacity of certain groups that are ideologically weak but structurally strong to adapt themselves to changing sociopolitical environments by transforming their organizational goals."[33] The new mafiosi lacked the Confucian urbanity of their predecessor. Chang Yuqing, known as Two-Ton Chang (although the crook in truth weighed a mere 150 kilos), was a former butcher and one of the principal leaders of the Subei (northern Jiangsu) clique within the Green Gang. The Japanese had already made use of him in 1932, at the time of their fleeting occupation of Zhabei. In 1938, they ordered him to assemble a thousand henchmen from the Yellow Way Society (*Huangdao hui*), which was taken over a few months later by the Anqing Society,* officially presented as the heir to and perpetuator of the Green Gang. Chang Yuqing and his acolytes were the tools of counterterrorism that the Nanjing government organized in opposition to Nationalist and Communist terrorist activities. Once installed in the New Asia Hotel in Hongkou, they converted all the bathrooms into execution chambers. These killers were professional criminals: they worked for whoever would pay them.

For Wang Jingwei and his immediate entourage, in contrast, the switch to collaboration represented a carefully considered political decision. Despairing of China's military weakness and hostile to the united-front policy and the Communist manipulations that this authorized, Wang Jingwei and his followers placed their hopes in cooperation with Japan. As they saw it, the salvation of their country lay not in the all-out resistance encouraged by the Chongqing government but in a "just peace" and support for "the New Order in East Asia" advocated by Tokyo. This choice seemed to them to conform with the doctrine of Sun Yat-sen, who until his death continued to extol the virtues of the struggle against Western imperialism within the

---

* Its full name was *Anguo qingmeng* (bringing peace to the country and enlightenment to the people). It referred to the name of an eighteenth-century secret society believed to be the forebear of the Green Gang.

framework of "Greater Asia."* By virtue of their former services to the revolutionary cause and the national government, the collaboration leaders determined that they had as much right as Chiang Kai-shek to pronounce on China's destiny. Since its establishment in 1927, the Nationalist regime had been disrupted by many factional clashes. The legitimacy of Chiang Kai-shek was repeatedly challenged, and the lawful basis of the state was fragile. A good citizen was not one who obeyed the law but one who acted for the good of China. Indecision and a confusion of loyalties explain why many links remained between the political staff in Chongqing and those in Nanjing and Shanghai—links that helped to blur the demarcation line between resistance and collaboration.

In some respects, the perverted patriotism of the Chinese collaborators puts one in mind of that of certain Vichyists. And, as in the case of the latter, disappointment was not far away. Far from treating their collaborators as partners, the Japanese made them their auxiliaries and left them with no financial resources. Both the Nanjing government and the Shanghai municipality lived by racketeering and, through the mediation of Number 76, extorting protection money from the casinos, opium dens, and houses of prostitution in the Badlands. The image of collaboration merged with that of vice and crime.

Violence was the collaborators' chief means of action. They opposed the terrorism of Nationalist and Communist networks with their own counterterrorism. The concessions became a battlefield in a faceless war that spread terror everywhere. The old law of "an eye for an eye" was given new twists, becoming "a banker for a banker" or "an editor for an editor."[35] Every execution perpetrated by one camp was immediately matched by others perpetrated by the other camp.

Unable to match the quality newspapers of the concessions by a press of comparable caliber, the collaborators hired Number 76 to eliminate the journalists themselves. In 1941, the blacklist of designated victims contained the names of seven foreigners and eighty Chinese. Each wave of assassinations was succeeded by another: there were half a dozen murders

---

* The doctrine of a "Greater Asia" (*Da Yazhou zhuyi*) was the theme of Sun Yat-sen's last great speech, delivered in Kobe in November 1924.[34]

in 1938, twenty more between 1939 and 1941. Newspaper headquarters-turned-fortresses were constantly raided. The mailbag would bring sinister warnings accompanied by severed hands or fingers. The heads of victims would be left dangling from lampposts or dumped in the gutters.

The purpose of the counterterrorism directed against bankers and their employees was to gain control of financial activities in the concessions, where Nationalist institutions were still present after 1937, and Chongqing money continued to be used despite the collaborators' efforts to impose the Central Reserve Bank's new dollar issued by the Nanjing government. Attacks against individuals gave way to collective slaughtering, raids were replaced by bombardments, and terrorism slid into guerrilla warfare. On the night of March 21, 1941, in response to a raid on the Central Reserve Bank, agents of Number 76 stormed the residence reserved for employees of the Bank of China and abducted 128 of them as hostages.

This counterterrorism made the protection that the concessions afforded the Chinese resistance ever more illusory; and at the start of the Pacific War, these fragile refuges disappeared. New fields of operation opened up for the collaborators, and the Nationalist and Communist networks of Shanghai were weakened while propaganda for the New Order in East Asia intensified and the population was reduced to submission. Despite symbolic gestures such as the retrocession of the concessions, collaboration lost its credibility even in the eyes of those who had been its promoters. Wang Jingwei and his entourage, overtaken by feelings of failure and culpability, increased their secret contacts with Chongqing. Discourse was swept away by the relation of forces. Faced with the militarism of the Japanese, now hardened by their setbacks in the war, collaboration spread but was in truth merely resignation to the inevitable and became increasingly confused with a simple desire to survive.

SURVIVAL

For the vast majority of the Shanghai population, the growing difficulties of material life compounded the humiliations and dangers of the occupation. Many foreigners, relatively spared until 1942, now also experienced the pangs of hunger and the agonies of exclusion. The question was, how to survive in the hell that Shanghai had become?

Yet at the beginning of the war, the Shanghai economy had retained its vitality. In 1938, the excellent rice harvest in the lower Yangzi basin had made it possible to keep the city supplied, and the influx of refugees and capital into the solitary island of the concessions had stimulated an industrial boom. But the situation had begun to degenerate in 1939 when the Japanese decided to cut the city off from its hinterland, thereby depriving it of its usual supplies of rice. At this point, Shanghai had resorted to imports, which increased from 308,000 tons in 1937 to 3.9 million tons in 1940.[36] Starting in 1941, the commercial blockade imposed by the Americans in the Pacific and the intensification of Japanese requisitioning in central China resulted in serious shortages in the city. The price of rice rose ever higher. A rationing system was introduced in the foreign concessions in 1941–1942 and was extended in the following year to the Chinese quarters. But it functioned badly: distributions covered only one-quarter of the official rations. The queues outside the licensed shops lengthened by day and night, and many riots broke out.

The black market supplemented the inadequate rations. But from 1942 on, illegal trafficking became increasingly dangerous, as the Japanese tightened their controls in order to retain the rice from the lower Yangzi for their own armies and civilian population. Smuggling, albeit much scaled down, nevertheless persisted. This was antlike trading: the rice entered Shanghai in minute quantities, hidden in the clothing of a multitude of small-scale transporters, most of them traveling by bicycle. This contraband rice sold at prices five or six times higher than that of the official rice and was beyond the means of many people. Never had there been so many dying of hunger in the streets of Shanghai. On some winter mornings, hundreds of corpses were collected, most of them children. In the summer of 1942, the city was ravaged by the full force of an epidemic of typhoid and cholera.

The city was also short of raw materials and coal. Electricity was hard to come by. Between 1937 and 1944, production in Shanghai fell by 80%. Factories in the concessions were forced to close; by 1942, only half were still functioning, at a reduced rate. In homes, electricity failures were more and more frequent, and the neon lights went out. Taxis had disappeared. Public transport operated for only a few hours a day. Unemployment took a general hold. Galloping inflation undermined the purchasing power of even those lucky enough still to have a job. Shortages, inflation, and unemployment fueled violence on every side: muggings, exactions, armed robbery, harassment of women queuing for food. Not all the insecurity could be blamed on the Japanese bayonets and the gangsters of Number 76.

In this city stricken by a creeping paralysis, strategies for survival varied according to social status, wealth, fame, and moral values. Entrepreneurs displayed their opportunism. The war and the occupation had upset their activities, but accustomed as they were to working in an unstable environment and running their businesses on a short-term basis, they proved clever at limiting their losses and seizing any opportunities for increasing their wealth offered by speculation in a time of shortages. The destiny of the Rong family and its Shenxin textile mills illustrates this ability to survive and sometimes even prosper in adverse circumstances.

In August 1937, the Rong brothers refused to move their seven Shanghai textile mills westward. They thought the conflict would be brief and were loath to disrupt their business networks and to fall under the authority of the Guomindang with which their relations were frequently strained. A few months later, they lost five mills situated in the zone of Japanese occupation. In an attempt to recover them, Rong Zongjing, the head of the family and business group, agreed to join the Association of Shanghai Citizens, designed to promote collaboration with the Japanese and restart production. For Rong Zongjing, this was not a political choice but the kind of maneuver customary for Chinese merchants, who in troubled times were always prepared to negotiate with whoever held the power. "The fact is that China now has no government.... If I do not take steps to protect my businesses, who will?"[37] However, the attacks being perpetrated by Guomindang agents against powerful collaborators frightened Rong Zongjing, and soon he fled to Hong Kong, where he died a few weeks later.

The patriarch's disappearance put his sons and nephews in the driver's seat. Such a handover from one generation to another and the division of shares that accompanied it generally represented a dangerous moment in the life of great Chinese family businesses. However, in the context of war and crisis, the increasingly autonomous management of their various production units conferred considerable flexibility upon the strategy of the Rongs. Mills no. 2 and no. 9, situated in the international settlement, were registered as foreign property for greater security and, as such, enjoyed great prosperity at the time of the solitary island, from 1938 to 1941. They worked for the local market and exported goods to the European colonies of Southeast Asia that were no longer supplied by their respective warring metropolises. At this time, Shanghai's concessions were still part of the network of international trade and so were able to import raw materials and coal that were no longer to be found in China. Production increased, as did profits: the Rongs reinvested their dividends (between 30% and 40% each year) in gold and foreign currencies.

After the occupation of the international settlement, the Rongs were permitted to relaunch production in return for large sums of money and the appointment of Japanese inspectors to both their textile mills. But times had changed. It was no longer possible to obtain from overseas whatever was unavailable locally. Furthermore, the Shenxin textile mills were threatened by the authoritarian policies of the Nanjing government, which was trying to set up a production system under state control. Mills no. 2 and no. 9 were operating at no more than 20% capacity, and the Rongs did not manage to restart production in the other mills that they had recovered from the Japanese. They therefore dismantled part of the machinery in those factories and proceeded to create scattered workshops that, being so much smaller, eluded controls and taxation more easily.

In all negotiations with the Japanese and the Nanjing government, the Rongs were extremely prudent, eschewing personal interventions and always acting through intermediaries. They further avoided the stigma of collaboration given that they transferred some of their textile mills (those in Hankou) to the western provinces where, supported by generous loans from Chiang Kai-shek's government, they turned out most of the textiles needed by free China.

By dispersing the family factories, each managed individually, the Rongs were able to pursue negotiations with both rival governments simultaneously. Each family member had a different role to play. As a result, despite the large profits that they made in Shanghai during the war, the Rongs were not regarded as traitors when the occupation came to an end. In truth, their loyalty had gone neither to the Japanese nor to the Nanjing government. Nor had it gone to Chiang Kai-shek's government.

In the great tradition of Chinese merchants generally, the Rongs had remained loyal only to their family and their businesses.[38]

The traditions of the intellectuals were quite different. While the Confucian ideal of moral rectitude led some of them into resistance, others took refuge in the detachment from earthly things encouraged by Daoism. They remembered how scholars of the past, forced to submit to usurping dynasties or invading foreigners, would deliberately condemn themselves to solitude and silence. But it was hidden away in the lilong that these latter-day hermits withdrew into their internal exile, not deep in the woods. The suppression of "Chinese newspapers under foreign management" and publishing houses favorable to the Nationalists, combined with the removal of a number of universities and institutes to the free zone, led to the flight of more intellectuals and deprived those who remained of their livelihoods: "We who are starving and are impotent to change . . . feel superfluous, becoming slaves to mere existence."[39] The revolts of 1938–1939 gave way to blanket discretion. Writers changed their names and professions and lived by performing little services when they could. If they ventured into print, they expressed their love for their country in an oblique fashion, through allusions to historical episodes and familiar dramas. Sometimes the allusions were so transparent as to fail to provide adequate protection: in the spring of 1945, the Japanese police arrested Li Jianwu; his courage under torture made a resistance hero of someone who claimed only that he tried to behave as an honest man.

Sometimes the passive resistance of the "hermits" became indistinguishable from the weak collaboration of the increasing numbers of people who gave in to their fear of reprisals, the need to earn some money, or the attraction of social recognition. But among these collaborating writers, it would be fruitless to seek men such as Brasillach or Drieu de la Rochelle, who put their faith in the destiny of Fascism and were eager to be associated with it and to guide it. Far from exalting the new order, the principal collaborating literary review, *Memory* (*Gujin*), hymned the nostalgia of days gone by: "Everything in the world is just traces and remains / Standing futilely in the West wind / I contemplate the past." These lines, with which the first issue of the review opened in March 1942, sounded the note of a collective disenchantment. The Nanjing government financed the publication, and even the regime's most august figures were prepared to send it contributions marked by a philosophical pessimism that ill concealed their sense of culpability. In October 1944, the Japanese, irritated by *Gujin*'s negative tone, closed it down.[40]

The foreigners, too, tried for the most part to survive without bothering too much about patriotic and philosophical considerations. The British, Americans, and French felt trapped by history, abandoned like wrecks on shores that they no longer dominated. Despite the threatening clouds that were gathering, the period of the solitary island had still been that of an easy, privileged life, with assured employment, homes full of servants, and high salaries paid in currencies with a purchasing power that rose as devaluation continued to affect Chinese money. Throughout 1941, the British and American governments urged the families of their expatriate nationals to leave Shanghai, but in vain: most wives rejected their pleas.[41]

The occupation of the international settlement brought about a progressive disintegration of this colonial society. Many Sikhs from India, employed by the municipal police, collaborated with the Japanese, considering them to be a scourge of Western imperialism and liberators of oppressed peoples. Other active collaborators came from among the Anglo-Chinese who had suffered from discrimination: for example, the lawyer Laurence Kentwell, who, although a graduate of both Oxford and Columbia universities, had never been able to gain membership in the Shanghai Club.[42] For others, traffickers living on the margins of Western society, money provided the determining motive. One was Hilaire du Berrier, a Franco-American arms dealer: after trying his luck with Chiang Kai-shek, he worked for the Japanese secret services and collaborated with Nazi magazines.

Most of the 10,000 British residents who were trapped in Shanghai (the diplomats were virtually the only residents whom it had been possible to repatriate) were concerned above all to preserve their livelihoods. To the benefit of the Japanese and under their control, they agreed to continue to work for the Municipal Council, the police, and the public and private utility services. However, this passive collaboration came to an end in 1943 when the Japanese decided to intern all nationals of enemy countries and fill their posts with Chinese or White Russians. Just like the Chinese in their lilong and the Jews in their ghetto, the British and Americans, in their internment camps, now suffered from hunger, cold, sickness, and humiliation.* Their relations with the Japanese were now simply those between prisoners and their jailors.

Until July 1943, when their concession was suppressed, the French were spared. The many concessions that the consul-general and the municipality made to the Japanese bought their tranquillity. However, every one of those measures was the object of painstaking negotiations. Vichyist though he was, Roland de Margerie was anti-Nazi and nurtured no particular sympathy for the Japanese. Under pressure from him and from Ambassador Henri Cosme, the authorities and elites of the concession had rallied to Marshal Pétain. The friendly society of World War I veterans, suspected of Gaullist sympathies, had been dissolved and replaced by the Pétainist Legion of Combatants, which nearly all the members of the French Chamber of Commerce joined. Caught between the Chongqing government, to which Ambassador Cosme was still accredited, the government of Wang Jingwei, with which France had no official relations, and the Japanese, who practiced a policy of indirect control, the authorities of the French concession had limited margins of maneuver.

Resorting to pragmatism, these authorities depended on the personal relations that existed between the chief of the municipal police, Colonel Fabre; and the commander of the Japanese Shanghai police force, a former fellow cadet at Saint-Cyr; and also on the relations that many elites had maintained with Chu Minyi, who had been an important player in Franco-Chinese cultural exchanges before becoming minister of foreign affairs in the Nanjing government. Case by case, they endeavored to limit Japanese encroachments and to preserve at least an appearance of French sovereignty. Although obliged to accept interventions by the Japanese police in their territory, they successfully arranged that such interventions should always take place in the presence of French policemen: those of the brigade commanded by Inspector Pierre Maron, who had to be informed of any projected operations and who, often enough, made the most of this to warn the designated victims. In the French concession, as

---

* Unlike the British, many Americans had been able to benefit from repatriation offers: no more than a few hundred were imprisoned in internment camps.

in the rest of the city, opportunism won out over every kind of principle, and ambiguity triumphed.

The restitution of the French concession to the Nanjing government simply increased that ambiguity. Unable to arrange for the repatriation of French employees who were now deprived of their livelihoods, the consul-general persuaded the collaborationist municipality to reengage about one-third of them with their former salaries, which were very much higher than those of their Chinese colleagues.* Thus, Roland Sarly, the ex–assistant director of the municipal police, became chief inspector of the Chinese police force of the eighth arrondissement of Shanghai, which covered the territory of the former French concession. At the same time, over one hundred Frenchmen became officials of the government of Wang Jingwei. Given that the Chinese municipality was already overstaffed, the new recruits seem not to have had much to do. But this arrangement made it possible for them to sit out the war without too many deprivations or too much suffering except, for the best of them, that of a moral nature, which, as compromise followed compromise, resulted in the obliteration of all their ideological references and moral values.

There were some in Shanghai who not only survived but actually lived it up. The disappearance of the concessions put an end to the collective hysteria associated with the quest for amusement and plentiful consumption that at the start of the war had propelled the wealthy into the smart restaurants, casinos, and luxurious nightclubs of the Badlands and attracted others into the Great World amusement center and the cinemas to enjoy films such as *Gone with the Wind* and *Mulan Joins the Army* (*Mulan congwu*). Once the curfew was imposed, there were no more dances, the lack of transport paralyzed movement, electricity cuts made it hard for restaurants to operate, and Japanese censorship banned the showing of American and Chinese films conveying a patriotic message.

Social life and the frenzied pursuit of luxury nevertheless persisted, although now it was reduced to a small circle of Nazi leaders; German, Italian, and Japanese officers; Chinese and foreign collaborators; and ad-

---

* The Municipal Council of the French concession employed 400 French citizens, who together with their families constituted a group about 1,000 strong.

venturers of many kinds. On the Avenue Joffre, Russian restaurants organized candle-lit dinners, and Princess Sumaire invited the cream of the collaboration to cocktails and receptions in her suite in the Park Hotel.* And Captain Pick (born Eugene Kojevnikoff, in Riga), a World War I veteran (in the Russian army) and talented artist, installed in the Hotel Cathay, divided his time between spying for the Japanese navy and appearing as a musician or actor at society receptions, where he was always hailed as a star.

The liberation of Shanghai in the summer of 1945 brought with it just as many ambiguities and contradictions as the occupation had. The capitulation took Chiang Kai-shek by surprise, far away in his Sichuan refuge. The Communist Party was keen to make the most of the situation and establish its control over the city. It was counting on a workers' uprising (planned for August 24) organized in liaison with the Communist New 4th Army, which was operating in Anhui and northern Jiangsu. Seven thousand men—artisans, skilled workers, and gangsters—were recruited, and the mayor-to-be, Liu Changsheng, one of the principal Communist trade-unionist militants, was already chosen.** But the insurrection never took place:[44] it was called off by the Soviets, who had just signed a treaty of friendship with the Chongqing government, and it was forestalled by Chiang Kai-shek himself, who asked the collaborationist mayor, Zhou Fuhai, to remain at his post until the arrival of the Nationalist troops. Despite the air route that the Americans had set up to link Sichuan with the east coast, the troops took three weeks to arrive.

During that time, life seemed to remain in suspension. Japanese soldiers continued to patrol and maintain order in the city. After its official surrender on September 7, the garrison eventually withdrew into camps organized and guarded by its own men. Nazi leaders continued to occupy the fine villas that they had requisitioned; meanwhile, thousands of internees waited to leave their camps. Seizing the chance offered by the political vacuum,

---

* Princess Sumaire, who claimed to be (and perhaps was) the daughter of a great Sikh family, lived the adventurous life of a demimondaine in Shanghai and sometimes worked as a spy.[43]
** Liu Changsheng (1904–1967). Thanks to this militant's clandestine actions in Shanghai under the Japanese occupation, the party had begun to recover influence in workers' circles.

a few French residents tried to return to the days of extraterritoriality: organized into small commandos, they began to stalk the avenues of the former French concession, settling old political and personal scores with their compatriots.[45] Shanghai took no part, even symbolically, in its own liberation. Far away from the events that were turning the world upside down, it seemed to be waiting for history to deign to remember it.

CHAPTER 12

Backward into Revolution

(1945–1952)

A FTER THE VICTORY, a Shanghai liberated from Japanese oppression and reunified after the disappearance of the foreign concessions seemed ready to resume its role as the pioneer of modernization within the framework of a system of international relations in which China would now be included as a full partner. In the summer of 1946, the civil war started up again, but it was waged far away from Shanghai. In the metropolis, a new golden age seemed to be in the offing. The cotton mills were enjoying an unprecedented prosperity, while worker militancy, now more autonomous, the activism of student and professional organizations, and the political commitment of the intelligentsia were all promoting the rebirth of an embryonic civil society.

But this upturn was simply the last flash of capitalism and the swan song of Chinese liberalism. It was no match for galloping inflation and the dictatorial measures that accompanied it. In 1947–1948, the Shanghai economy and society were paralyzed. This grave crisis spelled disaster for the Guomindang and at the same time brought about the miscarriage of an embryonic civil society. It resulted in Shanghai not creating the revolution but simply accepting it, lending credit to the idea that nationalism and modernization could now be achieved only through Communism. In May 1949, this city, so long in the avant-garde of revolutionary struggles, stood by, passive and consenting, as it was taken over by the peasants of the People's Liberation Army (PLA).

The ease of this conquest stood in sharp contrast to the difficulties that were to slow down the city's integration into the new revolutionary order. Behind its socialist facade, inland bureaucratic and xenophobic China was back. It was a China in which there was no place for Shanghai, with all its cosmopolitanism and entrepreneurial spirit. Three years of cautious maneuvers, carried out in the name of a united-front policy and punctuated by episodes of terror, were to pass before the Communists really made themselves masters of the city and took command of its economy and its society.

THE DESCENT FROM DREAMS INTO
DISILLUSIONMENT (1945–1949)

Along with many other peoples, the Chinese believed the Allies' victory was one for law and liberty and brought a promise of peace and prosperity. For many of them, the collapse of Japan in August 1945 brought with it the hope of profound change. It was the beginning of a new era in which China, relieved of the weight of unequal treaties and enjoying full sovereignty, was summoned to take its place among the world powers. The Chongqing government, as the government of free China, had been treated as an equal ally by the Westerners. As a founding member of the United Nations in 1944–1945, China enjoyed a permanent seat on the Security Council and ranked as one of the Big Five, alongside the United States, the Soviet Union, Britain, and France. Chinese nationalism, exacerbated by the trials of the war, was gratified by this new world order. The credit went to Chiang Kai-shek, the very symbol of patriotic resistance.

The victory over Japan conferred unprecedented prestige upon the leader of the Guomindang. It presented him with a new legitimacy that, it was hoped, he would use to renovate his regime, consolidate national unity, and at last achieve modernization and democratization. Shanghai was readying itself to play an essential role in the construction of this future. Delivered from the stigma of colonialism, it now claimed the rank of a Chinese metropolis, the economic and financial capital of an immense country destined for rapid development. "Now we have won the war. . . . With the unequal treaties abolished, Shanghai is now completely under Chinese sovereignty. From now on, no one in Shanghai, regardless of his nationality, is to observe any law other than that of this country,"* the commander-in-chief of the Nationalist forces reminded his listeners.[1]

---

* Declaration made by General He Yingqing at a press conference in Shanghai on September 17, 1945. It should be remembered that within the framework of their alliance with free China, Great Britain and the United States had renounced on October 10, 1942, all the rights given them by the nineteenth-century treaties. France, which had restored its concession to Wang Jingwei's puppet government in 1943, made that retrocession official in the treaty signed with the Chongqing government on February 28, 1946.

As soon as the maritime blockade was lifted, the port of Shanghai recovered its preeminence. The absence of military operations after the terrible battles of 1937 had allowed the city to rebuild and preserve its industrial potential during the war years. By 1945, the production capacity of Shanghai's Chinese textile mills was as great as it had been in 1936, that is, about 1.1 million spindles.[2] The confiscation of the Japanese factories raised hopes that this potential might be doubled, and the disappearance of Japanese competition held out a promise of happy days for Chinese entrepreneurs. However, this fund of optimism was soon eroded by the uncertainties that surrounded the takeover.

Was it a takeover or pillage? The term *jieshou*, which denoted the Guomindang's recovery of control over the regions that the Japanese had occupied, can mean either, depending on the characters in which it is written. When spoken, it is impossible to distinguish between the two meanings of the word. Nor could the Shanghainese discern any distinction as they watched the Nationalist troops make their spectacular entry and witnessed the triumphal return of the Chongqing émigrés.

September 1945 saw a veritable army of carpetbaggers descend upon the city. The Chinese returning from Chongqing had nothing but scorn for their compatriots who had remained in Shanghai and submitted to the authority of the occupiers and their collaborators. To "purge their ideological tarnish," intellectuals and "puppet students" were made to attend courses on the doctrine of Sun Yat-sen and study the speeches of Chiang Kai-shek. The confiscation of enemy property opened up opportunities for every kind of abuse. It took place amid the greatest confusion, with a multitude of different offices taking charge, their corruption matched only by their high-handedness. Officials made the most of the process, appropriating confiscated possessions for themselves, dismantling and selling industrial machinery, clearing out warehouses, and fabricating crimes of collaboration, the better to lay hold of whatever goods they fancied. Meanwhile, profiteers speculated on the depreciation of the dollar issued by the Reserve Bank (brought into circulation by the government of Wang Jingwei), which continued to be used for several months in parallel to the legal dollar (*fabi*) (issued by the Guomindang government), for which it could be exchanged only at a most unfavorable rate. Thanks to this disparity, those arriving from Chongqing with their pockets stuffed with fabi were in a position to buy up the possessions and properties of the local impoverished population at very low cost.

Those dreaming of beginning a new era now realized that the profiteers were still there, as always, and that nothing had changed except their uniforms and nationality. Indignation was widespread. Chiang Kai-shek himself declared that "the extravagances" of officials and Guomindang officers should be punished.[3] But how on earth could the regime repress abuses and manage to bring about the purge demanded by former members of the Resistance, victims of the occupation, and all those who wished to see justice done? Chiang Kai-shek was above all preoccupied with the threat of Communism and avoiding delegating power to his generals, all too deeply involved in factional struggles within the Guomindang. So he turned to the Japanese and their collaborators, relying on them to re-establish his authority in the coastal provinces.

In Shanghai, the mayor in office, Zhou Fuhai, was asked to remain in his post until the Nationalist troops arrived, which was not until one month after the Japanese capitulation. On October 3, he was arrested and taken to Chongqing. At his trial in 1946, his plea was that he had been playing a double game and maintained secret relations with the Chongqing regime throughout the occupation. There were many at this time who laid claim to a secret patriotism, for the ruling on punishment for traitors allowed for indulgence for those who had secretly been working against the enemy. Unfortunately for Zhou Fuhai, Dai Li, the head of the Guomindang information services, was killed in an air accident in March 1946. His death robbed Zhou Fuhai of the man he had designated as his principal secret contact, who might have acted as a witness to exonerate him. Chiang Kai-shek, however, did at least get the former mayor's death sentence commuted to life imprisonment.

The other two main leaders of collaboration in Shanghai, Chen Gongbo, mayor from 1940 to 1944, and Chu Minyi (who had negotiated the restitution of the French concession), were executed. But most collaborators eluded justice. Those most compromised were allowed to flee to Japan; the rest were allowed to return to the ranks of the Guomindang. Those who did face judgment were tried in a most irregular fashion, according to legal processes that fluctuated in both definition and application. For instance, under violent pressure from various political and military factions, Chinese courts sometimes did prove extremely determined, as in the trial of Roland Sarly, one of the former chiefs of police in the French concession.* But in this affair, the affirmation of national sovereignty and the desire to have done once and for all with extraterritoriality and the former privileges that went with it certainly counted for more than any notion of a purge.[4]

At the end of 1947, the Chinese authorities, increasingly absorbed by the civil war operations, brought the purging process to an end and were preparing for amnesty measures, even though Wang Jingwei's regime was still far from brought to account. The question of the responsibility and culpability of collaborators was never really examined. The frustration engendered by this inadequate purge compounded the bitterness aroused by the excesses of the carpetbaggers. It made the sense of a need for reforms more acute but did not fundamentally undermine the regime.

THE LAST FLASH OF SHANGHAI CAPITALISM

Shanghai now prepared to savor the fruits of victory. In 1945, the outlook seemed favorable. Maritime relations were being restored, and the port recovered its place in the circuits of international trade. The city imported from the United States, India, and Brazil the raw cotton it could no longer obtain from the northern provinces and found outlets for its cotton cloth in Southeast Asia. From July 1946 on, economic activity followed rhythms imposed by the unfolding civil war, but for the time being the fighting was all in the north and northeast, and things were going well for the Guomindang. Not until January 1949 did the Communist victory at Huaihai open up the path to the Yangzi basin and the impending outcome of the civil war become clear. In Shanghai, intensified trading with southern China and the markets of Southeast Asia compensated for the suspension of communications with the Manchurian provinces.

---

* After three years of legal proceedings and two appeals, Sarly was eventually acquitted in December 1948.

The government encouraged this international reorientation of trade. Until the end of 1946, the currency market was free, and at the official rate of exchange (2,000 fabis per 1 U.S. dollar), the U.S. dollar was relatively cheap. The government sacrificed a large proportion of its reserves in order to uphold the rate of its own currency. This was an imprudent policy, but the Guomindang knew that it could count on the support of the United States, which was keen to integrate China into the world market. Low-cost supplies provided by the United Nations' Relief Agency came in through the port of Shanghai, which was considered safer than ports in the north, and they were distributed locally.

Shanghai's recovery was also now favored by the absence of Japanese competition. The production capacity of the nineteen Japanese textile mills that the Shanghai authorities had confiscated in 1945 was greater than that of all the city's Chinese textile mills together.[5] The fate of those Japanese mills was a subject of altercation between the partisans of nationalization and those of privatization. The postwar economic reconstruction plan, inspired by the doctrine of Sun Yat-sen, favored the existence of a public sector to include infrastructures and heavy industry and a private one to consist of consumer industries. The Shanghai textile mill owners therefore argued that the Japanese factories be handed over to them, as compensation for war damages, or be sold to them at a low price. But the government rejected their views, not wishing to be denied the extremely large profits that the exploitation of the Japanese textile mills might bring it. Instead, it entrusted their management to the Company for the Development of the Chinese Textile Industry (CDCTI), set up in November 1945.

The cotton mills, an essential element of Shanghai industry, enjoyed a newfound prosperity. The private entrepreneurs profited from the heavy demand for textiles and their high prices and also from the high quality and low prices of imported raw cotton. Their profits had never been greater (82% of cost in 1946, in the case of the Shenxin textile mills). But the government's demand for free supplies for the army and other state agencies undermined the CDCTI profits. As in 1919–1921 and 1938–1939, this third golden age of Shanghai capitalism occurred at a time of extreme instability. But this time Shanghai was no longer a half-foreign city, and its destiny was now linked more closely to that of the rest of China.

The civil war that had broken out in the provinces of the north and the northeast soon plunged Shanghai's economy into a severe crisis that hastened a degeneration in the political situation. To finance the budgetary deficit caused by military expenses, the Nationalist government issued more and more banknotes. When inflation rapidly increased during 1946 and 1947, the government reacted with increasingly authoritarian measures that smothered commercial and industrial activities without, however, curbing inflation.[6]

At the end of 1946, the free currency exchanges were abandoned, imports were limited, and a system of quotas was introduced, which made supplies to companies dealing in raw materials dependent on the goodwill of the authorities. In February 1947, the government decreed a general price freeze accompanied by a wage freeze. This measure, which was rigorously applied in Shanghai itself but not in the surrounding region, led to the cessation of rice deliveries to the metropolis. The shortages that followed, the food riots, and the escalation of black-market prices forced the government to back down. Inflation grew ever more rampant. People tried to protect themselves by buying foreign currencies and gold ingots or other saleable merchandise. Stockpiling and speculation squeezed out regular investment. Production costs increased.

The effect of the proliferating commissions set up to control supplies, manufacturing, and retail prices was to slow down activity every bit as much as the inflation that they had been designed to rectify. So Shanghai entrepreneurs now started to move their capital and equipment abroad.

By the summer of 1948, when the battle zone was drawing closer, Shanghai was living in a situation of hyperinflation. Prices were jacked up, sometimes leaping 30% in a single day. The denomination of banknotes in circulation was set at 100,000 dollars or at an even higher level, and tips were calculated by the million. Printing presses could no longer cope with the demand for paper money. The least purchase, unless effected by bartering, required enormous quantities of banknotes. Suitcases and sacks replaced wallets. Shanghai was threatened by a general economic breakdown. The authorities, at last awakening to the danger, opted for a radical policy: on August 19, 1948, all banknotes were withdrawn from circulation and replaced by gold dollars, each worth 3 million paper dollars.*

This monetary reform, in principle applicable to the whole country, was accompanied by various measures intended to stabilize prices, combat stockpiling, reduce interest rates, and restore confidence.[7] However, these measures were applied only in Shanghai, where Chiang Kai-shek's eldest son, Jiang Jingguo, had received full power to implement the policy.** He set about it with a brutality maximized by his aversion to capitalists and exploiters. Under his direction, the monetary reform turned into some kind of revolutionary mass movement, prefiguring subsequent major Maoist mobilizations. To break the resistance of the "big tigers," that is, the major capitalists, Jiang Jingguo called upon certain paramilitary organizations loyal to him personally. Trucks drove throughout the city, and the rich were urged to hand over their treasures. When persuasion proved unproductive, 3,000 businessmen were arrested, including a number of leading figures, such as Du Yuesheng's son and the Shenxin Company's Rong Hongyuan. In this terrorized Shanghai, speculation simmered down, and for a few weeks prices stabilized.

However, Shanghai "had become a tiny island of controlled prices in the midst of a sea of raging inflation."[8] Breaking its promises, the government resumed its issue of banknotes and authorized increases in the prices of tobacco and alcohol (official monopolies), thereby dooming the reforms to failure. The population was seized by panic. In this city deprived of supplies, secret stockpiling continued, speculation resumed, and famine set in. At the end of October 1948, the policy of controls was officially abandoned, marking the end of all attempts to redress the situation. Shanghai's activities, much slowed down, staggered on while its capitalists deserted the city and the population awaited the arrival of the Communist troops.

---

* Although not convertible into gold, the gold dollar (or gold yuan) was to be guaranteed by a reserve made up of 40% precious metals and foreign currencies and 60% government bonds. Only 2 billion could be issued.

** Jiang Jingguo (Chiang Ching-kuo) had spent eleven years training in the USSR. When he returned to China in 1937, he served in the provincial administration of Jiangsu before moving on to head the Youth League of the Three Principles of the People. At this time, his reputation was one of integrity, efficiency, and brutality. Forty or so years later, this same Jiang Jingguo, succeeding his father, introduced the first elements of liberalization and democratization in the regime of Taiwan.

THE SWAN SONG OF CHINESE LIBERALISM

The last golden age of Shanghai capitalism coincided with a remarkable liberal upturn during which the intelligentsia, students, and workers, making the most of the government's tolerance, organized themselves in a more autonomous fashion, defended their interests, and took part in public debate and political life. Even half a century of civil and foreign warfare, all the chaos, and the dictatorship had not altogether smothered the embryo of a civil society that had been nurtured by the practices of modern capitalism, the thinking of a cosmopolitan intelligentsia, and a nationalistic consensus. But the lull was short-lived. By mid-1947, the changing balance of military power between Communists and Nationalists and the rapid degeneration of the economic situation caused the Guomindang to return to dictatorial methods and stamp out new forms of social organization and participation, well before triumphant Communism passed the death sentence on them.

Brief as they were, those liberal interludes that recurred decade after decade illuminate the history of Shanghai society and testify to its capacity to restructure itself and find a voice whenever circumstances permitted. The 1945–1947 period looked promising. The demise of the foreign concessions seemed to remove the threat that imperialism had posed to the Western model of modernization and democratization. In 1945, America, always keen to mark out its difference from the old European powers, presented itself as the champion of decolonization, liberty, law, and democracy and was regarded by much of the Chinese public as a protective and friendly power. The Guomindang, at the height of its popularity and legitimacy, seemed won over to the idea of self-renewal. A resurgence of political parties and trade unions and a series of parades, demonstrations, and strikes now enlivened Shanghai society. It even saw a revival of the feminist movement, which had been relegated to oblivion after the great revolutionary wave of the 1920s and the return to Confucian moralism in the 1930s.

The rebirth and emancipation of the workers' movement constituted but one of the signs of Shanghai society's newfound vitality. The movement had collapsed following the Japanese occupation of the international settlement in 1941. There were then no more trade unions, no more strikes.

Activity was limited to a framework of brotherhoods, mutual credit associations, and consumer cooperatives. Workers had played no part in the city's liberation, but they did return to center stage once the Japanese departed, at which point they organized 406 strikes between August and December 1945. They still numbered roughly 800,000, representing 20% of the city's population. However, their ranks now included hardly any children, and the proportion of skilled workers had increased, as had that of second- and third-generation workers. The working class had matured and no longer appeared as a semirural extension of urban society, as was proved by the protest marches that moved in from the distant industrial suburbs and now invaded the Bund and the former Avenue Joffre in the very heart of the city.

The working class had also become more autonomous, more impatient toward attempts at manipulation. Communist influence, having been fiercely opposed by first the Guomindang, then the Japanese, was very weak among workers. The foundations of official trade unionism had collapsed when the Nationalist government moved to Chongqing and the Green Gang declined. However, in the immediate aftermath of the war, the industrial revival made the workers' participation indispensable, and this prompted employers to make concessions. The Guomindang tried to regain political control of trade-unionist activities but was hampered by the fragmentation of mafioso societies that had in the past formed a federation around the Green Gang. Making the most of those divisions, workers' organizations concentrated on defending their own interests and making their management more democratic. In the spring of 1946, the elections of factory union leaders took place amid relative freedom and brought militants from a variety of origins into influential posts. Between 1945 and 1947, the trade-union revival found expression in an upsurge of strikes and in the successes won by its protest movements: in March 1946, the textile mill workers won their demand for wages indexed according to the cost of living as well as a number of other social concessions—maternity leave, health insurance, and so on—and these were soon extended to other major businesses.

The emergence of a measure of trade-union pluralism favored the return of Communist militants. Abandoning their 1930s doctrine, they now adopted a strategy of participation and infiltration in various workers' organizations, mutual aid societies, religious fraternities, and so on. In this way they extended their influence among the skilled workers in the public services (tramways, gas, electricity, postal) and the department stores but refrained from agitating for revolutionary mobilization. Now partially liberated from Guomindang control, the new trade unionism, a "Shanghai-type labor movement,"[9] regarded itself as an opposition force still loyal to the regime. Spiraling inflation forced workers to unite in order to survive the constant deterioration of their purchasing power. To this end, in 1947 workers demonstrated against the wage freeze and secured the reestablishment of a sliding scale.

However, after this show of strength, the Guomindang abandoned its policy of tolerance. Alarmed at the turn that the civil war was taking, it banned strikes, and since it was unable to control the trade-union movement, it repressed it. As the crisis deepened, the hunt for Communist militants and the repression of wildcat strikes became increasingly brutal. One thousand military policemen were mobilized against striking workers in the Shenxin Company's textile mill no. 9 on February 2, 1948. During the ensuing clashes, three young women were killed and hundreds more were wounded. To justify the violence of the police intervention, the authorities blamed Communist manipulation, which seems in truth not to have existed.[10] But the monetary crisis of August 1948, the economic debacle, and the Guomindang's consequent loss of legitimacy all played in favor of the militant Communists. These were becoming increasingly numerous among the workers: by the time Shanghai fell into the hands of the People's Liberation Army, they numbered more than 5,000. These militants discreetly kept a low profile. In conformity with the line adopted by their party since military victory seemed to be in the offing, they were anxious to preserve as much as possible of the machinery that was soon to pass under Communist control. Now that the Guomindang was already doomed, workers were clamoring for a distribution of aid. But this spontaneous agitation did not develop into a protest movement. Repressed as they were by the Guomindang, to which they no longer owed any loyalty, and held at a distance by the Communist Party, whose strategy was based on the mobilization of peasant soldiers, the Shanghai workers played no political role at all in rallying Shanghai to the revolution.

The political commitment of the intellectuals was equally indicative of the vitality of Shanghai society. During the Sino-Japanese War, Chiang Kai-shek, forced to depend on the unity of national forces and wishing to be seen as the embodiment of this union so as to strengthen his legitimacy, had not only established a united front with the Communists but had also granted elite economic and cultural groups a voice within the Political Council of the People created in 1938. Although it lacked any effective power, this council had nevertheless become a forum for major debates on politics in general, debates that had been echoed in the press. Liberal opinion supported the war of resistance and called for national unity. The better to effect mediation between the Communists and the Nationalists, most small parties had banded together to form the Democratic League. When the Sino-Japanese War came to an end, the liberals believed that the moment had come to realize their aspirations for modernization, liberty, and democracy.

After the victory, the hopes nurtured in Free China throughout the Japanese occupation developed into a powerful current that mobilized public opinion in the coastal towns. This movement united rather loosely around the Democratic League, which comprised a number of small independent groups, some influential reviews, and some influential figures. Its unity and identity lay in its rejection of Nationalist dictatorship and Communist totalitarianism: hence its name, the Third Way (*zhongjian luxian*). Naturally enough, this Third Way involved Shanghai. The outlook was encouraging. In January 1946, Chiang Kai-shek promised to transform the presidential system into one of ministerial responsibility, an end to the single party system, and the creation of a coalition government. However, the profound distrust between Chiang Kai-shek and his Communist partners, along with the violent factional rivalries within the Guomindang itself and the most conservative of its leaders' irreducible hostility to all reform, combined to derail this fine project. Applied in unilateral fashion, the January agreements were drained of all their content. As the civil war intensified, the liberals found themselves in an increasingly difficult position: the Communists condemned them for their wait-and-see attitude while the Nationalists regarded them as "fellow travelers." The mediation for which the Democratic League was striving became an impossible mission. In 1947, the league was banned, but its cause was taken up by the *Observer* (*Guancha*) review.

The burst of groups and publications that the postwar years produced made this one of the richest periods of modern Chinese political thought. *Guancha* and its editor, Chu Anping, played a part of prime importance. The success of this review and the courage and talent of its editor created a tradition that outlived the coming of Communism, and many Chinese intellectuals today acknowledge its influence.[11] The review was read widely throughout China, and many of Beijing's most famous writers and professors contributed to it, but *Guancha* nevertheless remained firmly anchored in Shanghai.

Chu Anping was born in 1909 in Jiangsu. He studied in Shanghai and Beijing, then went to complete his education at the London School of Economics. While in London, he observed English society and discovered the underlying principles of a state founded on law and freedom of expression, which he understood to be the basis of British power and a recipe for setting the Chinese nation back on its feet. After the war, he taught at Fudan University. When he founded *Guancha* in September 1946, he obtained the collaboration of several dozen eminent intellectuals, some in Shanghai, others elsewhere, some of whom—for instance, Zhang Dongsun and the sociologist Fei Xiaotong*—belonged to the Democratic League.[12] These intellectuals from different parts of China and with different perceptions and political aims came together under the *Guancha* banner in the name of peace, freedom, and modernization. Even if they gave up their hopes of seeing the establishment of a multiparty system and a coalition government, they clung to the idea of seeing a reformed Guomindang. Their view of their own role was influenced by the idea of the traditional authority of scholars and the notion of a "regular" opposition such as that found in a parliamentary system. *Guancha* thus became the emblematic mouthpiece of Chinese liberalism, upon which it conferred a last burst of brilliance.

---

* Zhang Dongsun (1886–1973), a philosopher and politician, played an active part in introducing China to Western political thought (including Marxism). In 1930, he became a professor of philosophy at Beijing's Yanjing University. The Japanese imprisoned him, but he regained his post after 1945. Fei Xiaotong, born in 1910 and educated in Great Britain and the United States, occupied the chair of anthropology at Beijing's Qinghua University.

This weekly review, which printed as many as 60,000 copies, served a large urban readership in Shanghai and other towns of the lower Yangzi basin. It was read by professors, students, members of the liberal professions, officials, and salaried members of the lower urban bourgeoisie (*xiao shimin*), all of whom had suffered greatly from inflation and were disgusted by corruption. Despite growing pressure from the Guomindang, the review survived until December 1948, striving to maintain a balance between criticism of the Nationalist regime and warnings against the totalitarian danger introduced by Communism.

The Third Way led along a narrow path that became more and more arduous to follow as the Communist threat became more specific and Nationalist repression grew more heavy-handed. Zhang Dongsun, for example, eventually reached the conclusion that freedom and modernization were incompatible. He hoped for Soviet-style planning, believing it to be the only way to ensure rapid and rational economic development, but he admitted that such planning implied a restriction of political liberties. He nevertheless clung to the hope that at least a measure of "creative" cultural liberty might be preserved for writers and artists.[13] Zhang Dongsun thus pointed the way forward for many liberals who, when confronted by the Communist victory, would—more out of nationalism than opportunism—accept the idea that economic and social rights took priority over civil rights and that the construction of the nation justified the sacrifice of individual liberties.

The mobilization of public opinion through a review such as *Guancha* was no more successful in achieving triumph for the liberal cause than was the intellectuals' commitment to small democratic parties. The impotence of liberalism resulted from the circumstances, the men involved, and the national political culture. Its failure, like that of capitalism, testified to the size of the gap that separated Shanghai from the rest of China. For in Shanghai itself liberalism did not seem all that impotent. The appeals launched by intellectuals did evoke a response in the many demonstrations, meetings, and marches of those protesting against war, oppression, hunger, and poverty. Liaisons between the intellectuals in their ivory towers and the demonstrators in the streets were mediated by students. While their elders engaged in thought, these engaged in action. The two groups shared the same corporatist concerns about objectives and methods of teaching and the status of their members; and until 1947, their common opposition to Guomindang policies did not imply that either group rejected the regime that was in power. But when the time came to rally to Communism, the students proved more prompt and more enthusiastic than their mentors.

Student activism had reemerged in 1945. In December of that year, in the wake of demonstrations in Kunming (Yunnan), large student demonstrations took place in Shanghai, protesting against any resumption of civil war. Like the workers' movement, the Shanghai student movement at that point enjoyed a measure of relative autonomy. The years of warfare had destroyed the mechanisms by which the Guomindang had previously controlled student organizations from within. The government showed tolerance so long as the young activists put forward mobilizing themes, such as nationalism, that overlapped with its own agenda. But as soon as the party felt threatened by rising student radicalism, it resorted to police methods, introducing moles into the university campuses and associations and encouraging young Guomindang loyalists to set up their own organizations and to join the Youth League of the Three Principles of the People (*Sanqingluan*).*

Once relaunched, Shanghai student activism recovered the vanguard position and federating role that it had assumed before the war. Not all the great movements that mobilized Chinese students in the late 1940s started in Shanghai: that of December 1946 began in Beijing, and that of May–June 1947 was centered in Nanjing. But once they reached Shanghai, these movements became radicalized and took on a national significance. The Shanghai students were skilled at organizing demonstrations in many large towns across the country and also knew how to establish a link between their own specific interests (the syllabus and schedules of studies and examinations) and the economic and social aspirations of the population in general. The demonstrations that they organized against the government in the spring of 1948 were also protests "against hunger" that took account of the suffering caused by inflation and recession.[14]

---

* The league was heir to the former Blue Shirts, and its members swore a personal oath of loyalty to Chiang Kai-shek.

The postwar Shanghai student demonstrations thus referred back to the movement of May 4, 1919, which had established the students as society's spokesmen. They took over the repertory of protest movements of previous generations: they made soapbox speeches, bombarded the authorities with petitions, organized strikes against lectures and examinations, and occupied public premises and services.[15] But history did not altogether repeat itself. The spokesmen of the young people of the May Fourth Movement had been intellectuals hardly older than themselves. The postwar students turned to their elders, theoreticians from the 1920s and 1930s. Chu Anping, who was not yet forty, stood out as an exception. The political consensus did not always bridge the generation gap. In 1948, it crumbled away as the students became more radical and rallied in increasingly large numbers to Communism. At this point, hostility flared up between the generations, paving the way for future Communist campaigns in which professors and liberal intellectuals would be denounced by their erstwhile disciples.

A striking feature of the Shanghai student movement was its extreme fragmentation, which stemmed both from its spontaneity and from its politicization. The disappearance of the foreign concessions and the end of Japanese aggression had deprived it of the usual themes of federation, rendering it more vulnerable to manipulation by both the Guomindang and the Communists. Given the gatherings organized by regular associations, the counterdemonstrations mounted by the Youth League of the Three Principles of the People, and the maneuvers of Communist militants seeking to reorient student activism in conformity with party strategy, it was sometimes hard to make out what was happening. All these groups chanted, "Down with imperialism!" but for some that imperialism was embodied by the United States, for others by the Soviet Union.

Some of the great postwar student demonstrations were motivated by particular events, as in January 1947, when the protest movement against "the brutalities of American military personnel" was a response to the rape of a female student in Beijing. But the movement also expressed the anti-American sentiments of much of the Chinese population, indignantly noting that even after the abolition of the nineteenth-century treaties, a new form of imperialism continued to ensure monopolies and privileges for foreigners. The influx of American merchandise into Shanghai represented serious competition for the products of Chinese industry, and the anger of the city's entrepreneurs coincided with the students relaunching the campaign to prioritize national goods (*guohuo*). Although there was no question of reestablishing extraterritoriality, the American soldiers based in China were exempted by special agreements from the jurisdiction of local authorities; meanwhile, foreign inhabitants advantaged by the exchange rate maintained their luxurious lifestyle. Right up until the eve of the Communist victory, for them the civil war remained one of those episodes that had, for decades, repeatedly disturbed life in the provinces without much affecting activities in Shanghai. As an Australian journalist admitted, "foreigners hardly remember that they now live in China . . . not in the international settlement."[16]

However, the demonstrations of May–June 1947 "against hunger and the civil war" were not provoked by any particular incident. They unfolded in an atmosphere of hyperinflation and economic chaos that affected the lives of all Shanghainese. Following the serious clashes in Nanjing on May 20 that set the forces of order in opposition to the student delegations that had come to present their petitions to the central government, committees dedicated to the support of victims proliferated in Shanghai. The breakdown of relations between the authorities and the Shanghai students was marked by hundreds of arrests and police raids on university campuses and dormitories. The Pan-Chinese Student Association, organized in Shanghai in the wake of these demonstrations, was banned and went underground.

Between April and June 1948, the movement "against oppression, hunger, and American aid to Japan" fit into the context of an incipient cold war and a worsening economic crisis. The students were protesting against the aid that the United States had decided to provide for the industrial reconstruction of Japan, which the Chinese public feared would pave the way for a resurgence of Japanese militarism. Chiang Kai-shek, although equally hostile to the new orientation of American policy, was accused of being nothing but a Washington puppet. By this time students had lost all faith in the regime, which they no longer believed to be indispensable to the construction of a new China. Now they were counting on the Communist Party to realize this objective and were turning to it not so much for ideological as for patriotic reasons. Certain of the military victory in the offing, the Communist Party was seeking not to provoke new disturbances on the urban front but to create conditions favorable for the coming handover of power. The return to relative calm in the major Shanghai educational establishments by the new academic year of 1948 indicated that the Communists were already in control of the students.

ON THE EVE OF THE COMMUNIST CONQUEST

In the spring of 1949, Shanghai was a city living on borrowed time and American subsidies, where a corrupt bureaucracy confronted a semi-emerged civil society. Cut off from the outlying countryside and seemingly unaffected by the convulsions in which this was caught up, Shanghai was pursuing its own dream. Daily life there assumed an unreal character, and farce rubbed shoulders with tragedy. The smallest transactions were settled with hundreds of millions of dollars. Bartering had become universal. The biggest capitalists had taken refuge in Hong Kong, and the highest-ranking officials of the Guomindang were already in Taiwan. Many White Russians took advantage of the aid provided by the Philippines to escape the Communist domination from which they had fled thirty years earlier.* The last trains, ships, and airplanes to depart were besieged by those who believed they had everything to fear from the incoming regime. Even more people, though, waited to see how things would turn out, with a lack of concern spiced with curiosity. "Maskee!"** the Shanghainese declared.[17] The precedents set by Beijing and Tianjin, where the entry of Communist troops and the switch of regimes had been carried out amid order and calm a few months earlier, encouraged the population's confidence. Many foreigners were equally optimistic. The British consul-general had "great confidence that the government of China will not fall into the hands of any but responsible men who will have the interests of their country at

---

* With aid from the International Refugee organization, the Philippines at this time took in 6,000 White Russians waiting to immigrate to other countries.
** This term, a derivation from Portuguese, was adopted by all the dialects spoken in Shanghai. With more optimistic overtones, it expressed the same indifference to immediate circumstances as the Russian *nitchevo*.

heart," the implication for him being that they would respect foreign interests in Shanghai.[18]

Given the press censorship that existed, it was not until the last moment, when the People's Liberation Army crossed the Yangzi on April 21, 1949, that the population of Shanghai became fully aware of the Communists' imminent arrival. Everyone knew that resistance was now pointless. For several months, Chiang Kai-shek had been solely concerned with ensuring his forces' retreat to Taiwan. He had even organized a raid on the gold reserves held by the Bank of China on the Bund. By night, files of coolies carried the

Censorship allowed very little news of the Communist troops' advance.

gold ingots to a cargo ship anchored on the Huangpu, while regular troops cordoned off the entire quarter and protected the operation.

But face had to be saved. On April 22, martial law was proclaimed, the hunt for real or supposed Communists intensified, and executions multiplied. Tens of thousands of poorly disciplined Nationalist soldiers invaded the city on the pretext of defending it, while their leaders made many heroic declarations. At the end of April, Chiang Kai-shek promised, "Shanghai will resist right to the end. There will be no surrender." Preparations for resistance went ahead with the construction of a palisade roughly 50 kilometers long to protect the west side of the city. This "Shanghai wall," a wooden Maginot line, was to prove completely useless. With the Communist guns rumbling in the suburbs, the remaining representatives of the Guomindang organized one last grand victory parade along the flag-lined Bund, complete with military bands and children's choirs. But during the night they fled the city before the arrival of the first detachments of the People's Liberation Army at dawn on May 25, 1949.

SHANGHAI BECOMES COMMUNIST (1949–1952)

Many people at this point predicted that the Communists would ruin Shanghai, and Shanghai would ruin the Communists. The fact was that the Chinese revolution had matured in the countryside. Its cadres and peasant soldiers were deeply distrustful of urban society and openly hostile to the Shanghainese. The metropolis embodied all that Communist dogma condemned: the triumph of capitalism, the arrogance of imperialism, and all the fruits of cosmopolitan culture. "Shanghai is a non-productive city. It is a criminal city. It is a refugee city. It is the paradise of adventurers."[19] Rao Shushi, the secretary of the Shanghai Party Committee, even suggested immediately transferring half the city's population, then 5 million inhabitants, to the Chinese interior to reduce Shanghai once again to an ordinary regional center.

However, Shanghai was also one of the cradles of the revolution and the place where the Chinese Communist Party had been founded in 1921. Furthermore, it was the country's foremost port, its principal industrial center, and the bastion of the working proletariat that symbolized the avant-garde of the revolution. So the metropolis was called upon to play an important role in the construction of the new China, particularly in its economic construction, which was one of the priorities of the Communist authorities. The Communist leaders, torn between the contradictory needs of both dogmatic purity and economic efficacy, decided in the first instance to implement a subtly mixed policy within the framework of a united front. It was designed to restore Shanghai's potential for production, but it also favored some unwelcome social and political trends.

The conquest or, to use the official terminology, the "liberation" of Shanghai was completed without a single blow being struck. At dawn on May 25, the first Communist soldiers entered the city and seized the already evacuated military posts without encountering any resistance. The municipal police gave them a warm welcome. The mayor had set up a welcoming banner, and the church bells were all ringing. The Shanghainese, who had gone to sleep under Guomindang law, awoke to the Communist regime. The changeover of power took place in a perfectly choreographed fashion, with the flight of one group preceding the arrival of the next by several hours. At nine o'clock in the morning, the shops opened their doors, and business and life generally proceeded as usual. The population, neither fearful nor enthusiastic, was above all curious to see these young peasants in their green uniforms and cloth sandals, whose disciplined behavior was in marked contrast to that of the fleeing Nationalist forces and looters and who gazed with wide-eyed astonishment at all the skyscrapers and elevators.[20]

New institutions were rapidly set in place. Thanks to the experience acquired in former Red bases and the now liberated regions of the north and the northeast, the mechanisms of Communist power were well organized. For the time being, military authority superseded the civil administration. General (soon to be Marshal) Chen Yi, whose 3rd Field Army had taken Shanghai, became president of the Military Control Commission in charge of the city and mayor. In this capacity, he supervised the operation of taking (*jieguan*) all administrative and economic institutions. In August, he called a conference of representatives of all social strata of the city to ensure liaison between the municipal government and the masses.

Following the overall victory of the Communists, in October 1949 municipal institutions were integrated under the authority of the new central government; at the regional level, they answered to the military and

Soldiers of the People's Liberation Army marching through Shanghai

administrative commission of East China. As always in Chinese Communist systems, a Party Committee reinforced each of these governmental organs. The cadres whom the new mayor appointed to Shanghai services came from his 3rd Field Army, mostly recruited in Subei (the northern part of Jiangsu). As has been noted previously, the Shanghainese were prejudiced against such provincials, whom they regarded as uncouth and stupid. Furthermore, there were not enough of these cadres, so the new administration was obliged to retain 80% of the former Guomindang personnel.

The man responsible for the administration of the city he had just conquered was a prestigious military leader. From his years of training in France, where he had worked from 1919 to 1921 in the Michelin factories, the new mayor had preserved his habit of wearing a beret clamped on his head and gripping an eternal cigarette between his teeth. After directing Communist military operations in Jiangsu Province during the Sino-Japanese War, General Chen Yi had launched the greatest battle of the civil war, that of Huaihai, in the winter of 1948, after which he had orchestrated the crossing of the Yangzi in brilliant fashion, opening up the PLA's route to Shanghai. He was a native of Sichuan. The presence in Shanghai of this "Outside Red," who had been a member of the central committee since 1945, testified to the strict control that party leaders were determined to retain over the metropolis. Until 1954, when other responsibilities called him to Beijing, Chen Yi continued as Shanghai's loyal representative of the central authorities, scrupulously obeying all directives from Beijing and President Mao Zedong.[21]

Absorbed by his many responsibilities, the mayor relied on his adjutant Pan Hannian for the day-to-day running of the metropolis. Pan, born in 1906, was from Jiangsu Province. But he was also a man of Shanghai, where he had mingled with progressive literary circles before going to Moscow in 1935. Upon his return one year later, Pan was instrumental in the formation of the united front between the Communists and the Guomindang and directed the party's underground activities in Shanghai during the Sino-Japanese War. Compared to Chen Yi, the veteran of guerrilla and civil warfare, he was the very epitome of a white-zone militant. His urbanity contrasted strongly with the plain speaking of the soldier. Chen Yi was favored by popularity and his membership in the highest party circles, Pan Hannian by his familiarity with Shanghai society. The two men complemented each other and got along well together.

The Shanghainese submitted without resistance but involved themselves very little in the new authorities' agendas. Although students provided a contingent of enthusiastic activists, there were few local cadres or militants, only about 9,000 in all, who were clandestine until the PLA's arrival. To broaden the regime's social base, the city's new masters created mass organizations and worked on honing their propaganda techniques.

Workers were gathered into a Shanghai General Labor Union directed by a former underground leader, Liu Changsheng, who was destined for a fine political career. By February 1950, the Shanghai General Labor Union had acquired 1 million members. The Shanghai Federation of Democratic Youth League recruited only 60,000, mostly students, and the Shanghai Federation of Democratic Women, 300,000. These associations organized parades, marches, and political education courses. At a more concrete level, 2,000 residents' committees were formed between 1950 and 1951, their role being to organize the participation of inactive elements of the population—the retired, the unemployed, and housewives—in tasks of civil management and public security.

Likewise, the party controlled associations and committees. Its directives reflected the themes developed by the propaganda apparatus. In Shanghai, this was based on eight daily newspapers, the most important of which, *The Liberation Daily* (*Jiefang ribao*), printed 100,000 copies. Every day these newspapers published a list of slogans to be copied onto blackboards set up at street corners and at the entrances to factories and administrative offices. These were then discussed in the course of the sessions of political education that were proliferating in workplaces and living quarters. Radio and cinema still played a limited role. American films, which continued to be shown but in steadily decreasing numbers, attracted more people than films imported from the Soviet Union or made in Chinese state studios. In these efforts at social mobilization, revolutionary themes were exalted less often than more consensual ones, such as public order, security, and patriotism. Street corners displayed as many portraits of Sun Yat-sen, the ardent defender of national unity and independence, as of Mao Zedong. But discreetly and insidiously, things were beginning to change.

The eradication of crime and debauchery and the reinculcation of a sense of moral values in a decadent society were the aims of a vast program that no previous holders of power—either foreign or Chinese—had ever succeeded in realizing. The Communists set about tackling them without more ado. Priority went to the struggle against secret societies, whose dissolution was ordered as early as July 1949 by the Public Security Bureau (the official name for the police force). The activities from which these societies derived their power—black marketeering, speculation, prostitution, drug trafficking—were tackled in a more or less rapid and rigorous operation of repression. In the weeks following the installation of the new regime, over 2,000 traffickers were arrested. The crowds were summoned to witness their execution, which took place on the racecourse in the heart of the city. Those condemned were hauled by a pulley up to the top of a tall mast, then dropped to the ground as many times as it took to kill them.[22]

Less brutal methods were adopted in the fight against prostitution. The prostitutes, who were regarded as proletarian victims of capitalist exploitation, were invited to leave their brothels and return to their villages or to turn to other professions. As a precaution, a number of procurers were persuaded to take the initiative themselves and renounce their erstwhile lucrative activities. Clients were intimidated, and their numbers declined. Casinos, dance halls, and opium dens began to close their doors.[23]

Gradually, austerity took over. The window displays of the department stores were scaled down. Wearing ties went out of fashion as the costume promoted by Sun Yat-sen (an upright-collared cotton tunic) and favored by Communist cadres gained ground. The ambitious Shanghainese familiarized themselves with the new political idioms and the meaning of terms such as "cadre" (*ganbu*) and "great popular masses" (*renming dachong*). In association with a simplification of syntax and the disappearance of classical literary language from all official texts, mastery of the new vocabulary—and the concepts conveyed by it—made it possible for one and all to "master the new language."[24] Revolutionary Puritanism had not triumphed yet, but already the city was losing its color, and its features were becoming blurred behind the veil of moralism.

The declining visibility of foreigners, still present but now more discreet, also changed the look of the city. Many Westerners had not waited for the entry of the Communist troops and had already left, in particular numerous Americans—businessmen, missionaries, and so on—after their consul-general, as early as November 1948, had counseled prudence. By May 1949, their community had shrunk from 4,000 to 1,200 people.[25] However, almost all the British had remained: "We will stand by Shanghai if we possibly can. . . . Shanghai is home to us as a community, not merely a trading post."[26] All the same, as a precautionary measure, many wives and children were sent back to their native land.

Nuns embarking, in flight from the advancing Communist troops

Except for the American businesses confiscated by the Communists in retaliation for the freezing of Chinese assets in the United States, foreign firms continued to function, albeit at a reduced rate. Their relations with the new authorities were complicated by the fact that official regulations were now published in Chinese only, not in a bilingual Chinese/English version, as had been customary even after the suppression of the international settlement. Furthermore, foreign employers now had to agree to huge wage increases for their workers and were not allowed to lay them off. They themselves could no longer obtain exit visas, nor could they shut down their businesses, which survived thanks only to funds sent from abroad by their company headquarters. The British government's recognition of the People's Republic of China in January 1950 did not result in the improvements that the Shanghailanders were hoping for. The British initiative was not imitated by other Western powers, most of which simply left a skeleton staff of uncertain status to guard their consulates. At the end of 1949, the foreigners celebrated Christmas and saw in the New Year with dancing and whiskey drinking. But already they were living as hostages.

Religious and educational institutions funded or run by foreigners also lived in uncertainty from one day to the next. The 1949 Common Program recognized freedom of belief and religious practice; although official policy advocated the Three Autonomies (administrative, financial, apostolic) of religious foundations, they sought to create so-called patriotic churches, that is, churches controlled by the new political authorities. Shanghai's two great missionary universities, the Protestant St. John's and the Catholic Aurora, were placed under close surveillance.

At St. John's University, problems arose not from the presence of extremely well-disciplined young PLA soldiers stationed on the campus but from the zeal of radical students who, in one general assembly after another, proceeded to take control of university courses and university life. Prevented as they were from carrying out their regular teaching in the course of the year following the city's switch to Communism, the American professors departed from Shanghai. At Aurora University, the Communist takeover of power proceeded in the same fashion but ran into greater resistance, which reflected the Catholic Church's opposition to any form of secular power that attempted to establish primacy over the spiritual power embodied by the papacy and the ecclesiastical hierarchy.* In the winter of 1949, the few hundred Catholic students gave up resisting the pressure that activists of the Youth League applied and abandoned the running of the university in order to carry the struggle into specifically religious terrain. Joining forces with the 2,000 pupils of Shanghai's Catholic colleges and other establishments and with the faithful in Catholic parishes, they banded together around foreign missionaries, Chinese priests, and Ignace Kung (Gong Pinmei), the first Chinese bishop of Shanghai, who was himself an old "Aurorian." In early 1951, Aurora University was confiscated by the Chinese authorities, who handed its management over to a Catholic "patriot." The presence of foreign missionaries was still tolerated in order for them to continue to teach, but arrests were multiplying. One of

---

* The Catholic Church of China could not become an autonomous and "patriotic" church without rejecting the spiritual authority of the pope, in other words, without contravening dogma and thereby excluding itself from the community of believers. Even when reduced to a matter of faith, the loyalty of Chinese Catholics to the pope—a foreigner!—exposed them to accusations of betrayal and revolutionary vindictiveness. The various Protestant churches, with a more decentralized organization, did not encounter such acute problems.

the first victims was the (Chinese) director of St. Ignatius College, which provided preparatory classes for entrance to Aurora University. The slow death throes of the university came to an end in 1952, when the whole establishment was dismantled, some of its departments integrated into other universities, and its faculty of medicine turned into the Shanghai Second Medical University.[27]

The Communist takeover had not been accompanied by any brutal breakdown of relations. There had been no rivers of blood, just pressures of a more or less direct nature and constraints more psychological than physical. The changes were gradual, in many cases scarcely perceptible. It was a smooth transition that reflected the prudent and clever policies of the new regime.

THE UNITED-FRONT STRATEGY

Mao Zedong considered the united-front strategy, that is, alliance with forces outside the party, to be "one of the three magic swords of the revolution."[28] In 1949, he was counting on this to impose his power over coastal China. The strategy was prompted by some very concrete motives: in the absence of competent cadres of their own, the Communists appealed to capitalists to continue to manage the private sector. "Chinese private capitalist industry is a force that should not be ignored," declared Mao Zedong in his report to the second plenary meeting of the VIIth Central Committee in March 1949. This same theme was taken up again by Liu Shaoqi in April–May, in his *Tianjin Talks*. It became a part of official policy in September 1949 in the promulgation of the Common Program that served as a charter for the new regime. Future economic construction would have to "take into account both public and private interests" (*gongsi jiangu*) and "serve both labor and capital" (*laozi liangli*).

So, unlike their Russian predecessors in 1917, the Chinese revolutionaries did not intend to liquidate the entrepreneurial class but would seek to use it for their own ends. This strategy, imposed by the existing circumstances, found a measure of theoretical justification in the policy known as the Democratic Dictatorship of the People, which called for a wide alliance of popular forces under the party's direction. Only "national" capitalists, that is, those who had collaborated with neither foreign imperialism nor the Guomindang bureaucracy, were considered to belong to the people. In reality, however, in 1949 any and every businessman prepared to cooperate with the new regime was labeled "a national capitalist." This political category, which corresponded to no economic or social criterion at all, was intended solely to legitimize an alliance that might, in some quarters, be considered unnatural.

Why did so many Shanghai capitalists agree to collaborate with the Communist cadres? Out of disgust for the Guomindang, or out of patriotism, as propaganda insisted? Possibly. But also out of a desire to preserve their own interests. Accustomed as they were to managing their businesses in a climate of extreme political and economic instability, they tended to take a short-term view and were always ready to negotiate with those in power, whoever they might be. The united-front policy was founded on multiple interactions: it would be mistaken to interpret it simply as an attempt on the part of the authorities to penetrate an autonomous, passive society.

The ideal field in which to implement this policy seemed to be Shanghai, where it could speed up economic reconstruction. In 1949, the city was home to about 20,000 private industrial businesses and almost 120,000 private commercial ones funded by Chinese capital. Thanks to a campaign organized as early as 1948 by clandestine militants and designed to safeguard industrial machinery, and thanks also to the swift retreat of Nationalist forces, the factories of Shanghai had not suffered when the Communist troops entered the city. All the same, they found themselves in a difficult position. For months they had been running at reduced speed and had been weakened by the monetary crisis. The civil war had cut them off from the domestic market. The strict blockade that the Guomindang naval forces had imposed on June 26, 1949, had paralyzed the port. Furthermore, on February 6, 1950, the Guomindang bombing raids on the central electricity stations caused a serious energy shortage. In that same month, the measures that the Beijing government adopted to stabilize the currency hampered recovery. All these economic difficulties were compounded by the flare-up of workers' demands. Despite the authorities' appeals for restraint, there were over 2,000 labor conflicts in July 1949 alone.

The new leaders endeavored to relaunch industrial activity without altering either production relations or social structures. They took control of the businesses that already belonged to the public sector (essentially the textile factories confiscated from the Japanese and nationalized in 1945) and set up various mechanisms to support the private sector. This aid helped firms to get back on their feet but also enabled the authorities to extend their power over them.

To win the cooperation of the capitalists, Pan Hannian threw himself into a great public-relations campaign, aided by cadres already familiar to Shanghai society, such as the Cantonese Xu Dixin, a former underground militant who during the war had been placed in charge of contacts with the industrialists who had retreated to Chongqing; and the publisher, journalist, and author Zhou Erfu, who left an account of these transitional years in his novel *Morning in Shanghai* (*Shanghaide zaochen*).* As early as June 2, 1949, Pan Hannian invited the principal businessmen of Shanghai to return to their normal rhythms of production. In the days that followed, he embarked on a round of visits and dinners in town. He appeared to the capitalists in the guise of a "good friend" with whom they could chat the more freely since he spoke the Shanghai dialect and shared the same culture as they did. At the end of a banquet, he was perfectly prepared to join his guests in singing airs from Beijing opera. When he paid a visit to Guo Dihuo, of the Wing On (Yong'an) Company, he took along his wife, the daughter of Cantonese bankers with whom the Guo family, also of Cantonese origin, had been connected for many years.

The targets upon whom Pan Hannian trained his powers of persuasion and charm were the leaders of the business community, through whom he hoped to extend his influence over the entrepreneurs as a whole. However, most of the great capitalists had left Shanghai before the arrival of the Communist troops and had taken refuge in Hong Kong, from where they observed how the situation was developing. Until 1952, the Shanghai–Hong Kong corridor remained open, and entrepreneurs who regarded themselves as temporary émigrés frequently shuttled between the two cities to keep an eye on their interests. Pan Hannian managed to persuade some of them to

---

* This novel was translated into English and published by the Foreign Languages Press, Beijing, 1962. Zhou Erfu was purged in the course of the Cultural Revolution but was later rehabilitated, and in 1978 was appointed minister of culture. He was later condemned for economic crimes.

send capital and equipment back to Shanghai. But the entrepreneurs returned only occasionally and temporarily, and eventually, disappointed by the new regime, they departed, this time definitively. Among them was Rong Erren, the principal executive of the Shenxin Company, who declared that he certainly did not consider himself "more backward than the workers."[29]

Unable to win over and use the men of influence whom it needed, the party was thus obliged to fabricate others. In exchange for their cooperation, it offered economic advantages and political standing to the younger scions of great families who had been left in Shanghai to watch over family assets that it had not been possible to transfer out of China. These included, for instance, Guo Dihuo and Rong Yiren, the young half-brother of Rong Erren.*[30] The party also appealed to entrepreneurs until then classed as bosses of small and medium-sized businesses. In some cases, it even picked "representatives of the capitalist party" recruited from among technicians and trade-union officials to take over factories deserted by their managers or proprietors. With political fictions brought in to substitute for socioeconomic realities, these men provided the missing links in the united-front policy.

As this policy made headway, it could no longer be contained within the framework of personal relations and dinners in town and so became institutionalized. Two mass organizations were made responsible for mobilizing entrepreneurs and keeping them under surveillance: the Shanghai Federation of Industry and Commerce (SFIC, *Shanghai gongshang lianhehui*), which was the successor to the city's former Chamber of Commerce and Industry, and the China National Democratic Construction Association, usually shortened to the Democratic Party (*Minjianhui*). After eighteen months, from August 1949 to February 1950, the SFIC was set up; meanwhile, the old associative structures were remodeled in such a way as to serve the regime's objectives, transmit official directives, and institutionalize the power of major entrepreneurs that had rallied to the united-front policy. The Democratic Party was an organization that was twinned with the SFIC. The membership and

---

* Rong Yiren, the son of a concubine, had been distanced from all important posts in the Shenxin-Maoxin Company by the sons of the first wife, which was no doubt why he decided to try his chances with the new regime. In a private interview in Paris in the early 1980s, Zhou Erfu confirmed this point for me.

leadership of the two organizations were identical, but while the SFIC took care of economic and financial problems, the Democratic Party concentrated on propaganda and political education.*

The propaganda-cum-seduction campaigns run by party cadres were accompanied by concrete measures. Aid to businesses took the form of orders passed to them by the municipal government or other official agencies. During the months following the arrival of the Communist troops, thousands of contracts were signed, saving the businesses concerned from paralysis. In some cases, official aid might take the form of loans from the People's Bank of China: these amounted to 98 billion renminbi in 1949 and 244 billion in the first three months of 1950, about one-third of these funds being absorbed by the cotton mills. The municipality also tried to help the private sector by restoring calm on the labor front. In various branches of industry, it set up "labor and capital" committees (*laozi xieshang*) with the task of preventing or resolving conflicts between employers and their staffs. The authorities did not hesitate to apply pressure to the trade unions, with a view to moderating their demands; they even advised workers to request wage reductions to make it possible for factories to continue production.

Because of these measures, the return of civil peace, and the government's general policy of reopening the railways and stabilizing the currency, Shanghai's industrial production took an upward turn: in 1951 it was 60% higher than in 1949. The private sector, which at this point accounted for 87% of industrial production (compared to 83% in 1949), played the most important role in this improvement. This relative increase in the importance of the private sector in Shanghai stood in contrast to its decline at the national level (from 65% to 41%). By the end of 1950, more businesses were starting up than were closing down.** In 1952, most

---

* Liberals in Chonqing created the Democratic Party during the Sino-Japanese War. In 1947, the Guomindang declared it illegal, and it went underground. In 1949, it was refounded in Beijing, and its leaders were given ministerial posts in the new government. Most of them were Shanghainese, but they became figures of national stature and their Shanghai identity was obscured. The Shanghai branch was but one of the party's provincial agencies.

** To stimulate the zeal of entrepreneurs, in December 1950 the government proclaimed a ruling that granted shareholders a fixed dividend of 8% (what was traditionally paid on all industrial investments, whatever the results of exploitation) and that allocated to them 60% of any surplus profits.

of the textile mills were making a profit and paying out dividends to their shareholders.[31]

The Communists had long been well versed in united-front strategies. The helping hand that they extended to the capitalists was an iron fist in a velvet glove. But the strategy was nevertheless a risky one. In 1951, private businesses were in full swing, capitalists were prospering, and Communist cadres and Shanghai employers were fraternizing. In the wake of 1949, as in that of so many other revolutions, a partial fusion of the elite groups of the old and the new regimes was beginning. However, a brutal reaction on the part of the party was in the offing; and when it came, it revealed the true nature of Communist power to Shanghai society. China's entry into the Korean War in the autumn of 1950 further hastened a radicalization of the Communists' political line.

FORCING SOCIETY TO TOE THE LINE

In 1951–1952, repression struck Shanghai society, its liberal intellectuals, and its private entrepreneurs. Seen from the West, it simply expressed the dictatorial nature of the regime and its determination to impose its authority by every possible means, including violence and terror. Chinese historians, on the other hand, have always maintained that what was involved was a struggle between, on the one hand, the people and the party, and on the other, a bourgeoisie bent on clinging to its own privileges and power.

In Shanghai, the vitality of a society still by no means completely under control perhaps provided arguments for those who regarded the repression as a defensive reaction on the part of the regime. In 1951, the ideological, political, and social trends authorized by the united-front policy strengthened the position of those within the central and local party apparatus who were hostile to even a temporary alliance with the elite groups of the past. Many things were still eluding the authority of the new regime, beginning with the demographic growth of the city, whose population increased from 5 million in 1949 to 6.2 million in 1952.

Two-thirds of this growth was due to the arrival of people from rural areas seeking better living conditions. The Communist cadres who dreamed of deporting half of Shanghai's population to the countryside proved unable to stem the flow of immigrants, which was far greater than the several 10,000 peasants sent back to their villages and technicians allocated to the development of China's interior. The great wave of immigration kept unemployment high and made it impossible for the labor bureaus set up in 1950 to control the labor market. Workers, particularly the youngest of them, recently arrived from the countryside and intractable to the discipline of industrial labor, tended to flit from one job to another. Former militants also criticized the Stakhanovist rhythms of production imposed upon them in order to speed up reconstruction and support the war effort in Korea. The situation in the labor market, where the demand for qualified cadres far exceeded the number available, also hampered the policy of assigning positions to newly qualified graduates of colleges and universities (*fenpei*) that was pursued by committees set up within educational establishments. This policy was resented among students who, however enthusiastic about the new regime, could not forget their traditions as protest leaders and were constantly organizing petitions and boycotts.[32]

As the party took control of schools, hospitals, the press, and publishing houses, many members of the xiao shimin became salaried officials. This reconversion to the public sector was partly aided by the fact that ways of ascending the political, economic, and social ladder were becoming increasingly scarce, but it was also encouraged by the prestige traditionally associated with a career as an official. There were many intellectuals and members of the liberal professions who, out of nationalistic sentiments, sacrificed considerations of material profit and personal prestige to the general objectives of modernization and national sovereignty.

But some writers and artists, even if they put their trust in the regime, refused to subordinate their creative activities to the directives that propaganda propounded. The period immediately following the 1949 Revolution saw a return of the debates that had fired the left-wing intelligentsia in the 1930s and had divided the Yan'an intellectuals at the time of the rectification campaign launched in 1942.* Shanghai appeared as the bastion of those who, even though they proclaimed their loyalty to the regime, wished

---

* In his *Talks on Art and Literature* of April 1942, Mao Zedong called upon Communist intellectuals to demonstrate their complete submission to the party.

to preserve a certain freedom of expression. They gathered around Feng Xuefeng, a Communist man of letters and head of the Shanghai section of the Writers' League, and Hu Feng, a fellow traveler of long standing, who continued to express his dissent by publishing articles in organs controlled by the party, a procedure he described as "the monkey's trick of crawling into the belly [of his opponents],"[33] a reference to *The Journey to the West.** Although not all intellectuals were as bold as Hu Feng, who for the time being was protected by his literary reputation and his friendship with Lu Xun, many did persist in applying to their professional work the methods that they habitually employed, most of which they had learned from the West. In so doing, they were seeking not to oppose the political authorities but simply to set beyond the latter's reach what they regarded as their own reserved domain, their own field of expertise.

For Shanghai's several thousand Catholics, it was faith that constituted their particular reserved domain. As all courses of religious education had been suppressed and the proselytizing activities of institutions such as the Legion of Mary were kept under close surveillance, the faithful organized many small catechism groups that, because of their dispersed nature, escaped the immediate notice of the authorities. Thanks to this strategy, the Catholic community managed to mobilize itself against the establishment of any "patriotic" church. The authorities, who defined themselves as a dictatorship (of the people), regarded all such reserved domains as a threat.

In particular, they regarded the independence and lack of discipline manifested by the private entrepreneurs as a threat. As the economic situation improved and the private sector grew stronger, entrepreneurs did indeed multiply their commercial transactions, neglecting or delaying official orders or attending to them in a slapdash fashion. In their view, the time for being told what to purchase and for what fixed-rate payments was over, and now they should return to complete freedom of production and marketing. Entrepreneurs were also trying by every means to evade the new taxation introduced by the law of December 1950. To increase

---

* *The Journey to the West* was an extremely popular sixteenth-century novel that told of the adventures of the pilgrim monk Xuan Zang, who went off to India in search of sacred Buddhist texts, accompanied and protected by a monkey of many wiles.

revenue from taxes on private businesses, the new regime began by requir-
ing employers to declare all their company assets. By means of thorough
monitoring, this policy was effective.* But fraud and tax evasion were still
common in Shanghai, even on the part of entrepreneurs who had entered
into alliance with the regime.[34]

To protect themselves, entrepreneurs tried to ingratiate themselves with
Communist cadres, whom they plied with presents and dinner invitations.
For the Chinese merchants, this was the traditional manner of going about
their business. For the party ideologues, it was quite simply corruption.
Sometimes resistance to Communist surveillance took a more concerted
form. Many groups were formed outside the official associations: study
societies, societies of friends, and discussion groups, whose members would
meet weekly in a restaurant or a tearoom to decide upon the best attitude
to adopt in the face of pressure from the cadres. The authorities likewise
regarded these well-established forms of conviviality as manifestations of
clandestine opposition.

To reduce what was not in all cases really resistance, but might become
just that, from 1951 on the Center launched a series of mass campaigns
that exalted discipline and patriotism and targeted counterrevolutionaries,
bourgeois intellectuals, the foreigners who had remained in Shanghai,
Christians, corrupt officials, and eventually, in the spring of 1952, the
entrepreneurial bourgeoisie.** In the Communist victory of 1949, social
divisions had played virtually no role at all, but given that Communist
propaganda purveyed the ideal of an egalitarian society, expectations
were certainly created. In response to them, the party tried to shore up
the party leaders' plans for change by ascribing the initiative to demands
from the masses. To this end, they organized movements (*yundong*) that
spilled over from the institutional frameworks of associations such as trade

---

* In the early 1950s, the private sector assured the state of a budgetary income (16% of the gross
domestic product) far greater than those of the imperial and Nationalist governments.
** In contemporary Chinese political texts and texts concerning contemporary China, the
"Center" is the term that designates the central organs of government (the State Council
and the ministries and commissions dependent upon it) and also those of the party (the
Political Bureau and the secretariat and departments of the Central Committee). The expression is interchangeable with others such as "the Beijing authorities" or "the central
government."

unions, women's unions, and the Youth League. These new movements were based on the principle of the mass line that Mao Zedong had first formulated in 1943 and that associated a quasi-mystical concept of the creativity of the people with the directional role of the party. The masses were called upon to recognize that directives issued by the Center in effect translated their own aspirations and, consequently, to mobilize with a view to seeing that they were implemented. This method of government short-circuited the hierarchical chain of party agencies and was to lead to the people's greater participation in political life. However, that participation, which committed every individual totally to the party line, was to be limited exclusively to the level of execution.

The series of mass movements in Shanghai in 1951 and 1952 were a response to national directives. The first targeted counterrevolutionaries, who were hunted down in accordance with the law of February 1951. By April–May, the movement was going full steam ahead in Shanghai. At first it was directed against active reactionaries such as spies, secret agents, and the members of criminal gangs, but it was not long before it turned against ex-Guomindang officials, former employees of foreign administrations and businesses, journalists and teachers trained in the West, and Catholics who had remained loyal to their church. A manhunt was organized, based on denunciations. During the night of April 27–28 alone, about 10,000 people were arrested. Roundups were followed by collective judgments passed in stadiums swarming with crowds. Popular juries, presided over by the highest-ranking local leaders, were supposed to identify not individual forms of behavior but typical cases. These hasty procedures were followed by mass executions: 293 victims on April 30; 208 on May 31.[35] After a few weeks, once all the real or potential political opponents of the new regime had been eliminated, the terror died down.*

Unprotesting, the terrified population went along with the movements that followed, which were less bloody and more precisely focused. The campaign for thought reform, launched in November 1951, targeted reformist intellectuals and liberals, inviting them to criticize themselves

---

* No official statistics exist on the overall number of victims of this movement in Shanghai. Nationalist sources suggest that it could be as high as 300,000.

and make their public confessions in the course of sessions of ideological reeducation. At about the same time, the movement of the Three Antis targeted corrupt cadres who covered up their criminal behavior by invoking "the need to develop social relations in order to implement united-front policies."[*36]

Corruption, on the increase in urban society, was a reality that party leaders could not afford to ignore. Nor could they ignore the role that private capitalists were playing in the corruption of Communist cadres. The campaign of the Five Antis, which targeted corrupters, started in the immediate wake of the campaign against those who had been corrupted. But those in charge were not in agreement regarding the meaning and objectives of the latest campaign. There were two views on the Five Antis. According to the more radical one, "the party had been undermined by bourgeois ideology and influences. . . . Relying on the bourgeoisie led to abandoning the working class."[37] This attitude amounted to a rejection of the united-front policy. According to the more moderate view, which the Central Committee adopted, it was necessary "to rely on the working class and at the same time unite with those members of the bourgeoisie who respected the law . . . , so as to launch a large-scale and resolute struggle against the bourgeoisie that did not respect the law."[38] With this perspective, the united-front policy was maintained, but its application became more restrictive. Such ambiguities allowed local cadres to stress whichever aspect of the new policy they chose.

In Shanghai, the Five Antis campaign took a very particular turn because of the city's large concentration of private businesses, the size of its industrial proletariat, and the important role played by the united-front policy in the strategy of local cadres. An initial moderate phase was succeeded by a radical one, both reflecting spontaneous reactions on the part of the Shanghai population and the local cadres. But in Shanghai, what was at stake both economically and politically was so important at a national level that the Center inevitably tried to take the movement in hand.

---

* The Three Antis (*Sanfan*) campaign targeted corruption, wastage, and bureaucracy. The Five Antis (*Wufan*) campaign targeted bribes, tax fraud, theft of state property, cheating involving labor, and the misappropriation of raw materials.

The campaign in Shanghai got under way around mid-January 1952, rather later than in northern and northeastern China. Local cadres invited industrial and commercial circles to "fight against themselves" (*ziji fan ziji*), adopting an extremely formal procedure. The Shanghai Federation of Industry and Commerce was to encourage its members to make confessions, formulate criticisms, and organize debates. To set an example, a number of important leaders of the SFIC confessed to having delayed honoring official contracts, betrayed economic secrets, entertained cadres, or even stockpiled foreign currencies and transferred capital abroad. But their action remained hesitant, and their ideas were still confused. "Was it corrupt to invite cadres to dinner?" and "What about doing business with other private firms—was that corruption?"[39] Most businessmen seemed indifferent rather than hostile to the movement. When asked to confess, they did so with bad grace, concealing their graver offenses and manipulating party rhetoric, which they had mastered.

On February 4, all this changed. This was the day when the SFIC lost control of the movement, which then plunged into violence and chaos. The development of factional clashes within the party seems to have caused the sudden reversal of the situation. "Some of the old cadres . . . were of a leftist inclination. They were keen to make the most of this opportunity [the movement of the Five Antis] to destroy private capitalism and establish socialism. Among those who supported a savage struggle against the capitalists was one of the leaders of Shanghai General Labor Union."[40] The views of such cadres were echoed among workers. The mayor, Chen Yi, now forced to adopt a more radical policy, proclaimed the Four Regulations, which ordered the directors and senior managers of private businesses not to leave their workplaces. The SFIC itself was purged. Posters, banners, caricatures, and loudspeakers all spread the new slogans. The general theme was "Well boss, have you confessed?" In a fervent atmosphere, the movement "for one denunciation per man" was launched.[41] Tension mounted. Confined to their offices, without food or sleep and subjected to a barrage of questions and accusations, many employers threw themselves out of windows. By the end of February, more than two hundred people had been arrested, forty-eight had attempted suicide but failed, and thirty-four were dead. The minister of finance, Bo Yibo, who was sent to Shanghai to assess the situation, determined that "the movement was not properly organized. . . . Every worker, every employee was fighting his own battle."[42]

This radical phase was short-lived. Economic difficulties multiplied, and unemployment increased. Central government decided to suspend the Five Antis campaign in Shanghai, reorganize it, and relaunch it one month later in conformity with strictly defined procedures. The mayor declared that Shanghai "should be no exception" and that all its erring capitalists would be punished; but the masses had to distinguish between entrepreneurs who respected the law and those who broke it. There must be criticism but no anarchy so as not to upset production.

The Five Antis campaign was thus restarted, this time under strict control by the party, which took many precautions designed to channel all interventions by the masses. In-depth investigations preceded the dispatch of inspection teams, mostly made up of members of the Youth League or workers' trade unions, which were accompanied by cadres specializing in united-front work and responsible for supervising the accusations against the capitalists. Three hundred of the most important capitalists received privileged treatment. They were assembled in one of the large buildings on the Bund (now the Peace Hotel), where they had to criticize one another and themselves under the supervision of their "good friend" Pan Hannian. The purpose of this scaled-down confrontation was to ensure the survival of Shanghai's principal entrepreneurs and thereby preserve the possibility of future cooperation between the regime and the private sector. Meanwhile, however, small and medium-scale entrepreneurs were exposed to physical attacks by the masses. The explanation for the difference in treatment was the local cadres' concern not to paralyze production completely; it also reflected the general line favored by the Central Committee, which was not yet prepared to abandon the united-front policy.

On April 30, *The Liberation Daily* announced that the Five Antis campaign had secured "an overall victory" in Shanghai. The entrepreneurs emerged from this ordeal shattered both physically and morally. Sentenced to pay out huge sums, either as fines or as tax readjustments, they were unable to meet the demands and were forced to turn to official banks for loans and to government offices for orders. The general establishment of consultative conferences between workers and employers and the increasing role played by the party secretaries implanted at the heart of their businesses eroded their control over their affairs. Despite the indulgence shown to the principal capitalists, who were declared to be "all in all respectful of the law," this campaign terminated the dominant role that the Shanghai business bourgeoisie had played for over half a century.

The decline of the bourgeoisie was reflected in that of the SFIC and the professional associations that composed it. The principal functions of those associations (fixing prices, processes of buying and selling, mediation, and so on) were now transferred to municipal offices. Cut off from their social bases, the leaders of Shanghai business circles became more and more dependent on their relations with cadres and their own status within the state and party apparatus.

The major Shanghai capitalists put up no resistance to their absorption into the bureaucratic apparatus, although in the earliest days of the regime in 1949–1950, they had certainly tried to negotiate rather than obey, without, however, attempting to enroll the small and medium-scale entrepreneurs in their support. Instead of defending the interests of the latter and behaving as responsible leaders of the Shanghai business community, they had simply endeavored to protect their own individual and family interests. In the hope of obtaining advantages and rewards, they had agreed to cooperate with the new authorities. Meanwhile, the smaller entrepreneurs became the principal victims of the Five Antis campaign. The fall of the bourgeoisie is certainly explained partly by the skill and brutality of the Communist cadres' policies, but equally by the fragmentation of Shanghai society and the prevalence of values such as family solidarity and the attraction that officialdom exerted within this, the most modernized sector of society.

The regime would have to organize further mass campaigns in order to overcome the intellectuals' inclinations toward critical independence and the entrepreneurs' bent for economic initiative. But the forces that had fired society had already been extinguished. The campaigns of 1951–1952 had brought to an end the regime of liberty under surveillance that the city had enjoyed immediately following its conquest by the PLA troops. The united-front policy had seemed to ward off the specter of terror, but now this had been adopted as the government's general method. Far from being limited to the regime's declared enemies, it had engulfed all those who, without opposing the authorities, sought not to become pledged to them. Shanghai now discovered the constraints of totalitarianism. As economic reconstruction neared completion and society was forced into line, it embarked upon its new life as a Communist metropolis.

PART FOUR

Shanghai under Communism

CHAPTER 13

Shanghai in Disgrace
under the Maoist Regime

A S THE COMMUNIST REGIME gained in strength and adopted the Soviet model of development, Shanghai entered a long period of disgrace. The city, punished for its colonial and imperialist past, fell victim to a policy that curbed urban development while advocating industrialization. Shanghai was no longer the erstwhile autonomous metropolis that had been more a partner of central government than its dependent. Now decisions elaborated by the hierarchy in Beijing dictated its rhythm of life. Shanghai, which had so often inflected the future course of the nation, was now simply one arena among many in which the factions struggling for control over central power fought it out.

In the Maoist period, the importance that Shanghai retained was measured by its contribution to the country's development. But even if it was one of the pillars of the centrally planned economy, it could no longer be its beacon, for that role was reserved for the capital, Beijing, the face of which was subjected to an upheaval designed to provide the Communist government with a setting suitably symbolic of its power. Shanghai's political discredit and unpopularity stripped it of the attributes of socialist greatness. But because of this, it was not disemboweled to make room for gigantic thoroughfares and cold Stalinist architecture.

Contrary to some predictions, Shanghai did not destroy Communism but was obliged to submit to it. But neither did Communism destroy Shanghai; it simply changed it. In a setting that remained intact, it engendered a new economy and a new society. Yet the minute controls were relaxed, as happened during the periodic clashes between rival factions at the top, certain features of the social activism characteristic of the old Shanghai resurfaced. The student demonstrations and workers' strikes that broke out in the winter of 1966–1967 at the beginning of the Cultural Revolution revived Shanghai's tradition of protest, but its radicalism now stemmed above all from the local party apparatus: it was a bureaucratic radicalism serving a senile dictator and his partisans in the shape of the Gang of Four.

A PILLAR OF THE CENTRALLY PLANNED ECONOMY

As soon as the Communist regime took power, the municipality of Shanghai, like all the rest of the country's administrative units, became part of a strictly hierarchical network; it held provincial rank and, as such, was directly answerable to Beijing.* In the centralized CCP system, relations between the provinces and the state apparatus were organized on a vertical axis. Shanghai thus received directives from Beijing that it then applied to the lower levels subject to its own authority. In contrast, horizontal connections between administrative units on the same level were discouraged to avoid any risk of collusion between local interests. Shanghai was thus deprived of the old, productive symbiosis that before 1949 had stimulated so many financial, commercial, and demographic interrelationships with the neighboring provinces of Jiangsu, Zhejiang, and Anhui.

The history of Shanghai was now conditioned by the policies of the central government. These fluctuated considerably but were generally unfavorable to Chinese towns because the Soviet model that inspired the First Five-Year Plan in 1953 was designed to develop industry while limiting urban development to reduce infrastructural costs. In ascribing a symbolic value to steel production and heavy industry, Beijing aimed to compensate for the imbalances bequeathed by the past and to do away with the predominance of both the processing industries and the coastal regions: the plan was to implant 156 major units of industrial production in key towns, but not one was assigned to Shanghai.

However, this strategy, which guzzled capital but created few jobs, engendered difficulties that soon brought the Soviet model into question. In 1956, Mao Zedong, in his report on "The Ten Great Relationships," was already in favor of no longer sacrificing the coastal regions to development of the country's interior, nor the manufacture of consumer goods to the growth of heavy industry. Accordingly, in the following year, investment

---

* Relations between Shanghai and the capital were sometimes mediated by the intermittent mediatory regional agency of East China, which played quite an important role in the 1950s and 1960s.

granted to Shanghai for industrial development reached 380 million yuans (more than the total sum granted over the first four years of the plan).[1] The Second Five-Year Plan was based on the same principles, but the Great Leap Forward paralyzed the launch of its implementation.*

The Great Leap Forward was a voluntarist strategy founded on the mobilization of the masses. Sadly, it became notorious for its catastrophic application in the Chinese countryside. Yet Mao Zedong underestimated neither the importance of financial investment nor that of advanced technology. At the time, he declared that it was necessary "to walk on both legs," in other words, boldly to develop different sectors by different means. In 1957–1958, state industrial investment rose from 12 billion to 21 billion yuans (51% of the national budget), while the number of workers employed in heavy industry (not counting small blast furnaces) increased from 4.5 million to 17.5 million. Shanghai benefited from such massive injections of capital and labor. Its industrial development intensified under the aegis of municipal authorities to whom administrative decentralization had restored power and at the same time granted increased resources:** in 1958, the metropolis could boast 698 new industrial projects in the making.[2]

But decentralization, badly managed, led to wastages that were soon denounced by Chen Yun.*** He reminded everyone that the country was "a single checkerboard" whose development must be guided by a central plan. The predominance of pragmatic considerations summed up in Deng Xiaoping's famous saying, "No matter whether the cat be white or black so long as it catches mice," was reflected by a new policy of "Readjustment and Consolidation" imposed in 1961. It restored certain coordinating measures while leaving a measure of initiative to local agents. At this

---

* Prime Minister Zhou Enlai presented this plan at the Eighth CCP Congress in September 1956.

** In November 1957, provincial (or in the case of Shanghai, municipal) authorities were given control over the industries producing consumer goods that operated in their territories, whereas previously they had been placed under the authority of the Ministry of Light Industries. Heavy industries continued to depend on central technological ministries, but supervisory rights were granted to regional agencies.

*** This typographical worker, born in Jiangsu in 1900, became one of the party's most important leaders. In the 1950s, he was one of the principal authorities on economic policies. He was distanced from power at the time of the Great Leap Forward and regained a position of importance only after the death of Mao Zedong, when reforms were introduced in 1978–1979.

point, Shanghai recovered some of its entrepreneurial flair, thanks to the abilities of the vast hierarchy of local managers that replaced the Soviet experts who were recalled home in 1960.

This upturn was short-lived. Since its break with the Soviet Union and America's commitment in Vietnam, China had felt isolated and under threat. For strategic rather than ideological reasons, Mao Zedong now returned to a policy of industrialization without urban development. From 1965 onward, his policy, known as the Third Front, advocated that units of production be dispersed among the mountainous regions of the interior, out of the range of possible invaders. Now Shanghai was not only not creating new businesses but actually becoming deindustrialized, as several hundred of its factories were transferred.[3] In the following year, the upheavals of the Cultural Revolution combined with the effects of the Third Front policy to paralyze all development. Shanghai was forced to a standstill that lasted until Mao Zedong's death in 1976.

Not only did the central government not encourage development in Shanghai but it even exploited the city's resources for the benefit of other Chinese regions. Given that the central budget was fed mostly by revenues from the public sector, Shanghai, with its many state businesses, was expected to be the foremost provider of funds for the regime. It is estimated that between 1950 and 1976, the city handed over to the Center funds thirteen times greater than those that it received for its municipal budget. On average, 87% of its tax revenues were siphoned off for Beijing. Shanghai was the regime's cash cow, the "pocket" (*koudai*) into which the regime's hands never ceased to dip.

It is sometimes claimed that this exploitation was offset by the privileges that benefited the city in an economic system that tended to finance industrialization by confiscating agricultural resources. That confiscation was engineered through the discrepancy between the very low prices that the state fixed for agricultural products destined as food for the towns and the very high ones set on manufactured goods sold to the peasants. But even if this discrepancy increased the profits of factories, what it increased even more were the resources available to the government, which controlled the factories. Shanghai "acted like a sponge, soaking up rural resources for the national budget."[4]

Technicians and equipment were also plundered. At first, material and staff were moved to Manchuria to reinforce heavy industry there. Later they were relocated to the far west, where industrialization was one of the priorities of the Five-Year Plan. Within just a few years, 170,000 skilled workers and 30,000 engineers and technicians from Shanghai factories were thus dispersed throughout the interior.[5] In the early 1960s, transfers slowed down, only to be resumed and increased within the framework of the relocations envisaged by the Third Front industrial policy. Furthermore, between 1949 and 1976, engineers and technicians trained in the universities and institutes of Shanghai were regularly sent off to work in other regions. This organized brain drain led to lower standards among those in positions of responsibility in Shanghai factories.

The municipality devoted its investments to developing the production apparatus but neglected infrastructure (transport, equipment, lodgings). This imbalance between productive and nonproductive investments was particularly marked during the Great Leap Forward (84% as against 16%). Beijing cared little about the improvement of urban infrastructure and services, and more surprisingly, local leaders were equally unconcerned. Until 1978, Shanghai was systematically disadvantaged by its political cadres: these were concerned above all with ensuring that Beijing received all the taxes it demanded and, in order to ingratiate themselves with the Center, they usually supported policies that were contrary to local interests. In 1953–1954, however, one of them, Rao Shushi, attacked the program of industrial readjustment to the detriment of Shanghai.* It was an imprudent move that led to his being accused of seeking to construct "an independent kingdom" and being swiftly purged. In contrast, Ke Qingshi, who dominated Shanghai politics from 1954 to 1965 as mayor and secretary to the party's municipal committee, owed his local ascendancy to his personal relations with Mao Zedong and his support for the latter in all factional disputes at the top.

---

* In 1950, Rao Shushi became the head of the regional apparatus of East China. In 1953, he was promoted to head the Organization Department of the Central Committee in Beijing and acquired a seat on the State Planning Commission. He was accused of colluding with Gao Gang, the party leader responsible for the Northeast region, and in 1954 was purged and disappeared.

A brilliant career in Beijing was his reward for the zeal he had shown in Shanghai.*

As a great economic and cultural center, Shanghai still preserved a measure of influence at the national level, but that influence was simply used as a stake in the major ideological and political clashes of this period. The left-wing position with which it was credited at the time of the Great Leap Forward and during the Cultural Revolution was essentially that adopted by local cadres, who were committed to the support of Mao Zedong's clique. In China generally, provincial cadres played the role of intermediaries and endeavored to conciliate the demands of the party with the interests in their care. But in Shanghai, the municipal administrators were first and foremost agents of the central power.

A GREAT INDUSTRIAL BASE

From 1949 on, many of the economic activities of Shanghai declined. The city lost its position as a financial and commercial center. The introduction of a centrally planned economy made many services redundant, while others were now run by the administration, with government bureaus taking the place of private businesses. Nevertheless, the industrial sector continued to develop vigorously: the share of the secondary sector of Shanghai GDP rose from 52% in 1952 to 77% in 1975 with industry alone accounting for 76%.[6] During this period, industrial production registered a 10% annual rate of increase, only marginally lower than the national rate of 11%. But in consequence of this slight disparity, Shanghai's share in Chinese production thereafter tended to decline, dropping from 19% in 1952 to 14% in 1971.

This decline testified to the intense efforts to develop industrialization being made at a national level rather than to any backwardness on the part of Shanghai. The city's 25,600 private firms had emerged much weakened from the Five Antis movement, but at the start of the First Five-Year Plan they were still turning out 63% of all industrial production. But maintaining a private economic sector, even one controlled by the central authorities,

---

* Ke Qingshi entered the political bureau in May 1958 and became deputy prime minister in 1965, a few months before his death.

seemed incompatible with the huge effort required to make the plan successful and with the doctrinal bases of the regime. Beijing's new political line, that of a transition to socialism, called for a radical transformation of the structures of production and the establishment of state capitalism founded on extremely large production units.

The decision to nationalize Shanghai businesses was made at the end of 1955, and by January 1956 the operation was completed. The capitalists themselves, organized into working teams directed by party cadres, carried it out, and its completion was greeted by huge parades during which the crowds acclaimed "the patriotic national capitalists courageously heading along the path to socialism." In the space of a few weeks, the great factories became state-owned (*guoying*) or mixed enterprises managed under state control. Meanwhile, smaller firms were amalgamated and turned into collective enterprises.[7]

The state-owned enterprises were placed under either the direct authority of central ministries or that of eighty-three Shanghai corporations (*gongsi*) responsible for supervising and coordinating the management of various production units. In many cases, the territorial authorities—of the municipality, arrondissement, or district—retained a right of surveillance over the firms in their area. The larger collective enterprises were also kept under tight control. Their management differed very little from that of the state-owned firms, except that their employees' conditions were less favorable. The various overseeing authorities were responsible for both supplying raw materials and finding outlets for the manufactured products. All that was left to the local managers were immediate problems concerning the manufacturing process.

Nationalization coincided with the extension to Shanghai of the system of directors imitated from the Soviet model. In this system, the authority of a single director, who was appointed by the government, replaced the responsibilities of the committees set up in the aftermath of the 1949 Revolution. The committees, in which workers, employers, technicians, and party cadres were represented, had allowed for a measure of democratization in the management of these firms. The adoption of single directorial responsibility was a mark of the growing bureaucratization of the system of production.

Nationalization made it possible for the party/state to extend the rhythms and processes of development that political leaders defined to the entire production apparatus. In Shanghai, this led to a diversification of the industrial sector. Its share of heavy industry steadily increased, rising from 21% to 52% of the total value of production between 1952 and 1975,[8] with more and more steelworks, oil refineries, chemical factories, and electric power stations making their appearance. During the Great Leap Forward, the movement speeded up, mainly by means of the installation of huge units of production. The campaign for steel production, in which Shanghai was deeply involved, also led to the installation of many small, traditional blast furnaces, but these turned out to be as useless and ephemeral here as they were elsewhere.

Thanks to the local authorities' consolidation policy, the crisis that followed the Great Leap Forward was more or less successfully averted in Shanghai: the city thus entered the 1960s with an increased production capacity and a better-balanced industrial structure. It was by now the second-largest steel-producing center in China. After Sino-Soviet relations were broken off in 1960, it benefited from the importation of Japanese or European turnkey factories and developed new branches of activity, such as the manufacture of chemical fertilizers and electrical equipment.

In the space of ten or so years, the industrial geography of the metropolis was transformed. It is true that in the old Shanghai some quarters, such as Zhabei in the northwest, Yangshupu in the northeast, and Nanshi to the south of the old Chinese town, had been particularly oriented toward industrial production, but factories and workshops had also been scattered throughout the city, squeezed in between living quarters. As soon as it had the means to do so—that is, after the industrial redeployment of 1956—the municipality tried to introduce a more rational distribution of industrial activities. First it removed to the periphery a number of factories that posed a risk to the public or the environment. Then it marked out new zones in the inner suburbs for specialized industries: in the north, Pengpu and Dachang were designated as steel-production centers, Taopu in the west was to accommodate chemical and pharmaceutical industries, and oil refineries were to be established in Gaoqiao close to the mouth of the Huangpu River.[9]

The removal of industrial activities to the periphery speeded up in December 1958, with the adoption of a program to build satellite towns inspired by the Soviet example. Seven sites were selected within a radius of several dozen kilometers around the built-up city of Shanghai. However, unlike the Soviets, the Chinese were averse to creating towns from scratch, preferring to transform already-existing large country towns: by 1960, Minhang, to the southeast, had become a manufacturing center for boilers, turbines, and pumps. But with inadequate funding, this program soon ran out of steam. It was interrupted by the Cultural Revolution but resumed in the 1970s, when a couple of chemical industries were set up in Jinshawei to the south, and an iron and steel complex was set up in Wusong-Baoshan to the north.

By the end of the 1970s, Shanghai was thus surrounded by several concentric zones of industrial activities. However, this attempt at relocation had been hampered by insufficient funding and had run into bureaucratic obstacles rendered the more redoubtable by the vertical structure of the economic bureaucracy and its division into departments that did not communicate. Decongestion within Shanghai had not really been achieved. In the early 1990s, industrial activities still occupied 8% of the surface of the city center, for even as relocation and peripheral installations went ahead, small workshops continued to spring up inside the city. Most were under collective management and designed to absorb surplus labor. Their proliferation at the time of the Great Leap Forward was accompanied by the creation of urban communes.* Unlike the latter, the small workshops survived the collapse of the Great Leap Forward and became integrated into the urban fabric. In the late 1960s, the city center, where density was as high as 41,000 inhabitants per square kilometer, still included over 10,000 units of industrial production, and the muddle that resulted from the mixture of factories and dwellings continued to cause serious difficulties.[10]

TOWN PLANNING SHELVED

The Communist regime closed down the erratic real estate market, ended the wild speculation that was forcing the price of land and buildings ever higher, and halted the city's chaotic growth caused by the appearance of more and

---

* These urban communes, created at the end of the Great Leap Forward, hardly survived it, unlike the rural communes, which disappeared only in 1984.

more factories and shantytowns. To deal with daily problems and rationalize how land was occupied, the municipality created a number of bureaus—one for Land and Real Estate, another for Urban Construction, and so on. There was no shortage of experts in Shanghai. But the improvement plan of 1949, inspired by projects prepared during the Guomindang period, was never applied; nor was that of 1953, drawn up with the aid of Soviet experts.[11] Town planning was not a priority for the First Five-Year Plan.

Yet the life of the metropolis had to continue, and the problems bequeathed by the former regime had to be resolved, as did new ones created by the city's demographic and spatial growth. Between 1949 and 1957, the urban population increased from 5 million to over 7 million inhabitants. A rigorous controlling policy reduced this to 6.5 million in the early 1960s and to fewer than 6 million in the following decade.* During this same period, the municipal territory was extended: in 1949, the city's twenty urban arrondissements and six suburban districts covered 80 square kilometers; following a series of expansions, the largest of which took place as early as 1958, this territory increased to 5,910 square kilometers, incorporating rural zones that were less densely populated than the city proper.** With the populations of the neighboring countryside and country towns added to that of Shanghai itself, the number of inhabitants under municipal management came to 10 million.

It was with this scale in mind that several plans were devised and implemented. They involved industrial and residential decentralization, food supplies from the agricultural periphery of the urban center, and improved means of transport. But the diversity of the administrative units controlled by the municipality (urban arrondissements, suburban districts, and rural districts), the divisions that separated them, and the difference in status between agricultural land (classed as collective property) and urban territory all combined to make the task of establishing a complementary bal-

---

* These figures relate to the urban population and do not take into account the residents of rural zones incorporated into the municipality. The establishment and interpretation of demographic statistics are complicated by great variations in the area of the municipal territory and by the sudden oscillations in official policies concerning the planning of births and enforced immigration.[12]

** In 1958, ten districts were attached to the Shanghai municipality: Jiading, Baoshan, Shanghai, Chuansa, Nanhui, Fengxian, Jinshan, Songjiang, Qingpu, and Chongming.

ance between Shanghai and its hinterland extremely difficult. The greatest obstacle, however, remained the meager financial resources allotted to the municipality's nonproductive investments. The needs of its population were sacrificed to the government's policy, which strongly favored productivity. Over the first three decades of the Communist regime, the upkeep of urban structures absorbed no more than 3.85% of the municipal budget, and housing suffered accordingly.[13] Beijing was thus responsible for the degeneration of infrastructure along with the entire urban framework. The fact that Shanghai survived this programmed paralysis testifies to the advantages that it had inherited from the previous regime, the chief one probably being the competence of its local administrators, who managed to preserve new wine in old flasks.

Starved of funds, Shanghai was obliged to fall back as best it could on its own resources. The network of water pipes and the drainage system inherited from the former concessions were maintained, and the supply of energy was tripled, thanks to the enlargement of the old Nanshi power station and the creation of new production units in the suburbs. Without means to construct a subway system (plans for which had been drawn up in 1958), the municipal authorities multiplied bus routes and the number of buses.

No new buildings were constructed to house the new administration units, so the properties along the Bund, now deserted by foreign firms, were converted into offices for them. The most majestic of all, the Hong Kong and Shanghai Bank, now became home to the municipal government. The police force established its "Circulation" department behind the columns of the former Bank of Indochina. The import-export Textile Corporation took possession of the premises of the Chartered Bank. In similar fashion, the villas of former Chinese and foreign notables became the residences of high-ranking Communist leaders. In the early 1950s, Chen Yi, mayor of Shanghai, lived in the home of a former official of the French municipality. Later, whenever Mao Zedong's wife, Jiang Qing, visited Shanghai, she installed herself in the former residence of T. V. Song, the minister and brother-in-law of Chiang Kai-shek.

No new thoroughfares were built to compete with the avenues of the former concessions: the Bund, renamed Sun Yat-sen Avenue; Avenue Joffre, now Huaihai Street; and the Nanjing Road, which retained its name. The creation of a park and the layout of People's Square on the site of the former racecourse altered the urban landscape very little and preserved a central oasis of greenery and a large empty space now dedicated to political demonstrations.[14] The only prestigious building that the new regime erected was the Exhibition Palace, built in the mid-1950s on Yan'an Street (formerly Edward VII Avenue) on the boundary between the two former foreign concessions. Its rigid lines, its series of colonnades and steeples, and the upward thrust of its high spire made this palace a fine specimen of the Stalinist style and testified to the short-lived Sino-Soviet friendship, which its construction had celebrated.

The lilong of old Shanghai also survived. Unlike the edifices in the finer quarters, these buildings retained their functions as homes and businesses, although the many small businesses squeezed into the network of its alleyways were no longer private but part of the collective sector. The city center thus looked more or less unchanged. Foreigners revisiting Shanghai in the late 1970s would be transported by a series of flashbacks. From behind the flags, red stars, and slogans that now adorned the facades, the entire capitalist and cosmopolitan past of the city would assail them. The Shanghainese themselves appeared oblivious to the silent presence of that past, unknown to the younger generation and deplored or repressed by the rest. The urban patrimony that was thus preserved or, to be more precise, escaped destruction, was an object not of pride but embarrassment or, at best, indifference.*

The survival of an urban framework at odds with the regime's political philosophy was one, but not the most serious, of the many problems

---

* In 1981, my colleagues at the Shanghai Academy of Social Sciences reacted with considerable reserve to my plan of embarking on a quasi-archaeological exploration of the city. Seeing that I could rely only on myself and my own old maps (brought from France), I set about exploring the city and relocating the old names of its streets and buildings. It was very slow work until my Chinese colleagues, satisfied now that no imperialistic nostalgia was involved on my part and that I was simply researching urban history, put a car at my disposal and a guide, in the shape of a colleague familiar with the Shanghai dialect and willing to interview old residents on street corners, with a view to identifying old sites. Equally appreciated was the help offered me by Mlle. Micheline Gewitsch, who was born and brought up in Shanghai and worked for the consulate-general of France once it had reopened in 1981. This longtime resident's enduring and accurate recollection of places and names made her a living memoir of the French concession.

resulting from the lack of funds. Others, in particular the housing short-age, produced dramatic consequences for the lives of the population. In 1949, the habitable surface area was definitely inadequate: about 23 mil-lion square meters (including slums and shantytowns), that is, roughly 4 square meters per person.[15] The confiscation and redistribution of hous-ing occupied by foreigners or "counterrevolutionaries" did not greatly im-prove the situation. Although dozens of families were now crammed into the old villas, whose reception rooms were divided and subdivided and whose garages and annexes were converted into apartments, Shanghai did not contain enough bourgeois residences to lodge all the city's inhabitants living in shocking conditions. The situation deteriorated even further in the early 1950s, when general demographic growth introduced a further influx of immigrants.

The municipality, which had become the principal proprietor of real estate in the city and the sole manager of its housing, made an effort to face up to the crisis and launched several construction programs. These, which were to spread over fifteen years, absorbed 487 million yuans. They added 8 million square meters to the habitable surface area by creating new residential zones in the city's more or less distant outskirts. The aim was to reduce density in the city center and to locate particular activities in areas specially designated according to their functions.

The first construction program dated from 1952 to 1953. This was still the honeymoon period of the revolution. The promises that it held out were beginning to be realized in the promotion of social housing. The plan was to construct nine workers' towns, known as New Villages (*Xincun*), on agricultural land on the immediate periphery of the city's built-up area, close to the old industrial quarters of Zhabei and Yangshupu, in order to do away with three hundred zones of precarious housing. Each new town, made up of four- to five-story buildings, was to accommodate about 400,000 inhabitants. A total of 22,000 lodgings of roughly 30 square meters each were built at this stage. During my first visit to Shanghai in October 1957, I had the opportunity to visit Caoyang, to the northwest of the city, cre-ated in 1952 to accommodate families then living in extremely precarious conditions. "Thirty thousand people are living in these small gray cubes, linked by paths bordered by young trees. We visited one apartment: three tiny rooms, inhabited by a family of six. On the landing, there was a communal kitchen used by three housewives in the building."[16]

These towns, with poor internal links and equally poor bus services to Shanghai's city center and without general social services, testified to the overwhelmingly quantitative preoccupations of the local authorities. Construction continued over forty years, with stops and starts dictated by whatever funding was available. Little by little, the height of the buildings increased and the comfort of lodgings improved. Although many kitchens continued to be shared, at least individual plumbing and bathroom equipment appeared. By 1973, these towns—all seventy-six of them—represented one-quarter of the habitable surface area of Shanghai. In the housing domain, they constituted the principal contribution of the Maoist regime.[17] Springing up in the fields all around the city, they formed a belt of gray and gloomy suburbs. But they did at least fulfill the purpose for which they were intended: they housed as many families as possible at the lowest possible cost. To that extent, the New Villages program could be considered a success.

The same could not be said of the program for satellite settlements launched in 1958, which coincided with the stepping up of industrial development. The dispersed production units were supposed to be surrounded by housing zones. Medium-sized urban centers were to be developed around the new factories, far enough away from the metropolis for them not to merge with its spreading suburbs. The policy advocated at this time earmarked the immediate suburbs for intensive market-gardening and pushed the construction of satellite towns toward a distant periphery, between 20 and 70 kilometers from the main Shanghai complex.[18] These towns were not supposed to be dormitory towns. They were intended to be organized around new, specialized industrial units. Their population, which was not supposed to exceed 300,000 or 400,000 inhabitants, was to be distributed among quarters well equipped from a social point of view, each of which a particular group of factories would dominate. Greenbelts were supposed to separate industrial zones from residential ones.

In Shanghai, an extension of the municipal territory facilitated implementation of this policy. The network of the seven satellite towns envisaged by the town planners overlapped that of the large country towns of Jiangnan. The satellite towns were arranged around a basin of heavy mechanical industries. The first to be completed was Minhang. It benefited from large investments and, in particular, from the construction of a four-lane highway linking it with Shanghai. At the time, the press ran an insistent propaganda campaign to encourage families to settle in the new town. It praised the quality of the air, the abundant supply of fresh vegetables, and the spacious accommodation (9 square meters per person). Yet barely one-quarter of the workers assigned to Minhang were willing to settle their families there. The rest preferred to continue living in Shanghai, even if it meant a long journey every day to get to work. Their reluctance to make the move stemmed partly from Minhang's inadequate social services and means of transport. The mediocre quality of its local schools constituted another negative factor. Anxious to further their children's chances in the future, families preferred to send them to Shanghai schools with good,

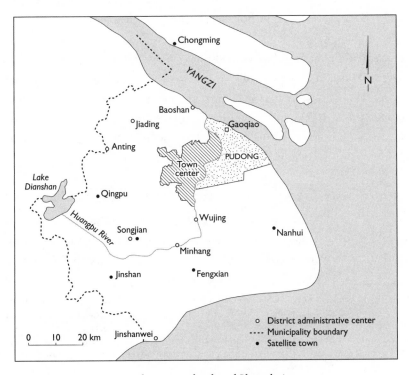

The new suburbs of Shanghai

well-established reputations. Finally, at a time when a family needed two salaries to make ends meet, the isolation of the satellite town and the extremely specialized nature of its production units complicated the search for employment for wives and elder children.[19]

After the Great Leap Forward, lack of funds slowed the construction of satellite towns. Construction was interrupted by the Cultural Revolution, then resumed in the early 1970s, but continued to run into the same difficulties. According to the 1990 census, the inhabitants of the seven satellite towns totaled only 680,000, less than 10% of Shanghai's population. Furthermore, those inhabitants had not come from Shanghai's city center but from the neighboring Jiangsu and Zhejiang countryside.

Despite very real efforts, the housing problem had not been resolved. The housing shortage grew even worse. In 1957, the habitable surface area fell to less than 3 square meters per person.* At this time, over 1 million people were still living in shantytowns or in thatched huts. Not until the late 1970s did the habitable area per person recover more or less its 1949 level. The acute and chronic housing shortage weighed more heavily on the lives of Shanghai residents than any of the disadvantages resulting from the weakness of nonproductive investment. Some 129,000 resident families were still without any form of housing in 1980, and over 400,000 young people, though legally married, were unable to live together, as they had nowhere to settle down.[20] Creating a proletarian society that could be a showcase and symbol of the regime proved a far more difficult undertaking than turning Shanghai into a bastion of heavy industry.

A SOCIETY UNDER CLOSE SURVEILLANCE

Turning Shanghai into a proletarian citadel meant obliterating its past, wreaking revenge on all exploiters, and loudly proclaiming the role of the workers, who were now the country's symbolic "new masters." Although

---

* In *The Attic: Memoir of a Chinese Landlord's Son*, Cao Guanlong provides a humorous and compassionate description of the life of his parents and their four children in the attic in which the family lived when they took refuge in Shanghai in the early days of the revolution. From their home, reached by a ladder and a trapdoor, it was easier to reach the roof than the lower stories. The beams were so low that there was no room for furniture except mattresses and a small stove; space was in such short supply that at night the sleepers, with their arms and legs intertwined, could not move without waking one another.

the Communist regime may not have created the Shanghai working class, under its influence such a class increased in numbers and acquired a status that it had thitherto lacked.* However, the constitution of this working aristocracy was accompanied by processes of exclusion that closed the door in the faces of many unlucky people. The unemployed, immigrants who had but recently arrived from the countryside, soon joined the ranks of those disappointed by socialism. Their discontent, along with that of many others, found expression at the time of the crisis of the One Hundred Flowers in 1957.

On May 2, 1956, Mao Zedong called for "the blooming of a Hundred Flowers" and urged the party to show more moderation in its exercise of power. In the spring of 1957, after months of equivocation and debate, there was a brief period of liberalization. But so violent was the manifestation of discontent that after eight weeks the authorities halted the experiment and launched an "anti-right-wing" repression of exceptional scope and severity. What historians especially noted were the political aspects of this crisis, that is, the factional struggles within the Communist apparatus and all the ideological and bureaucratic clashes. Social troubles seemed to them far less important, given that the Maoist regime, which deprived society of its autonomy, thereby minimized the importance of social matters in the evolution of history. Furthermore, at the time, protesting intellectuals and the more liberal politicians made hardly any mention of economic and social difficulties—a fact that appeared to indicate that social unease had very little to do with political discontent. All the same, this fleeting dislocation of the political leadership did allow this aspect of social reality, usually masked by official discourse and censorship, briefly to surface.

Insofar as it is possible to understand Shanghai society at the time of the Hundred Flowers, it does not appear to tally with the flattering image of a workers' paradise that the Communist leaders sought to present. On the contrary, society seems to have been riven by many dissatisfactions, foremost among them those preoccupying the workers, supposedly the class of the elect. In the spring of 1957, a wave of strikes hit Shanghai.

---

* Speedy industrialization created new jobs, and the number of Shanghai workers rose from 500,000 in 1949 to 770,000 in 1957.[21]

Most erupted in mixed enterprises formed after the nationalizations of the preceding year, for in these employees were not granted the same advantages reserved for workers in the public sector. The strikes took the form of spontaneous demonstrations prompted by wage claims and demands for better status and social protection. Apprentices were among the most determined of the strikers, protesting against the extension of the period of training, which kept them longer on the lowest of wages; meanwhile, temporary workers were revolting against the precarious nature of their situation. This unrest took place outside the framework of the trade unions, which, the workers claimed, had become mere agencies for keeping them under control, simply "tongues of the bureaucracy and tails of the administration." It produced no explicit criticisms or political complaints. But the frequency and violence of horizontal conflicts between different categories or generations of workers did highlight the cleavages that divided the workers' world internally.[22]

"Capitalists" were not so much disappointed by socialism as nostalgic for the ancien régime. Dispossessed of their businesses by the nationalizations of 1956 (but preserving the classification and status of capitalists that had been attributed to them in the aftermath of the revolution), they had received compensation (*dingxi*) calculated in proportion to the capital that had been appropriated from them. Although the commissions of inquiry had systematically underestimated its value, compensation paid out to the most important heads of firms certainly assured them of a living standard incomparably superior to that of the Shanghai masses. Furthermore, many of them had been invited to continue their activities within their former businesses, for which they received far higher salaries than those of the cadres appointed by the authorities, under whose direction they now worked. Coexistence was not easy either for the state representatives, many of whom were not qualified for the positions they held, or for the former bosses, who had now lost their authority. The latter were indignant at the position to which they had been relegated. Their anger boiled over in March 1957 when one of them, the erstwhile proprietor of a pharmaceutical factory, was physically attacked by one of his former apprentices, now the firm's director. The former employers demanded "fairer treatment," the restoration of responsibilities to those employers who had been "politically reformed," an increase in their salaries, and a prolongation, from seven to twenty years, of the period during which they were to be paid compensation.

The former smaller-scale employers—shopkeepers, independent craftsmen, and so on—were less well treated, and the fates of many of them were lamentable. The small sums of compensation allotted to them did not suffice to provide for their families, and their continued classification as capitalists disqualified them from seeking employment and rejoining the ranks of the workers. Their anger was directed not so much against the government but against the big capitalists who had entered into alliance with the regime without sparing a thought for their humbler colleagues. They complained that in business circles nothing had changed since the days before 1949: "The big fish continued to eat the small fry."

In contrast to the intellectuals and students of Beijing, who played a role of major importance in the reexamination of ideological and political questions in the spring of 1957, those of Shanghai proved more reserved. Not that their fate was any better. In 1957, the universities of Shanghai decided to reduce the number of admissions. While university doors were closing and administration departments, already fully staffed, were also cutting down on new employees, many college students could see their hopes of a career evaporating. Meanwhile, those already accepted by universities complained of the ideological pressures to which they were subjected and the authoritarian way in which jobs were assigned to them when their studies were over, most of which were totally unrelated to their particular skills and required them to move to posts far away from Shanghai. The bitterness of these young people found expression in various demonstrations but did not lead to a veritable intellectual revolt, as it did in Beijing. It was in the Chinese capital that the leaders of the former liberal intelligentsia, such as Chu Anping, spoke out in the One Hundred Flowers period. In Shanghai, figures of note were still crushed by the terror created by the 1955 campaign against Hu Feng. This longtime fellow traveler, author of a report attacking the dogmatism and intolerance of cultural bureaucrats, had at that time been accused of collusion with the Guomindang and the United States and had then been thrown into prison. The Communist campaign had then turned upon and hunted down the vanished Hu Feng's colleagues and friends, many of whom lived in Shanghai. In 1956, the authorities softened their approach to intellectuals, but fear and distrust remained. At the time of the One Hundred Flowers, most Shanghai intellectuals of any standing remained silent, fearful of a trap and a brutal reversal of the new political line.

Their fears were justified. Faced with the violent criticism that this liberalization unleashed and the threat that it posed for the authorities in power, the factions were reuniting. In early June 1957, the party performed a brutal U-turn. The anti-right-wing purge that followed dispatched hundreds of thousands of people to the gulag camps and shattered the ideal of a social consensus founded on patriotism. The social unrest did not convert into political mobilization, nor was any attempt made to link up with the demonstrations of discontent and the political protests then developing in Beijing among liberal intellectuals and the leaders of small democratic parties. The absence of determined social protest resulted from the nature of Chinese society at this time as much as from the political system: society was still fragmented, parochial community interests dominated, and the Maoist dictatorship now made it impossible for great popular movements to develop, temporarily unifying the masses, as they had in the 1920s and 1930s.

For the relations between society and the authorities in power 1957 marked a turning point that was just as important as that of 1949, if not more so. In the course of the anti-right-wing campaign unleashed in June, hundreds of thousands of intellectuals, cadres, and experts were sent away to camps as a result of arbitrary decisions, as was permitted by the new law on reeducation through work. Protected against any legal interference, the Chinese gulag became the regime's flexible and effective instrument for strengthening its control over society.

To keep the population under its thumb, the regime resorted to three types of administrative measures, which combined to produce the required effect: household registration (*hukou*), rationing of basic foodstuff and cloth, and allocation of jobs by labor bureaus. The hukou system made it compulsory for every home to register every member of the family with the Public Security Bureau (the police). Registration gave Chinese people the right to live and work where they were born but prevented them from settling elsewhere. In other words, it fixed peasants to the land and urban residents in their towns. The destiny of an individual was now determined by his or her birthplace. This system interacted with the rationing of cereals, oil, and other essential foodstuffs. In towns, coupons were distributed every month, but only to residents registered in the regular manner. Illegal residents had no option but to turn to free markets or the black market, and it was hard for them to find work since the labor bureaus reserved regular work for legal residents.

In Shanghai, these regulations were applied particularly strictly. The growing population was one of the main problems facing the municipal administration. The by no means negligible progress achieved in the early 1950s in the creation of jobs and construction of housing was totally eroded by strong demographic growth fueled partly by peasant immigration (1.8 million new arrivals between 1949 and 1957) and partly by natural causes: at 4.6%, Shanghai's birthrate was higher than that of any other Chinese province. It therefore seemed essential to limit population growth.

The first plan for the city's demographic development, in 1957, fixed the level at which the population should stabilize at 7 million and advocated a reduction in immigration. The hukou system, which prevented peasants from settling in the city, was accompanied by a systematic program for returning peasants to the countryside (*xiaxiang*). At first, there were massive deportations of recently arrived immigrants, in particular the unemployed, coolies, and laborers. At the Northern Station in Zhabei and on the wharves of the Huangpu, police supervised group departures. In 1955, about 850,000 people were moved in this way, and in 1958 another 500,000 (7% of the population).[23] Further deportations took place in the 1960s. Now the peasants and coolies were replaced by surplus workers, disgraced cadres, intellectuals, and entire classes of secondary school pupils. The number of enforced emigrants fell little by little until the eve of the Cultural Revolution, but it always exceeded the number of immigrants.

The high priority ascribed to population control in Shanghai was also reflected in the 1957 implementation of a program designed to reduce the birthrate. Business cadres and residents' committees threw themselves into campaigns providing information and means of birth control. The birthrate now declined regularly, reaching .9% in the mid-1970s and leading to a

parallel fall in the rate of natural growth (from 4% to .3%). This spectacular reduction in the number of births, which stood in sharp contrast
to the difficulties encountered in the rest of China, suggests that in Shanghai it was welcomed by a better-educated population, keen to preserve or
improve its standard of living and to ensure the future of its children.[24]

The provincial labor bureaus set up in the aftermath of the revolution
appeared initially to lack authority and be condemned to inefficiency by
the multiplicity and confusion of the tasks assigned to them and their inadequate funding. But from 1957 on, as the public sector was extended
and economic management was decentralized, their role increased. They
were now given greater powers and the authority to allot jobs to graduates and to both temporary and tenured workers. Public-sector businesses
had to apply to these bureaus when recruiting staff; when it proved necessary to appeal for a supplementary labor force from the countryside,
it could only be done within the framework of collective contracts negotiated between the agricultural cooperatives (or later, the people's communes) and the concerned businesses, and always under the supervision
of the labor bureaus. The labor bureaus furthermore barred all residents
without legal status from regular employment.

These "vertical" controls that various administrative offices exercised
were complemented by "horizontal" controls that operated within the
work units (*danwei*), where both the professional and the personal life
of every employee was kept under surveillance by his or her colleagues
and within the framework of neighborhood committees. One woman in
Shanghai who used to belong to one such committee has explained that
its members would be recruited from among older women who were either unemployed or retired and many of whom, herself included, were illiterate. Under the direction of local party cadres, these committees were
responsible for organizing community life, keeping the residents' political
attitudes under surveillance, and raising everybody's political consciousness. As our witness herself admitted, committee members were not popular. People distrusted them, accusing them of sticking their noses in where
they were not wanted; at their approach, conversations tended to dry up.
Our informant, who was responsible for a gray block of apartments in
the inner suburbs that was home to two hundred people, was constantly

scurrying from one meeting or interview to another. Despite assistance from activists, each one detailed to keep one of the doors to the building under surveillance, she often found no time to look after her own home and family. One of her chief tasks was to note the presence, in the building or near it, of any strangers who might be miscreants or secret residents. She also had to take part in a series of campaigns designed to encourage hygiene and vaccinations, to teach young wives contraception methods, and to win round their unwilling husbands. She sometimes found it hard to impose her authority, despite the support that party cadres were supposed to provide. For instance, she failed to liberate an apartment in which a widow was squatting, fed up with sharing a single room with her children and grandchildren and having to sleep in the kitchen or on a balcony, both of which were too narrow. Nor was she successful in restoring peace in the relationship between a fickle worker and his "silly goose" of a country wife. No aspect of the private lives of her neighbors escaped the surveillance that she maintained in the name of socialist morality and community harmony.[25]

Under such controls, Shanghai gave the impression of a society without problems. Shanghainese were privileged in comparison to peasants and the residents of smaller towns, and they shared living conditions that, although austere, appeared to be relatively egalitarian. A young Australian expert, recruited in 1965 to teach English there, was pleasantly surprised to find a city that was "refreshingly unsophisticated, more like a big country town than a great metropolis" and Shanghainese who felt "obvious pride in Shanghai's achievements" and were full of a "naïve confidence in the future."[26] However, beneath this tranquil surface, new inequalities were developing, now founded not upon wealth but status, on which access to goods and services depended.

THE NEW INEQUALITIES

The social order established after the 1949 Revolution accommodated people with privileges, actively engaged in maintaining the status quo, but incorporated others who were excluded from it. It furthermore preserved some small areas in which inequalities left over from the previous regime were perpetuated.

As in all Communist countries, the *nomenklatura* (members of the party/state apparatus) tended to constitute a class apart. Party cadres lived among themselves, in residences reserved for them. They bought their supplies in special shops and sent their children to the best schools. Longtime revolutionaries were now above all concerned with their own well-being and the future of their families; they were resting on their laurels. One such was Zhou, a Yan'an veteran who had become vice-president of the Institute of Foreign Languages, who regularly absented himself on Thursdays to avoid the sessions of manual labor scheduled for that day.[27] The egalitarianism that prevailed obliged Chinese cadres to act with more discretion than their counterparts in the Soviet Union. The frequent campaigns of criticism and self-criticism made them more vulnerable and therefore more prudent. But in Shanghai, until the Cultural Revolution in 1966, careers remained stable, governed by the principle of seniority, and cadres were never replaced.

Many Shanghai workers were also actively involved in preserving both a status quo that favored them and a system that made them not only dependent on but also supportive of the cadres.[28] The development of heavy industry and the installation of large production units had resulted in the emergence of a working aristocracy made up of those with permanent jobs in the public sector. Workers who enjoyed this status accounted for about 40% of the Chinese industrial working force, or probably rather more in Shanghai, where many large state-owned enterprises were concentrated. Apart from possessing a job guaranteed for life, they earned higher wages and benefited from bonuses, insurance, and other social advantages (medical costs that were covered and retirement pensions); they also had access to housing and services such as canteens and crèches that were either refused or offered on less generous terms to other categories of workers. The status of a permanent state worker was inaccessible to nonregistered residents and, increasingly, even to some who were legal. Around the mid-1960s, when the baby boomers born in the wake of the revolution arrived on the labor market, the number of jobs available in the public sector had fallen even lower in relation to all the new job seekers.

In Shanghai, as in all large Chinese towns, the goods and services upon which living standards depended were obtained essentially through distributions made within the work unit, whether this was a firm or an administrative office. The work unit thus became the focal point of both the professional and the private and family life of every employee.[29] This was where links of dependency between the party/state and elite workers were forged. The party apparatus, which was distinct from yet very close to the administrative hierarchy, exerted its influence in work units through the action of its members, who could rely on small groups of activists driven by either conviction or ambition. It was these activists who proposed who should be granted privileges, promotion, bonuses, and other advantages. They also had a hand in drawing up the personal files of employees (*dang'an*), containing professional, moral, and political evaluations based upon their behavior (*biaoxian*) at the many political meetings held during working hours or in daily life generally. The best way to improve one's living conditions was to ingratiate oneself with these petty bosses. Constraints were omnipresent—all firms were equipped with a department of Public Security that was directly attached to the municipal Public Security Bureau—but party power also, in fact above all, rested upon these "clientist" networks that, in a situation of general shortages, made one's work unit the direct source of both goods and services. Workers' loyalty (inspired by self-interest) was rewarded by the paternalism of unit leaders who were bent on strengthening their own popularity by negotiating directly with other production or administrative units for the supply of foodstuffs and other consumer goods to their own staff.

Work units were thus the citadels of a working-class elite who supported the regime that had turned them into a privileged caste. However, the excluded outnumbered the elect, and their ranks were constantly swelling. In the wake of the black years that followed the failure of the Great Leap Forward, industrial employment declined and surplus labor was either barred from the labor market or subjected to unfavorable conditions of employment and status.

In 1964, the "sending down" program in operation since the mid-1950s was given a new boost. Its objective now was to remove from Shanghai and send to the countryside all the young graduates from secondary school education who were about to become job seekers.[30] Municipal officials would preside over gatherings of several thousand young people and exalt the generosity of those about to depart for distant regions in order to further the construction of their socialist country and the improvement of peasant education and, in return, to learn from those peasants all the revolutionary virtues. In the heat of the moment, hundreds of their listeners signed up for departure to the countryside. Volunteers were also recruited in the various town quarters by committees of representatives of the Youth League, police, and local schools. At the end of each school year, colleges and universities drew up lists of candidates for departure. At the Northern Station, college graduates, in their own college groups, solemnly bade farewell to their parents. Many went off to Xinjiang (Sinkiang) on the desert northwestern borders of China where 50,000 of them by 1965 were working on state farms managed by paramilitary units. The atmosphere of forced enthusiasm surrounding their departures did nothing to mitigate the sorrow of all the families, who were distressed at the thought of their children exiled to such distant and inhospitable lands.

For the young people of Shanghai who refused to leave, the future looked very unpromising. A few managed to find employment in some of the collective businesses that had multiplied at the time of the Great Leap Forward. These were small-scale enterprises (in Shanghai in 1963, most employed, on average, no more than thirty-two people), most of which were managed by the local arrondissement or district authorities, paid low wages, and were unable to provide their staff with any of the advantages enjoyed by those employed in the public sector. Such young job seekers might, alternatively, find employment on a temporary basis, in which case they were paid by the day or given short-term contracts. Either way, they were relegated to unskilled and poorly paid work alongside laborers of peasant origin.

The peasant-worker system was introduced in the early 1960s. Contracts negotiated with people's communes made it possible for urban enterprises (state owned or collective) to call upon a rural labor force whenever the need to do so arose. The peasant workers did not have the right to settle definitively in Shanghai and had to hand over a proportion of their wages to their native people's commune. Not only were they much lower paid than other workers but they were offered no protection of any kind nor any social advantages. Initially, businesses called on them only to cope with unexpected fluctuations in production, whether or not of a seasonal nature. But from 1964 on, in conformity with national directives, these rural workers tended to be substituted for permanent workers to reduce the cost of staff. This policy was supposed to close the gap that separated towns from the countryside by making it possible for peasant workers to improve their skills and by facilitating the transfer of better-qualified workers to the interior. In practice, however, it increased the discontent of permanent workers, whose positions were thus threatened, of job seekers whom it deprived of employment, and of the peasant workers themselves, who were jealous of the working conditions available to other categories of employees.

Finally, on the margins of the new society, there still existed niches where the privileges of the former bourgeoisie were perpetuated to varying degrees. Some "red capitalists," with pensions and in some cases government salaries and still able to access dividends from family businesses that had moved out of China, managed to maintain a luxurious lifestyle. They simply had to be very discreet about it.[31] Even more astonishing was the situation of Nien Cheng, the daughter of a big landowner and widow of a Nationalist diplomat who, in the early 1960s, was still living in a vast family home, crammed with ancient silverware and porcelain and English books and magazines. Still served by her former domestic staff, the lady watched carefully over her daughter, who, after completing her studies at Municipal College no. 2, one of the best in Shanghai, became a cinema actress and would relax at home playing Chopin nocturnes and amusing herself with her pet Persian cat.*

---

* Because of food shortages, pets were officially banned. Nien Cheng left an extremely detailed account of her life in Shanghai and the misfortunes that befell her during the Cultural Revolution in *Life and Death in Shanghai*. Nien Cheng studied at the London School of Economics from 1935 to 1938. She then followed her husband to a post in Australia, where the couple lived until 1948. After the 1949 Revolution, her husband became the director of the Shanghai agency of the Shell Petroleum Company, one of the few foreign firms to have retained an office in Shanghai. Widowed in 1957, Nien Cheng was then herself employed by the company as an assistant director/translator until the local office was closed in 1966. During the Cultural Revolution she was arrested as a spy and thrown into prison, where she remained for six years. When she was released, she learned that her daughter had been beaten to death by the Red Guards. Her memoirs record the cruel days of the Cultural Revolution with intelligence and humanity.

Not all Shanghai's former bourgeois had managed to negotiate their survival so successfully, nor did they possess healthy bank accounts in both China and abroad. But in the universities, many ancien régime intellectuals retained their teaching responsibilities (which they carried out under surveillance from cadres of varying levels of competence), and some even managed to pursue their vocations. One such was the head of the English Department at the Institute of Foreign Languages, who seldom put in an appearance in the workplace but devoted all his energies to translating the complete works of Chaucer; another was the head of piano studies at the Municipal Conservatory, who devoted herself entirely to preparing her students for great international music competitions.[32] These people caused the regime very little trouble and were, to a certain extent, useful to it, so they led relatively protected lives. They came under threat only when major popular mobilization campaigns occurred, as happened from time to time. They would then invariably be picked on as targets for mass criticism. They became the unfortunate victims of the campaigns launched against counterrevolutionaries in 1951, against Hu Feng in 1955, and against right-wingers in general two years later. But at the beginning of the next decade, such violence abated and life returned to a more normal course.

The 1949 Revolution had profoundly changed Shanghai society, rendering it more egalitarian within the framework of collective privilege represented by the status of an urban resident. Party members and their clients dominated this society. It advantaged them and, in certain cases (up to a point), a larger worker-aristocracy. Members of the old elite groups, if they still existed, now played no role at all, but their children learned how to live in the system and, thanks to their good school results, moved on to the best secondary schools, where they rubbed shoulders with the children of cadres.* Those who were excluded were the unfortunate workers of the collective sector, temporary and illegal residents, and the xiaxiang deportees. The stability of society rested on the support of huge numbers of people and the constraints that were imposed upon everyone. There appeared to be no reason why Shanghai should become the bastion of radicalism.

---

* Neale Hunter notes that at the Institute of Foreign Languages, the children of working-class or peasant origin made up only half the total number of students and were frequently assigned to classes with inferior teachers and equipment.

THE CULTURAL REVOLUTION AND
SHANGHAI RADICALISM

It was in Shanghai in November 1965 that the first press attack against Mao Zedong's enemies was launched; and it was there in November 1966 that for the first time workers took part in a massive movement of rebellion. It was also there that, as early as the spring/summer of 1967, a relative calm returned, more than a year before it did so in the rest of the country.

Shanghai also stands out because the factional clashes there did not degenerate into civil war. There was no heavy fighting, nor were there thousands of corpses. Finally, Shanghai was remarkable for the role that the leftist faction continued to play there until Mao Zedong's death. Right from the start, part of the local apparatus was won over to the Maoist objectives, that is, the struggle against any institutionalization of the revolution that might drain it of its purpose and, more concretely, the elimination of leaders and cadres who opposed the will of the president. Thanks to the close relations between Mao Zedong and those who were to become known as the Gang of Four but were at the time simply "the Shanghai group,"* the city became the principal base and laboratory of the Cultural Revolution Group.**

After the failure of the Great Leap Forward, the political struggle at the top intensified. Ranged against Mao Zedong, considered to be responsible for the catastrophe, were most of the top party leaders. They were anxious to restore production and social order by means of pragmatic, relatively liberal policies. However, they did not oppose the president openly, for his popularity and charisma rendered him untouchable; instead, they blocked the application of Maoist directives designed to relaunch the class struggle. Isolated within his party, Mao Zedong turned to the masses to save his concept of the revolution and his own power. Unable to operate in Beijing, where the central administration eluded his influence and the

---

* This group centered on Jiang Qing, Mao Zedong's wife, and included three of the principal leaders of the Maoist clique, all of them Shanghai cadres: Zhang Chunqiao, Yao Wenyuan, and Wang Hongwen.
** The Cultural Revolution Group, made up of members of Mao Zedong's family and personal entourage, joined by a few other cadres of tried and tested loyalty, replaced the discredited central apparatus in 1966 and took over direction of the activities of revolutionary rebels in the provinces.

mayor, Peng Zhen, was hostile to him, he decided to launch his offensive in Shanghai.

Why Shanghai? The choice may be explained by certain of its local leaders' unwavering loyalty to Mao Zedong personally and to his policies. Ke Qingshi, the mayor and first secretary of the Shanghai Party Committee, was foremost among them, but his sudden disappearance in April 1965 was a severe blow to the Maoist camp. His successor, Cao Diqiu, was certainly a Communist loyal to the party and to its leader, but his managerial temperament did not incline him to embrace Maoist Utopias. The real heirs to Ke Qingshi were his former collaborators from the Propaganda Department, Zhang Chungqiao and Yao Wenyuan.

As the director of that department, Zhang Chunqiao had tried to pursue an in-depth program for correcting the attitudes of intellectuals.* He supported Jiang Qing, Mao's wife, in her endeavors to eliminate traditional Chinese opera, with its cohorts of kings, ministers, and courtesans, and to popularize revolutionary opera with contemporary themes. In 1963, he organized a festival in Shanghai, during which the new models of opera were presented. He gathered around him a team of young cultural bureaucrats, among whom Yao Wenyuan stood out by virtue of his dogmatism and the violence of his attacks during a series of campaigns to intimidate intellectuals.[33]

Yao Wenyuan fired the first salvos of the Cultural Revolution when, on November 10, 1965, he published in a local newspaper a very critical review of a play titled *Hai Rui Dismissed from Office*.** Masquerading as a piece of literary and historical criticism, the article, written with the help of Jiang Qing, constituted a political attack on the mayor of Beijing, Peng

---

* Zhang Chungqiao, born in 1917 in Shandong, came from a family of local elites. He arrived in Shanghai in 1935 and became an active member of its League of Leftist Writers. During the Japanese occupation, he joined Mao Zedong in Yan'an and became a member of the CCP. After the 1949 Revolution, he returned to Shanghai where, under the protection of Ke Qingshi, he headed the party local committee supervising literary and artistic activities, was made the general manager of the *Liberation Daily*, and rose rapidly in the local hierarchy.

** This was a play about the misfortune of a mandarin under the Ming dynasty in the sixteenth century who was made destitute for having criticized the emperor's policy of land confiscation. The fate of Hai Rui evokes that of Marshal Peng Dehuai, who was purged in 1959 for having opposed Mao Zedong. The mayor of Beijing, Peng Zhen, protected the author of this essay, the historian Wu Han.

Zhen. It took Mao Zedong six months to get rid of this powerful leader, but once that was done, the Cultural Revolution really took off.

In Shanghai, the universities mobilized. They were reacting to a declaration made by Mao Zedong on May 16, 1966, in which he called for a battle to root out "people of the Khrushchev brand still nestling in our midst." On university campuses, many aggressive meetings took place. The students attacked cadres, administrators, and professors who had become so absorbed in their studies that they neglected political activities. Among the earliest victims were individuals who had had occasion to cross swords with Yao Wenyuan, in particular the director of the Municipal Conservatory, who rejected the "politicization" of music.[34] Like the high-ranking leaders in Beijing, the mayor of Shanghai encouraged the movement but at the same time tried to control it by filling the campuses with work teams made up of tried and tested cadres to prevent the protests from targeting the party itself.

In August, Mao Zedong, in his Sixteen-Point Decision, criticized the role of the work teams and made it clear that the aim of the Cultural Revolution was indeed "to overthrow those persons in authority who are taking the capitalist road" and to eliminate the "Four Olds" (old ideas, old culture, and old customs and habits). At this, the revolution spilled over from the universities into the streets under the momentum created by the Red Guards. In Shanghai, as in Beijing, these were mostly recruited from among university and college students organized into propaganda teams to spread the thought of Mao Zedong and to exercise terror among representatives of the bourgeois order. To the sound of drums and gongs, they distributed tracts, hung posters, delivered soapbox speeches, and chanted slogans. They would halt and molest passersby who sported hairstyles or clothes inspired by Western fashions, demanding, "Why do you wear those shoes with pointed toes?" "Why do you wear narrow trousers?" "Why do you have oiled hair?"[35] They destroyed architectural features that evoked the old Western presence, stripped sanctuaries of their old cult objects, invaded the Municipal Museum looking for "feudal relics," then continued their search in the houses of former bourgeois. In the evening of August 30, a gang of thirty or so college students invaded the home of Nien Cheng and rummaged through it, smashing the precious porcelain, emptying drawers of their treasures, the refrigerator of its provisions, and the library of its books, all the while heaping insults and blows on their owner.[36] The Red Guards searched a total of 150,000 homes and confiscated 900,000 pounds of gold and silver jewelry, 300,000 pounds of pearls and jade, 3.3 million U.S. dollars and other currencies of nearly equal value, and so on.[37]

The summer of the Red Guards, with its succession of violent attacks, humiliations, and suicides, was different from previous mass campaigns because of the youth of the actors and the preeminence accorded to the thought of Mao Zedong, whose sayings were to be found inscribed everywhere, even on bicycle handlebars! But the targets were the same as ever: former bourgeois, ex-capitalists, old intellectuals, and all those who, in some capacity or other, had had contacts with the Guomindang or foreigners. The mayor, Cao Diqiu, did not or would not accept that the Cultural Revolution also targeted the party itself and, although he provided the Red Guards with all the material they required (ink, paper, paintbrushes, loudspeakers, trucks), he was watchful, anxious to ensure that local cadres were not attacked. A few particularly active radicals on the Fudan campus complained that the movement was heading in the wrong direction and simply "tilting at dead tigers" (that is, survivors from the bourgeoisie),[38] but they convinced neither the youthful Red Guards nor the general population, who continued to place their trust in the party and its principal representative, the city's mayor.*

It fell to the radical Red Guards who arrived from Beijing in three successive waves, in August, September, and October, to "light a fire" (*dianhuo*) and set their Shanghai comrades on the correct revolutionary path. The newcomers from Beijing came to Shanghai within the framework of a program for the exchange of revolutionary experiences (*chuan lian*), which was at that time congesting the roads and railway stations with millions of Red Guards. "Why are you folks here so civil, without

---

* Cao Diqiu enjoyed particular freedom in imposing his strategy given that Zhang Chunqiao and Yao Wenyuan had both been recalled to Beijing to join the Cultural Revolution Group entrusted by Mao Zedong to direct the movement nationwide. The two men nevertheless kept a close eye on developments in Shanghai and were later to intervene with a heavy hand there.

even a bit of revolutionary spirit?" they asked their Shanghai comrades, as they taught them the art of beating their victims with leather belts. Thus admonished, the Red Guards of Shanghai brought about 354 deaths and 704 suicides in the month of September alone.[39]

On the university campuses, radicals led the assault to lay hands on the "black books," the personal files that recorded the details and actions of both cadres and ordinary citizens. They were after information on which to base accusations against cadres, which would cause one of the bureaucracy's principal weapons to rebound against itself. Coordination was established between one university and another, across the board from Fudan to Jiaotong and the Shanghai Second Medical University, and new organizations emerged: the Red Revolutionaries, the Third Red Headquarters, and a group known as Fire on the Headquarters, all three toeing the line of the Beijing Guards.

Until this point, the organizers of the Cultural Revolution had accepted the principle that it should not affect production, and the Red Guards had been ordered not to enter any factories. However, in November the Red Guards of Beijing overrode the official ban and the reluctance of local radicals and proceeded to spread propaganda in the workshops of Shanghai, thereby precipitating workers onto the revolutionary stage and ushering in a new phase of the Cultural Revolution. The Workers' General Headquarters, which they helped to set up on November 6, had soon rallied several hundred thousand members, recruited from among the most disadvantaged apprentices and temporary workers. When the mayor refused to recognize their organization, several thousand representatives of the Workers' General Headquarters requisitioned a train to carry their complaints to Beijing. On September 10, the train was halted at Anting (in the suburbs of Shanghai), where a decisive clash took place. Zhang Chunqiao, who had arrived from Beijing, now usurped the mayor's authority and accepted the workers' demands. These now played an increasingly important role. On December 3, when the Incident of the *Liberation Daily* occurred, they fought to free Red Guards who had forced their way into the newspaper's premises and were now trapped there, besieged by members of the Shanghai population. After this, the workers, rather than the students, became the principal actors in the revolution.

On the one hand, these incidents discredited the municipality's authority, and on the other, aroused the indignation of the population. In reaction, a conservative workers' organization known as the Scarlet Guards was formed. It mustered 800,000 members, mostly drawn from among permanent public-sector workers. Clashes between the two workers' movements multiplied, workshops were deserted, and the municipality was paralyzed.[40] Meanwhile in Beijing, the Cultural Revolution Group lost no time in backing the initiative of the Shanghai radicals: on December 9, a national directive urged all workers to join the struggle alongside the Red Guards, and on December 26 an official decision condemned the peasant-worker system and ordered the financial compensation and reemployment of those who had lost their jobs. This immediately prompted other categories of Shanghai workers to present their own demands for pay increases, resorting to strikes in order to get their way. Either impotent or complicit, the cadres agreed to all demands and handed out many bonuses and wage increases.*

The proletariat's return in force to the political stage was one of the distinctive features of the Cultural Revolution in Shanghai. The workers' protest movement certainly shows that, even twenty-five years or more after the establishment of the Communist dictatorship, Shanghai society still preserved remarkable initiatory and mobilizing powers. These activists clashing in the factories and streets were nothing like the model workers celebrated by propaganda. Gathered beneath the banner of the Workers' General Headquarters were many young rebels from the northern provinces. They came from the very poorest classes and from broken families, had grown up in shantytowns with very little schooling, expressed themselves in streams of swearwords, and believed themselves wronged by their hierarchical superiors and society itself. They resembled those whom General de Gaulle, in the Paris of 1968, described as "the chaotic dregs of society." Nevertheless, among them were to be found a number of strong personalities whose talents as leaders were to be revealed by the Cultural Revolution. One was Wang Hongwen. He was born into a peas-

---

* According to official Chinese historiography, which deplores "the evil wind of economism," the cadres of Shanghai had used these handouts to demobilize the working class and create chaos.

ant family in Manchuria in 1935 and was a veteran of the Korean War and a member of the Communist Party. When demobilized, he had been taken on as a mechanic in Shanghai's Textile Factory no. 17, where he had subsequently been promoted to its Security Department. His rival, Geng Jinzhang, who was ten years his senior, was also from northern China, the son of poor Shandong peasants, a Communist Party member, and a former soldier who had served in the Guomindang armies before joining the People's Liberation Army. In the Shanghai paper-pulp factory that had employed him since 1957, his reputation as a womanizer and no doubt his outspokenness had impeded his promotion: at the time of the Great Leap Forward, for example, he had been free with his criticisms of "the cadres who eat their fill while the peasants are driven to throw themselves in their own wells."[41]

The Scarlet Guards, who took up the defense of the Shanghai Party Committee, were for the most part more orderly people, lower cadres of state-owned enterprises, natives of Shanghai, labor models, and zealous activists committed to the networks of patronage that afforded them influence and material advantages. The millions of strikers who were demanding higher wages and better working conditions were apprentices and contractual workers but were soon joined by others who were tenured veterans.*

The mobilization of all these workers shows that, even when in the grip of totalitarianism, society was still alive, suffering but still hopeful. But the way that things turned out also shows that mobilization made little impact on the course of history, apart from the use put to it by the political forces manipulating it.

The masses disappointed the hopes of the Maoists, for they mobilized not so much against revisionism but rather in the hope of improving their

---

* These analyses of the social trajectories of workers in revolt are borrowed from the very rich monograph by Perry and Li Xun, *Proletarian Power*. However, I do not agree with the authors' theoretical conclusions. The distinctions that they draw between three kinds of activism—that of marginal rebels, of conservative clients, and of protesting strikers—seem too systematic. The sense of social exclusion, the solidarity of client networks, and the bitterness of exploited workers are motivations shared to varying degrees by all the workers in revolt, as is shown by the frequent and massive swings of allegiance from one organization to another.

living conditions. Their spontaneous movements could develop thanks to the prevalent disorder, eluding the control of the radicals of the party apparatus, who soon began decrying them, condemning them as a product of bureaucratic manipulation. In the meantime, the revolutionary festival took the form of a stampede for the shops, where everybody hurried to spend the bonuses that had just been distributed.

The economically inspired strikes spread rapidly from the factories to the port and then, in early January, to the railways. Supplies of water and electricity faltered. The situation was degenerating into a general strike. The banks ran out of funds. The neighboring countryside was providing increasingly inadequate supplies for the city, whose population had been swollen by the arrival of a million Red Guards and the return from Xinjiang of thousands of "sent down" youths. The policies of the Cultural Revolution Group and the masses' spontaneous surge of protest led to the disappearance of any form of public authority and to economic paralysis. The municipal authorities were powerless, and despite his mandate from Beijing and the support provided by the local garrison, Zhang Chunqiao found it difficult to impose his authority. In more and more plants, administrative offices, and teaching establishments, rebel groups were seizing power. The lowest-level cadres were eliminated and replaced by committees whose elected members could be dismissed at any time.* In the various city quarters, residents' committees were toppled by a population that blamed them for having been in favor of sending young volunteers off to Xinjiang.

There were over a million rebels, divided into many separate groups. The Workers' General Headquarters was weakened by numerous schisms and attracted little support from the population, but it did have the advantage of the protection of Zhang Chunqiao and the leadership of Wang Hongwen. The Scarlet Guards were more popular, but their organization collapsed when the Shanghai Party Committee did. On December 28, in a pitched battle fought in Kanping Road, they could muster only 20,000 against 100,000 activists from the General Workers' Headquarters. After this defeat, several hundreds of thousands of Scarlet Guards rallied to

---

* Zhou Enlai was later to criticize "the style of workers taking over management as they have done in Shanghai."[42]

the opposite camp, placing themselves under the authority of Geng Jin-zhang. Except for the General Workers' Headquarters, the various rebel organizations shared a common hostility to Zhang Chunqiao, deploring his low-class origins, his long career as a bureaucrat in the service of the party apparatus, and his policy of restoring order with the support of the armed forces. Their own slogan was "Doubt everything and overthrow everything!"[43] The masses had certainly liberated themselves, but far from seeing themselves as a springboard for a Maoist reconquest of power, they were still dreaming of a society that could elude state power altogether.

Zhang Chunqiao's mission was to restore order in Shanghai, but without preventing the masses from expressing themselves. This was no easy task, and it led to both a use and an abuse of rhetoric that classified as counterrevolutionaries and enemies of Mao all those who refused to return to work and discipline. Responsibility for the chaos was shunted onto the leaders of the former municipality, who were subjected to humiliating sessions of self-criticism before the masses. On January 9, Zhang Chunqiao launched an "Urgent Appeal" to the population, urging it to halt the strikes, give up its economic claims, and repay the exceptional bonuses received over the past weeks. At the same time, he called upon the garrison troops to restore order and security. The military did not resort to force but did make themselves conspicuously omnipresent, occupying banks, the radio station, and the airport. On February 5, Zhang tried to institutionalize his power by setting up a Shanghai Commune, claimed to be inspired by the Paris Commune of 1871.

Frequent references to the Paris Commune during the Cultural Revolution seem to have been used as a Marxist-Leninist means to justify a remarkably unorthodox Maoist strategy.[44] Like the French *communards*, the Maoists called for the destruction of the existing apparatus (the difference being, however, that what they were targeting was not the apparatus of a bourgeois state but that of the Communist Party); they wanted to set up direct dictatorship by the masses and were rejecting all official technical and administrative hierarchies. At the very moment when he was fulminating against Soviet revisionism and striking out along a path untrodden by his predecessors, Mao Zedong used the memory of an episode exalted by Marx and Lenin to integrate his own procedure into the continuity of revolutionary tradition. However, although Mao made use of the commune as an ideological weapon, he was too knowing and pragmatic a statesman to make it a model for action. Had he ever been tempted to do so, the Shanghai experience would soon have dissuaded him.

The Shanghai Commune functioned through consultation with delegates from the rebel organizations, the number and identities of which varied from one day to the next and depending on the subjects of discussion. Many rebel organizations, hostile as they were to Zhang Chunqiao, took no part in such consultations, and the system found little support among the general population. So Mao Zedong refused to sanction it, even though his confidence in Zhang Chunqiao remained unimpaired; and under the latter's direction, on February 24 one of China's first revolutionary committees was set up. This new structure, which emerged out of the Triple Alliance between the masses, the army, and the party (or at least those of its cadres who had escaped criticism or had declared themselves repentant), was gradually extended throughout the entire country.

Zhang Chunqiao, who headed this committee, on the strength of the authority conferred upon him by Mao Zedong's official recognition now imposed his policy of a return to order and mass demobilization. The rebel institutions that were hostile to him were dissolved. Geng Jinzhang, who had become altogether too independent and too powerful at the head of his Second Regiment was soon arrested (on February 25). The last pockets of resistance were crushed on August 4, when an attack was launched against a coalition of revolutionary rebels (*Lian Si*) in the Shanghai Diesel Engine Factory. This faction, which had emerged from struggles within the factory, had managed to band together all those with complaints against Wang Hongwen and his General Workers' Headquarters and those who, having been excluded from the new structures of power, likewise opposed them. "People say we are bombarding the city revolutionary committee. So what? With the city revolutionary committee madly oppressing the revolutionary masses . . . we have to bombard."[45] After eight hours of hand-to-hand fighting, Wang Hongwen's rebels, with the aid of the garrison soldiers, routed the Lian Si partisans. Zhang Chunqiao was now in a position to implement his policy for the restoration of order without serious opposition.

The young people who had escaped from Xinjiang were sent back to their state farms; the peasants went back to the countryside. The former cadres, particularly those at the lowest and intermediate levels, were rehabilitated and, in exchange for a hasty confession, recovered their posts. New residents' committees were set up. Opposition had not disappeared completely, but it had become fragmented and had gone to ground in a number of basic units—factories, administrations, schools, and city neighborhoods. Tracts continued to appear criticizing Zhang Chunqiao for not fighting the class war and demanding a return to revolutionary "chaos."[46] Zhang Chunqiao's policies also met with resistance from the cadres themselves. Party Committee secretaries, factory managers, and college principals were unwilling to resume their responsibilities, fearing to become once again the targets of future mass campaigns. They adapted the official slogan "Struggle, criticism, transformation" to suit their own situation: "Struggle, criticism, departure."

Despite these difficulties, by the summer of 1967, Shanghai had recovered a measure of calm. It was spared the terrible clashes that were then causing blood to flow in many large Chinese towns. Nevertheless, the consequences of the upheavals of the winter of 1966–1967 turned out to be deep and lasting. For the next decade, the city found itself once more at the mercy of the Gang of Four. When the Shanghai Party Committee was reestablished in 1971, Zhang Chunqiao became its first secretary, with Yao Wenyuan as its first vice-secretary. When national responsibilities called these two leaders to Beijing (where they joined the Political Bureau and in 1973 became members of the bureau's permanent committee), the management of Shanghai was entrusted to Wang Hongwen. He proceeded to make the most of this by filling the municipal administration with cadres devoted to the Maoist cause. The promotion of some of them was so rapid that it was said that "they went up by helicopter." Wang Hongwen also extended his control over the trade unions when these were reorganized in 1973, and he set up an armed force of 1 million men, consisting of workers' militias equipped with heavy weaponry and answerable solely to the Shanghai Party Committee. Everything was now ready for the Gang of Four to seize supreme power, with Shanghai's support, at Mao Zedong's anticipated death.

The workers whose rebellion had made this changing of the guard possible found themselves, despite all their efforts, neither better represented nor better treated. The Cultural Revolution did not allow the Shanghai proletariat to accede to power any more than the 1949 Revolution had,[47] and furthermore, society continued to suffer from its traumatic experiences during the Cultural Revolution. Order and public security had never been fully restored, let alone the consensus that used to ensure cohesion within the social body. What with its frustrated workers, intimidated cadres, disenchanted young, and intellectuals reduced to silence, society was now split into fragmented groups with little understanding between them. In work units, coexistence between the more or less rehabilitated victims of the Cultural Revolution and their tormenters, who were still in their posts, was uneasy. This revolution left in its wake a discouragement and cynicism reflected in a general rejection of discipline, hierarchies, and effort. In the factories, absenteeism and slapdash work expressed passive resistance to all authority. At the lowest level, factionalism remained rife but was for the most part drained of all ideological content and reflected only personal resentments and conflicts between immediate interests. All these economic and social difficulties affected daily life. Shanghainese were spending more and more of their time and effort trying to buy food, clothing, and equipment. They were increasingly tempted or obliged to "use the back door" (*zou houmen*), in other words, to resort to the black market or corruption. Society was sinking into one of those latent crises characteristic of reigns that are coming to an end.

When Mao Zedong died on September 9, 1976, the Maoist faction disintegrated. Many highly placed civilians and military men who had been loyal to the president turned away from Jiang Qing and her acolytes. Shanghai remained the Gang of Four's principal base of support, but when its members were arrested in early October, there was no reaction from the city and troops sent out from Beijing forestalled any attempts at mobilization on the part of the militia and trade unions. Shanghai radicalism had disappeared along with the elimination of the leaders with whom it was identified. However, it left the city with a bad reputation. Deng Xiaoping and the reformers who came to power in 1978 continued to be wary of Shanghai.

CHAPTER 14

The Rebirth of Shanghai
(1990–2000)

A S SOON AS HE CAME TO POWER IN 1978, Deng Xiaoping set China on a radically reformist path. The policy of the Four Modernizations that was soon introduced was essentially pragmatic, designed to speed up economic development and raise the Chinese population's standard of living. The scale of central planning was reduced and market forces took over, so actors in the social scene regained a margin of initiative. The country now opened up to foreign products, techniques, and capital.

Success was not long in coming. In the mid-1980s, rural decollectivization resulted in a spectacular increase in agricultural production; progressive freedom from price controls and the partial autonomy restored to firms stimulated industrial production; and the creation of "special economic zones" facilitated the importation of foreign capital and know-how. Despite the turbulence that accompanied these measures, toward the end of the decade they resulted in the emergence of a mixed economy. Shanghai, with its strong entrepreneurial and cosmopolitan traditions, looked set to become a major beneficiary of these innovations, a pioneer of reform and increasing openness. Yet for ten years Shanghai, on the contrary, lagged behind other provinces in the implementation of the new policy.

SHANGHAI: A LAGGARD

There were many reasons why Shanghai did not leap on the reformist bandwagon set in motion in 1979, first because of the legacy of its radical past. Deng Xiaoping, who had been struggling to impose his authority over the heirs to Mao Zedong from 1976 to 1978, was wary of the Shanghai bureaucracy, which was full of cadres appointed by the Gang of Four.* Despite a purge that removed roughly one-third of those cadres, the apparatus re-

---

* Almost immediately after Mao Zedong's death in September 1976, the Gang of Four was eliminated, but it took Deng Xiaoping over two years to put aside the moderate Maoists, who had regrouped around the new but short-lived president of the CCP, Hua Guofeng.

mained unwelcoming to reform policies.[1] So Deng Xiaoping turned to other regions, particularly those in the south, for support for his plans.

Until 1985, Shanghai remained distanced from the national political scene. But when the Shanghai leadership team was reshuffled and Jiang Zemin was appointed mayor, that isolation came to an end. The new mayor, born in Jiangsu in 1926 and a graduate of the famous Shanghai Jiaotong University, had completed his training in the Soviet Union and then launched himself into a career as an engineer and a manager, during which he rose to become head of the Ministry of Electronic Industry in 1983. In Shanghai, he surrounded himself with cadres who were likewise university graduates and experts, among them Zhu Rongji, who soon became the mayor's right-hand man. He was two years younger than Jiang Zemin and was also an engineer. He had studied at the prestigious Qinghua University in Beijing but fell victim to the anti-rightist purge of 1957, when he was expelled from the party. His career then suffered a long eclipse. In 1979, he was rehabilitated and came to occupy a series of economic management posts in the central government. In 1988, when Jiang Zemin became secretary of the Shanghai Party Committee, Zhu Rongji succeeded him as mayor of Shanghai. These new leaders were both energetic and intelligent, but they did not open up as many opportunities for the city as they might have. Shanghainese complained that Jiang Zemin always had his eyes fixed on Beijing; and it is quite true that the national leadership did not wish to see its reforms developed first and foremost in Shanghai. This was not out of political distrust, for the new Shanghai team had the approval of the Center, but because the general strategy of reform and the immediate preoccupations of the government inclined it to favor the maintenance of the status quo in the metropolis.

The program of reforms that Deng Xiaoping introduced supported gradual change. It felt its way forward carefully, adopting lines of least resistance and favoring flexibility to avoid clashes with the conservative faction and reduce the resistance of vested interests. Its earliest applications affected the periphery of the system. In 1979, distant southern provinces such as Guangdong and Fujian were chosen as fields of experimentation in the installation of special economic zones and the development of non-public enterprises; and sectors such as agriculture, small-scale industry, and labor-intensive service industries were the first to be reformed. The heart of the system—the major state industries that the bulk of production depended on and that were linked to the destiny of the elite groups of workers—was hardly affected at all. Because of its geographical and political proximity to the Center and its role as a pillar of the centrally planned economy, Shanghai was ruled out as a pilot area of reform. Success there would have been harder to achieve and failure more dangerous.

Maintenance of the status quo in Shanghai can also be explained by the size of the revenues that it provided for the Center, for the reforms were accompanied by a decentralization at both the administrative and fiscal levels, allowing local authorities to retain a greater proportion of their income in order to finance their new investments. For years Shanghai had been providing roughly one-sixth of the central government's entire resources.[2] Had its contribution diminished, state finances would have been destabilized. It was therefore out of the question to alleviate fiscal pressure on the metropolis; consequently, well into the mid-1980s it continued to pass on 80% of its fiscal income to Beijing.

Shanghai thus lagged behind. While the regions benefiting from reforms were enjoying annual growth increases of 10% or more, growth in Shanghai was increasing by no more than 7.5%. Between 1978 and 1990, as its share in Chinese industrial production fell from 12% to 7%, its contribution to the national budget declined.[3] By 1984 it was overtaken by Jiangsu and in 1988 by Guangdong. Apart from the reasons mentioned previously, three main factors caused the relative backwardness of the city: the weakness of foreign investment, the absence of reform in its state-owned enterprises, and weak development in the private sector.

During the first decade of reforms, foreign investors in Shanghai did not benefit from the advantages offered in the special economic zones of the southern provinces: tax and customs exemptions and funding by the local authorities for the creation of infrastructures. In consequence cumulative foreign direct investment in Shanghai between 1978 and 1990 rose to only 1.2 billion U.S. dollars (as opposed to 6.7 billion in Guangdong).[4] The predominance of the public sector, which in 1987 still accounted for 98% of Shanghai's industrial production, also hampered growth. The relatively high wages and the welfare benefits that work units had to provide kept production costs high. The "iron bowl of rice" system (that is, the guarantee of jobs for life) that tenured workers enjoyed forced state-owned enterprises to retain a high proportion of surplus labor. The ponderous hierarchy and the inflexibility of bureaucratic management impeded innovation and the manufacture of products better adapted to market demands. New national regulations that gave firms a certain autonomy replaced the remittance of all revenues to the state with a tax on profits, and subsidies with bank loans. But such measures did not suffice to transform the style of management. About one-third of the Shanghai state-owned enterprises showed deficits that had to be made good by official subsidies: in 1987 about 600 million yuans were required to keep Shanghai businesses afloat; by the early 1990s, five times more were needed.[5] The Center decided to place a few giant production units in Shanghai, such as the Baoshan steelworks and the automobile factory created in collaboration with the German Volkswagen company, but even this did not remedy the situation. Meanwhile, private firms were subjected to a particularly rigorous system of authorization and taxation (which appropriated over 80% of profits), which inevitably curbed their development.[6]

The treatment to which their city was subjected did not pass unnoticed by the Shanghainese. Intellectuals, administrative cadres, and firm managers all spoke up in defense of local interests. This was unusual, for the defense of such interests was generally left to internal maneuvers within the bureaucracy, either bargaining between the various parties concerned or services rendered to political clients. The matter now mobilized the population and, with the press abetting, was brought into the public domain.[7] Those most involved were research associates of the Shanghai Academy of Social Sciences and former officials and experts who belonged to committees attached to the People's Municipal Congress.* They came together in seminars to discuss problems such as "What kind of Shanghai should we be endeavoring to construct?" and they published their findings in the

---

* The peoples' municipal and provincial assemblies played the same role in relation to local executive authorities (mayors, governors) as that played by the People's National Assembly in relation to the Beijing government. They were registering chambers rather than the sources of laws or regulations, and their importance was no more than secondary, although not altogether negligible.

academy's monthly review, *Social Sciences* (*Shehui Kexue*) or in a national weekly, *The World Economic Herald* (*Shijie jingji dabao*), also published under the aegis of the academy. They criticized the role that the Center allotted to Shanghai and expressed their jealousy of new urban developments in Beijing—all the skyscrapers and highways that, they suspected, had been built with Shanghai money. They demanded more autonomy for their city, convinced that it would prove just as successful as the southern provinces if only given a chance. They wanted it to contribute to national development not only by increasing production but also by introducing new technology and helping the economy to modernize. Singing the praises of their city's past, they called for a renewal of the spirit of enterprise that the Communist system had destroyed.

However, society's intervention in a debate until then confined to members of the bureaucracy did not herald the emergence of a public sphere in which the agents of central power and representatives of society would be free to negotiate or argue. The institutions and men that came to the defense of Shanghai interests were of course dependent upon the party, their own legitimacy stemming only from their particular skills and whatever official recognition they enjoyed. The defenders of Shanghai interests were able to speak out to the extent that a number of local cadres shared their points of view and allowed them expression. The ambiguity of the official position is brought out by the contradictions of the *Liberation Daily*, the organ of the Shanghai Party Committee: having initially deplored the "weak points" of Shanghai in 1980, it performed a U-turn in the following year and instead criticized "the arrogance" and egotism of the Shanghainese.*

It was probably not so much the battle waged by intellectuals and experts but the obstacles blocking the expansion of local industrial enterprises that persuaded the Center to moderate its opposition to reform in Shanghai. The competition from the reformed provinces and their increasingly frequent refusals to supply Shanghai with raw materials because they found it more profitable to process them themselves were curbing the activity of many Shanghai businesses and causing their profits to fall, and the funds

---

* Among the "weak points" enumerated were the tardiness of urban infrastructures and the shortage of housing and green spaces.

transferred to Beijing to diminish. To remedy this situation, Shanghai was allowed a small dose of reform.

Such half measures produced very little effect, however. An "economic zone of Shanghai" was created in 1982, but starved of administrative and financial means, it vanished without a trace by 1990. In 1984, Shanghai was one of four coastal towns declared open to foreign trade and capital, and this resulted in the appearance of three tiny "zones of economic and technological development" in Hongqiao in the city's western suburbs, and in Minhang and Caohejing in the southern suburbs. A tax reform in 1985 lowered the percentage of local revenues that had to be passed on to the Center, but this brought no improvement to the city's situation since the effects of this measure were counterbalanced by the general decline in the profits of its industrial enterprises. Eventually, in 1988, Shanghai was conceded the same contractual fiscal system as that of Jiangsu and Guangdong. The municipality's autonomy and resources were thereby increased, but this still did not enable Shanghai to catch up with the pioneer provinces. After a full decade of reforms from which, thanks to the Center's decisions, it had benefited hardly at all, Shanghai seemed to be slowing down. Much of its urban equipment was out of date, and a conservative bureaucracy still controlled its productive apparatus. Shanghai was a kind of dinosaur that had not found a place in the entrepreneurial China that was reemerging along the coastline.

THE HEAD OF THE DRAGON

In the 1990s, the reform movement took off anew. Shanghai was now designated its pivot, the head of a dragon that symbolized the Yangzi basin and, more generally, the entire Chinese economy. The city's return to the forefront of the national economy took place in the context of a political environment deeply disturbed by the Tian'anmen demonstrations and the brutal repression that in 1989 stamped out popular dissent and restored the old conservative guard to power.

However, Deng Xiaoping did not allow the achievements of reform to be brought into question, and reversion to a hard political and ideological line did not stop him from declaring that not only did reform remain the order of the day but, furthermore, it must be speeded up. During January and February 1992, the old leader paid a highly symbolic visit to the special economic zone of Shenzhen (in Guangdong), where he preached the cause of an open market, private initiative, and international cooperation. In the face of the reticence of the politicians of the north, he set up the model of an entrepreneurial and cosmopolitan south upon whose success his visit conferred the stamp of legitimacy. He also emphasized the role that fell to Shanghai in the new phase of reforms: "In the areas of talented personnel, technology, and administration, Shanghai has an obvious superiority that radiates over a wide area. Looking back, my one major mistake was not to include Shanghai when we set up four special economic zones (in 1979). Otherwise the situation of reform and opening to the outside in the Yangtze [sic] river delta, the entire Yangtze river valley, and even the entire nation would have been different."[8] In an earlier visit to Shanghai in February 1990, Deng Xiaoping had already encouraged local leaders to speed up development in the city. The message conveyed in the spring of 1992 was repeated by the Fourteenth Communist Party Congress in the following October, thereby converting that encouragement into national policy.

The fact that Shanghai was restored to grace in the eyes of the highest ranks of leadership was largely explained by the way that the political situation had evolved in Hong Kong. The popular demonstrations on the island in the wake of the Tian'anmen Square repression, and the independence that Chris Patten, Hong Kong's new governor, manifested in his dealings with Beijing caused the Chinese leadership to fear that the contagion of a spirit of protest would spread to the provinces of southern China situated close to the colony. Prudence thus dictated shifting the center of reform from Guangdong and Fujian to the region of Shanghai and the lower Yangzi basin, which was closer to the Center and more under its political control.

Shanghai's now-acknowledged importance also resulted from the evolution of relations of strength within the party. Since reforms began in 1979, Deng Xiaoping had consistently encouraged decentralization and striven to mobilize the provincial bureaucracy in order to combat the aging central leaders' opposition to a transition to a market economy. At the time of the events in Tian'anmen Square, Deng Xiaoping had turned for support to Shanghai, namely, to the secretary of the Shanghai Party Committee, Jiang Zemin, and the mayor, Zhu Rongji, who between them had managed to calm down local unrest without resorting to armed force. Jiang Zemin was rapidly promoted within the party, becoming secretary-general of the Chinese Communist Party in June 1989; Zhu Rongji became vice-premier in April 1991 and prime minister in March 1998. The two of them formed the nucleus of a faction that was further strengthened when numerous other Shanghai cadres were also transferred to Beijing. The rise of this "Shanghai clique" reflected general recognition of the importance of the metropolis in national life and held out possibilities of patronage that would play an essential role in the recovery of the Shanghai economy.

In 1990, the central government gave its approval to the extension of Shanghai on the right bank of the Huangpu and the creation of the new zone of Pudong (*xinqu*) that was to enable Shanghai to reemerge as an international metropolis.* To speed up its development, "Ten Preferential Policies" were adopted. Most of these were dispositions already operating in other special economic zones, such as exemption from tax and customs dues for foreigners. But some seemed privileges that were peculiar to Shanghai or shared only with Shenzhen, in particular the creation of a free zone, the installation of foreign banking agencies, and the acceptance of foreign capital in branches such as major distribution networks and services. The creation of a Stock Exchange in that same year was also an advantage only to Shanghai and its southern rival, Shenzhen. In 1995, Beijing introduced yet more incentives when it authorized foreign banking agencies established in Pudong to handle transactions involving yuans.** Finally, the government designated Shanghai as the location of extremely large concerns with foreign funding, whose contracts the Center negotiated: the General Motors automobile factory in 1997 and the Krupp steelworks in the following year.

Thus stimulated, the economy of Shanghai made a formidable recovery: growth speeded up, activities were restructured, and the new zone of Pudong was set up. By 1992, the municipality's growth rate had caught up with that of the southern provinces: it reached over 14% in 1995 and remained

---

* Pudong, which means "to the east of the Huangpu," faced the Shanghai agglomeration, now increasingly frequently referred to as Puxi ("to the west of the Huangpu"). The Pudong district had already fallen under the remit of the Shanghai Municipal Council in 1990, but at that time it was only partly built up.
** Until then, foreign banks operating in China had had the right to deal only in foreign currencies, essentially for foreign firms.

above 10% until the end of the decade, at a time when the Asian crisis was causing Chinese growth generally to fall to 7%–8% per year. This boom was sustained by the influx of foreign capital: overall, the total of foreign direct investments reached 36 billion U.S. dollars in 1999. In that same year, Sino-foreign firms were responsible for 39% of the value of Shanghai's industrial production. French and Japanese department stores opened on the central streets of the city, as did supermarkets a bit further out. Property promoters flocked to Shanghai, from Hong Kong in particular, and sixty or so multinationals set up shop in Pudong.[9] The return of foreign banks was crowned by the reinstallation of the Chinese headquarters of the Hong Kong and Shanghai Bank.[10] Among the investors and entrepreneurs of all nationalities who rushed to Shanghai were over 3,000 Taiwanese. Their number was to increase in January 2002, when the Taipei government lifted the ban on transfers of capital to the Chinese mainland.[11]

All this growth was accompanied by a restructuring of economic activities, with service industries accounting for 48% of local gross domestic product in 1998. The Shanghai Stock Exchange stood as the symbol of this rise of the tertiary sector. Since 1997, it had been located in a twenty-seven-story tower in Pudong, with the most modern equipment. Its capitalization (128 billion U.S. dollars in 1999) and the number of companies listed exceeded those of Shenzhen, and the volume of its transactions in 1996–1997 on some days exceeded that of Hong Kong.[12] Industry, despite its relative decline in importance, still constituted one of the bases of the Shanghai economy. Textile factories, suffering from competition with those of neighboring provinces, were in decline, but the six "pillar industries"— steel, energy, petrochemicals, automobiles, telecommunications, and domestic appliances—that the authorities designated as priorities continued to expand. New manufactured goods appeared: integrated circuits, electronic and computer components. Information industries still accounted for only 7% of gross domestic product, but Shanghai leaders were dreaming of turning the lower Yangzi into China's "silicon delta."*

---

* In 2000, Jiang Mianheng, the son of President Jiang Zemin, and Winston Wang, the son of one of the major Taiwanese entrepreneurs, worked together to obtain an investment of 1.6 billion U.S. dollars in a factory designed to produce electronic components to be set up in the vicinity of Shanghai.[13]

Alongside Sino-foreign joint ventures, state-owned companies dominated industrial production. Rather than allow the private sector free rein, the authorities of Shanghai, obeying directives from the Center, decided to reform the public sector and ensure its survival by improving its performance. It was thus in Shanghai that an experimental "modern enterprise system" was introduced in 1992. It limited state interference to the exercise of its rights as proprietor and left the management of businesses, now turned into joint-stock companies, to their directors. Financial holding companies were made responsible for protecting and promoting state assets by ruling on mergers and bankruptcies. By 1996, over half of the Shanghai assets in the public sector were managed in accordance with this new system that introduced a certain flexibility and facilitated restructuring.

However, firms still remained under state control, for most of the directors of the new holding companies were picked from former officials, and these were concerned not so much with rationalizing production and increasing profitability of the assets that they managed but with preserving jobs and thereby social stability in order to win the goodwill of the cadres upon whom the future of their careers depended.[14] In the face of foreign and public-sector competition, private firms also had to cope with the Shanghai administration's policies, which, although now somewhat less rigorous, were still discriminatory. Whether it was a matter of bank loans or listing on the stock exchange, which would enable them to raise capital, the interests of private businesses were always made to play second fiddle to state enterprises. Although extremely numerous—over 60,000—they remained small concerns, concentrated in branches such as catering and labor-intensive service industries.

PUDONG AND URBAN REDEPLOYMENT

From 1990 on, residential quarters and port and industrial plants spread eastward, along the right bank of the Huangpu. This expansion was regarded as a way both to create a new international economic center and to resolve the serious town-planning problems that were checking progress in Shanghai.

Sun Yat-sen had been the first to launch the idea of a "great eastern port" with a deep-water harbor on the Pacific coast that would serve as an outer port to a town remodeled by diverting the Huangpu River and connecting Pudong physically with the Bund quarter of Shanghai. As Sun Yat-sen saw it, this plan would resolve the alluvial problems that the river port was constantly facing and, by depriving the foreign concessions of access to maritime traffic, would eventually bring about their disappearance. Guomindang town planners had subsequently, on several occasions, reintroduced this possibility, particularly in 1946, when they were elaborating an overall urban development plan for Shanghai. During the Maoist period, the project had been forgotten; but in the early 1980s, cadres timidly resurrected it. Eventually the Center sanctioned it, and in 1990 it began to be implemented.

Despite references to "the dreams of those who cherished the noble ideals of building a modern nation,"[15] in many respects the aims of the project differed from Sun Yat-sen's vision. Nevertheless, they testified to an abiding confidence in the future of Shanghai and also confirmed the need to appeal for international investment. The 1990 project was ambitious. Its objectives were realized thanks partly to the huge financial resources that were mobilized and partly to the support forthcoming from the Center and the zeal of local cadres. On an area of 170 square kilometers, four priority zones of development were marked out: (1) the duty-free zone of Waigaoqiao, associated with a new deep-water harbor on the Yangzi estuary; (2) the industrial zone of Jinqiao; (3) the Zhangjiang high-technology park; and (4) the financial center of Lujiazui, situated on a promontory jutting out into the Huangpu River, immediately opposite the Bund. To set up the proposed installations, it was necessary to rearrange Pudong and to develop communications between the new zone and Shanghai, which were separated by the river, at this point between 400 and 500 meters wide. Most of these operations were completed in less than ten years.

Pudong is now linked with Puxi by several underwater tunnel crossings and the two cable-stayed bridges of Nanpu and Yangpu, whose elegant forms are silhouetted against the Shanghai sky.* Connecting with the bridges on the left bank (Puxi) are a 47-kilometer-long inner-ring road,

---

* These two bridges were built between 1988 and 1993. Subsequently, two more were built: the Xupu bridge, upstream, serving the southern sector of the outer-ring road; and more recently, the Lupu bridge, completed in 2002.

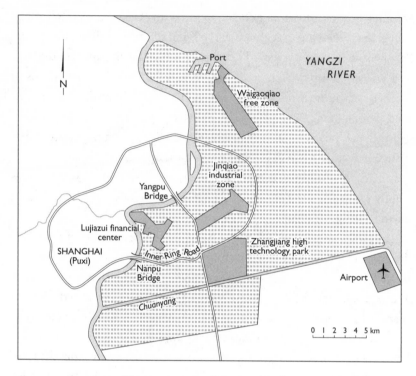

The new economic zone of Pudong

itself fed by the elevated expressway grid that crosses the city center, creating a two-story city. Seen from the upper level, at which traffic circulates, the monuments of the old Shanghai are indistinguishable. The bell towers, domes, and even the Stalinist spire of the Exhibition Palace are hardly visible: only the new skyscrapers stand out on the horizon. In 2004, this inner-ring road was circled by an outer one. This new 90-kilometer-long road surrounds a zone of 610 square kilometers and leads to Pudong in the north through a four-lane tunnel and to a southern outlet over a new bridge. The construction of the no. 1 underground line (running from north to south) in 1995 was followed by that of two other lines in 2003. These three lines total about 80 kilometers in length.[16]

On the other side of the river, Century Avenue, also known as the Pudong Champs-Élysées, is a huge artery 5 kilometers long and 100 meters wide, which forms the central axis for the Lujiazui Financial District. It was completed in 2000, shortly before the first terminal of the new international airport positioned close to the seashore to the southeast of Pudong. The building, with its curved pale blue roof, has all the elegance of a seagull about to take flight. The next building project, at the mouth of the Yangzi, is to be the huge deep-water harbor, able to accommodate 10,000-ton ships, that will make Shanghai one of the world's largest container ports, at an estimated cost of 12 billion U.S. dollars. Construction work began in the spring of 2002.

The Pudong project, whose ambitious nature originally gave rise to skepticism on the part of many observers, thus became a reality within one decade. The colonnaded buildings of the Bund are balanced by the high towers of Lujiazui on the other side of the Huangpu River. In the foreground is the "Pearl of the East," the 430-meter-high television tower, whose shape resembles a rocket on its launching pad. Behind it cluster over two hundred skyscrapers, dominated by the Jin Mao tower, whose pyramid-shaped tip is 420 meters high.

The development of Pudong produced serious repercussions for the urban fabric of Puxi. The type of funding adopted for the construction of the new zone's infrastructure sparked feverish property speculation that tore into the urban fabric of the metropolis. Contributions from the central and municipal governments and loans from international institutions—the World Bank and the Asian Development Bank—far from covered costs that amounted to tens of billions of U.S. dollars. The shortfall was made up by thirty- to eighty-year leases of the urban land, ownership of which had been taken up by the state after the 1949 Revolution. This was made possible by the 1987 law that transfers land-use rights and accompanying initiative and profits to the relevant local municipalities. The scarcity of land in the city center and the strong demand for premises by foreigners attracted by the new prospects for local development had inflated prices. Many foreign property developers acquired leases. A number of Hong Kong companies were hoping to renew the speculation that since the 1960s had contributed so much to their profits in the ex-colony. Local Chinese companies (including those in the public sector) were even keener and not only invested their own capital but also ran up debts to banks in the hope of profits from their speculation. As a result, between 1992 and 1995 as many office buildings were constructed in Shanghai as had been in Hong Kong over the past four decades,[17] not including large hotels and luxury residences. Skyscrapers took over the Nanjing Road, and a huge commercial complex was set up in Xujiahui, formerly the Jesuits' Zikkawei.

All this construction inevitably involved destruction. Neither time for reflection nor the quandaries of choice were allowed to residents who were ousted from their quarters: the district or arrondissement authorities, by dint either of persuasion or coercion, got them to move to residential blocks in the outer suburbs, many of these built by property speculators who had acquired plots of land in the city center. Within a single decade, with astonishing speed and apparent ease, one-tenth of Shanghai homes had by these means been transferred elsewhere.[18] It is true that these removals were accompanied by financial compensation and material advantages: the new apartments made available for families were larger and better equipped than their former lodgings, which in many cases had fallen into the category of "precarious accommodation" (penghu). Regardless, this transplantation to the other side of town, to zones still badly served by public transport, did represent a painful break from the past, former habits, and neighborly relations; and many of those affected tried hard to resist it. The media's silence on the subject testified to the pressure that the authorities were bringing to bear in their efforts to effect this urban redeployment.

The growth of Shanghai in the 1990s thus resulted from determined efforts both at the Center and at the local level. The city then enjoyed the active patronage of the regime, whereas after 1949 Beijing had mainly been intent on restricting its growth. The need to appeal to foreign investors and the freedom allowed to local initiatives nevertheless introduced hazards in the realization of official ambitions. The municipality took a number of measures designed to avoid regrettable eventualities: the bureaucratic procedures to which foreign entrepreneurs were subjected were tougher in Shanghai than anywhere else in China; furthermore, the arrondissement and district authorities, who had the right to grant leases and could therefore initiate many projects, were under surveillance by the municipality's technical commissions (Town Planning, Economy and Statistics, and so on), whose task was to ensure that the Center's approved main lines of action were respected. However, in a system in which personal relations and corruption played an important part, those precautions were not always effective, and wastage was not always avoided. It was the market itself and the collapse of property prices, rather than any official interventions, that in 1996 put an end to speculation on the construction of offices and large hotels.

THE NEW SHANGHAINESE

In the 1980s, the Four Modernizations policy began to clear the way for a renewal of society. Ten years later, market socialism was authorizing real autonomy for society vis-à-vis the state and the party. In their private and professional lives and also in community activities, the Chinese recovered their freedom. The line that was still not to be crossed was that of political protest and militancy, for those who held power were determined to retain their monopoly over it. But aside from that forbidden perimeter, there now stretched vast zones of party/state tolerance, thanks to which Chinese society could be itself once more.

There were more Shanghainese than ever wanting to make the most of the new possibilities opened up by economic growth and the regime's relative liberalization. In 1993, there were estimated to be 13.5 million legal residents, of whom 9.5 million lived within the urban zone. Natural growth played an extremely limited role in the population increase: so successful was the one-child policy that the birthrate rate fell (even reaching negative values in 1993 and 1994). On the other hand, the relaxation of residency rules (*hukou*) allowed for a slight increase in official immigration. Added to this was the illegal variety: workers in an illegal situation, who therefore eluded any census, numbered around 2 million to 3 million.

Overall, Shanghainese in the urban zone were in a privileged position. With over 6,000 yuans per inhabitant in 1991, their average annual income was the highest in the country, except for the special zone of Shenzhen. By the end of the decade it had reached 8,700 yuans,[19] but the gap separating the upper strata (in which the average was 15,000 yuans) and the lower (3,700 yuans) was widening. The affluent category included the young graduates recruited by foreign firms: their salaries were two or three times as high as those of their relatives who worked for state enterprises.

It also included certain stockbrokers, "millionaires" (*dakuan*) who, in a market still poorly regulated, owed their success not so much to their own financial flair but to inside information. And then there were all those who exploited their position or connections within the apparatus to pull off profitable deals. Private enterprise, which was subject to too many controls and exactions, was seldom a source of enrichment.

At the bottom of the pile, illegal immigrants were obliged to accept the most unpleasant and worst-paid jobs. For no more than a few hundred yuans a month, they labored on building sites or dangled at the end of a rope dozens of meters above the ground, cleaning the glass skyscraper windows. Female cleaners and workers were recruited from among young peasant girls, recent arrivals in town, who, as illegal immigrants, were forced to drudge fourteen hours a day for a monthly wage of 200 yuans. The impoverished also included increasing numbers of former state employees, victims of the massive layoffs that accompanied the restructuring of the public sector. One million workers lost their jobs between 1990 and 1998, the majority of them women who had worked in the textile industries that were now in rapid decline. These unemployed people were not totally abandoned: the municipal government allowed them a monthly sum of 230 yuans and had set up several hundred retraining centers to facilitate their reemployment. But neither their education nor their experience prepared them for the jobs available in the lucrative sectors of the new economy: if they did find work, it was usually in unskilled occupations such as restaurant waiters or waitresses or in other service roles. Some launched themselves into one of the many micro-businesses that crowded the sidewalks, selling doughnuts or offering all kinds of repair services, but they were unable to recover either the standard of living or the social status that membership in their work unit (*danwei*) had conferred upon them.

However, many public-sector workers did still have their jobs and their wages, which they supplemented by working for private enterprises in the evenings or on weekends. They realized that the advantages attached to their status were bound to disappear sooner or later, that state-owned enterprises were abandoning the social responsibilities that they had assumed over the past half century and were about to stop providing coverage for the risks of sickness, to finance retirement, and to provide lodgings. The municipality was already trying to set up a new pension system, financed by the combined contributions of employers and employees, and since 1994 work units had been gradually getting rid of the lodgings that they owned by making it easy for their occupants to buy them. Thanks to these measures and, to a lesser extent, to the increasing sales of the new apartments that had come onto the market, more and more Shanghainese were becoming homeowners.*

Part of the Shanghai workers' aristocracy was thus turning into a middle class.** For this class, consumerism represented compensation for the past years of rationing and shortages. It was also a way of proclaiming their modernity: in a society still bearing the marks of the Maoist egalitarianism, the cultural symbolism of the new forms of consumerism was perhaps not so much that of social distinction but rather that of membership of a contemporary worldwide society. Generation differences were as determining as disparities in income: when they spent an evening in a suburban discotheque or went to McDonald's for a hamburger, cash-strapped adolescents were asserting their membership in that society just as much as those who were purchasing costly electrical household equipment.

Shanghainese were reverting to the aspirations that their grandparents had embraced in the 1930s and setting their sights on a contented family in a comfortable home. The advertisements of housing agents extolled the charm of little properties immersed in leafy surroundings, summoning up a mirage of fresh "oases" in the midst of the urban hubbub.[22] Few Shanghainese could afford such luxury, even though in the late 1990s purchasers of new lodgings were able to benefit from the lower prices that followed the bursting of the speculative bubble of 1994–1996. But they all wanted to make the most of the 9.6 square meters per person that they now, on average, possessed.[23] "When people move into an empty flat, they want

---

* The price of lodgings put up for resale by work units represented, on average, the equivalent of a family's annual income. The sale of an estate of danwei apartment blocks was far more instrumental in enabling Shanghainese to become property owners than the appearance on the market of luxurious apartments reserved for a clientele made up principally of foreigners or overseas Chinese.[20]

** According to the "Report on the Study of Social Strata in Contemporary China" produced by the Chinese Academy of Social Sciences in 2000, this middle class represented around 100 million people, about half of all urban workers.[21]

to remodel it. . . . Some people see a particular style and want to imitate it by remodeling yet again. . . . Reinforced concrete integrates an apartment building as one body. . . . The noises of sawing wood, cutting water pipes, and sudden pounding on the wall mix together from different directions . . . with no end and no finish, no way to hide . . . a cacophony of torment."[24] This feverish activity was accompanied by a craze for electrical domestic appliances. The ambition of every household in the 1980s, for decades limited to the acquisition of a sewing machine and a bicycle, extended to the possession of a refrigerator, a washing machine, a color television set, and a video recorder. Ten years later, people began to buy microwave ovens and air conditioners.

Chinese families began going out to restaurants. Their rising standard of living was reflected by many new establishments that were a far cry from the drab eating places with wooden benches and canteen food of twenty or thirty years ago. The success of fast-food chains such McDonald's and Kentucky Fried Chicken rested not so much upon the menus available as upon the settings: with their bright lights, soft music, and the vibrant colors of their furnishings, these restaurants could initiate one and all into modern society. Parents took their children along to prepare them for the world of tomorrow. There was nothing these parents, who had themselves grown up in the gloomy period of the Cultural Revolution, would not do for their only child. On him or her, they would spend, on average, 600 yuans a month—the equivalent of one parent's basic wage. Nothing was too good for these children: sweets, clothes, educational toys, video games, private tuition in English, computer skills, piano playing. Public places catered assiduously for these little emperors/empresses who ruled over their families: every department store and every fast-food outlet offered special zones devoted to their amusement.[25]

Shanghainese also reembraced the tradition of elegance that had been theirs before blue cotton overalls imposed their proletarian uniformity. Women recovered their charm, streets their colorful atmosphere. Whether influenced by the memory of the English suits of the international settlement or the fashionable French boutiques of the former Avenue Joffre, the Shanghai style was characterized by its good taste and sobriety. Both at work and on the streets, the modern look predominated. The qipao, with

its high collar and split skirt, was for the most part kept for parties, ceremonies, and weddings—all opportunities for a display of high elegance.
Often enough a bride would change costumes four or five times in the
course of the wedding celebration, moving on from her wedding dress to
a qipao and then to an evening gown. For couples who could not afford
such a wardrobe, special studios would rent out dresses and ornaments
to slip on just for a photo session.

Since the appearance of the earliest of these studios, the Venus, many
more have appeared and have diversified their services, now offering hair-
styling, makeup, organized reception buffets, the hire of cars and chauffeurs,
and so on. All this is expensive; the photographs alone cost the equivalent
of 300 U.S. dollars or sometimes even twice as much. But young couples,
particularly the brides, are eager to immortalize the memory of their beauty
and, in some cases, their happiness. Their parents go along with this, themselves regretting that their only wedding souvenirs are drab black-and-white
snaps in which, as in identity photographs, their faces look out from a bare,
gray background. Many older couples cannot resist the temptation to be
photographed anew, but this time in festive clothing and romantic poses
in a flower-decked setting. Wreathed in bridal veils, their smiling wrinkled
faces are very moving in their Proustian quest for lost time.[26]

PLEASURE, MONEY, AND FREEDOM

Higher incomes and, since 1997, the official reduction of working hours
to five days a week provide Shanghainese with a chance to have fun: what
a change from the old days when their free time was taken up by compulsory political meetings and household chores with the aid of no domestic
appliances! Today's Shanghainese are eager to descend on a town that once
more beckons all who love outings, shopping sprees, dancing, and entertainment. More and more go off to spend weekends in the vicinity and
to sample the joys of Jiangnan towns: Songjiang, Jiading, Nanxiang, and
Suzhou, with all their old pagodas, temples, and gardens. They go boat-
ing on Lake Dianshan, 50 kilometers west of Shanghai, and stroll along
its shores, through villages still steeped in rich traditions, or, attracted by
the lure of exoticism, even visit the church that the Jesuits built in 1930
on Mount Sheshan, close to Songjiang.[27]

Nightlife has recovered all its dazzle. The Shanghai sky is again ablaze with multicolored neon lights. Karaoke bars, dance floors, and discotheques abound, to suit all pockets and all tastes, ranging from halls with subdued, romantic lighting, where middle-aged couples waltz or tango in each other's arms, to discotheques where adolescents in black leather and purple makeup are engulfed in an explosion of decibels; from smart establishments on the Nanjing Road or Huaihai Road, where disc jockeys from Hong Kong preside and the entry fee is 100 yuans or more, to little dives where the local kids can hang out for an evening, paying ten times less.[28]

In the bars, hostesses are once again at their posts. Like their predecessors of the 1930s, most are little country girls under the wing of a "madam," who offer clients their company or sometimes rather more. Each one dreams of meeting a businessman, preferably an overseas Chinese who will set her up as his "canary" in a luxurious apartment, give her 20,000 yuans a month, and between visits, leave her free to keep a "toy boy" of her own. Drugs have also made a reappearance: about 20,000 people in Shanghai are on heroin imported from Xinjiang or Yunnan. At 200 yuans a fix, ecstasy is still a luxury beyond the means of most night owls. But never mind; they will swing their heads back and forth like anyone else once they get onto the dance floor.[29]

Up to a point, the police turn a blind eye to these excesses, for after all, business must continue to thrive and the economy must continue to develop; besides, the system of connections and protection offers plenty of possibilities of coming to a profitable arrangement of some kind. All the same, there are precautions to be observed and limits that must not be overstepped, on pain of arrest or being sent to a rehabilitation center or, in the case of persistent offenders, to a labor camp or, in the case of proprietors of gambling joints, having their establishments permanently closed down. Routine checks and periodic spectacular "mopping-up" operations do not suffice to eradicate all evils, but they do limit them and prevent the mafia from acquiring a monopoly over the vice industry such as that which made the Green Gang so powerful in the 1930s. The Center keeps a strict eye on Shanghai, the head of the dragon and the model of reform, so it cannot afford such grave indiscretions as can Shenzhen or the island of Hainan in the south.

"Grow rich!" Deng Xiaoping told his compatriots when he launched his program of reforms, and Shanghainese clearly got the message. They have well and truly buried the disinterested "new man" entirely devoted to the public good whom Mao dreamed of creating. Now it is money that rules, governing the whole of social life. To earn it, Shanghainese work hard, holding down two or even three jobs at a time. They speculate on the Stock Exchange; one out of every two Shanghainese is now a shareholder, and they also resort to manipulating influence and corruption. Matrimonial strategies are likewise ruled by money: the most desirable fiancés are those with well-lined pockets. Research workers abandon their studies to retrain for more lucrative activities, and as a result, numerous venerable institutes of learning are now deserted save for aging professors and a few doctoral students.

The education system, of which Shanghai has always been so proud, is evolving to meet new aspirations. Technical secondary education now competes with classical secondary schools. In universities, programs are changing: literature and history are being abandoned in favor of economics, international law, foreign languages, computer skills, and biological engineering. Private schools (*minban*), which first appeared in 1978, have been the first to introduce new disciplines, as well as hiring good teachers whose high salaries are financed by the substantial tuition fees paid by students. But elitism and financial profitability are not restricted to the small private sector. The public sector, too, has its pilot schools and colleges that are attended by the most talented pupils, and most state establishments try to raise funds to complement their municipal subsidies. Primary schools and colleges, where attendance is compulsory but which cannot count on the limited contributions required from parents, are throwing themselves into a variety of activities designed to increase their budgets. They rent out part of their premises to local companies and enter into relationships with business enterprises, offering advice and expertise. Meanwhile, since 1995 universities have been charging fees, which cover around 30% of their budgetary expenditure.[30] Shanghai is endeavoring to maintain its tradition of academic excellence and at the same time put it at the service of economic growth and the aspirations of the latest generation, for whom education comes down simply to the acquisition of qualifications that promise high salaries and incomes.

Individualism is making progress alongside materialism. In the 1980s, some groups, in particular student groups, continued to mobilize—against Japanese imperialism in the autumn of 1985, in favor of democracy and freedom in the winter of 1986. Fifty thousand students invaded the People's Square on December 21, 1986, to demand improvements in their treatment and a liberalization of the regime. Their protest movement, which spread rapidly to Beijing, contributed to the fall, in the following January, of Hu Yaobang, the secretary-general of the Party and presumptive heir to Deng Xiaoping. In May 1989, students in Shanghai supported the protests of their Beijing comrades, but the workers did not follow them and the movement was suppressed, without bloodshed, by the local leaders at that time, Jiang Zemin and Zhu Rongji. Since 1989, Shanghainese, like many other Chinese, have taken less and less interest in politics. Liberated from party control and intent upon material success as they are, what they tend to think of now are their families and, more and more, themselves.

Since the point in the 1980s when the party gave up trying to rule hearts and minds, Confucian morality has once again become a structuring force in society. Communist cadres no longer seek to thwart developments that, as they see it, offer them a means of shedding social responsibilities, such as support of the elderly, who are now often at the mercy of the filial piety of their descendants. They are not averse to reinstituting an ethic that poses no threat to the established order, even if it does not stem from Marxist-Leninist doctrine. All the same, economic prosperity and the opening to foreign influences are beginning to engulf society in a whirl of freedom and emancipation. Sex is no longer taboo, the cohabitation of engaged couples before marriage is no longer a crime, and divorce is on the increase: in 1998, divorces totaled 13,000, most of them caused by adultery or incompatibility, sexual or otherwise. Paradoxically enough, fifty years on from the Communist Revolution, this new freedom of behavior clashes not so much with party rules as with those of a resuscitated Chinese tradition. That, at least, is the finding of psychological consultations provided by telephone networks that are open twenty-four hours a day, with anonymity making it possible for each and every one to express problems freely. Most callers are young adults seeking help in their quest for a compromise between their desire for emancipation and their strong and abiding belief in the importance of family stability.[31]

THE GHOST OF HAIPAI

Over the past two decades, cadres have become increasingly aware of the value of Shanghai's urban legacy. They are seeking to preserve it, not so much out of sentimental attachment to the past but in order to profit from it and to revitalize the seduction that attracted so many foreigners in the nineteenth century and, with them, their capital, to the banks of the Huangpu. This preservationist policy, which is associated with plans for economic growth, has been adopted with an eye to profitability: the objective is to resuscitate the Haipai spirit and make it serve both business interests and the mass tourism boom that each year brings over 1 million visitors to the city.

One merit of this policy is that it has saved from destruction a number of buildings that appear on a preservation list drawn up in 1991. However, the policy is applied in a very uncoordinated fashion, which accounts for the many discordances between protected buildings and the totally transformed sites juxtaposed to them: for example, the Xujiahui (Zikkawei) cathedral and the gigantic commercial center alongside it; and between the neoclassical buildings of the Bund and the road that now cuts them off from the riverbank.* The 1991 list also designated entire quarters for conservation, but many of these have been renovated in a way that appalls those who loved the old Shanghai. For instance, in Nanshi, the old walled town, the whole of the northern part has been converted into a kitsch theatrical scene: the alleyways have been widened to accommodate tourist buses, and the low houses have been replaced by several-story shops whose facades are adorned with many wood-carved window frames and whose roofs display an abundance of curved eaves. On official holidays, this pastiche town, now one of Shanghai's favorite tourist spots, receives 500,000 visitors. The sight of all this bogus

---

* The buildings along the Bund, evacuated by the municipal services that had occupied them since 1949, were handed over to the foreign companies that were the highest bidders for them, on condition that they would restore them to the condition prescribed by the conservation offices.

chinoiserie makes one feel almost relieved that the rest of the old walled town is scheduled to disappear and be replaced by a clutch of skyscrapers.[32] The renovation of the Nanjing Road, part of which is now a pedestrian precinct, has been a more successful operation. But what of the destruction of the alleyways (*lilong*) in the Luwan arrondissement of the former French concession and their replacement by a leisure center complete with an artificial lake and a luxurious shopping mall near the site where the Chinese Communist Party was founded in 1921? No doubt it seemed easier to create a new Manhattan in Lujiazui than to revive the traditional Paris of the East.

Shanghai cadres are not indifferent to culture, but they conceive of it above all in terms of splendid and functional constructions. In that they set more store by modernity than by historical authenticity, they are no doubt more faithful to the spirit of Haipai. At any rate, the prestigious monuments that they have raised in the city since the mid-1990s testify to their determination to make Shanghai's intellectual and artistic influence worthy of its economic preeminence. Efforts have been concentrated upon the People's Square in particular: the vast concrete esplanade that for fifty years served as the stage for all the city's mass demonstrations has become its cultural and artistic center. Between 1994 and 2000, a museum, a city hall, an opera house, and an information center on town planning have all been established there. The museum, shaped like a great urn, was conceived and constructed through the determination and skill of its director and assistant director. These two sixty-year-olds managed to get the bureaucrats of Shanghai and Beijing to work together, and they themselves found extra funding from overseas Chinese capitalists and American foundations in order to build and equip what is, in the opinion of experts, "the finest museum of Chinese art in the world."* The opera house, which faces the museum, is a beautiful building of steel and glass, with a roof that rests upon six pillars and machinery and acoustic equipment that are products of the most advanced technology.

The relative apathy of Shanghai cultural life stands in marked contrast

---

* That was the judgment passed on Shanghai's new museum by the conservationist of the department of Asian Arts of the Metropolitan Museum of New York.[33]

to the magnificence of these new buildings. Where painting, music, cinema, and literature are concerned, Shanghai does not attract as many talents as Beijing, perhaps because the metropolis became receptive to international artistic trends a decade later and also because its regional pride, often condemned as arrogance by its detractors, makes it less attractive than the cosmopolitan capital to artists from other provinces. The fussy control that the Shanghai Party Committee's Propaganda Department maintains over intellectual life also makes Shanghai a "politically correct" city that does not encourage creativity. The banning of a production of the opera *The Peony Pavilion* in a complete and modernized version provides but one of many examples of the obstructive nature of bureaucratic interventions. This work, which dates from the sixteenth century and was written in the very refined but now moribund *kunju* style, was to have been performed in 1998 during the Lincoln Center Festival in New York after being rehearsed in Shanghai. Either because the modern staging was shocking to purists or for other reasons best known to the Shanghai authorities, at the very last moment the authorities banned the entire project.*

The Haipai spirit, which its detractors dismissed in the 1920s and 1930s on account of its popular and commercial nature, is no doubt still vibrant in other sectors—erotic literature, for example. The best seller *Shanghai Baby* tells the story of an impossible love affair that unfolds amid Shanghai's gilded bohemian circles that mingle with foreigners, drift from bars to discotheques, and live for sex and drugs.[35] The official banning of the book in 2000 and accusations of plagiarism leveled at its author, Zhou Weihui, a pretty young woman of twenty-seven, simply increased the scandal that surrounded it and its success. Did Zhou Weihui really copy *La, la, la*, another book of similar inspiration? The matter was debated on Chinese websites. However, there can be no doubt that, although the author never names them, she was inspired by the modernist authors of the 1920s. The descriptions of the city, with its lights, its sounds, and its crowds, which alternate with the book's erotic scenes, are reminiscent of the visions of writers such as Liu Na'ou and Mu Shiying, even if they lack

---

* An abridged version of the play was later presented in New York and Paris, using different actors and different scenery.[34]

the symbolic power of the latter. The work's insistent references to the Shanghai of the concessions and the 1930s are perhaps designed to link it with the Haipai literary tradition but in truth seem more like an alibi, a means of conferring a modicum of intellectual respectability on a text based mostly on pornography.

Shanghai's rebirth is spectacular. In the space of ten years, a new city has sprung up and traces of the old Shanghai are fast vanishing from the urban scene. Not that the past is deliberately concealed as it was for forty years: on the contrary, it is constantly evoked and mythologized so as to legitimate the role that the present Chinese leadership has chosen to attribute to the city—that of a great economic and financial metropolis of the twenty-first century. In this era of ongoing technological revolution and globalization, will Shanghai be up to that role and succeed in recovering the preeminence that it possessed in the days of steamships and colonial empires? At the dawn of the twenty-first century, the outlook seems uncertain.

Epilogue

Shanghai at the Dawn of the Twenty-first Century

S HANGHAI'S REBIRTH, however spectacular, prompts a number of questions. Might not the bureaucratic interventions upon which the city's present growth depends slow down progress in the future? Might not competition from other Chinese regions also now developing at full speed prevent Shanghai from recovering its national and international preeminence? Can the spirit of enterprise, for half a century lambasted by the regime, bloom once more among the new Shanghainese?

In September 1999, the annual forum organized in Pudong by *Fortune* magazine, attended by 350 representatives of large multinational companies, was presented as the apotheosis of new Shanghai capitalism. The foreigners were invited to admire its achievements and support its development. But the selection of Chinese participants—two hundred directors of state-owned enterprises designated by the authorities—and the selective nature of the statements put out by the Municipal Information Office drew attention to the ambiguous and bureaucratic nature of this new capitalism. At the dawn of this twenty-first century, present among the Shanghai entrepreneurs were none of those independent capitalists heading small or medium-sized businesses whose initiatives had ensured the rise of the economies of Taiwan and Hong Kong, leaving only party secretaries, managers of a public sector now reconverted to business affairs on the orders of their hierarchical superiors. The way that the Shanghai Stock Exchange operates illustrates the bastard system engendered by this coupling of bureaucracy and business. Its acceptance of companies depends on authorization from the Center—authorization that is granted almost exclusively to state-owned enterprises. Companies showing a permanent deficit continue to be listed, and rates vary according to rumors that reflect whatever official interventions are being made with a view to rescuing this or that ailing company. What is presented as a triumph for Shanghai capitalism in truth seems more like a triumph for effective bureaucratic management. For example, labor-force layoffs in Shanghai are less brutal than elsewhere; they are accompanied by measures that attenuate the social consequences and forestall episodes of violence such as those that have erupted in the northeast, Hunan, and Sichuan. But the subordination of businesses to the power of the party/state does have its drawbacks, as growth depends upon political vagaries that are hard to predict in a regime so lacking in transparency.

When China joined the World Trade Organization, it undertook to bring its economic system into harmony with that of its partners. It is not possible to foresee how the Beijing government will fulfill its obligations or to what extent regional authorities will comply with the undertakings to which the Center commits itself. Will state-owned enterprises in Shanghai be reformed, or will the entrepreneurial cadres, relying on their bureaucratic connections and their network of clients, seek to preserve their privileges and monopolies? The discipline that the Shanghai apparatus has always demonstrated with regard to the Center operates in favor of the first of those two hypotheses, but the persistent size of the public sector and the weight of personal interests and powers that are at stake make it impossible to rule out the second.

The economic progress of other reformed regions in China, essentially the coastal ones, tends to reduce the relative importance of Shanghai. It seems unlikely that the city will recover the absolute preeminence that it enjoyed before 1949, when it constituted an island of modernity in an underdeveloped world. Today, Shanghai contends with competition from its immediate neighborhood. As land prices and wage levels rise in the metropolis, investors are turning to other towns in the lower Yangzi basin: Suzhou and, a little further to the east, Kunshan are attracting more and more Taiwanese and Westerners, and factories there are multiplying. In the end, though, the development of these towns is bound to strengthen the importance of the region as a whole and consequently that of its metropolis, in the face of the competition from other coastal provinces. For Shanghai must certainly also contend with the "golden coastline" that, stretching all the way from Guangdong to Shandong, is home to half the population of China and responsible for half the country's industrial production. Furthermore, Shanghai has not yet eclipsed Hong Kong; despite the support now forthcoming from the Beijing government, it will no doubt not be easy to assert itself in the face of the former colony, which, since 1997, has become a special administrative zone that benefits from the economic system and legal frameworks bequeathed to it by the British.*

Finally, there is after all no certainty that the new Shanghainese will recover the open-mindedness, the ability to adapt, and the taste for risk taking through which their predecessors made both their own fortunes and that of their town.[1] Because of the falling birthrate and longer life expectancy, the population of Shanghai is aging. In 1990, 17% of Shanghainese were aged sixty or older; by 2020, that percentage will likely have risen to 37%. Moreover, virtually all of them are only children who are all the more closely bound to the family home, since in the absence of brothers and sisters, it will fall solely to them to shoulder the heavy personal and financial obligations prescribed by filial piety and rendered imperative by the weakness of public assistance—pensions, medical aid, and so on—in the transition period. Another consequence of the reign of the only child is a shrinking of the kinship networks upon whose solidarity the triumphant capitalism of the golden age was founded. As they grow older and the pressure of their obligations to half a dozen or so forebears increases, the new Shanghainese's appetite for risk taking seems to be waning.** Most still work for the public sector. They manifest considerable prudence when it comes to branching out from the well-trodden, familiar paths and tend to hedge their bets heavily before taking the plunge into "the sea of business" (xiahai). If a husband does opt for the private sector, his wife will remain faithful to her danwei, and vice versa. Alternatively, an individual will endeavor to combine security and a large paycheck by working simultaneously for a state-owned enterprise and Sino-foreign companies or rural businesses set up in the vicinity. Because of their skills and intelligence, Shanghai managers are much in demand and highly paid. But one may perhaps wonder whether the conformism that the regime has

---

* On July 1, 1997, the British colony was returned to Chinese sovereignty but retained a considerable measure of autonomy, summed up by the expression, "One State, two systems."
** After several decades of strict birth control, more and more of today's only children belong to parents who were themselves only children. In such cases, the scion of the youngest generation is duty bound to take care of not only both parents but also both paternal and maternal grandparents.

so long demanded of them has not withered a taste for adventure that is inherent in the entrepreneurial spirit. After all, following so many trials and tribulations, why should they not now be dreaming above all of securing a comfortable and protected life?

Furthermore, by banning immigration, the system of household registration (*hukou*) has contributed to drying up the reservoir of energy that fueled the rise of Shanghai in the last century. As we have seen, the greatest Shanghai entrepreneurs were merchants who hailed from Guangdong, Zhejiang, and other provinces, and their native-place associations constituted one of the principal forces behind local capitalism. The hukou system, which halted the arrival of new immigrants, saved Shanghai from turning into a huge shantytown like so many other metropolises in Asia and Africa, but at the same time it checked the renewal of its vital forces and turned its population into an inward-looking group. The 2 or 3 million illegal immigrants that the reforms have brought into the city over the past twenty or so years have provided an indispensable labor force, but their presence has not nurtured a spirit of enterprise. With neither resources nor training, rejected by society, and living in fear of police checks, these immigrants have at the moment little chance of becoming entrepreneurs except, occasionally, micro-entrepreneurs in the form of street vendors or repairmen.

Now that China is a member of the World Trade Organization, it is considering unifying the labor market by restoring the population's freedom of geographical movement. The phasing out of hukou announced in August 2001 is to be spread over five years. Will Shanghai be able once again to attract provincials greedy for success? That is by no means sure, since entrepreneurs in the coastal provinces already find a local outlet for their talents and energies, while others, discouraged by the Shanghainese's reputation for arrogance, prefer to move to towns that are more welcoming, such as Shenzhen, which in the past twenty years has absorbed several million migrants from all over China.* The conservative mood of a population anxious to preserve its advantages appears then to accept the

---

* In the special economic zone of Shenzhen, the diversity of communities and hence regional languages is such that *putonghua*, the national language officially taught in schools, is the language in which they communicate with one another. In Shanghai, the local Wu dialect, used in daily transactions, operates as an exclusion factor for non-Shanghainese.

management provided by an enlightened local bureaucracy. What appears to be in the offing is not capitalist growth in the Hong Kong manner but a Singaporean type of development, dominated by official initiatives that the population goes along with.

However, Shanghai, unlike Singapore, is not a city-state isolated at the tip of a peninsula, the hostility of which forces it toward the sea. Shanghai's position on the coast, yet at the heart of the geopolitical hub of the country, invests it with a particular function of mediation between, on the one hand, a China that stems from a maritime, commercial, and cosmopolitan tradition and, on the other, an inland China, the seat of power and ideological orthodoxy: in other words, between blue China and yellow China.* Like the coastal communities of southern China, the metropolis knows how to open up to foreign influences, but it does so in a less extensive, less spontaneous manner. Since the nineteenth century, many innovations in Shanghai—whether in trading methods, economic and political institutions, or artistic practices—have been imported via Hong Kong and Canton. Before 1949, as after 1979, the intense flow of trade along the coastline from south to north introduced many foreign and modernizing influences. The geographical situation of their province at the southern tip of the mainland favored contacts between the Cantonese and foreigners, and the pragmatism of the Cantonese encouraged them to profit from those contacts and develop them further. Yet the Cantonese were regarded by their compatriots not as messengers of a new era but as defectors, ready to sell their own country (*mai guo*), that is, abandon values judged to be essential to the Chinese identity: loyalty to the emperor and later, the nation, submission to the bureaucracy, exaltation of the official ideology. At the vanguard of Westernism and modernization, the Cantonese did not carry the country along in their wake; instead, they were carried away by developments that affected them alone and that nurtured their separatist tendencies.**

---

* The blue of the ocean waves symbolizes coastal civilization, while the yellow of the loess plateaus of northern China, the cradle of the first dynasties, is the symbol of imperial majesty.[2]
** The recurrent separatist tendencies at the beginning of the republic, which gave rise to several political regimes in competition with that of Beijing, were still very much alive under the Nationalist regime and produced a number of serious revolts in the 1930s. They were repressed by Communism, but reappeared with the reforms, leading some observers to predict that Chinese unity would be broken apart. However, history has not confirmed that view.

In contrast, Shanghai, though open to the sea, was also rooted in the mainland. Far more than Canton and, a fortiori, Hong Kong, in the nineteenth century and the first half of the twentieth, it preserved a solidarity with inland China and shared in the traditions that the latter embodied. Although the presence of the foreign concessions conferred upon it a large measure of autonomy, the ideological and administrative grip of the central power maintained its hold, albeit sometimes in very degenerate forms. The lower Yangzi, the cradle of Chinese capitalism, was also the region that supplied first the empire, then the republic, then the Communist regime with many of their best leaders and administrators. By the end of the nineteenth century, scholar-officials and modernized elite groups were in close communication there and were fusing to form a single dominant class, that of the merchant mandarins (*shenshang*). When they adopted innovations introduced by the Cantonese, Shanghainese rendered them more acceptable to the rest of China and thereby helped to transform foreign borrowings into the very stuff of Chinese modernity.

Since it reopened to the West at the end of the twentieth century, China has seen development that has been rapid but very uneven from one region to another, thereby incurring the risk of weakened national cohesion. To the extent that modernization today suits the Nationalistic plan to restore the country's past grandeur and strengthen the legitimacy of the regime, the party/state is careful to maintain unity by imposing its decisions and controls by means of propaganda or, if necessary, force. Yet, given that the Beijing government has decided to put market forces at the service of this nationalistic modernization, its authoritarian stance may prove counterproductive; it may even smother the very development it claims to be serving. In this situation, the function of mediation and legitimation that Shanghai has assumed in the modern history of China ought to recover its full importance. Much has been said about the rivalry between the metropolis and the Canton/Hong Kong region in the race for economic and financial preeminence. But positioned as they are, at either end of the coastal corridor, both seem instead destined to continue to assume their respective specific and complementary roles. While private initiatives continue to flourish in the south, Shanghai could well once again become the place where raw capitalism and political and cultural tradition meet and coexist in harmony.

Ultimately, the destiny of Shanghai, like that of China as a whole, depends on how the political regime evolves. If it changes and embraces democracy, propelled by economic and social forces that it has itself set in motion, the metropolis, forgoing protection but liberated from outside controls, will have to fall back on its own entrepreneurial spirit. In the meantime, within the framework of the mixed system that dominates its development, Shanghai capitalism will continue to draw upon the elements that have always constituted its strength: the presence of foreigners, its special geographical position, and its unique historical and cultural traditions.

The businesses of Shanghai, in partnership as they are with great foreign companies that provide capital and advanced technology, appear well placed to dominate the liberated national market that should open up to competition now that China has become a member of the World Trade Organization. Thanks to its geographical position at the mouth of the huge Yangzi basin, which has been one of the essential trump cards for its development since the mid-nineteenth century, Shanghai is still the principal doorway to China, giving access to and serving as the outlet of not just a few coastal plains hemmed in by mountains (as in the cases of the ports of the south and southeast) but some of the country's largest and most densely populated provinces: Sichuan, Hunan, Hubei, and Jiangsu. Finally, positioned midway between the mandarinal traditions of Beijing and the compradorial ones of Canton,* Shanghai itself represents a third tradition, created by a century and a half of vicissitudes: the tradition of a regulated westernization adapted to the means and aims of the society that it transforms even as that society transforms it, the tradition of a modernity to which over 1 billion Chinese aspire and to which they are learning to adapt.

---

* The compradorial tradition is that of the local merchants who had dealings with merchants from elsewhere in Asian ports that were open to foreign trade. The term "comprador" is frequently, although unjustly, used in a pejorative sense by both Nationalist and Communist Chinese historians to denigrate the acculturation of those intermediaries.

Reference Matter

Notes

INTRODUCTION

1. In a classic article, Lucien Bianco compared the conditions of organized trips in China during the Maoist period to the programmed circuit of a goldfish, constantly coming up against the glass walls that surround it, much as travelers came up against a series of more or less explicit prohibitions. See Bianco, "Voyage en Chine."

2. See Murphey, *The Outsiders*.

3. Johnson, *Market Town to Treaty Port*.

4. Bergère, "'Shanghai,'" pp. 1039–1068.

CHAPTER 1

1. Hauser, *Shanghai*, p. 10.

2. Jurien de la Gravière, *Voyage en Chine*, vol. 1, pp. 252–254.

3. Fredet, *Quand la Chine s'ouvrait*, p. 41.

4. Ibid., pp. 42–43, 124.

5. Ibid., p. x.

6. Letter from Montigny to Baron Forth-Rouen, chargé d'affaires envoy to China, cited in Cordier, *Les origines de deux établissements français*, p. 61.

7. Moges, *Souvenirs*, p. 185.

8. A report by Montigny, cited by Fredet, *Quand la Chine s'ouvrait*, pp. 101–102.

9. Fredet, *Quand la Chine s'ouvrait*, pp. 106–108.

10. Moges, *Souvenirs*, p. 185; Fredet, *Quand la Chine s'ouvrait*, pp. 112–120.

11. Consul Montigny, Shanghai, May 23, 1849, to Baron Forth-Rouen, chargé d'affaires envoy in China, cited in Cordier, *Les origines de deux établissements français*, p. 9.

12. John K. Fairbank has described how Westerners replaced the tributary system, which they neither could nor would operate, by the treaty system. The interpretation is challenged in particular by Japanese historian Takeshi Hamashita, who stresses the dynamism and the survival of the tribute system over a thousand-year period. He suggests that it was not so much the shock of opening up to Westerners that governed the modernization of East Asia but the internal evolution of the system, its hegemonic structure, and its organization into a series of networks. See Hamashita, "Intra-regional System in East Asia," pp. 113–135.

13. Fairbank, "Creation of the Treaty System," pp. 216–217.

14. See Fairbank, *Chinese World Order*, p. 261.

15. Jurien de la Gravière, *Voyage en Chine*, vol. 1, p. 255. Captain Jurien de la Gravière was in command of the corvette *La Bayonnaise* sent by the French government.

16. Johnson, *Market Town to Treaty Port*, pp. 8–10; "An Emerging Jiangnan Port," pp. 151–181.

17. Lindsay and Guztlaff, "Amherst Expedition," pp. 549–552.

18. Leung, *Shanghai Taotaï*, p. 30.

19. Johnson, *Market Town to Treaty Port*, p. 206.

20. Cited in Maybon and Fredet, *Histoire de la concession française*, p. 30.

21. Letter from Montigny, Shanghai, April 25, 1849, cited in ibid., p. 37.

22. "French Consular Ground at Shanghai," Chinese Repository, vol. XVIII, 1849, p. 332, cited from Cordier, *Les origines de deux établissements français*, p. xxxiii.

23. Pott, *Short History of Shanghai*, p. 63.

24. Ged, "Shanghai. Habitat," chap. 2, "Le mode de cession des terrains," pp. 59–63.

25. Letter from the Consul Benoît Edan, Shanghai, August 2, 1853, cited from Maybon and Fredet, *Histoire de la concession française*, p. 63.

26. La Servière, *Histoire de la Mission du Kiang-nan*, vol. I, pp. 203–212; Delande, "Une entreprise d'exception," pp. 28ff.

27. La Servière, *Histoire de la Mission du Kiang-nan*, vol. I, p. 206.

28. Montalto de Jesus, *Historic Shanghai*, p. 58.

29. See Dyce, *Personal Reminiscences*, pp. 32–33.

30. That is what is suggested by Linda Johnson, *From Market Town to Treaty Port*, pp. 320–321.

CHAPTER 2

1. See Goodman, *Native Place*, in particular chap. 2, the basis for many of the following remarks.

2. Fairbank, *Trade and Diplomacy*, p. 428.

3. Maybon and Fredet, *Histoire de la concession française*, p. 97.

4. *Taiping Revolution*, London, 1866, cited in La Servière, *Histoire de la Mission du Kiang-nan*, vol. I, p. 292.

5. Ibid., p. 293.

6. Montalto de Jesus, *Historic Shanghai*, p. 84.

7. Launay, July 24, 1860, cited from La Servière, *Histoire de la Mission du Kiang-nan*, vol. II, p. 20. The given name of Launay is not cited in La Servière. Launay was an obscure missionary.

8. Among many memoirs, see those of Commander de Marolles, "Souvenirs."

9. Ibid., vol. 4, no. 1, p. 3. Chinese sources mention a gift of one hundred mink skins. The value of 10,000 francs that Marolles attributes to "sheepskins" suggests that the gift in truth did consist of mink skins. See Tang et al., *Jindai Shanghai dashiji* [A Chronology of Modern Shanghai], p. 172.

10. Feetham, *Report*, vol. I, p. 32.

11. See Ged, "Shanghai. Habitat," p. 139.

12. Cited by Montalto de Jesus, *Historic Shanghai*, p. 102.

13. See Ged, "Shanghai. Habitat," p. 138.

14. Letter from Consul Edan to the daotai Wu Jianzhang, October 19, 1853, cited in Maybon and Fredet, *Histoire de la concession française*, p. 140.

15. Editorial in the *North China Herald*, September 17, 1853, cited in Fairbank, *Trade and Diplomacy*, p. 525, note 30.

16. Memoirs of the daotai Xue Huan, cited by Leung, *Shanghai Taotaï*, p. 58.

CHAPTER 3

1. Ding, *Shanghai jindai jingjishi* [Economic History of Shanghai in the Modern Period], vol. 1, p. 154; vol. 2, pp. 26–27.

2. Ibid., vol. 1, p. 168; vol. 2, p. 26.

3. Ibid., vol. 2, pp. 39–40.

4. Ibid., vol. 1, p. 57.

5. *China Yearbook*, 1912, p. 448.

6. Ding, *Shanghai jindai jingjishi*, vol. 1, pp. 167–179; vol. 2, p. 34.

7. Ibid., vol. 2, p. 32.

8. Feuerwerker, *Foreign Establishment in China*, p. 93.

9. Pott, *Short History of Shanghai*, p. 156.

10. *Shanghai qianzhuang shiliao* [Materials for the History of Shanghai's *qianzhuang* Banks], pp. 33, 94.

11. See the memorial of Sheng Xuanhuai, cited by Feuerwerker, *China's Early Industrialization*, p. 227.

12. Extracts from the correspondence of Consul Edan, April 28, May 15, July 11, 1861, cited from Maybon and Fredet, *Histoire de la concession française*, p. 227.

13. Hao, *Commercial Revolution in Nineteenth-Century China*, p. 279.

14. Ding, *Shanghai jindai jingjishi*, vol. 2, p. 366.

15. The statistics presented here are from Jiang, *Yangwu yundong yu gaige kaifang* [The Foreign Affairs Movement, the Reforms, and Opening Up], p. 60. The sources are neither complete nor reliable, so figures vary considerably from one author to another.

16. Ding, *Shanghai jindai jingjishi*, vol. 1, pp. 499–500. See also Cornet, *État et enterprises en Chine*.

17. Ding, *Shanghai jindai jingjishi*, vol. 1, pp. 255–263.

18. Ibid., p. 261.

19. Pott, *Short History of Shanghai*, p. 74; Maybon and Fredet, *Histoire de la concession française*, p. 290.

20. Zhang, *Jindai Shanghai chengshi yanjiu* [Research on the History of the Town of Shanghai in the Modern Period], p. 334.

21. Ibid., p. 353.

22. *China Yearbook*, 1912, p. 46.

23. Yan et al., *Zhongguo jindai jingjishi tongji ziliao xuanji* [A Selection of Statistical Material on the Economic History of Modern China], pp. 162–163.

24. Ding, *Shanghai jindai jingjishi*, vol. 1, pp. 261–262.

25. Bergère, *L'âge d'or*, pp. 176–178.

26. Feuerwerker, *Chinese Economy*, pp. 39–42.

27. Ding, *Shanghai jindai jingjishi*, vol. 1, pp. 69–70.

28. Augustine Heard, cited by Hao, *Comprador in Nineteenth-Century China*, p. 168.

29. Motono, *Conflict and Cooperation in Sino-British Business*, pp. 7–10; Goodman, *Native Place*, pp. 129–133.

30. Motono, *Conflict and Cooperation in Sino-British Business*, pp. 92–116; Goodman, *Native Place*, pp. 132–133.

31. Cited by Pott, *Short History of Shanghai*, p. 101.

32. Hao Yen-p'ing, *Comprador in Nineteenth-Century China*, pp. 166–167.

33. Ibid., pp. 168–169.

34. Hou, *Foreign Investments*, p. 115.

35. Ibid., pp. 122–123; Wang, "Shijiu shiji waiguo qing Hua qiyezhongde Huashang fugu huodong" [Complementary Investments Made by Chinese Merchants in the Foreign Companies That Invaded China in the Nineteenth Century].

36. Motono, *Conflict and Cooperation in Sino-British Business*, p. 37.

37. Cited by Hao, *Commercial Revolution*, p. 263.

38. Motono, *Conflict and Cooperation in Sino-British Business*, pp. 79–80.

39. Hunt, *Making of a Special Relationship*.

40. Cited by Fairbank, *Trade and Diplomacy*, p. 455.

41. The businessmen of the British China Association are cited from MacPherson, *Wilderness of Marshes*, p. 263.

42. Statement by Sir Claude MacDonald to the Shanghai Commerce of China Association in the 1890s, cited by MacPherson, *Wilderness of Marshes*, p. 263.

43. Cited from Kuo, "Self-Strengthening," pp. 496–497.

44. These statistics may be compared with those relating to the private and foreign sectors: official and semi-official Chinese enterprises had capital of 14 million dollars and employed 14,600 workers, 46% of the total capital and 30% of the workforce of the Shanghai modern industrial sector; private Chinese enterprises, 4.3 million dollars (14%) and 10,500 workers (22%); foreign enterprises, 12.2 million dollars (40%) and 23,000 workers (48%). The three sectors totaled 30.5 million dollars in capital and 48,100 workers. Information from Jiang, *Yangwu yundong yu gaige kaifang*, pp. 59–61. Numbers were rounded off and percentages worked out by the author.

CHAPTER 4

1. See in particular Wakeman and Yeh, *Shanghai Sojourners*, p. 5.

2. See Betta, "Marginal Westerners in Shanghai," pp. 38–54; and Markovits, "Indian Communities in China," in ibid., pp. 55–74.

3. Feuerwerker, *Foreign Establishment*, pp. 17–18.

4. See Brunnert and Hagelstrom, *Present Day Political Organization of China*.

5. MacPherson, *Wilderness of Marshes*, pp. 60–61.

6. Pott, *Short History of Shanghai*, p. 88; Darwent, *Shanghai*, p. 116.

7. Kuo, "Self-Strengthening," p. 535; MacPherson, *Wilderness of Marshes*, p. 261.

8. Maybon and Fredet, *Histoire de la concession française*, pp. 273, 283.

9. Darwent, *Shanghai*, p. 44; Henriot, *Belles de Shanghai*, p. 437, note 18.

10. Henderson report, cited by Henriot, *Belles de Shanghai*, p. 305. Most of the prostitutes visited by foreigners were of Chinese origin. Before World War I, there were about two hundred prostitutes.

11. MacPherson, *Wilderness of Marshes*, p. 268.

12. Deng, *Survey of Shanghai*, p. 71.

13. Dyce, *Personal Reminiscences*, p. 200.

14. Darwent, *Shanghai*, pp. 7, 80; Brossolet, *Français de Shanghai*, pp. 245–248.

15. Dyce, *Personal Reminiscences*, pp. 200–221.

16. Ibid., pp. 95–115.

17. Deng, *Survey of Shanghai*, p. 196.

18. Darwent, *Shanghai*, p. 149.

19. Cordier, *Catalogue*. Henri Cordier's father had opened and run the Comptoir d'Escompte in Shanghai, which operated from 1859 to 1864.

20. Fairbank et al., *H. B. Morse*, pp. 93–94.

21. Pan, *Shanghai*, pp. 28–29, 31.

22. Zou, *Jiu Shanghai renkou bianqiande yanjiu* [Study on the Evolution of the Population of Old Shanghai], p. 90.

23. Sanford, "Chinese Commercial Organization and Behaviour," p. 183.

24. Leung, "Regional Rivalries," p. 33.

25. See the excellent definition of the various regional groups present in Shanghai

in Goodman, *Native Place*, chap. 1, "Introduction. The Moral Excellence of Loving the Group," pp. 1–46.

26. See Hönig, *Creating Chinese Ethnicity*.

27. See Goodman, *Native Place*, chap. 3, "Community, Hierarchy and Authority," pp. 84–118.

28. Cited by ibid., p. 5.

29. Wakeman and Yeh, *Shanghai Sojourners*.

30. Ding, *Shanghai jindai jingjishi*, vol. 1, p. 674; vol. 2, p. 492.

31. The Hanlin or Imperial Academy was attended by the most brilliant of the successful candidates in the official examinations, those who graduated with top marks in the Imperial Palace examinations, the last and most daunting hurdle in the mandarin cursus, and earned the title of "Doctor" (*jinshi*).

32. On courtesans and the role that they played in the lives of Shanghai's literate elite, see Henriot, *Belles de Shanghai*, pp. 42–58.

CHAPTER 5

1. *North China Herald*, April 15, 1879, p. 352; cited in Elvin, "Mixed Court." On the administration of Shanghai by Chinese local elites, cf. Elvin, "The Gentry Democracy in Chinese Shanghai" and "The Administration of Shanghai, 1905–1914."

2. *North China Herald*, February 2, 1880, p. 159.

3. Cited by Feetham, *Report*, vol. 1, p. 141.

4. Maybon and Fredet, *Histoire de la concession française*, p. 372.

5. Cited by Xiao-Planes, "La Société générale d'éducation du Kiangsu," p. 282.

6. See Xiao-Planes, *Éducation et politique en Chine*, pp. 256–262.

CHAPTER 6

1. Chen Tienhua, cited from Young, "Ch'en Tien-hua," pp. 120–121.

2. Tsou, *Revolutionary Army*, p. 60.

3. Shenbao, cited by Goodman, *Native Place*, p. 192.

4. Bergère, *Une crise financière à Shanghai*.

5. Rankin, *Early Chinese Revolutionaries*, chaps. 3, 4, 5; and Elvin, "Revolution of 1911 in Shanghai," pp. 119–161.

6. Rankin, *Early Chinese Revolutionaries*, p. 212.

7. Zhang, *Jindai Shanghai chengshi yanjiu*, p. 675.

8. Perry, *Shanghai on Strike*, pp. 41–43.

9. Gipoulon, *Qiu Jin*.

10. *North China Herald*, July 26, 1913.

CHAPTER 7

1. Most of the information presented in this chapter comes from an earlier work, Bergère, *L'âge d'or de la bourgeoisie chinoise*. Only complementary references are indicated in the present notes.

2. Hsiao, *China's Foreign Trade Statistics*, p. 176.

3. Xiong, *Shanghai tongshi* [General History of Shanghai], p. 11.

4. Ding, *Shanghai jindai jingjishi*, vol. 2, p. 123.

5. Ibid., vol. 2, pp. 19–20, 123.

6. Yen, "Wing On and the Kwok Brothers," pp. 47–65.

7. Chan, "Personal Styles," p. 76.

8. Cochran, *Encountering Chinese Networks*, pp. 124–127.

9. Xiong, *Shanghai tongshi*, pp. 111–114.

10. Coble, *Shanghai Capitalists*, p. 159.

11. Quoted in Remer, *A Study of Chinese Boycotts*, p. 167. The classic study on relations between Chiang Kai-shek and the Shanghai capitalists is that by Coble, *Shanghai Capitalists*. The following remarks are inspired by that work.

12. See Kirby, "Continuity and Change in Modern China," p. 128.

CHAPTER 8

1. Roux, "Espace et politique dans la Shanghai," pp. 20ff.

2. For a critical interpretation of these traditional solidarities in the working class, see Chesneaux, *Le mouvement ouvrier chinois*; for a more positive appreciation, see Perry, *Shanghai on Strike*.

3. Goodman, *Native Place*, pp. 263–265.

4. Wasserstrom, *Student Protest*, pp. 57–71.

5. Perry, *Shanghai on Strike*, pp. 70–72.

6. Cited in Bergère, *Sun Yat-sen*, p. 344. [Reference is to the French edition.]

7. Van de Ven, *From Friend to Comrade*, pp. 59–64. See also Smith, *A Road Is Made*, pp. 13–19, 24–25.

8. This was the term used by the American journalist Harold Isaacs in the title of his magnificent report *The Tragedy of the Chinese Revolution*. For Isaacs, the tragedy perhaps lay not so much in the repression itself but in the impotence to which, he believed, the policies of the Comintern and Stalin reduced the insurgents.

9. *Shanghai gongren sanci wuzhuang qiyi yanjiu* [A Study of the Shanghai Workers' Three Armed Uprisings].

10. Archives of the Ministère des Affaires étrangères (MAE), series E515-4, vol. 342, section on the foreign press, "Monsieur Naggiar," correspondence on Shanghai.

11. Ibid.

12. Ibid., vol. 341, letter addressed to the Ministry of Foreign Affairs by the French Tram Company, March 27, 1927.

13. Ibid., vol. 342, telegram from Paul-Émile Naggiar, consul-general of Shanghai, May 29, 1927.

14. That is what is suggested by Alain Roux's research on Shanghai workers, *Grèves et politique à Shanghai*, pp. 59–60. Roux's interpretation, followed here, also draws on the work of American historians, Hönig, *Sisters and Strangers*; and Perry, *Shanghai on Strike*.

15. Martin, *Shanghai Green Gang*, pp. 113ff.

16. Roux, *Grèves et politique à Shanghai*, p. 149.

17. Ibid., p. 149.

18. Ibid., p. 77.

19. Cited by Stranahan, *Underground*, p. 120.

20. Wakeman, *Policing Shanghai*, pp. 146–149, 371 note 97.

21. On the history of the 1931 boycott and the participation of various social strata in the movement, see Wasserstrom, *Student Protest*, pp. 174–175; Coble, *Facing Japan*, pp. 32–55, 330–342; and Henriot, *Shanghai*, pp. 83–86.

22. Stranahan, *Underground*, p. 197.

23. Coble, "National Salvation Association," pp. 139–140.

CHAPTER 9

1. On these problems, see Henriot, *Shanghai*, pp. 199–204.

2. Wakeman, *Policing Shanghai*, p. 7.

3. Ibid., p. 25.

4. See Wong et al., *Culture and State in Chinese History*, pp. 1–26.

5. For a detailed study of the government of Greater Shanghai, see Henriot, *Shanghai*, chaps. 5, 6, 7, on which this paragraph is based.

6. Christian Henriot has shown the influence that the provincial origin of the mayor exerted upon the recruitment of directors of municipal offices. See Henriot, *Shanghai*, pp. 130–131. [Reference is to the French edition.]

7. Wakeman, *Policing Shanghai*, p. 53. Most of the material that follows is inspired by this remarkable study.

8. Wakeman, "A Revisionist View," pp. 394–432.

9. Wakeman, *Policing Shanghai*, pp. 232–233.

10. Xu Xiaoqun, "National Salvation and Cultural Reconstruction," pp. 66–69.

11. Roux, *Grèves et politique à Shanghai*, pt. 3: "La paradoxale vitalité du mouvement ouvrier, 1928–1932," pp. 151–258.

12. Goodman, "Creating Civic Ground," pp. 164–177.

13. Wakeman, *Policing Shanghai*, pp. 132–138.

14. On the inadequacy of the financial resources of the municipality and its causes, see Henriot, *Shanghai*, pp. 167–183.

15. On the Green Gang, see the authoritative study by Martin, *Shanghai Green Gang*, on which the material that follows is based.

16. The expression is borrowed from Fabre, *Les prospérités du crime*.

17. Martin, *Shanghai Green Gang*, p. 61.

18. Archives of the MAE, series E515-4, vol. 336, telegram from M. A. Wilden, consul-general in Shanghai, February 18, 1924. The total of the bribes paid out each month to officials of the municipal services varied between 3,500 dollars (for the head of police) and from 150 to 1,000 dollars for French staff. Chinese staff received between 40 and 500 dollars. The official salaries of these employees ranged from several dozen to several hundreds of dollars per month. See Shieh [Xue], *Dans le jardin des aventuriers*, pp. 63–64.

19. Archives of the MAE, series E515-4, vol. 336, telegram from M. A. Wilden, consul-general in Shanghai, February 18, 1924.

20. The existence of an opium farm has never been officially confirmed, and the French diplomatic archives record no trace of one. However, some French documents—apparently authentic—preserved in the American archives and various other testimonies attest to it, in particular that of the former Chinese detective employed by the French police force of Shanghai, Joseph Shieh [Xue Gengxin]. See Martin, *Shanghai Green Gang*, p. 241, note 25.

21. In the wake of many more or less unreliable reports, accounts, and depositions, Martin's study, *Shanghai Green Gang*, pp. 112–134, for the first time provides a truly historical analysis of the relations between the Green Gang and the French concession.

22. For a portrait of Du Pac de Marsoulies and a description of his activities, see the Archives of the MAE, series 515-4, vol. 336, report by the plenipotentiary minister D. Martel, February 10, 1925. The elected council, disbanded in 1927, was never reestablished, and the Provisional Municipal Commission continued to function throughout the existence of the French concession.

23. For an in-depth analysis of these strikes, see Roux, *Grèves et politique à Shanghai*, pp. 189–250.

24. On the provocation set up by Du Yuesheng, with the complicity of certain of the French police, to obtain the arrest of Xu Anmei, see Shieh, *Dans le jardin des aventuriers*, pp. 80–81.

25. The income that the central government derived from the opium monopoly was officially recorded as 100 million dollars in the 1934 budget. However, in reality it was doubtless considerably higher. Wakeman, *Policing Shanghai*, pp. 260–263.

26. Marshall, "Opium and the Politics of Gangsterism," p. 34.

27. Ibid., pp. 36–37.

28. Martin, *Shanghai Green Gang*, pp. 191–192.

29. Marshall, "Opium and the Politics of Gangsterism," p. 38.

30. Ibid.

31. Ibid., p. 32.

CHAPTER 10

1. On the history of the term *Haipai* and its successive meanings, see Li, "*Haipai*. Jindai shimin wenhua zhi lanshang" [*Haipai*. The Source of Modern Urban Popular Culture], pp. 1130–1159.

2. On the quarrel between advocates of the Shanghai School and the Beijing School, see Rabut, "École de Pékin et école de Shanghai," pt. 1, chap. 1, pp. 1–59.

3. On the renovation of the urban landscape after World War I and the technological and institutional circumstances of that renovation, see Ged, "Shanghai. Habitat," chap. 4, "Shanghai à son apogée," pp. 165–250; and Ged and Péchenart, "Shanghai: images," pp. 1–96. See also Delande, "Une culture d'ingénieur," pp. 138, 1-38, 1-49; and Delande, "Décor-déco," pp. 46–52.

4. Zou, *Jiu Shanghai renkou bianqiande yanjiu*, p. 90, tab. 1.

5. Roux, "La vie quotidienne des anonymes," pp. 110–114, quotation on p. 113.

6. Cited by Lee, *Shanghai Modern*, p. 13.

7. See Chan, "Selling Goods," pp. 19–36.

8. Cochran, "Transnational Origins of Advertising," pp. 40–46.

9. Mu, *Five in a Nightclub*, cited from Trumbull, "The Shanghai Modernists," pp. 265–266.

10. Cited by Benson, "Consumers Are Also Soldiers," pp. 124–125.

11. Ibid., p. 97.

12. Ibid., p. 109.

13. Cited by Lee, *Romantic Generation*, p. 33.

14. Hu, "Shanghai xinwenzhi de bianqian" [Transformations of the Shanghai Press], pp. 379–397.

15. Drège, *La Commercial Press de Shanghai*, pp. 50, 215 note 47. Many of the Commercial Press's collections were destroyed in the Japanese bombardment of 1932.

16. Report from the Alliance française, cited in Brossolet, *Les Français de Shanghai*, p. 216.

17. On Yu Dafu's experiences in Japan, see Lee, *Romantic Generation*, pp. 87–92; on Dai Wangshu, see Trumbull, *Shanghai Modernists*, pp. 35–36, 107–143.

18. On Shao Xunmei, see Lee, *Shanghai Modern*, pp. 241–254.

19. Hu, "Shanghai dianyinguande fazhan 1907–1936" [The Development of Cinema Halls in Shanghai, 1907–1936], pp. 532–556.

20. Lee, *Shanghai Modern*, pp. 89–90, 95–96, 118–119.

21. See Lu, "'The Seventy-two Tenants,'" pp. 133–184. The author stresses the disparity

between the lifestyle of the traditional alleyways and that of the modern residential quarters. He returns to this theme and elaborates it in *Beyond the Neon Lights*.

22. On the evolution of social time, see Roche, *La France des Lumières*, chap. 3: "Le temps et l'histoire." On the coexistence of traditional time and modern time in Chinese calendars, see Lee, *Shanghai Modern*, p. 79.

23. Lee, *Shanghai Modern*, pp. 69–72.

24. Yeh, "Corporate Space, Communal Time," pp. 97–122.

25. Chang, "The Good, the Bad and the Beautiful," p. 137.

26. Cao Juren, cited in Cochran, *Inventing Nanjing Road*, p. 63.

27. Liu, *De l'inconvénient d'avoir tout son temps* [Two Men Impervious to Time], quotation based on the translation by Lee, *Shanghai Modern*, p. 204.

28. Hönig, *Sisters and Strangers*, pp. 182–184.

29. Mao, *Midnight*, quoted in Lee, *Shanghai Modern*, p. 30.

30. Lee, *Shanghai Modern*, pp. 17–22.

31. *Les causeries du café* [Café Conversations] is a collection of essays by the Francophile aesthete Zhang Ruogu. *Une nuit au café* [A Night in a Café] is a play by the filmmaker and playwright Tian Han.

32. Wakeman, *Policing Shanghai*, p. 317, note 28; and Henriot and Roux, *Shanghai*, pp. 68–69.

33. Lee, *Shanghai Modern*, pp. 23–24.

34. Henriot, *Belles de Shanghai*, pp. 319–339; and Wakeman, *Policing Shanghai*, pp. 114–115.

35. Henriot, *Belles de Shanghai*, p. 226.

36. Flaubert, *Correspondance générale*, vol. 4, p. 314.

37. On this literary genre, see Link, *Mandarin Ducks and Butterflies*. That study inspired the paragraphs that follow.

38. Lee, *Romantic Generation*, p. 190.

39. Ibid., p. 24.

40. The history of this literary trend is studied in Trumbull, "The Shanghai Modernists."

41. See Lee, *Shanghai Modern*, pp. 32–34.

42. Zeng, cited from Lee, *Shanghai Modern*, p. 19. The Francophile publisher Zeng Pu did not belong to the group of modernists but shared their taste for literary exoticism (even if he does not appear to have had much understanding of Molière's characters!).

43. Liu N'aou, cited by Trumbull, "The Shanghai Modernists," p. 19.

44. Cited by Li, "Le néo-sensationnisme et le cinéma chinois," p. 298.

45. Liu, *De l'inconvénient d'avoir tout son temps*, French translation by Rabut and Pino, *Le Fox-Trot de Shanghai*, pp. 297–300.

46. Mu Shiying, "Le Fox-Trot de Shanghai," French translation by Rabut and Pino, *Le Fox-Trot de Shanghai*, p. 192.

47. Mu Shiying, *Five in a Nightclub*, cited from Trumbull, "The Shanghai Modernists," p. 264.

48. Mu Shiying, *Craven A*, cited from Lee, *Shanghai Modern*, pp. 215–216.

49. The exclamation served as an introduction to his story, "Le Fox-Trot de Shanghai," French translation by Rabut and Pino, *Le Fox-Trot de Shanghai*, p. 191.

50. Ibid., p. 196.

51. Ibid. On the influence of cinema on the narrative technique of the modernists, see Li, "Le néo-sensationnisme et le cinéma," pp. 283–318.

NOTES TO CHAPTERS 10–11

52. On the history of the league, see Wong, *Politics and Literature in Shanghai*.

53. On this somewhat neglected subject, see the pioneering study by Waara, "Invention, Industry, Art," pp. 61–89.

54. Barbizet and Vincent-Vidal, *Le contexte économique et social d'une production culturelle*.

55. See Zhang, "Tea House, Showplay, Bricolage," pp. 27–50.

56. On the history of the Mingxing Company, see Quiquemelle and Passek, *Le cinéma chinois*, pp. 45ff., 64.

57. For a cultural interpretation of the major 1930s films, see Zhang, *The City in Modern Literature and Film*.

58. See the analysis by Zhang, "Prostitution and Urban Imagination," p. 168.

59. Cited by Li, "Le néo-sensationnisme et le cinéma," p. 287.

CHAPTER 11

1. On Shanghai's Japanese community, see Henriot, "'Little Japan' in Shanghai," pp. 146–169; Peattie, "Japanese Treaty Port Settlements," pp. 181–186, 190–191; and Vogel, "Shanghai-Japan," pp. 927–950.

2. Guillain, *Orient extrême*, pp. 41–42.

3. Farmer, *Shanghai Harvest*, pp. 42–43, cited from Fu, *Passivity, Resistance, and Collaboration*, p. 3.

4. Robert Guillain, *Orient extrême*, pp. 40–41.

5. Powell, *My Twenty-five Years in China*, p. 301.

6. See Fu, *Passivity, Resistance, and Collaboration*, p. 171, note 9.

7. Auden and Isherwood, *Journey to a War*, p. 252. The two English poets visited Shanghai in May 1939.

8. Barnett, *Economic Shanghai*, p. 152, tab. 10.

9. Tang et al., *Shanghai shi* [History of Shanghai], pp. 800–805; Barnett, *Economic Shanghai*, pp. 101–103.

10. Archives of MAE, Series Guerre 1939–1945, subseries E-Vichy, vol. 142, Henri Cosme, ambassador, Shanghai, July 31, 1940; vol. 143, Cosme, Beijing, March 2, 1941; Margerie, Shanghai, June 16, 1941, and September 12, 1941; Cosme, Beijing, August 29, 1941; MAE, Vichy, to the French Embassy in Tokyo, May 20, 1941.

11. See Ristaino, "Russian Diaspora Community in Shanghai," pp. 203–206.

12. See Kranzler, *Japanese, Nazis and Jews*; Kreissler, "Exil ou asile à Shanghai?"

13. Kreissler, "In Search of Identity," pp. 213–220.

14. See Wasserstein, *Secret War*, pp. 90–91.

15. In his autobiographical novel, *Empire of the Sun*, J. G. Ballard provides an unforgettable description of this episode, pp. 30–31.

16. Cited by Wasserstein, *Secret War*, p. 102.

17. See Fu, *Passivity, Resistance, and Collaboration*, pp. 121–122.

18. See the testimony of Collar, *Captive in Shanghai*. On internment conditions, see also Carey, *War Years at Shanghai*.

19. Archives of MAE, Series Guerre 1939–1945, subseries E-Vichy, vol. 143, Margerie, Shanghai, December 9, 1941; vol. 144, Margerie, Shanghai, April 3, 1942; Margerie, Beijing, October 10, 1942; Margerie, Shanghai, November 5, 1942.

20. See Archives of MAE, Series Guerre 1939–1945, subseries E-Vichy, vol. 144, Margerie, Shanghai, June 17, 1943.

21. On the preparations for and conditions of the retrocession, see Archives of MAE, Series Guerre 1939–1945, subseries E-Vichy, vol. 144, Cosme, Beijing, April 17 and June 16, 1943; Cosme, Shanghai, July 23, 1943. Note from Direction politique/Asie, Vichy, June 1943.

22. On the suicide of Colonel A. J. F. Artigue, see Guillermaz, *Une vie pour la Chine*, pp. 136–137.

23. On the history of this rebellion, see the series of reports written by Colonel Artigue, Archives of MAE, Series Asie-Océanie 1944–1955, subseries Chine, vol. 14, Shanghai, June 4, July 23, and September [n.d.] 1945.

24. However, some foreign and Chinese historians working abroad (such as Fu Poshek, Frederic Wakeman, and Bernard Wasserstein), partly inspired by works produced on occupied France, set about analyzing the complex reactions of the population of Shanghai in the face of the moral and political dilemmas thrown up by war and defeat.

25. Rousso, *Le syndrome de Vichy*, pp. 38–40.

26. Yeh, "Urban Warfare," p. 118.

27. Wakeman, *Shanghai Badlands*, pp. 25, 48, 64, 97.

28. See Fu, *Passivity, Resistance, and Collaboration*, pp. 74, 77–96.

29. See ibid., pp. 56–58.

30. On the foundation and activities of "France Quand même," see the testimony of R. Pontet (himself a member of this group): "En Chine," pp. 20–22. According to Pontet, 239 volunteers were recruited for the Free French forces, but most of their files were burned before the Japanese troops entered the international concession. On the movements of R. Egal, see Cornille, "La résistance en Chine."

31. Archives of the Foreign Office (FO) 371 28335, a document appended to the letter from M. Le Rougetel, Shanghai, October 1, 1941.

32. See Marsh, "Chou Fo-hai," pp. 313, 320–321.

33. Rowe, "The Qingbang and Collaboration under the Japanese," p. 498.

34. See Bergère, *Sun Yat-sen*, pp. 460–461. [Reference is to the French edition.]

35. The expression is borrowed from Boyle, *China and Japan at War*, p. 283.

36. Henriot, "Rice, Power and the People," p. 43.

37. Cited by Bergère, "Chinese National Enterprises."

38. On the history of the Shenxin group under the occupation, see Poncin, "Une grande enterprise shanghaienne face à la guerre." For a more general study of merchants' attitudes, see Coble, "Chinese Capitalists and the Japanese," pp. 69–76.

39. Cited by Fu, *Passivity, Resistance, and Collaboration*, p. 140.

40. On the history of Gujin, see the subtle and sensitive study by Fu Poshek, ibid., pp. 126–154. The lines are cited on p. 130.

41. Carey, *The War Years*, p. 109.

42. Wasserstein, "Ambiguities of Occupation," pp. 34–36.

43. See Wasserstein, *Secret War*, pp. 41–44, 110–113.

44. On the episode of the clandestine workers' army of Shanghai, see Perry, *Shanghai on Strike*, p. 117. This abortive project possibly testifies to the desire of some Communist activists in white zones to recover the strategic initiative that had long since passed to the camp of Mao Zedong and partisans of the rural guerrilla force. See Roux, "Chine 1945–1949," pp. 8–44.

45. On the slowness of the liberation of Shanghai and the disturbances that accompanied it, see Bergère, "L'épuration à Shanghai," p. 34.

NOTES TO CHAPTER 12

CHAPTER 12

1. Cited in Bergère, "L'épuration à Shanghai," p. 35.

2. See the calculations of Wang, *Jindai Shanghai mianfangye zuihou guanghui* [The Last Thriving Days of the Shanghai Modern Cotton Industry], pp. 10, 265–266.

3. Pepper, *Civil War in China*, p. 20.

4. Bergère, "L'épuration à Shanghai," pp. 35–39.

5. Wang, *Jindai Shanghai mianfangye zuihou guanghui*, pp. 25–31.

6. The evolution of the index of gross prices in Shanghai from 1945 to 1948: 100 (September 1945); 1,475 (September 1946); 12,534 (September 1947); 142,468 (May 1948); 755,165 (July 1948); 1,368,049 (August 1948). The source for this information is Eastman, *Seeds of Destruction*, p. 174.

7. See ibid., chap. 5, "Chiang Ching-kuo and the Gold Yuan Reform."

8. Ibid., p. 189.

9. The expression is from Roux, "Le Guomindang et les ouvriers de Shanghai," pp. 69–95. The material that follows is based on that study.

10. Roux, "La 'tragédie du 2 février 1948,'" in Bergère, *Aux origines*, p. 64; Perry, *Shanghai on Strike*, pp. 124–125.

11. The complete works of Chu Anping were reprinted in Shanghai in 1998.

12. On Chu Anping and the creation of *Guancha*, see Castelino, "Les intellectuals non engagés."

13. Castelino, "Zhang Dongsun," p. 133.

14. Lutz, "Chinese Student Movement," pp. 102–103.

15. On student protests, see Wasserstrom, *Student Protests*.

16. Cited by Barber, *Fall of Shanghai*, p. 113.

17. See ibid., p. 29.

18. Ibid., p. 60.

19. *Jingji Zhoubao* [Economy Weekly], August 25, 1949, cited from Gaulton, "Political Mobilization in Shanghai," p. 46, in Howe, *Shanghai*, pp. 35–65, citation p.46.

20. For a detailed account of the Communist troops' entry into Shanghai, see Barber, *Fall of Shanghai*, pp. 144–159.

21. On loyalty to the central authorities on the part of "Outside Reds" (so called to distinguish them from local militants or whites coopted by the new administration), see Chamberlain, "Transition and Consolidation in Urban China," pp. 256–257.

22. Barber, *Fall of Shanghai*, pp. 160–161.

23. Henriot, "La Fermeture," pp. 470–473. It was to take several more years and far more repressive measures to install the reign of virtue in Shanghai.

24. Gaulton, "Political Mobilization in Shanghai," p. 56.

25. Wilkinson, "Shanghai American Community," p. 245.

26. Statement by the consul-general of Great Britain at the end of 1948, cited in Barber, *Fall of Shanghai*, p. 60.

27. On the history of Aurora after 1949 and Shanghai Catholics' resistance to the new regime, see Lefeuvre, *Shanghai*.

28. Cited in Bergère and Wang, "Du capitalisme au communisme," p. 83. The paragraphs that follow are based on this chapter and on Bergère, "Les capitalistes shanghaiens," pp. 7–30.

29. Rong, "Rong Erren tan shengchan" [Rong Erren on Production], p. 5.

30. See Loh, *Escape from Red China*, pp. 118–119.

31. See Howe, *Employment and Economic Growth*, p. 13; and Sears, "Shanghai's Textile Capitalists," pp. 115–120.

32. On the demographic growth of Shanghai in the early 1950s and the consequences of that growth on the labor market, see Howe, *Employment and Economic Growth*, pp. 33–44.

33. Cited by Goldman, *Literary Dissent*, p. 132.

34. See Wang, "Construction of State Extractive Capacity," pp. 252–258.

35. See Guillermaz, *Le parti communiste*, pp. 32–33.

36. Kao Kang (Gao Gang), "Oppose Corruption and Decay, Oppose Bureaucracy," *Survey of China Mainland Press* (SCMP), no. 247 (January 3, 1952), pp. 9–10.

37. Statement by Gao Gang, SCMP, no. 270 (February 7, 1952), p. 7.

38. Kau and Leung, *Writings of Mao Zedong*, p. 287, presents this statement as being part of a directive issued by Mao Zedong on February 8, 1951. Bo Yibo, *Ruogan zhongda juece yu shijiande huigu* [Memories concerning Certain Important Decisions and Developments], vol. 1, pp. 164–165, cites it as an extract from directives issued by the Central Committee of the CCP on January 26, 1952.

39. Rong, "Yi ge ziwo gaizaode yundong" [A Movement of Self-Reform], vol. 3, no. 2.

40. Bo, *Ruogan zhongda juece yu shijiande huigu*, vol. 1, p. 171. Bo Yibo, the minister of finance and one of those chiefly responsible for economic reconstruction, was sent by the Center to Shanghai to supervise the Five Antis movement there. His memoirs contain a detailed report of this episode. The trade-union leader whose name is not mentioned by Bo Yibo is Liu Changsheng.

41. Gardner, "Wu-fan Campaign in Shanghai," pp. 477–539, quotation on p. 510.

42. Bo, *Ruogan zhongda juece yu shijiande huigu*, vol. 1, pp. 170–171.

CHAPTER 13

1. Fung, "Spatial Development of Shanghai," pp. 283–284.

2. MacFarquhar, *Origins of the Cultural Revolution*, vol. 2, p. 164.

3. See Cheung, "Political Context of Shanghai's Economic Development," p. 64.

4. White, *Shanghai Shanghaied?* pp. 3, 9, 13, 30–31, quotation on p. 3. In nautical parlance, the verb *to shanghai* means to force someone to board a ship; hence its more general meaning of "to constrain," "to bluff," "to cheat."

5. Gipouloux, *Les Cent Fleurs à l'usine*, pp. 28–29.

6. Mok, "Industrial Development," p. 203.

7. Evolution of the structure of industrial property in Shanghai: in 1952, there were 228 state and mixed enterprises, 37 collective enterprises, and 25,613 private enterprises; in 1962, there were 3,529 state and mixed enterprises, 5,280 collective enterprises, and no private enterprises. Source for this information is *Shanghai tongji nianjian* [Annual Statistics of Shanghai], 1993, 1994. Quoted from Mok, "Industrial Development," p. 206.

8. Mok, "Industrial Development," p. 200.

9. Fung, "Spatial Development of Shanghai," pp. 286–287.

10. Chan, "Urban Development and Redevelopment," p. 302.

11. On town planning and housing problems, see Ged, "Shanghai. Habitat," chap. 7, "Le Logement (1949–1979). Une pénurie de longue date."

12. For a systematic study of these statistics, see Howe, "Industrialization," pp. 153–187.

13. See Fabre, "Le réveil de Shanghai," p. 16; and Ged, "Shanghai. Habitat," chap. 7, p. 308.

14. On changes in the occupants of the principal Shanghai premises, see Shanghai Municipal Tourism Association, *Tour of Shanghai's Historical Architecture.*

15. In the absence of systematic statistics, these figures have been estimated on the basis of a comparison between numerous sources so are inevitably no more than approximate. Christopher Howe is to be congratulated on his patient labor of statistical reconstruction, published in "The Supply and Administration of Urban Housing in Mainland China," pp. 73–97.

16. Bergère, "Choses vues en Chine," p. 18.

17. Reynolds, "Changes in the Standard of Living," pp. 233–234.

18. Fung, "Satellite Towns," pp. 323–324.

19. Ibid., pp. 327–328.

20. White, "Shanghai's 'Horizontal Liaisons,'" p. 430.

21. Howe, "Industrialization," p. 161, tab. 6.6.

22. On the history of these strikes, see Gipouloux, *Les Cent Fleurs à l'usine,* pp. 202ff.; and Perry, "Shanghai's Strike Wave of 1957," pp. 1–27.

23. White, "Shanghai's 'Horizontal Liaisons,'" p. 423.

24. Ibid., p. 426, tab. 17.2.

25. "My Neighborhood. City Life and the Resident Committee," in Frolic, *Mao's People,* pp. 240–241.

26. Hunter, *Shanghai Journal,* pp. 9–10.

27. Ibid., pp. 50–52.

28. On the relations between Chinese workers and cadres, see Walder, *Communist Neo-traditionalism.* On the situation in Shanghai itself, see the same author's *Chang Ch'un-ch'iao.*

29. On the role of danwei in the creation of the client networks of businesses, see Walder, *Communist Neo-traditionalism.* According to Walder, these networks owed nothing to traditional solidarities but were the product of new power relations that the regime had created within Chinese society.

30. White, "Road to Urumchi," pp. 481–510.

31. For a description of the lifestyle of these former capitalists, who drove around in Jaguar cars, traveled abroad, and were attended by many domestic servants, see Richman, *Industrial Society,* chap. 12, "Communist China's Capitalists."

32. Hunter, *Shanghai Journal,* pp. 45–47; and Cheng, *Life and Death in Shanghai,* pp. 70–71.

33. See the full biography of Zhang Chunqiao compiled by W. Zafanolli in Bianco and Chevrier, *Dictionnaire biographique,* pp. 737–744. By the same author in the same work, see also the biography of Yao Wenyuan, pp. 712–717.

34. See Walder, *Chang Ch'un-ch'iao,* p. 13. The material that follows is based on this remarkable monograph.

35. Cited in Cheng, *Life and Death in Shanghai,* pp. 85–86.

36. Ibid., chap. 3, "The Red Guards."

37. Statistics established by the Bank of China, cited in Perry and Li, *Proletarian Power,* p. 12. These figures represent only a portion of the booty entrusted for safekeeping to the bank.

38. Cited by Hunter, *Shanghai Journal,* p. 90.

39. Perry and Li, *Proletarian Power,* pp. 10–11.

40. On the establishment of the rebel and conservative groups, the clashes between them, and the background of their leaders, see Perry and Li, in ibid., chaps. 2 and 3.

41. Cited by Hunter, *Shanghai Journal*, p. 225.

42. Cited by White, "Leadership in Shanghai," p. 359.

43. See Walder, *Chang Ch'un-chiao*, p. 62.

44. See Bergère, "La Chine," pp. 512–535.

45. Cited by Perry and Li, *Proletarian Power*, p. 139.

46. White, "Leadership in Shanghai," pp. 359–360.

47. That is the conclusion that Perry and Li seem to draw, despite the title of their study, *Proletarian Power*.

CHAPTER 14

1. Cheung, "Political Context of Shanghai's Economic Development," p. 69.

2. Ho and Tsui, "Fiscal Relations," p. 154.

3. Sung, "'Dragon Head,'" p. 181, tab. 7.3; Mok, "Industrial Development," p. 200, tab. 8.1.

4. Computed from Sung, "'Dragon Head,'" p. 186, tab. 7.5.

5. Cheung, "Political Context of Shanghai's Economic Development," p. 54.

6. White, *Shanghai Shanghaied?* p. 26.

7. Lam, "Local Interest Articulation," pp. 123–152.

8. Cited by Yatsko, *New Shanghai*, p. 22. In 1994, the author opened the first Shanghai office of the *Far Eastern Economic Review*, which she directed until 1998. She provides a lively and well-informed account of changes in the city during this period.

9. *Moniteur officiel du commerce international*, no. 1406 (September 9–15, 1999). See also Nagy, "Pudong ou Shanghai-Rive droite," pp. 28–36.

10. Since the early 1950s, China's oldest foreign bank had reverted to its mid-nineteenth-century practice of conducting its business in China from its headquarters in Hong Kong.

11. *South China Morning Post*, September 28, 2001; and *Far Eastern Economic Review*, November 22, 2001, p. 36. The ceiling of 50 million U.S. dollars imposed upon Taiwanese investments in China and obstructive authorization procedures had hardly checked Taiwanese transfers but had in many cases obliged them to take diverted routes, through Hong Kong in particular.

12. Yatsko, *New Shanghai*, pp. 60–61.

13. *The Economist*, December 2, 2000, p. 85.

14. McNally, "La marche en avant de Shanghai," pp. 33–39.

15. Cited in MacPherson, "La nouvelle zone de Pudong," p. 208. On the development of Pudong, see Ged, *Shanghai*, pp. 51–52.

16. Rowe, "Privation to Prominence," pp. 61, 68–71.

17. Chan, "Urban Development and Redevelopment," p. 316.

18. Yatsko, *New Shanghai*, p. 33.

19. Jacobs and Hong, "Shanghai and the Lower Yangzi Valley," p. 225; and Yatsko, *New Shanghai*, p. 94.

20. See Lu, "To Be Relatively Comfortable," pp. 133–135; Laurans, "Logements et confort à Shanghai," pp. 37–46; and *The Economist*, September 30, 2000, p. 77.

21. *The Economist*, January 19, 2002, p. 51.

22. Fraser, "Inventing Oasis," pp. 25–53.

23. Yatsko, *New Shanghai*, p. 33. In comparison to 1990, the habitable space per inhabitant had increased by 3 square meters. That increase resulted principally from the transfer of residents from the city center to more spacious accommodation on the outskirts.

24. Article in *Ximmin wanbao*, cited by Fraser, "Inventing Oasis," pp. 25–26.

25. Davis and Sensenbrenner, "Commercializing Childhood," pp. 54–79.

26. *International Herald Tribune*, June 27, 2001.

27. For a detailed description of these sites, see Ged, "Les environs de Shanghai," pp. 712–714.

28. Farrer, "Dancing through the Market Transition," p. 233.

29. Yatsko, *New Shanghai*, pp. 186–187, 195–197.

30. Mak and Lo, "Education," p. 390.

31. Erwin, "Heart-to-Heart," pp. 145–170.

32. Ged, "Shanghai: du patrimoine identitaire," pp. 79–88; also, by the same author, *Shanghai*, pp. 54–55.

33. Cited by Yatsko, *New Shanghai*, p. 142.

34. Ibid., pp. 158–168.

35. Zhou, *Shanghai Baby*.

EPILOGUE

1. Wong, "Entrepreneurial Spirit," pp. 25–48.

2. On the opposition between the traditions of coastal and inland Asia, see Bergère, *Le mandarin et le compradore*.

Bibliography

Archives of the Foreign Office (FO). Vol. 371 (28333, 28334, 28335) (January–August 1941); vol. 391 (2704, 31677).

Archives of the Ministère des Affaires étrangères (MAE). Series Guerre 1939–1945, subseries Vichy-Asie, vols. 142, 143, 144; Series Asie-Océanie 1944–1945, subseries Chine, vol. 14; Series E515-4, vols. 341, 342.

Auden, W. H., and Christopher Isherwood. *Journey to a War.* New York: Octagon Books, 1972. First published 1939.

Ballard, J. G. *Empire of the Sun.* London: Victor Gollantz, 1984.

Banister, Judith. "Mortality, Fertility and Contraceptive Use in Shanghai." *The China Quarterly,* no. 70 (June 1977), pp. 255–314.

Barber, Noël. *The Fall of Shanghai. The Communist Takeover of 1949.* London: Macmillan, 1979.

Barbizet, Laure, and Serge Vincent-Vidal. *Le contexte économique et social d'une production culturelle: la gravure sur bois dans la Chine des années trente et quarante.* Paris: Centre de recherches sur la Chine contemporaine de l'université de Paris VIII, 1981.

Barnett, Robert W. *Economic Shanghai: Hostage to Politics, 1937–1941.* New York: IPR, 1941.

Benson, Carlton. "Consumers Are Also Soldiers. Subversive Songs from Nanjing Road during the New Life Movement." In Cochran, *Inventing Nanjing Road,* pp. 91–132.

Bergère, Marie-Claire. *L'âge d'or de la bourgeoisie chinoise.* Paris: Flammarion, 1986. English translation: *The Golden Age of the Chinese Bourgeoisie.* Translated by Janet Lloyd. Cambridge: Cambridge University Press, 1989.

———, ed. *Aux origines de la Chine contemporaine. En hommage à Lucien Bianco.* Paris: L'Harmattan, 2002.

———. *La bourgeoisie chinoise et la revolution de 1911.* Paris: Mouton, 1968.

———. "Les capitalistes shanghaiens et la période de transition entre le régime Guomindang et le communisme (1948–1952)." *Études chinoises* 8, no. 2 (Autumn 1989), pp. 7–30.

———. "La Chine. Du mythe de reference au modèle d'action." In *1871. Jalons pour une histoire de la Commune de Paris,* ed. Jacques Rougerie et al., pp. 512–535. Assen, Holland: Van Gorcum.

———. "Chinese National Enterprises and the Sino-Japanese War: The Shenxin Cotton Mills of the Rong Family." Paper presented at the International Colloquium on Republican China, Nanjing, October 7–10, 1987. Published in Chinese: "Zhongghuode minzu qiye yu Zhong Ri zhanzheng; Rongjia Shenxin fangzhi chang." In *Minguo dang'an yu Minguo shixue shu taolun hui lunwen ji* [Collection of Articles on the Study of Archives of the Republican Period and on Republican History], ed. Zhang Xianwen et al., pp. 533–544. Beijing: Dang'an chubanshe, 1988.

———. "Choses vues en Chine" (2). *Techniques, Art, Science,* no. 17 (April 1958), pp. 11–20.

————. *Une crise financière à Shanghai à la fin de l'ancien régime.* Paris: Mouton, 1964.

————. "L'épuration à Shanghai (1945–1946). L'affaire Sarly et la fin de la concession française." *Vingtième siècle. Revue d'histoire,* no. 53 (January–March 1997), pp. 25–41. English translation: "The Purge in Shanghai, 1945–1946: The Sarly Affair and the End of the French Concession." In Yeh, *Wartime Shanghai,* pp. 157–178.

————. *Le mandarin et le compradore.* Paris: Hachette Littératures, 1998.

————. "'Shanghai' ou 'l'autre Chine,' 1919–1949." *Annales, Economie, Sociétés, Civilisations* 5 (September–October 1979), pp. 1039–1068.

————. *Sun Yat-sen.* Paris: Fayard, 1994. English translation: *Sun Yat-sen.* Translated by Janet Lloyd. Stanford: Stanford University Press, 1998.

Bergère, Marie-Claire, and Wang Ju. "Du capitalisme au communisme: cadres et entrepreneurs à Shanghai de 1949 à 1952." In Bergère, *Aux origines de la Chine contemporaine,* pp. 83–140.

Betta, Chiara. "Marginal Westerners in Shanghai: The Baghdadi Jewish Community, 1845–1931." In Bickers and Henriot, *New Frontiers,* pp. 38–54.

Bianco, Lucien. "Voyage en Chine." *Esprit,* March 1975, pp. 430–436.

Bickers, Robert, and Christian Henriot, eds. *New Frontiers. Imperialism's New Communities in East Asia, 1842–1953.* Manchester: Manchester University Press, 2000.

Bo Yibo. *Ruogan zhongda juece yu shijiande huigu* [Memories concerning Certain Important Decisions and Developments]. 2 vols. Beijing: Zhonggong zhongyang dangjiao chubanshe, 1990.

Boyle, John H. *China and Japan at War, 1937–1945. The Politics of Collaboration.* Stanford: Stanford University Press, 1972.

Brossolet, Guy. *Les Français de Shanghai, 1849–1949.* Paris: Belin, 1999.

Brunnert, Ippolit Semenovich, and V. V. Hagelstrom. *Present Day Political Organization of China.* Revised by N. Th. Kolessoff. Translated from the Russian. Shanghai: Kelly and Walsh, 1912. First published in Beijing, 1910.

Cao Guanlong. *The Attic: Memoir of a Chinese Landlord's Son.* Berkeley: University of California Press, 1996.

Carey, Arch. *The War Years at Shanghai 1941–48.* New York: Vantage Press, 1967.

Castelino, Noël. "Les intellectuals non engagés et l'opinion publique en Chine." Thèse du 3e cycle, Paris, EHESS, 1983.

————. "Zhang Dongsun. L'évolution d'un social-démocrate de 1919 à 1945." *Cahier d'études chinoises,* no. 5 (Paris, Publications Langues O, 1986), pp. 127–135.

Chabot, François. "La fin de la presence française à Shanghai, 1937–1945." In *La France en Chine, 1843–1943,* ed. Jacques Weber, pp. 233–245. Nantes: Presses académiques de l'Ouest: Ouest editions, 1997.

Chamberlain, Heath B. "Transition and Consolidation in Urban China: A Study of Leaders and Organizations in Three Cities, 1949–1953." In *Elites in the People's Republic of China,* by Robert A. Scalapino, pp. 245–301. Seattle: University of Washington Press, 1972.

Chan, Roger C. K. "Urban Development and Redevelopment." In Yeung and Sung, *Shanghai,* pp. 299–320.

Chan, Wellington K. K. *Merchants, Mandarins and Modern Enterprise in Late Ch'ing China.* Cambridge, Mass.: East Asian Research Center, Harvard University Press, 1977.

————. "Personal Styles, Cultural Values and Management. The Sincere and Wing On Companies in Shanghai and Hong Kong, 1900–1941." In *Asian Department Stores,* ed. Kerrie L. MacPherson, pp. 66–89. Honolulu: University of Hawaii Press, 1998.

————. "Selling Goods and Promoting a New Commercial Culture: The Four Premier Department Stores on Nanjing Road, 1917–1937." In Cochran, *Inventing Nanjing Road*, pp. 19–36.

Chang Kuo-T'ao (Zhang Guotao). *The Rise of the Chinese Communist Party, 1928–1938*. 2 vols. Lawrence: University Press of Kansas, 1972.

Chang, Maria Hsia. *The Chinese Blue Shirt Society: Fascism and Developmental Nationalism*. Berkeley: Institute of East Asian Studies, University of California, 1985.

Chang, Michael. "The Good, the Bad and the Beautiful: Movie Actresses and Public Discourse in Shanghai, 1920s–1930s." In Zhang, *Cinema and Urban Culture*, pp. 128–159.

Chen, Joseph. *The May Fourth Movement in Shanghai*. Leiden, The Netherlands: R. J. Brill, 1971.

Cheng, Nien. *Life and Death in Shanghai*. London: Grafton Books, Collins Publishing Group, 1986.

Chesneaux, Jean. *Le Mouvement ouvrier chinois, 1919–1927*. Paris: Mouton, 1962. Reprint, Paris: Éditions de l'EHESS, 1998.

Cheung, Peter T. Y. "The Political Context of Shanghai's Economic Development." In Yeung and Sung, *Shanghai Transformation and Modernization*, pp. 49–92.

The China Yearbook. Annual. 1912–1939, ed. H. G. W. Woodhead, London: G. Routledge; 1912–1919, New York: E. P. Dutton; 1921–1939, Beijing: Tientsin Press.

Chine. Collection: Guides Bleus. Paris: Hachette, 1998.

Chow, Tse-Tsung. *The May Fourth Movement. Intellectual Revolution in Modern China*. Cambridge, Mass.: Harvard University Press, 1960.

Clifford, Nicholas R. *Spoilt Children of Empire. Westerners in Shanghai and the Chinese Revolution of the 1920s*. Hanover, N.H.: University Press of New England, 1991.

Coble, Parks M. "Chinese Capitalists and the Japanese: Collaboration and Resistance in the Shanghai Area." In Yeh, *Wartime Shanghai*, pp. 62–85.

————. *Facing Japan: Chinese Politics and Japanese Imperialism, 1931–1937*. Cambridge, Mass.: Council on East Asian Studies, Harvard University, 1991.

————. "The National Salvation Association as a Political Party." In Jeans, *Roads Not Taken*, pp. 135–146.

————. *The Shanghai Capitalists and the Nationalist Government, 1927–1937*. Cambridge, Mass.: Council on East Asian Studies, Harvard University, 1980.

Cochran, Sherman. *Encountering Chinese Networks. Western, Japanese and Chinese Corporations in China, 1880–1937*. Berkeley: University of California Press, 2000.

————, ed. *Inventing Nanjing Road. Commercial Culture in Shanghai, 1900–1945*. Ithaca, N.Y.: Cornell University, East Asia Program, 1999.

————. "Transnational Origins of Advertising in Early Twentieth-Century China." In Cochran, *Inventing Nanjing Road*, pp. 37–58.

Collar, Hugh. *Captive in Shanghai. A Story of Internment in World War II*. Hong Kong: Oxford University Press, 1990.

Cordier, Henri. *Catalogue of the Library of the North China Branch of the Royal Asiatic Society*. Shanghai: Chin-foong General Printing Office, 1872.

————. *Les origines de deux établissements français dans l'Extrême-Orient, Chang-hai et Ning-po*. New documents published with an introduction and notes. Paris, 1896.

Cornet, Christine. *État et enterprises en Chine XIXe–XXe siècles. Le chantier naval de Jiangnan (1865–1937)*. Paris: Arguments, 1997.

Cornille, Jean. "La Résistance en Chine." *Journal des combattants*, April 26, 1947.

Darwent, C. E. *Shanghai. A Handbook for Travellers and Residents*. Shanghai: Kelly and Walsh, 1920.

David-Houston, J. V. *Yellow Creek: The Story of Shanghai*. London: Putnam, 1962.

Davis, Deborah S., ed. *The Consumer Revolution in Urban China*. Berkeley: University of California Press, 2000.

Davis, Deborah S., and Julia S. Sensenbrenner. "Commercializing Childhood: Parental Purchases for Shanghai's Only Child." In Davis, *Consumer Revolution*, pp. 54–79.

Delande, Natalie. "Une culture d'ingénieur. Origine de l'architecture moderne de Shanghai." Mémoire de DEA, Université de Paris I. 2 vols., 1994.

———. "Décor-déco: Shanghai 1920–1930." *Perspectives chinoises*, no. 3 (July–August 1995), pp. 46–52.

———. "Une entreprise d'exception: l'architecture jésuite de Shanghai pendant la période moderne." Ms., 1997.

Deng, Ming. *Survey of Shanghai 1840s–1940s*. Bilingual edition. Shanghai: Shanghai People's Fine Arts Publishing House, 1994.

Ding Richu, ed. *Shanghai jindai jingjishi* [Economic History of Shanghai in the Modern Period]. 2 vols. Vol. I: 1843–1894; vol. II: 1895–1927. Shanghai: Shanghai renmin chubanshe, 1994, 1997.

Dirlik, Arif. "The Ideological Foundations of the New Life Movement: A Study in Counterrevolution." *Journal of Asian Studies* 34, no. 4 (August 1975), pp. 945–980.

Drège, Jean-Pierre. *La Commercial Press de Shanghai, 1897–1949*. Paris: Collège de France, IHEC, 1978.

Dyce, Charles M. *Personal Reminiscences of Thirty Years' Residence in the Model Settlement, Shanghai 1870–1900*. Shanghai: Chapman and Hall, 1906.

Eastman, Lloyd E. *The Abortive Revolution, China and Nationalist Rule 1927–1937*. Cambridge, Mass.: Harvard University Press, 1974.

———. *Seeds of Destruction. Nationalist China in War and Revolution, 1937–1949*. Stanford: Stanford University Press, 1984.

Elvin, Mark. "The Administration of Shanghai, 1905–1914." In *The Chinese City between Two Worlds*, ed. Mark Elvin and William Skinner, pp. 239–269. Stanford: Stanford University Press, 1974.

———. "The Gentry Democracy in Chinese Shanghai, 1905–1914." In *Modern China's Search for a Political Form*, ed. Jack Gray, pp. 41–65. London: Oxford University Press, 1969.

———. "The Revolution of 1911 in Shanghai." In *Papers on Far Eastern History*, no. 29, pp. 119–161. Canberra: The Australian National University, Department of Far Eastern History, 1984.

Erwin, Kathleen. "Heart-to-Heart, Phone-to-Phone: Family Values, Sexuality, and the Politics of Shanghai's Advice Hotlines." In Davis, *Consumer Revolution*, pp. 145–170.

Fabre, Guilhem. *Les prospérités du crime. Trafic de stupéfiants, blanchiment et crises financières dans l'après-guerre froide*. La Tour d'Aigues: Editions de l'Aube, 1999.

———. "Le réveil de Shanghai. Stratégies économiques, 1949–2000." *Le Courrier des Pays de l'Est*, no. 325 (January 6, 1988), pp. 3–40.

Fairbank, John K. *The Chinese World Order*. Cambridge, Mass.: Harvard University Press, 1968.

———. "The Creation of the Treaty System." In *The Cambridge History of China*, vol. 10, *Late Ch'ing China 1800–1911*, pt. I, ed. Denis Twitchett and John K. Fairbank, pp. 213–263. Cambridge: Cambridge University Press, 1978.

————. *Trade and Diplomacy on the China Coast. The Opening of the Treaty Ports, 1842–1854.* Cambridge, Mass.: Harvard University Press, 1953.

Fairbank, John K., Martha Henderson Collidge, and Richard J. Smith. *H. B. Morse: Customs Commissioner and Historian of China.* Lexington: University Press of Kentucky, 1995.

Faligot, Roger, and Rémi Kauffer. *Kang Sheng et les services secrets chinois.* Paris: Robert Laffont, 1987.

Farmer, Rhodes. *Shanghai Harvest: A Diary of Three Years in the China War.* London: Museum Press, 1945.

Farrer, James. "Dancing through the Market Transition. Disco and Dance Hall Sociability in Shanghai." In Davis, *Consumer Revolution*, pp. 226–249.

Feetham, Richard. *Report of the Hon. Richard Feetham to the Shanghai Municipal Council.* 2 vols. Shanghai: North-China Daily News and Herald, 1931.

Feuerwerker, Albert. *China's Early Industrialization. Sheng Hsuan-huai (1844–1916) and Mandarin Enterprise.* Cambridge, Mass.: Harvard University Press, 1958.

————. *The Chinese Economy ca. 1870–1911.* Michigan Papers in Chinese Studies, no. 5. Ann Arbor: University of Michigan, 1969.

————. *The Foreign Establishment in China in the Early Twentieth Century.* Michigan Papers in Chinese Studies, no. 29. Ann Arbor: University of Michigan, 1976.

Fewsmith, Joseph. *Party, State and Local Elites in Republican China: Merchant Organizations and Politics in Shanghai, 1890–1930.* Honolulu: University of Hawaii Press, 1985.

Flaubert, Gustave. *Correspondance générale.* Vol. 4. Paris: Gallimard, Pléiade, 1998.

Fraser, David. "Inventing Oasis: Luxury Housing Advertisements and Reconfiguring Domestic Space in Shanghai." In Davis, *Consumer Revolution*, pp. 25–53.

Fredet, Jean. *Quand la Chine s'ouvrait . . . Charles de Montigny, consul de France.* Paris: Sté de l'histoire des colonies françaises, 1953.

Frolic, Michael B. *Mao's People. Sixteen Portraits of Life in Revolutionary China.* Cambridge, Mass.: Harvard University Press, 1980.

Fu Poshek. *Passivity, Resistance, and Collaboration. Intellectual Choices in Occupied Shanghai.* Stanford: Stanford University Press, 1993.

Fung Ka-iu. "Satellite Towns: Development and Contributions." In Yeung and Sung, *Shanghai*, pp. 321–340.

————. "The Spatial Development of Shanghai." In Howe, *Shanghai*, pp. 269–300.

Gardner, John. "The Wu-fan Campaign in Shanghai. A Study in Consolidation of Urban Control." In *Chinese Communist Politics in Action*, ed. Doak Barnett, pp. 477–539. Seattle: University of Washington Press, 1969.

Gaulton, Richard. "Political Mobilization in Shanghai 1949–51." In Howe, *Shanghai*, pp. 35–65.

Ged, Françoise. "Les environs de Shanghai." In *Chine*, pp. 712–714.

————. "Shanghai: du patrimoine identitaire au décor touristique." *Les Annales de la recherché urbaine*, no. 72 (1996), pp. 79–88.

————. "Shanghai. Habitat et structure urbaine 1842–1995." 3 vols. Thèse, EHESS, Paris, 1997.

————. *Shanghai.* Paris: Institut français d'architecture, collection: "Portrait de ville," 2000.

Ged, Françoise, and Emmanuelle Péchenart. "Shanghai: images d'architecture. Unité-Diversité." Research report. Paris: Institut parisien de recherche: architecture, urbanistique, société, 1991.

Gipoulon, Catherine. *Qiu Jin. Femme et révolutionnaire en Chine au XIXe siècle*. Paris: Éditions des femmes, 1976.

Gipouloux, François. *Les Cent Fleurs à l'usine. Agitation ouvrière et crise du modèle soviétique en Chine, 1956–1957*. Paris: Éditions de l'EHESS, 1986.

Goldman, Merle. *Literary Dissent in Communist China*. Cambridge, Mass.: Harvard University Press, 1967. Reprint, New York: Atheneum, 1971.

Goodman, Bryna. "Creating Civic Ground. Public Manoeuverings and the State in the Nanjing Decade." In *Remapping China. Fissures in the Historical Terrain*, ed. Gail Hershatter, Emily Hönig, Jonathan N. Lipman, and Randall Stross, pp. 164–177. Stanford: Stanford University Press, 1996.

———. *Native Place, City, and Nation. Regional Networks and Identities in Shanghai, 1853–1937*. Berkeley: University of California Press, 1995.

Guillain, Robert. *Orient extrême*. Paris: Le Seuil, 1986.

Guillermaz, Jacques. *Le Parti communiste au pouvoir (1er octobre 1949–1er mars 1972)*. Paris: Payot, 1972.

———. *Une vie pour la Chine. Mémoires 1937–1989*. Paris: Robert Laffont, 1989.

Hamashita, Takeshi. "Intra-regional System in East Asia in Modern Times." In *Network Power. Japan and Asia*, ed. Peter J. Katzenstein and Takashi Shiraishi, pp. 113–135. Ithaca, N.Y.: Cornell University Press, 1997.

Hao Yen-p'ing. *The Commercial Revolution in Nineteenth-Century China. The Rise of Sino-Western Mercantile Capitalism*. Berkeley: University of California Press, 1986.

———. *The Comprador in Nineteenth-Century China: Bridge between East and West*. Cambridge, Mass.: Harvard University Press, 1970.

Hauser, Ernest O. *Shanghai: A City for Sale*. New York: Harcourt, Brace, 1940.

Henriot, Christian. *Belles de Shanghai. Prostitution et sexualité en Chine aux XIXe–XXe siècles*. Paris: CNRS Éditions, 1997. English translation: *Prostitution and Sexuality in Shanghai. A Social History, 1849–1949*. Cambridge: Cambridge University Press, 2001.

———. "La Fermeture: The Abolition of Prostitution in Shanghai, 1949–1958." *The China Quarterly*, no. 142 (June 1995), pp. 467–486.

———. "'Little Japan' in Shanghai: An Insulated Community." In Bickers and Henriot, *New Frontiers*, pp. 146–169.

———. "Rice, Power and People: The Politics of Food Supply in Wartime Shanghai (1937–1945)." *Twentieth Century China* 26, no. 1 (November 2000), pp. 41–84.

———. *Shanghai 1927–1937. Élites locales et modernisation dans la Chine nationaliste*. Paris: Éditions de l'EHESS, 1991. English translation: *Shanghai 1927–1937: Municipal Power, Locality, and Modernization*. Translated by Noël Castelino. Berkeley: University of California Press, 1993.

Henriot, Christian, and Alain Roux. *Shanghai, années 30. Plaisirs et violences*. Paris: Éditions Autrement, 1998.

Hershatter, Gail. *Dangerous Pleasures: Prostitution and Modernity in Twentieth-Century Shanghai*. Berkeley: University of California Press, 1997.

Ho Lok-sang and Tsui Kai-yuen. "Fiscal Relations between Shanghai and the Central Government." In Yeung and Sung, *Shanghai*, pp. 153–170.

Hönig, Emily. *Creating Chinese Ethnicity: Subei People in Shanghai, 1850–1980*. New Haven, Conn.: Yale University Press, 1986.

———. *Sisters and Strangers. Women in the Shanghai Cotton Mills, 1919–1949*. Stanford: Stanford University Press, 1986.

Hou Chi-ming. *Foreign Investment and Economic Development in China, 1840–1937.* Cambridge, Mass.: Harvard University Press, 1965.

Howe, Christopher. *Employment and Economic Growth in Urban China, 1949–1957.* Cambridge: Cambridge University Press, 1971.

———. "Industrialization under Conditions of Long-Run Population Stability: Shanghai's Achievement and Prospect." In Howe, *Shanghai,* pp. 153–187.

———. *Shanghai. Revolution and Development in an Asian Metropolis.* Cambridge: Cambridge University Press, 1981.

———. "The Supply and Administration of Urban Housing in Mainland China. The Case of Shanghai." *The China Quarterly,* no. 33 (January–March 1968), pp. 73–97.

Hsiao Liang-lin. *China's Foreign Trade Statistics, 1864–1949.* Cambridge, Mass.: Harvard University Press, 1974.

Hu Daojing. "Shanghai dianyingyuande fazhan 1907–1936" [The Development of Cinema Halls in Shanghai, 1907–1936]. In *Shanghai yanjiu ziliao xuji* [Supplement to Research Materials on Shanghai], pp. 532–556. Shanghai: Shanghai tongshe, 1939. Reprint, Taipei: China Press, 1973.

———. "Shanghai xinwenzhi de bianqian" [Transformations of the Shanghai Press]. In *Shanghai yanjiu ziliao* [Research Material on Shanghai]. Shanghai: Shanghai tongshe, 1936. Reprint, Taipei: China Press, 1973.

Hunt, Michael H. *The Making of a Special Relationship. The United States and China to 1914.* New York: Columbia University Press, 1983.

Hunter, Neale. *Shanghai Journal. An Eyewitness Account of the Cultural Revolution.* New York: Frederick Praeger, 1969.

Isaacs, Harold. *La tragédie de la Révolution chinoise, 1925–1927.* London: Secker and Warburg, 1938. Reprint translated from the American edition published by Stanford University Press, Paris: Gallimard, 1967.

Israël, John. *Student Nationalism, 1927–1937.* Stanford: Stanford University Press, 1966.

Jacobs, Bruce, and Hong Lijiang. "Shanghai and the Lower Yangzi Valley." In *China Deconstructs,* ed. David S. Goodman and Gerald Segal, pp. 224–252. London: Routledge, 1994.

Jeans, Roger B., ed. *Roads Not Taken. The Struggle of Opposition Parties in Twentieth-Century China.* Boulder, Colo.: Westview Press, 1992.

Jiang Duo. *Yangwu yundong yu gaige kaifang* [The Foreign Affairs Movement, the Reforms, and Opening Up]. Shanghai: Shanghai shehui kexueyuan chubanshe, 1992.

Johnson, Linda C. "Shanghai: An Emerging Jiangnan Port, 1683–1840." In *Cities of Jiangnan in Late Imperial China,* ed. Linda C. Johnson, pp. 151–181. New York: State University of New York Press, 1993.

———. *Shanghai. From Market Town to Treaty Port, 1074–1858.* Stanford: Stanford University Press, 1995.

Johnston, Tess. *A Last Look: Western Architecture in Old Shanghai.* Hong Kong: Old China Hand Press, 1993.

The Jubilee of Shanghai 1843–1893. Shanghai: Past and Present, and a Full Account of the Proceedings on the 17th and 18th November, 1893. Shanghai: North-China Daily News Office, 1893.

Jurien de la Gravière (rear-admiral), Jean-Pierre Édouard. *Voyage en Chine et dans les mers et archipels de cet empire pendant les années 1847–1848–1849–1850,* by J. de la Gravière, commander of *La Bayonnaise* sent to these shores by the French government. 2 vols. Paris: Charpentier, 1854.

Kau, Michael, and John Leung, eds. *The Writings of Mao Zedong, 1946–1976*. Armonk, N.Y.: M. E. Sharpe, 1968.

Kirby, William. "Continuity and Change in Modern China: Economic Planning on the Mainland and on Taiwan, 1934–1958." *The Australian Journal of Chinese Affairs*, no. 24 (July 1990), pp. 121–141.

Kranzler, David H. *Japanese, Nazis and Jews: The Jewish Refugee Community of Shanghai, 1938–1945*. New York: Yeshiva University Press, 1976.

Kreissler, Françoise. "Exil ou asile à Shanghai? Histoire des réfugiés d'Europe centrale, 1933–1945." Thèse de doctorat d'État, Université de Paris VIII, Paris, 2000.

———. "In Search of Identity: The German Community in Shanghai, 1933–1945." In Bickers and Henriot, *New Frontiers*, pp. 211–230.

Kuo Ting-yee. "Self-Strengthening. The Pursuit of Western Technology." In Twitchett and Fairbank, *Cambridge History of China*, vol. X, pt. 1, pp. 491–542.

Lam Tao-chiu. "Local Interest Articulation in the 1980s." In Yeung and Sung, *Shanghai*, pp. 123–152.

Lanning, G., and S. Couling. *The History of Shanghai*. Shanghai: Kelly and Walsh, 1921.

La Servière, Joseph de. *Histoire de la mission du Kiang-nan. Jésuites de la province de France (1840–1899)*. 2 vols. Zi-ka-wei: Imprimerie de l'Orphelinat de Tsou-sè-wè, 1914.

Laurans, Valérie. "Logements et confort à Shanghai. L'exemple de Wanli, ensemble residentiel moderne." *Perspectives chinoises*, no. 68 (November–December 2001), pp. 37–46.

Lee, Leo Ou-fan. *The Romantic Generation of Modern Chinese Writers*. Cambridge, Mass.: Harvard University Press, 1973.

———. *Shanghai Modern. The Flowering of a New Urban Culture in China 1930–1945*. Cambridge, Mass.: Harvard University Press, 1999.

Lefeuvre, Jean. *Shanghai. Les enfants dans la ville*. Paris: Casterman, 1956.

Leung Yuen-sang. "Regional Rivalries in Mid-Nineteenth-Century Shanghai: Cantonese versus Ningpomen." *Ch'ing-shih wen-t'i* [Questions on Qing History] 4, no. 8 (1982), pp. 29–50.

———. *The Shanghai Taotaï Linkage Man in a Changing Society, 1843–1890*. Honolulu: University of Hawaii Press, 1990.

———. "The Shanghai-Tientsin Corridor. A Case Study of Interprovincial Relations in Late Nineteenth-Century China." In *Proceedings of the First International Symposium on Asian Studies*, vol. I, pp. 209–218. Hong Kong: Asian Research Service, 1979.

Leyda, Jay. *Dianying/Electric Shadows: An Account of Films and the Film Audience in China*. Cambridge, Mass.: MIT Press, 1972.

Li Jin. "Le néo-sensationnisme et le cinéma." In Rabut and Pino, *Pékin-Shanghai*, pp. 283–318.

Li Tiangang. "'Haipai.' Jindai shimin wenhua zhi lanshang" [Haipai. The Source of Modern Urban Popular Culture]. In Zhang Zhongli, *Jindai Shanghai chengshi yanjiu* [Research on the Modern History of Shanghai], pp. 1130–1159. Shanghai: Shanghai renmin chubanshe, 1990.

Lindsay, Hugh Hamilton, and Karl Guztlaff. "Amherst Expedition." *Chinese Repository* 2, no. 12 (1834), pp. 549–552.

Link, Perry. *Mandarin Ducks and Butterflies. Popular Fiction in Early Twentieth-Century China*. Berkeley: University of California Press, 1981.

Liu Ta-chün. *Growth and Industrialization in Shanghai. Growth and Industrialization in Shanghai.* Shanghai: China Institute of Pacific Relations, 1936.

Loh, Robert. *Escape from Red China.* New York: Coward McCann, 1962.

Lu Hanchao. *Beyond the Neon Lights: Everyday Shanghai in the Early Twentieth Century.* Berkeley: University of California Press, 1999.

———. "Creating Urban Outcasts: Shantytowns in Shanghai, 1920–1950." *Journal of Urban History* 21, no. 5 (July 6, 1995), pp. 563–596.

———. "'The Seventy-two Tenants.' Residence and Commerce in Shanghai's Shikumen Houses, 1872–1951." In Cochran, *Inventing Nanjing Road,* pp. 133–184.

Lu Hanlong. "To Be Relatively Comfortable in an Egalitarian Society." In Davis, *Consumer Revolution,* pp. 124–141.

Lust, John. "The Su-pao Case." In *Bulletin of the School of Oriental and African Studies,* vol. 27, pt. 2, pp. 408–429. London: University of London, 1964.

Lutz, Jessie. "The Chinese Student Movement of 1945–1949." *The Journal of Asian Studies* 31, no. 1 (1971), pp. 89–110.

Macfarquhar, Roderick. *The Origins of the Cultural Revolution.* Vol. 2: *The Great Leap Forward,* 1958–1960. New York: Columbia University Press, 1983.

MacPherson, Kerrie L. "La nouvelle zone de Pudong et le développement urbain de Shanghai: une mise en perspective historique." In *Les métropoles chinoises au XXe siècle,* ed. Christian Henriot and Alain Delissen, pp. 191–208. Paris: Éditions Arguments, 1995.

———. *A Wilderness of Marshes. The Origin of Public Health in Shanghai.* Hong Kong: Oxford University Press, 1987.

Mak, Grace C. L., and Leslie N. K. Lo. "Education." In Yeung and Sung, *Shanghai,* pp. 375–398.

Mann, Susan. *Local Merchants and the Chinese Bureaucracy, 1750–1950.* Stanford: Stanford University Press, 1987.

Markovits, Claude. "Indian Communities in China ca. 1842–1949." In Bickers and Henriot, *New Frontiers,* pp. 55–74.

Marolles (Commandant Jules-Auguste de). "Souvenirs de la révolte des T'ai P'ing (1862–1863)." *T'oung Pao* 3, no. 4, ser. II (1902), pp. 201–221; 4, no. 1 (1903), pp. 1–18. Leiden, The Netherlands: E. J. Brill.

Marsh, Susan H. "Chou Fo-hai: The Making of a Collaborator." In *The Chinese and the Japanese: Essays in Political and Cultural Interactions,* ed. Iriye Akira, pp. 304–327. Princeton, N.J.: Princeton University Press, 1980.

Marshall, Jonathan. "Opium and the Politics of Gangsterism in Nationalist China, 1927–1945." *Bulletin of Concerned Asian Scholars* 8, no. 3 (July–September1976), pp. 19–48.

Martin, Brian G. *The Shanghai Green Gang. Politics and Organized Crime, 1919–1937.* Berkeley: University of California Press, 1996.

Maybon, Charles B., and Jean Fredet. *Histoire de la concession française de Shanghai.* Paris: Plon, 1929.

McNally, Christopher A. "La marche en avant de Shanghai, un prélude vers une nouvelle étape des réformes." *Perspectives chinoises,* no. 43 (September–October 1997), pp. 33–39.

Moges (marquis de). *Souvenirs d'une ambassade en Chine et au Japon en 1857 et 1858.* Paris: Hachette, 1860.

Mok, Victor. "Industrial Development." In Yeung and Sung, *Shanghai,* pp. 199–224.

Montalto de Jesus, Carlos Augusto. *Historic Shanghai.* Shanghai: The Mercury Press, 1909.

Motono, Eiichi. *Conflict and Cooperation in Sino-British Business, 1860–1911. The Impact of the Pro-British Commercial Network in Shanghai.* New York: St. Martin's Press, 2000.

Murphey, Rhoads. *The Outsiders. The Western Experience in India and China.* Ann Arbor: University of Michigan Press, 1977.

Nagy, Leon. "Pudong ou Shanghai-Rive droite: nouvelle vitrine de la Chine?" *Perspectives chinoises,* no. 68 (November–December 2001), pp. 28–36.

Pan Ling. *Old Shanghai. Gangsters in Paradise.* Hong Kong: Heinemann Asia, 1984.

———. *Shanghai. A Century of Change in Photographs 1843–1949.* Hong Kong: Haigeng Publishing, 1993.

Le Paris de l'Orient. Présence française à Shanghai, 1849–1946. Catalogue produced by the Albert-Kahn Museum, Paris, Spring 2002.

Peattie, Mark R. "Japanese Treaty Port Settlements in China, 1895–1937." In *The Japanese Informal Empire in China, 1895–1937,* ed. Peter Duus, Ramon Myers, and Mark R. Peattie, pp. 166–209. Princeton, N.J.: Princeton University Press, 1989.

Pepper, Suzanne. *Civil War in China. The Political Struggle, 1945–1949.* Berkeley: University of California Press, 1978.

Perry, Elizabeth J. *Shanghai on Strike. The Politics of Chinese Labor.* Stanford: Stanford University Press, 1993.

———. "Shanghai's Strike Wave of 1957." *The China Quarterly,* no. 137 (March 1994), pp. 1–27.

Perry, Elizabeth J., and Li Xun. *Proletarian Power. Shanghai in the Cultural Revolution.* Boulder, Colo.: Westview Press, 1997.

Poncin, Marie-Christine. "Une grande entreprise shanghaienne face à la guerre: la famille Rong et ses filatures de cotton." Thèse de doctorat de 3e cycle, Paris, INALCO, 1985.

Pontet, R. "En Chine. France Quand même, Comité des Français libres de Shanghai." *Revue de la France libre. Les Comités de l'étranger (1940–1944),* no. 126 (June 1960), pp. 20–22.

Pott, F. L. Hawks. *A Short History of Shanghai, Being an Account of the Growth and Development of the International Settlement.* Shanghai: Kelly and Walsh, 1928.

Powell, John B. *My Twenty-five Years in China.* New York: Macmillan, 1945.

Quiquemelle, Marie-Claire, and Jean-Loup Passek, eds. *Le cinéma chinois.* Paris: Centre national d'art et de culture Georges Pompidou, 1985.

Rabut, Isabelle. "École de Pékin et école de Shanghai." In Rabut et Pino, *Pékin-Shanghai,* pp. 13–59.

Rabut, Isabelle, and Angel Pino. *Le Fox-Trot de Shanghai et autres nouvelles chinoises.* Paris: Albin Michel, 1996.

———, eds. *Pékin-Shanghai. Tradition et modernité dans la littérature chinoise des années trente.* Paris: Bleu de Chine, 2000.

Rankin, Mary B. *Early Chinese Revolutionaries. Radical Intellectuals in Shanghai and Chekiang, 1902–1911.* Cambridge, Mass.: Harvard University Press, 1971.

Rawski, Thomas G. *Economic Growth in Prewar China.* Berkeley: University of California Press, 1989.

Remer, Charles Frederick. *A Study of Chinese Boycotts: With Special Reference to Their Economic Effectiveness*. Taipei: Ch'eng-wen Publishing, 1966. First published by Reed in 1933.

Reynolds, Bruce. "Changes in the Standard of Living of Shanghai Industrial Workers, 1930–1973." In Howe, *Shanghai*, pp. 222–240.

Richman, Barry M. *Industrial Society in Communist China*. New York: Random House, 1969.

Ristaino, Marcia R. "The Russian Diaspora Community in Shanghai." In Bickers and Henriot, *New Frontiers*, pp. 192–210.

Roche, Daniel. *La France des Lumières*. Paris: Fayard, 1993.

Rong, Erren. "Rong Erren tan shengchan" [Rong Erren on Production]. *Shanghai gongshang* [SHGS, Shanghai Industry and Trade] 1, no. 2 (November 1949), p. 5.

Rong, Yiren. "Yi ge ziwo gaizaode yundong" [A Movement of Self-Reform]. *Shanghai gongshang* [Shanghai Industry and Trade] 3, no. 2 (January 31, 1952).

Rousso, Henry. *Le Syndrome de Vichy, 1944–198—*. Paris: Seuil, 1987. English translation: *The Vichy Syndrome: History and Memory in France since 1944*. Translated by Arthur Goldhammer. Cambridge, Mass.: Harvard University Press, 1991.

Roux, Alain. "Chine 1945–1949: la classe ouvrière dans une révolution à l'envers." *Cahiers d'histoire de l'Institut de recherches marxistes*, no. 28 (1987), pp. 8–44.

———. "Espace et politique dans la Shanghai de la première moitié du XXe siècle." Manuscript, January 2002.

———. *Grèves et politique à Shanghai. Les désillusions (1927–1932)*. Paris: Éditions de l'EHESS, 1995.

———. "The Guomindang and the Workers of Shanghai (1938–1948): The Rent in the Fabric." Paper presented at the conference "China's Mid-century Transitions," Harvard University, September 8–11, 1994.

———. "Le Guomindang et les ouvriers de Shanghai (1938–1948): la déchirure." *Le mouvement social*, no. 173 (October–December 1995), pp. 69–95.

———. "Les ouvriers et ouvrières de Shanghai, 1927–1949." 3 vols. Thèse de doctorat d'État, Paris, Université de Paris I Panthéon-Sorbonne, 1991.

———. *Le Shanghai ouvrier des années trente. Coolies, gangsters et syndicalistes*. Paris: L'Harmattan, 1993.

———. "La 'tragédie du 2 février 1948' à la Shenxin no. 9: une grève de femmes?" In Bergère, *Aux origines de la Chine contemporaine*, pp. 47–81.

———. "La vie quotidienne des anonymes." In Henriot and Roux, *Shanghai*, pp. 109–129.

Rowe, Peter G. "Privation to Prominence: Shanghai's Recent Rapid Resurgence." In *Shanghai. Architecture and Urbanism for Modern China*, ed. Seng Kuan and Peter Rowe, pp. 54–83. Munich: Prestel, 2004.

Rowe, William. "The Qingbang and Collaboration under the Japanese, 1939–1945." *Modern China* 8, no. 4 (October 1982), pp. 491–499.

Sanford, James C. "Chinese Commercial Organization and Behaviour in Shanghai of the Late Nineteenth and Early Twentieth Century." Ph.D. dissertation, Harvard University, 1976.

Sargeant, Harriet. *Shanghai: Collision Point of Cultures, 1918–1939*. New York: Crown Publishers, 1990.

Sears, Katrin E. "Shanghai's Textile Capitalists and the State. The Nationalization Process in China." Ph.D. dissertation, University of Michigan, 1985.

Shanghai gongren sanci wuzhuang qiyi yanjiu [A Study of the Shanghai Workers' Three Armed Uprisings]. Edited by Xu Yufang and Bian Xingying. Shanghai: Zhishi chubanshe, 1987.

Shanghai Municipal Tourism Association. *Tour of Shanghai's Historical Architecture*. Shanghai: Henan Fine Art Publishing House, 1994 (bilingual Chinese-English edition).

Shanghai qianzhuang shiliao [Materials for the History of Shanghai's *qianzhuang* Banks]. Shanghai: Zhongguo renmin yinhang Shanghaishi fenhang [People's Bank of China, Shanghai Branch], Shanghai renmin chubanshe, 1960.

Shanghai Shehui kexueyuan Jingji yanjiuso [Institute of Research on the Economy of the Shanghai Academy of Social Sciences]. *Shanghai zibenzhuyi gongshangye de shehui gaizao* [The Nationalization of the Capitalist Industrial and Commercial Businesses of Shanghai]. Shanghai: Shanghai renmin chubanshe, 1980.

Shieh, Joseph [Xue Gengxin], with Marie Holzman. *Dans le jardin des aventuriers*. Paris: Seuil/mémoire, 1995.

Shih Shu-mei. *The Lure of the Modern: Writing Modernism in Semicolonial China*. Berkeley: University of California Press, 2001.

Smith, Stephen Antony. *A Road Is Made. Communism in Shanghai, 1920–1927*. Richmond, U.K.: Survey Curzon Press, 2000.

Stranahan, Patricia. *Underground: The Shanghai Communist Party and the Politics of Survival, 1927–1937*. Lanham, Md.: Rowman and Littlefield, 1998.

Sullivan, Lawrence R. "Reconstruction and Rectification of the Communist Party in the Shanghai Underground: 1931–1934." *The China Quarterly*, no. 101 (March 1985), pp. 78–97.

Sung Yun-Wing. "'Dragon Head' of China's Economy?" In Yeung and Sung, *Shanghai*, pp. 171–198.

Tang Zhenchang et al., eds. *Shanghai shi* [History of Shanghai]. Shanghai: Shanghai renmin chubanshe, 1989.

Tang Zhijun et al., eds. *Jindai Shanghai dashiji* [A Chronology of Modern Shanghai]. Shanghai: Shanghai cishu chubanshe, 1989.

Trumbull, Randolph. "The Shanghai Modernists." Ph.D. dissertation, Stanford University, 1989.

Tsou Jung (Zou Rong). *The Revolutionary Army. A Chinese Nationalist Tract of 1903*. Introduction, translation, and notes by John Lust. Paris: Mouton, 1968.

Van de Ven, Hans J. *From Friend to Comrade. The Founding of the Chinese Communist Party, 1920–1927*. Berkeley: University of California Press, 1991.

Vogel, Joshua. "Shanghai-Japan. The Japanese Residents Association of Shanghai." *The Journal of Asian Studies* 59, no. 4 (November 2000), pp. 927–950.

Waara, Carrie. "Invention, Industry, Art. The Commercialization of Culture in Republican Art Magazines." In Cochran, *Inventing Nanjing Road*, pp. 61–89.

Wakeman, Frederic, Jr. *Policing Shanghai 1927–1937*. Berkeley: University of California Press, 1995.

———. "A Revisionist View of the Nanjing Decade: Confucian Fascism." *The China Quarterly*, no. 150 (June 1997), pp. 395–432.

———. *The Shanghai Badlands: Wartime Terrorism and Urban Crime, 1937–1941*. New York: Cambridge University Press, 1996.

Wakeman, Frederic, Jr., and Yeh Wen-hsin, eds. *Shanghai Sojourners*. Berkeley: Institute of East Asian Studies, University of California, 1992.

Walder, Andrew. *Chang Ch'un-ch'iao and the January Revolution in Shanghai.* Ann Arbor: University of Michigan Press, 1978.

———. *Communist Neo-traditionalism: Work and Authority in Chinese Industry.* Berkeley: University of California Press, 1986.

Wang Jingyu. "Shijiu shiji waiguo qing Hua qiyezhongde Huashang fugu huodong" [The Complementary Investments Made by Chinese Merchants in the Foreign Companies That Invaded China in the Nineteenth Century]. *Lishi yanjiu,* no. 4 (1965). Article reprinted in *Zhongguo jindai jingjishi lun wenxuan,* ed. Huang Yiping, vol. 1, pp. 193–257.

Wang Ju. *Jindai Shanghai mianfangye zuihou guanghui* [The Last Thriving Days of the Shanghai Modern Cotton Industry]. Shanghai: Shanghai shehui kexueyuan chubanshe, 2004.

Wang Shaoyang. "The Construction of State Extractive Capacity. Wuhan 1949–1953." *Modern China* 27, no. 2 (April 2001), pp. 229–261.

Wang, Y. C. "Tu Yuesheng (1881–1951): A Tentative Political Biography." *The Journal of Asian Studies* 26, no. 3 (May 1967), pp. 433–455.

Wasserstein, Bernard. "Ambiguities of Occupation: Foreign Resisters and Collaborators in Wartime Shanghai." In Yeh, *Wartime Shanghai,* pp. 24–41.

———. *Secret War in Shanghai, Treachery, Subversion and Collaboration in the Second World War.* London: Profile Books, 1998.

Wasserstrom, Jeffrey. *Student Protest in Twentieth-Century China: A View from Shanghai.* Stanford: Stanford University Press, 1991.

White, Lynn T., III. *Careers in Shanghai. The Social Guidance of Individual Energies in a Developing Chinese City.* Berkeley: University of California Press, 1978.

———. "Leadership in Shanghai, 1955–1969." In *Elites in the People's Republic of China,* ed. Robert A. Scalapino, pp. 302–377. Seattle: University of Washington Press, 1972.

———. *Policies of Chaos. The Organizational Causes of Violence in China's Cultural Revolution.* Princeton, N.J.: Princeton University Press, 1989.

———. "The Road to Urumchi . . . Pre-rustification from Shanghai." *The China Quarterly,* no. 79 (September 1979), pp. 481–510.

———. *Shanghai Shanghaied? Uneven Taxes in Reform China.* Hong Kong: Center of Asian Studies, University of Hong Kong, 1989.

———. "Shanghai's 'Horizontal Liaisons' and Population Control." In Yeung and Sung, *Shanghai,* pp. 419–467.

———. "Shanghai's Policy in Cultural Revolution." In *The City in Communist China,* ed. John W. Lewis, pp. 325–372. Stanford: Stanford University Press, 1971.

Widmer, Ellen, and David Der-wei Wang, eds. *From May Fourth to June Fourth: Fiction and Film in Twentieth-century China.* Cambridge, Mass.: Harvard University Press, 1993.

Wilkinson, Mark F. "The Shanghai American Community, 1937–1949." In Bickers and Henriot, *New Frontiers,* pp. 231–249.

Wong Bin, Theodore Huters, and Pauline Yu, eds. *Culture and State in Chinese History: Conventions, Accommodations and Critiques.* Stanford: Stanford University Press, 1997.

———. "Introduction: Shifting Paradigms of Political and Social Order." In Wong, Huters, and Yu, *Culture and State in Chinese History,* pp. 1–26.

Wong Siu-lun. "The Entrepreneurial Spirit: Shanghai and Hong Kong Compared." In Yeung and Sung, *Shanghai,* pp. 25–48.

Wong Wang-chi. *Politics and Literature in Shanghai. The Chinese League of Left-Wing Writers, 1930–1936*. Manchester: Manchester University Press, 1991.

Wong Young-tsu. "The Fate of Liberalism in Revolutionary China. Chu Anping and His Circle, 1946–1950." *Modern China* 19, no. 4 (October 1993), pp. 457–490.

Wu Tian-wei. "Chiang Kai-shek's April 12th Coup of 1927." In *China in the 1920s*, ed. Gilbert Chan and Thomas H. Etzold, pp. 147–159. New York: New Viewpoints, 1976.

Xiao-Planes, Xiaohong. *Éducation et politique en Chine. Le rôle des élites du Jiangsu, 1905–1914*. Paris: Éditions de l'EHESS, 2001.

———. "La Société générale d'éducation du Kangsu et son rôle dans l'évolution socio-politique chinoise de 1905 à 1914." 2 vols. Thèse de doctorat, Paris, INALCO, March 1997.

Xiong Yuezhi, ed. *Shanghai tongshi* [General History of Shanghai], vol. 8, *Minguo jingji* [The Economy in the Republican Period]. Shanghai: Shanghai renmin chubanshe, 1999.

Xu Xiaoqun. *Chinese Professionals and the Republican State. The Rise of Professional Associations in Shanghai, 1912–1937*. Cambridge: Cambridge University Press, 2001.

———. "National Salvation and Cultural Reconstruction. Shanghai Professors' Response to the National Crisis in the 1930's." In *Chinese Nationalism in Perspective: Historical and Recent Cases*, ed. George C. X. Wei and Xiaoyuan Liu, pp. 53–74. Westport, Conn.: Greenwood Press, 2001.

Yan Zhongping et al. *Zhongguo jindai jingjishi tongji ziliao xuanji* [A Selection of Statistical Material on the Economic History of Modern China]. Beijing: Kexue chubanshe, 1955. Reprint, Stanford: Stanford University Press, 1991.

Yang Dongping. *Chengshi jifeng* [Monsoon over the Town]. Beijing: Dongfang chubanshe, 1994.

Yatsko, Pamela. *New Shanghai. The Rocky Rebirth of China's Legendary City*. New York: John Wiley, 2001.

Yeh Wen-hsin. "Corporate Space, Communal Time: Everyday Life in Shanghai's Bank of China." *American Historical Review* 100, no. 1 (February 1995), pp. 97–122.

———. "Urban Warfare and Underground Resistance: Heroism in the Chinese Secret Service during the War of Resistance." In Yeh, *Wartime Shanghai*, pp. 111–132.

———, ed. *Wartime Shanghai*. London: Routledge, 1998.

Yen Ching-hwang. "Wing On and the Kwok Brothers. A Case Study of Pre-war Overseas Chinese Entrepreneurs." In *Asian Department Stores*, ed. Kerrie L. MacPherson, pp. 47–65. Honolulu: University of Hawaii Press, 1998.

Yeung, Y. M., and Sung Yun-Wing, eds. *Shanghai. Transformation and Modernization under China's Open Door Policy*. Hong Kong: The Chinese University Press, 1996.

Young, Ernest. "Ch'en Tien-hua (1875–1905): A Chinese Nationalist." In *Papers on China*, vol. XIII, pp. 113–163. Cambridge, Mass.: Center for East Asian Studies, Harvard University, 1959.

Zafanolli, W. "Yao Wenyuan." In *Dictionnaire biographique du mouvement ouvrier international. La Chine*, ed. Lucien Bianco and Yves Chevrier, pp. 712–717. Paris: Éditions ouvrières, Presses de la FNSP, 1985.

———. "Zhang Chunqiao." In *Dictionnaire biographique du mouvement ouvrier international. La Chine*, ed. Lucien Bianco and Yves Chevrier, pp. 737–744. Paris: Éditions ouvrières, Presses de la FNSP, 1985.

Zhang Yingjin, ed. *Cinema and Urban Culture in Shanghai, 1922–1943*. Stanford: Stanford University Press, 1999.

———. *The City in Modern Literature and Film: Configurations of Space, Time and Gender*. Stanford: Stanford University Press, 1996.

———. "Prostitution and Urban Imagination." In Zhang, *Cinema and Urban Culture*, pp. 160–180.

Zhang Zhen. "Tea House, Showplay, Bricolage: 'Laborer's Love' and the Question of Early Chinese Cinema." In Zhang, *Cinema and Urban Culture*, pp. 27–50.

Zhang Zhongli, ed. *Jindai Shanghai chengshi yanjiu* [Research on the History of the Town of Shanghai in the Modern Period]. Shanghai: Shanghai renmin chubanshe, 1990.

Zhou, Weihui. *Shanghai Baby*. Translated from the Chinese. Paris: Philippe Picquier, 2001.

Zou Yiren. *Jiu Shanghai renkou bianqiande yanjiu* [Study on the Evolution of the Population of Old Shanghai]. Shanghai: Shanghai renmin chubanshe, 1980.

Index

University of Fudan, 128, 179, 335, 398, 399
University of Shanghai, 187
urban communes, 374, 375*n**

Verdier, Marcel, 233
Versailles peace conference, 164*n**, 178, 181
Vietnam War, 370
Voitinsky, Grigori, 183
volunteer corps, 134–35

Waigaoqiao, 417
Wakeman, Frederic, 453*n*24
Walder, Andrew: *Communist Neo-traditionalism*, 456*n*29
walled town, 23, 32, 111, 126, 243
Wang, Winston, 415*n**
Wang Hongwen, 395*n**, 400–401, 402, 404, 405
Wang Jingwei: as head of collaborationist government, 7, 291*n**, 293, 295, 299, 301, 303, 310, 313, 319, 320, 325; relationship with Chiang Kai-shek, 209–10, 310
Wang Keming, 75
Wang Shouhua, 190–91, 197
Wang Xiaolai, 240
Wang Yiting, 125, 138
Ward, Frederick T., 43, 97
warlords, 147*n**, 162, 188, 190–91, 195, 200, 214, 215, 229
Washington Conference of 1921–22, 151–52
Wasserstein, Bernard, 453*n*24
water supply, 62, 113, 119–20, 224
Western imperialism, 228, 304, 311–12, 318; and *Haipai*, 243, 255, 260; relationship to modernization, 2, 50, 64–65; and treaty ports, 21–22. *See also* anti-imperialism
Western management practices, 155, 158–59
Western science (*xixue*), 121, 122
Western technology, 37, 44, 50, 123, 155
West Gate Stadium, 179, 208
White Russians, 296, 307–8, 340

Wilden, Auguste, 231
Wild Flower (Yecao xianhua), 283
Wing On cotton mills, 154, 166, 352
Wing On Department Store, 154, 250, 252
women: and fashion, 263, 424–25; fashion, 263, 424–25; feminism among, 139–40, 331; and *Haipai*, 260, 263, 263–66, 276, 283–84; in West, 93; Women's League for Political Participation, 140; women's unions, 359. *See also* prostitution
wood engraving, 281–82
Woodhead, H. G. W., 307
workers, 103, 211, 222, 263, 323; during anti-Japanese boycott of 1931, 207; during Cultural Revolution, 367, 395, 399–403, 404, 406; during May Fourth Movement, 178, 180, 181; in middle class, 423; during movement of May 30, 1925, 186, 187, 188, 189; relations with Communists, 186, 187, 189, 190–91, 198, 201, 321, 322, 331–33, 342–43, 345–46, 351, 362, 382–84, 453*n*44; during Shanghai Commune, 190–91, 196–97, 198, 201; social status of, 390, 394, 409, 421–23; workers' quarters of city, 244–45. *See also* trade unions
Workers' General Headquarters, 399–401, 402–3, 404
work units (*danwei*), 191, 388–89, 397, 406, 409–10, 423, 435, 456*n*29
World Bank, 419
World Economic Herald, The (Shijie jingji dabao), 411
World Trade Organization, 434, 436, 439
World War I, 147–48, 158; Versailles peace conference, 164*n**, 178, 181
World War II: Japanese attack on Pearl Harbor, 287, 298, 299; outbreak in Europe, 287, 288, 293. *See also* occupation of Shanghai by Japanese; Sino-Japanese War of 1937–45
Writers' League, 205–6, 357
Wu Dingchang, 175
Wu Han, 396*n***
Wu Jianzhang, 39, 45, 46, 47, 48–49